Models and Cognition

Models and Cognition

Prediction and Explanation in Everyday Life and in Science

Jonathan A. Waskan

A Bradford Book
The MIT Press
Cambridge, Massachusetts
London, England

© 2006 Massachusetts Institute of Technology

For information on quantity discounts, please email special_sales@mitpress.mit.edu.

Set in Stone sans and Stone serif by SNP Best-set Typesetter Ltd., Hong Kong. Printed and bound in the United States of America.

Library of Congress Cataloging-in-Publication Data

Waskan, Jonathan A.
  Models and cognition : prediction and explanation in everyday life and in science / Jonathan A. Waskan.
      p. cm.
  "A Bradford book."
  Includes bibliographical references and index.
  ISBNS: 978-0-262-23254-8, 0-262-23254-5 (alk. paper)
  1. Philosophy of mind. 2. Cognitive science. I. Title.

BD418.3.W37   2006
128′.2—dc22

                                                            2006043842

10 9 8 7 6 5 4 3 2 1

To my wife Laurie, for making me a better, happier man.

Contents

Preface

This book has been written so as to be intelligible to philosophers and cognitive scientists at all levels of expertise. In it you will find defended a range of provocative theses. Many of them will be immediately intelligible to professors and advanced graduate students in the aforementioned fields, but it is—for reasons on which I elaborate below—my intention to make all these theses, and the arguments for them, intelligible not only to professors and graduate students, but also to advanced undergraduates in philosophy and cognitive science.

Here are some of the claims I defend:

• Folk psychology provides only limited predictive and explanatory leverage with regard to everyday human behavior, but cognitive science has amply vindicated folk psychology.

• Cognitive science is succeeding brilliantly, but it is, despite frequent lip service to the contrary, not in the least committed to the computational theory of mind or to the discovery of intentional generalizations.

• For purposes of (at least much of) cognitive-scientific research, folk semantics can, and must, be replaced with an ahistorical theory of content. This means that contents can be naturalized without any appeal to natural selection.

• Although the appeal to mental contents that are fixed ahistorically plays an essential and legitimate role in the explanation for one of the most important facts about human behavior, contents are devoid of relevant causal powers.

• The capacity to engage in the truth-preserving manipulation of representations may be what most clearly differentiates humans from other creatures. The Intrinsic Cognitive Models (ICM) hypothesis—which, crudely put, amounts to the proposal that humans harbor and manipulate the cognitive counterparts to scale models—supplies the only viable explanation for this capacity.

• The ICM hypothesis can be distinguished from sentence-based accounts of truth preservation in a way that is fully consistent with what is known about the brain.

• Some computational systems (e.g., appropriately programmed personal computers) also harbor non-sentential models, and these representations are immune to the frame problem for the same reasons that scale models are. There is, in other words, an extant computational solution to the frame problem.

• A model of explanation grounded in the ICM hypothesis, termed the *Model model*, can resolve, in a way that no other model can, the many problems that beset the Deductive-Nomological model of explanation.

• The frame problem of artificial intelligence is intimately related to the ceteris paribus problem and the surplus-meaning problem in the philosophy of science. The upshot is that the aforementioned solution to the frame problem explains both how it is that scientists can always find a way to hang onto their pet theories in the face of otherwise countervailing evidence and how it is that scientists are able to use their theories to formulate countless new predictions.

• In what is perhaps the most important respect of all (i.e., the capacity to supply genuine, enlightening explanations), the special sciences are (at present) far superior to fundamental physics.

• If the ICM hypothesis is correct, then Kant was also basically correct in claiming that there is synthetic *a priori* knowledge (at least in geometry).

• In the near future, humans or non-humans may come to understand the nature of reality in its full, hyper-dimensional glory.

For a quick discussion of how many of these claims fit together, see the final paragraph of chapter 2 and the first few paragraphs of chapter 9.

It would be foolhardy for me to expect that, after reading the arguments of this book, flocks of previously unsympathetic graduate students and professors will suddenly come around to my way of thinking. I do think it reasonable to expect, however, that those of you who are interested in these topics will recognize the strength of the arguments advanced here and the elegance of my overarching position. It is in this spirit that I direct this book to the attention of even my least sympathetic peers.

There will also be those among you who already think that folk psychology has good scientific credentials, that folk semantics doesn't work for science but another semantics might, that we harbor and manipulate non-sentential mental models, or that having an explanation for an event or a regularity is having a mental model of what might have produced it. Those of you who fall into one or more of these categories are likely to find in this book a good deal more grist for your particular mill.

Finally, and most importantly, I direct this book to the attention of those of you who are just starting out in philosophy or cognitive science, for it is you newcomers who are the ultimate arbiters of the disputes addressed herein. (See section 2.6.) It is my hope—because my central theses are, after all, basically correct!—that the next generation of philosophers and cognitive scientists will include many who champion the position advanced in this book. It is largely for this reason that I have tried to write in a way that presupposes very little prior knowledge of these fields. Be advised, however, that this is no mere textbook, and you will sometimes need to put in a good deal of time and effort in order to understand the positions described and the arguments for them. It may help to know that there are many good resources that, if kept at the ready, will help you along the way. On the philosophy end of things, there are the Stanford and Routledge Encyclopedias of Philosophy. The former is a free (but incomplete) online resource; the latter is an online resource to which most university students ought to have electronic access. On the cognitive science end, you might try *A Companion to Cognitive Science* (edited by William Bechtel and George Graham) and *The MIT Encyclopedia of the Cognitive Sciences* (edited by Robert Wilson and Frank Keil). In the end, if you do put in the time and effort, you will—even if you disagree with the claims advanced here —surely learn a great deal about philosophy and cognitive science.

Acknowledgements

Much of the material presented in chapter 2 was first published as "Folk Psychology and the Gauntlet of Irrealism" (*Southern Journal of Philosophy* 41, 2003: 627–655).

A highly condensed version of the material presented in chapters 4 and 6 was published as "Intrinsic Cognitive Models" (*Cognitive Science* 27, 2003, no. 22: 259–283).

The following individuals and groups deserve special thanks for their role in this project: Bill Bechtel, the friend and able mentor who found me at GSU and dusted me off at WUSTL; the Philosophy Department at the University of Illinois at Urbana-Champaign for giving me the time and resources to complete my work; and the creators of Ray Dream Studio 5.02 and PlastFEM.

Formal and informal comments from, and discussions with, the following individuals and groups helped to shape the thoughts expressed in this manuscript: Dave Balota, Bob Barrett, Mark Bickhard, Bill Brewer (the esteemed psychologist), Kyle Broom, Ron Chrisley, Gary Dell, Daniel Dennett, Gary Ebbs, Rick Grush, Brian Keeley, Patrick Maher, Pete Mandik, Jesse Prinz, Mark Rollins, Dave Rosenthal, Whit Schonbein, Laurie Waskan, Desiree White, Tad Zawidski, the Department of Philosophy at CSU in Long Beach, the Department of Philosophy at OU in Athens, participants in my Cognitive Basis of Science course, the Philosophy Department at William Paterson University, the PNP Program at Washington University in St. Louis, and the Southern Society for Philosophy and Psychology.

And there are others to whom I am indebted. I spend a great deal of time expressing my disagreement with, most notably, Carl Hempel and Jerry Fodor. I could not, however, even begin to think the thoughts expressed herein without them. Indeed, they are, for their very rare gifts of clarity and ingenuity, my philosophical heroes. Fodor, in particular, is one to whom I frequently turn when I want to learn the lay of a particular tract of land in my own area. Indeed, after having thought about what I am trying to do in this book, and upon learning more about the broader philosophical community of which I am a part, I have begun to recognize that I agree with Fodor on far more points than I disagree. Thank you, then, Professor Fodor; the profession is far better off for having you around. Thanks also to Professor Zenon Pylyshyn for keeping us image and model theorists honest.

Models and Cognition

1 | Thoughts about the Mind: Past, Present, and Future

In this chapter, I set the stage for later chapters by introducing some important ideas in a way that should be intelligible to philosophers and cognitive scientists alike (albeit at the risk of coming across as pedantic to both). I begin with a very brief overview of some of the influential claims made about the human mind by philosophers in the seventeenth, eighteenth, and nineteenth centuries. I then consider the origins and nature of some of the major disciplines of cognitive science. I focus on claims that are relevant to the theses I will defend in the rest of the book. (For this reason, each of the three sections provides only a partial discussion of the topic under consideration.) At the close of the chapter, I propose that philosophy and the comparatively new science of the mind can help one another in some very specific ways.

1.1 Philosophy, the Mind, and the Mechanical Worldview

Many of the questions that currently befuddle Anglo-American philosophers took on their present shape around four centuries ago in the intellectual climate that developed after great men such as Galileo Galilei (1564–1642) and Johannes Kepler (1571–1630) distinguished themselves by all but inventing science as we know it. There were, of course, earlier fits and starts for science, but it was men such as these that truly got the engine of scientific discovery up and running for the first time.[1] Kepler, for instance, devised a predictively powerful model of the solar system that had the planets orbiting the sun in accordance with three elegant geometrical laws. Similarly, Galileo utilized geometrical theorems to characterize the motions of terrestrial bodies. He also made telescopic observations of the heavens which enabled him to discover that other planets have satellites and that Venus has phases similar to those of the Earth's moon, all of which lent powerful support to Kepler's model of the solar system. These and other achievements marked the ascendancy of the view that the universe is made up entirely of matter in mathematically ordered motion[2] and of the practice of systematically testing theories by determining and evaluating their implications. This proved to be a real formula for success, and it was soon used in attempts to discern the mechanisms governing nearly every facet of nature.

These developments would, of course, raise serious concerns about earlier work in natural philosophy and about the concomitant answers given to core philosophical questions. Many of these questions would thus have to be asked anew, from within the framework of the new mechanistic worldview. To take one highly germane example, philosophers of this period were driven to ask "Are minds, too, just the product of matter in motion?" At least on the face of things, an affirmative answer to this question would seem to suggest that it is possible to make real progress in the scientific study of the mind. On the other hand, an affirmative answer would also seem to suggest that there is no life after death, free will, or moral responsibility, and that Judaism, Christianity, and Islam have gotten things all wrong. In no small part because the mechanistic view of the mind seemed to carry with it these anti-religious implications, it would take centuries before a true science of the mind would be allowed to develop and flourish. In the interim, philosophers who were interested in the mind would have to content themselves with the "armchair" consideration of minds, principally their own.

Although the study of the mind was thus not significantly informed by science during this period, philosophers did believe that the study of science could be significantly informed by an accurate model of how the mind works. Philosophers hoped, specifically, to discern the principles of operation governing the device (i.e., the human mind) that we use to obtain knowledge (scientific or otherwise). This, they hoped, would allow a better understanding not only of science, but of the reach of the human intellect more generally. Philosophers of this persuasion who worked in the seventeenth and eighteenth centuries are traditionally divided (albeit at clear risk of glossing over important similarities and differences) into two main groups: the empiricists and the rationalists.

The empiricists (e.g., Thomas Hobbes, John Locke, George Berkeley, and David Hume) generally held that all of our thoughts about the world originate in experience and that our predictions about what will happen in the world under specific circumstances are the result of expectations borne of those selfsame experiences. For instance, my expectation that dropping an egg will lead to its breaking could, according to an empiricist, be explained by my tendency to associate (on the basis of experience) falling eggs with broken eggs. Because they believed that all knowledge was attained in this general fashion, they tended to take the reach of the human intellect to be quite restricted and to hold that human intellectual capacities do not differ in any qualitative way from those of other animals.

Unimpressed by the minimalist psychology of the empiricists, the rationalists (e.g., René Descartes, Benedict de Spinoza, and Gottfried Wilhelm Leibniz) emphasized the importance of the human capacity to reason, which they thought could not be explained by mere associations borne of experience. It was the capacity to reason, above all else, that rationalists took to separate man from beast. Leibniz, for instance, argued as follows: "It is, indeed true that reason ordinarily counsels us to expect that we will find in the future that which conforms to our long experience of the past; but this . . . can fail us when we least expect it, when the reasons which have maintained it change. This is why the wisest people do not rely on it to such an extent that they do not try to probe into the reason for what happens (if that is possible), so as to judge when exceptions must be made. . . . This often provides a way of foreseeing an occurrence without having to experience the sensible links between images, which the beasts are reduced to doing." (1705/1997, p. 52) On Leibniz' view, in other words, beasts may be capable of expecting that certain experiences will be followed by others (e.g., that an experience of a falling egg will be followed by an experience of a broken egg). Unlike humans, however, they are incapable of understanding when exceptions to a regularity (viz., exceptions that they have not experienced) might occur (e.g., if the egg is frozen or is falling into a bucket of non-dairy whipped topping).

If beasts cannot engage in the same kind of mechanical reasoning that humans can, they are clearly even more deficient in the abstract reasoning department. Consider, for instance, the properties of equiangular, closed planar figures that have an even number of sides. After a bit of thought, you may come to believe that for any given side of such a figure there is another side that runs parallel to it, but it seems implausible that any non-human terrestrial animal has ever come to believe this. Rationalists typically held that beliefs of this sort are unique in that any (unimpaired) person willing to spend the necessary time and effort can come to appreciate that they are necessarily and eternally true, and they denied that someone could come to appreciate this fact solely on the basis of associations borne of experience. As an alternative, rationalists typically maintained that some knowledge (e.g., mathematical knowledge) is innate, though they disagreed over the extent of this nativism and had some difficulty explaining why the exercise of reason would be required in order to "discover" what one already knows.

Late in the eighteenth century, a German philosopher by the name of Immanuel Kant would offer a new model of the human psyche in an attempt to resolve the problems of both rationalism and empiricism. He too believed that the limits of human knowledge could be determined if we understood the device (i.e., the human mind) that we use to obtain it, and, like the rationalists, he was dissatisfied both with the minimalist psychology of the empiricists and with their conclusions regarding the limited reach of the human intellect. If their minimalist psychology were correct, Kant claimed, we could not even have the experience of seeing an object, let alone the experience of seeing an object persist through time. More specifically, if our minds did not play an active role in the ordering of sensory inputs, we would have disconnected sensations of the parts and properties of objects (e.g., their color, shape, location, and so forth). For instance, instead of experiencing a solid table that persists through time, we would see light brown there-and-now, feel impenetrability here-and-now, hear a knocking sound, etc. If there were nothing more to experience than raw sense data, the world would appear as a chaotic, disjointed series of sensations. Nor could we be aware of our own existence, let alone experience our own persistence through time. To borrow a phrase from William James (1890, p. 462), the world would appear to us "as one great blooming, buzzing confusion." But experience is not like this, and so, Kant concludes, the mind must somehow synthesize the diverse bits of information it receives in order to generate the kind of coherent experiences of objects with which we are all familiar.[3]

Because Kant took there to be a good deal more to the mind than the empiricists maintained, he also held that the empiricists were wrong to place such severe limits on the extent of possible knowledge. At the same time, he believed that the reach of the intellect was far less than what rationalists frequently proposed, and he denied that we have a store of innate mathematical ideas. (See chapter 9.)

Late in the nineteenth century, a legitimate science of psychology was still nowhere to be found. There were some important precursors, but philosophers and self-professed scientific psychologists continued to rely heavily on introspection as a tool for investigating the mind. The work of the latter would largely be forgotten, but one introspective philosopher, Franz Brentano, drew attention to a feature of human thought processes that has been a source of controversy ever since. Brentano claimed, specifically, that mental phenomena are always *about* something.[4] That is, when we think, we think *about* things—for instance, we think about our families, activities that we hope to accomplish, tasty foods, parallelograms, and so on. Borrowing terminology from the scholastics (see note 1), Brentano described this feature of mental phenomena as their containing objects "intentionally within themselves" (1874/1995. p. 124). He also called it their exhibiting a "reference to a content" (ibid.), all of which terminology continues to be used by philosophers to this very day.[5]

In sum: From the time of Galileo and Kepler until late in the nineteenth century, there was an ongoing and fruitful philosophical inquiry into the nature of the human mind. A legitimate science of the mind would, however, not be forthcoming until the middle of the twentieth century, and only after some major miscues. Before we consider how philosophers and practitioners of this new science of the mind ought to regard one another, let us review just how it was that this science came about.

1.2 The History of the Science(s) of the Mind

The story of the latter-day science of the human mind—cognitive science—is the story of several separate contributors and of their interactions. I will not attempt to tell the whole story here, but I will present its bare outlines, both in order to get the many philosophers who are unfamiliar with it up to speed and because some of the details will prove important in later chapters.

1.2.1 The Neurosciences

The neurosciences include neuroanatomy (the study of the structure of the nervous system), neurophysiology (the study of the functioning of neurons and neural ensembles), and neuropsychology (the study of how brain structures and activities are related to high-level cognitive processes). This, at any rate, is not an uncommon way of dividing things up.

1.2.1.1 Neuroanatomy

The origins of neuroanatomy can be traced to the writings of Aristotle (circa 350 B.C.) and Galen (circa 150 A.D.). Galen's thoughts, in particular, were widely taken for gospel until Galileo and company got the engine of discovery up and running again in the seventeenth century. Galen believed that the brain was responsible for sensation and movement and that the brain's interaction with the body's periphery was hydraulic in nature. He believed that nerves were conduits for carrying liquid to and from the brain's ventricles (liquid-filled cavities).

A major breakthrough for neuroanatomy was the invention of the compound-lens microscope late in the sixteenth century. By the middle of the seventeenth century it would be discovered that all plants are made of cells, though there would be no conclusive evidence that all living things are made of cells until the middle of the nineteenth century, and not until late in the nineteenth century would the minute structure of the nervous system begin to be revealed. Camillo Golgi (1843–1926), in particular, can be credited with uncovering many details of the fine-grained structure of the nervous system. Golgi had invented a new staining technique. His method, involving the impregnation of nervous tissue with silver, made it possible to visualize the structure of neurons (the principal type of cell found in the nervous system). Because the nervous tissue he studied appeared to be connected in an intricate and seamless network, Golgi disagreed with the contention that the nervous system is composed of many distinct cells. Santiago Ramón y Cajal (1852–1934) found a way to adapt Golgi's technique to the staining of single neurons, and he was in this way able to refute Golgi's theory with his own invention.[6]

The subsequent study of the different types of neurons and their distribution culminated early in the twentieth century with the proposal by Korbinian Brodmann (1868–1918) that the cortex, the wrinkled outer surface of the brain, divides up into roughly 52 anatomically distinct areas. Brodmann's accompanying map of the distinct brain areas is still widely used today.

1.2.1.2 Neurophysiology A major step toward the development of present-day neurophysiology was Luigi Galvani's (1737–1798) discovery, late in the eighteenth century, that muscle cells have electrical properties. By the middle of the nineteenth century, it was discovered that the activity of the nervous system is also electrical in nature. Hermann von Helmholtz (1821–1894) managed to clock the speed at which nervous impulses travel. He found that the rate of conduction was, despite the electrical nature of the process, quite slow. Indeed, he found that the rate of conduction was not only slower than light (the suspected speed) but also slower than sound. Early in the twentieth century, it would also be revealed that the electrical activity of individual neurons is an all-or-none process (i.e., there is a sharp divide between their active, "firing" state and their quiescent state) and that the propagation of neural impulses involves the movement of ions across the cell membrane through gated channels. The process begins with depolarization at the body of the cell. If a threshold is exceeded, it sets off a chain reaction of depolarization that travels down lengthy projections, called *axons*, which terminate close to the surfaces of other neurons. In the typical case, when the electrochemical signal reaches the terminus of an axon, chemicals (i.e., neurotransmitters) are released that excite or inhibit activity in the next cell.

1.2.1.3 Neuropsychology Franz Josef Gall (1757–1828) was among the first to attempt relating brain structures to high-level cognitive processes. Gall, an able anatomist, is widely credited with some fundamental insights into the structure of the nervous system. He is, however, best known, and often ridiculed, for his now-defunct theory of phrenology. Gall noticed that some of his childhood friends had bulging eyes and that they also tended to have good memories. He speculated that both were consequences of enlargement of the area of the brain that is responsible for memory and that the heightened development of other mental abilities might also give rise, in a similar manner, to external characteristics— namely, bumps on the skull. He eventually developed an entire system for reading mental abilities and deficits from the shapes of people's skulls, and he and his followers came up with various maps that purported to represent the anatomical loci of particular abilities. Phrenology was soon adopted as a standard medical practice, and phrenological analyses of criminals would even be considered admissible evidence in American courts as late as the beginning of the twentieth century.

Unfortunately for phrenology, the theory behind the practice would begin to lose favor once its implications were tested. An early and influential attempt to do just this was carried out by Pierre Flourens (1794–1867) in experiments that (he claimed) involved the highly selective destruction of specific regions of the cortex in animals. Flourens found that the destruction of cortical areas hypothesized to be responsible for specific mental abilities did not result in the selective diminishment of those abilities; instead there seemed to be an across-the-board diminishment of higher mental abilities (perception, memory, and volition) proportional to the amount of cortex destroyed (Wozniak 1995).

Flourens' work contributed to the view that the cortex does not contain functionally distinct regions, but this view was soon called into question by, among others, Paul Broca (1824–1880), who reported in 1861 that the destruction of a particular part of the human brain (in the front of the left half) results in a specific set of speech abnormalities. In particular, patients with lesions to this area typically speak very little, and when they do it is only with great effort. Moreover, the speech that they do produce tends to be marred by grammatical errors. In 1874, in another classic localization study, Carl Wernicke (1848–1904) reported that a different linguistic disorder, one that is more semantic than grammatical in nature, results from the destruction of a more posterior part of the left half of the brain. Patients with damage to this area produce grammatical sentences quite readily, but these sentences are remarkably devoid of content. These patients also have great difficulty comprehending speech.

Though the debate over the possible localization of cognitive functions persisted well into the twentieth century, Gall's proposal that physical differentiation parallels functional differentiation had been permanently revived as a plausible hypothesis. With the completion of Brodmann's map early in the twentieth century, it was natural to try to associate particular cognitive functions to particular, anatomically distinct areas of the brain. Brodmann's map thus began to be used, as it is still used today, to correlate neural structures with cognitive functions.

1.2.1.4 More Recent Advances The aforementioned disciplines continue to utilize many of the same basic methods discussed above, but these methods have generally undergone vast improvement. And many new methods have been developed.

In neuroanatomy, many researchers continue to use various forms of microscopy and staining, but new stains and staining techniques have been developed that allow selective staining of the paths of particular axons (which can be quite lengthy), particular types of cells, and particular types of connections between neurons (e.g., those that utilize a particular neurotransmitter). These new staining methods have, in concert with electron microscopy and computerized equipment for generating images of the larger-scale structures of the brain (e.g., PET, CT, MRI), resulted in the creation of highly detailed neural wiring diagrams.

Neurophysiologists continue to study the electrical properties of neurons, but they are able to study the levels of electrical activity exhibited by particular neurons both in vitro and in vivo (e.g., in live, non-human primates) and even to study the opening and closing of particular ion channels. Single-cell recording techniques have also been scaled up in recent years, and it is now possible to study the electrical activity of entire populations of neurons at the same time. Neurophysiologists have also begun to study the functional roles played by each of the many different forms of neurotransmitter and to "knock out" specific genes in order to get a clearer picture of the mechanisms involved in the development of, and the functional differentiation in, neural networks.

The correlation of cognitive functions with anatomical structures through the study of impaired patients is still a very important source of evidence in neuropsychology. One major advance, however, has been the utilization of the computerized imaging techniques such as those mentioned above in order to determine ante-mortem which areas of the brain have been damaged. Other advances in brain imaging technology enable *functional* neuroimaging, which is the study of which areas of the brain are most active when particular cognitive abilities are being utilized. Most of this research involves the synthesis of techniques from neuroscience and experimental psychology, so I shall forestall further discussion of it until after I have covered the latter's long and storied history.

1.2.2 Experimental Psychology from the Middle of the Nineteenth Century to the Middle of the Twentieth

The discipline of experimental psychology got its start in nineteenth-century Germany, where the intellectual climate in the nineteenth century was conducive to the development of experimental psychology for a couple of reasons. The first was the enduring influence of that gargantuan figure in the history of philosophy, Immanuel Kant, who, as I noted earlier, had proposed an intricate and highly influential model of the human psyche. The second was the state of the university system in Germany (Hearnshaw 1987). In other places, the prospect of scientifically studying the mind still provoked (for the aforementioned reasons) harsh reactions from theologians, who remained a powerful force in university administrations. Early in the nineteenth century, however, German universities began to look very much like the universities of today. They were not only of places of learning, but the locus of much empirical research as well. German universities also began to emphasize the importance of academic freedom, so faculty members were free to teach and conduct their research in whatever manner they desired. Indeed, not only did German faculty members have great freedom; their research was often supported by generous grants. Now the quest for a genuine experimental psychology could begin in earnest.

In order to become a full-fledged science, however, psychology would have to exhibit a critical mass of the hallmarks of a genuine science. These have traditionally been taken to include the following:

a determinate subject matter
a means of gathering, quantifying, and analyzing data in a way that enables inter-subjective agreement
a method for testing competing theories (e.g., by controlling some experimental conditions while manipulating others)
replicability of findings

control over the object of study
connections with other sciences
formulation of a body of laws
accurate and novel predictions
understanding of the possible whys and the hows of (i.e., having explanations for) the phenomena under investigation.

Precisely when that critical mass was first attained in psychology is difficult to discern, but there were some clear milestones along the way, and a few major gaffes.

1.2.2.1 Mid-to-Late-Nineteenth-Century European Psychology

One of the earliest examples of the gathering and analysis of quantified psychological data was Ernst Weber's (1795–1878) use of the method of just-noticeable differences in the first half of the nineteenth century. Weber would, for example, study the ability of blindfolded subjects to discriminate between two weights in order to determine just how great the difference between the weights would have to be in order for subjects to detect a difference and how that difference increased with an increase in the weight of the items used. The results were quantified and expressed in terms of a law relating just-noticeable differences to stimulus magnitude. A similar method was employed for other sensory modalities, and the same law-like relationship was found. This marked the beginning of *psychophysics*, a line of inquiry whose methods would be refined by Gustav Fechner (who coined the terms "just-noticeable difference" and "psychophysics"). One of Fechner's enduring insights was that statistical analyses of data could be used to factor out uncontrollable variations in the outcomes of individual trials.

Around the same time, Helmholtz was discovering that the rate of nerve conduction is quite slow. This finding helped experimental psychology to take another huge step forward. What this finding meant, in particular, was that different mental processes might take measurably different amounts of time. This fact would not be of much use, however, without a device for measuring very short time intervals. Just such a device had recently been developed for military applications—specifically, to measure the velocity of projectiles at the time of launch. The first two researchers to take advantage of this new technology were Franciscus Donders (1818–1889) and Wilhelm Wundt (1832–1920)—friend and student, respectively, to Helmholtz.

Donders developed an ingenious experimental technique, known as the *subtraction method*, in order to study the time it takes for a particular mental process to occur. The basic strategy is to subtract the time it takes to perform a simple task from the time it takes to perform a more complex task, where the former is a component of the latter. For instance, as a simple task, subjects might be asked to depress a lever when a single light bulb is lit. For a more complex task, subjects might be asked to press the lever only when one particular light from a display of five lights is lit. The complex task is very much like the simple task except for the addition of a discrimination process. Thus the time of discrimination can, it was thought, be determined by subtracting the time it takes to perform the simple task from the time it takes to perform the more complex task.

Wundt and his students would co-opt the techniques of both Donders and Fechner. Wundt was also a creative genius in his own right when it came to devising experimental apparatus, and this resulted in the creation of a large number of devices and what many consider to be the first experimental psychology laboratory. The lab, which was little more than a storage room, is generally said to have been established in 1879 at the University of Leipzig, though in fact it developed over a period of time.

Research in the Wundt lab that involved Donders' subtraction method focused on the temporal onset of "apperception" (conscious awareness and recognition). This research had a heavy introspective component, as did research involving psychophysical methods. The third research strategy pursued by Wundt and his students was, however, introspective through and through. It is not very surprising that Wundt, a mind/body dualist, came to prefer this last method over the others as his career progressed.

In addition to conducting empirical research, Wundt contributed to the discipline of experimental psychology by founding scholarly journals and societies and by instructing a large number of students, many of them Americans. When American universities began, late in the nineteenth century, to follow the German model, and as students of Wundt began to arrive, psychology departments and laboratories sprouted up across the United States.

While most psychological experiments were geared toward the study of conscious perception, Hermann Ebbinghaus (1850–1909) devised a truly ingenious set of experiments on memory and learning, using only himself as a subject. He created a huge list of nonsense syllables (of the form "consonant vowel consonant") in order to factor out the effects of content on learning and memory. He then measured the number of times a list had to be studied in order for him to be able to repeat it without error. As a measure of his ability to retain this information over time, he would measure at various intervals the number repetitions that would be required in order to once again repeat a given list without error. Using these methods, and over the course of about two years of painstaking research and replication, Ebbinghaus discovered many important facts about learning and memory. He was able to determine, for instance, that the relationship between list length and learning was non-linear; instead, the number of repetitions required to learn a list increased dramatically as the list increased in length. He also found that it would take fewer repetitions to learn a list if those repetitions were spread out over time, that memory was better for items near the beginning and end of a list, and that learning was greatly facilitated by the use of contentful material.

1.2.2.2 Late-Nineteenth-Century American Psychology One of Wundt's most successful students, Edward Tichener (1867–1927), brought his teacher's introspectionist approach to the United States, where it would prevail for a time as the structuralist movement in psychology. Structuralists had as their goal the formulation, for states of consciousness, of something analogous to chemistry's periodic table of the elements. In the end, however, the attempt to classify the mental elements and the manner of their synthesis would lead to seemingly insoluble disputes.

American structuralists were initially opposed by functionalists, who were more concerned with the adaptive value of states of consciousness, and hence, to a far greater extent than structuralists, with behavior. William James (1842–1910) was a leader of the functionalists; he was also one of the few non-Germans of the late nineteenth century to have a lasting influence on experimental psychology. James himself did little to advance the techniques of psychological investigation, but he was well versed in, and personally acquainted with, the latest research in both Europe and the United States.[7] Drawing on this background and on his own armchair consideration of the mind, James wrote a landmark text, *Principles of Psychology*, which would eventually help to delineate the central topics of investigation in experimental psychology (e.g., perception, attention, declarative and procedural memory, learning, reasoning, and concepts). Before this could happen, however, psychology would have to take an important detour through its most conservative form: behaviorism.

1.2.2.3 Behaviorism The transition to behaviorism in American psychology was partly motivated by the success of the animal-behavior experiments conducted by Russian physiologist Ivan Pavlov (1849–1936). The findings for which Pavlov is most famous concern the amount of saliva secreted by dogs under various conditions. Pavlov found that, as a normal reaction (called the *unconditioned response*) to the taste of food (called the *unconditioned stimulus*), dogs are known to increase their rate of salivation. This can be measured by attaching a tube to the salivary duct in the animal's mouth. In addition, Pavlov found that an increase in level of salivation can be elicited even when food is not present. If, for instance, one repeatedly pairs the presentation of food and a seemingly irrelevant sensory stimulus (the *conditioned stimulus*), such as a whistle, one can subsequently elicit the salivary response (which has now become a conditioned response) merely by presenting the conditioned stimulus. The effect was, moreover, found to diminish at a steady rate when the conditioned stimulus was no longer paired with food.

The data from Pavlov's experiments were neatly quantified, and the results were easily replicated. Unlike other popular research strategies of that period, the behaviorist strategy did not treat introspection as a datum. Instead data were restricted to observable stimuli and responses, and these data could be quantified and the law-like relationships between them revealed.

Pavlov-style research exhibited nearly all the characteristics of genuine science. In no small part because of this, Pavlov's methods became tremendously popular in the United States. The theoretical basis for this research was a pair of assumptions about human psychology that were reminiscent of the associationistic psychology of the empiricists. Like empiricists, behaviorists emphasized the importance of associations borne of experience and downplayed the differences between man and beast.[8] John Watson (1878–1958) was one of the founders of this new, more scientific psychology. In a classic exposition of the tenets of behaviorism, he wrote: "Psychology as the behaviorist sees it is a purely objective experimental branch of natural science. Its theoretical goal is the prediction and control of behavior. Introspection forms no essential part of its methods, nor is the scientific value of its data dependent upon the readiness with which they lend themselves to interpretation in terms of consciousness. The behaviorist, in his efforts to get a unitary scheme of animal response, recognizes no dividing line between man and brute." (1913, p. 158)

The work of Pavlov and the polemic of Watson spurred a new generation of researchers to study the relationships between observable stimuli and behaviors. Nevertheless, many psychologists, Watson among them, found it difficult to eschew talk of the kinds of states that might intervene between stimuli and behaviors. In this regard, one of the more liberal of the early-twentieth-century behaviorists was Edward Tolman (1886–1959), who was quite explicit about his intent to use facts about stimuli and behaviors in order to make inferences about the intervening processes. He readily spoke of internal states such as goals, and of behavior-guiding structures such as cognitive maps (Tolman 1948). He even proposed that the new behaviorist research program would enable researchers to salvage many of the accurate, though methodologically suspect, proposals emanating from introspection-laden psychology (Tolman 1922).

At the opposite end of the spectrum was Burrhus F. Skinner (1904–1990). with his "radical" behaviorism. On Skinner's view, psychologists should study stimuli, responses, and their law-like connections and avoid all reference to conscious experience or any other supposed intermediaries. Skinner is perhaps the best-known figure in the history of experimental psychology, and his renown can be attributed in part to the extent to which he was able to control animal behavior. In contrast to the methods of Pavlov, which only enabled elicitation of automatic responses such as salivation, the methods of Skinner enabled the elicitation of virtually any kind of behavior of which an animal was naturally capable. Skinner found that behaviors (called *operants*) that resulted in particular effects (e.g., the depression of a lever) could, whether they appeared spontaneously or were caused to occur, be made more likely to occur in the future through the introduction of a reinforcer (e.g., food, water, or social contact). In small increments, an animal's behavior could be molded to take on almost any desirable form.

Much of Skinner's research centered on the law-like relationships between schedules of reinforcement and the frequency of operants. This research exhibited nearly all of the hallmarks of science described above, with the notable exception of clear connections to the ongoing work in the rest of science. The failure to be connected with the neurosciences was, of course, just a corollary of the denial that psychology need interest itself in intermediaries in general, or brains in particular. As we have already seen, however, neurophysiologists were already making great strides in the localization of cognitive abilities to particular areas of the brain; they were, in other words, studying the very intermediaries whose existence radical behaviorism denied. This did not bode well for the longevity of radical behaviorism. In the middle of the twentieth century, to make matters worse, radical behaviorism's agenda was challenged by its apparent failure when it came to linguistic development, by research in the new field of computer science, and by the brilliant work of a new breed of experimental psychologists.

1.2.3 The Cognitive Revolution

The aforementioned developments led to the emergence of a more inclusive, more interdisciplinary science whose determinate subject matter was the complicated set of systems intervening between sensory stimulation and behavior. The focus, more specifically, would be on "cognitive" processes, which are just the processes involved in the generation, storage, retrieval, manipulation, and utilization (for guidance of behavior) of representations.[9]

1.2.3.1 Language Development: Chomsky's Critique of Skinner It is commonly claimed, and not without some justification, that Noam Chomsky's critique of B. F. Skinner's theory of language development (e.g., as set out in his 1959 review of Skinner's 1957 book *Verbal Behavior*) delivered the death blow to behaviorism in American psychology. Whether or not this is the case, Chomsky's work in linguistics certainly raised serious concerns about the behaviorist proposal that a single set of learning principles are manifest in all forms of human and non-human learning.

Chomsky's most influential arguments against the Skinnerian model of language learning include the poverty-of-the-stimulus (POS) argument, the no-precedent output (NPO) argument, and the productivity argument. The POS argument emphasizes just how quickly, easily, and automatically language learning occurs in children despite the fact that their speech community typically affords them only meager evidence of the complicated principles governing the production and comprehension of their native language. The NPO argument is based on the observation that children undergo a fairly standard developmental progression that includes utterance of sentences that are neither grammatical nor like any sentences the child has ever heard. The productivity argument starts with the recognition that humans are finite creatures who are capable of producing and comprehending a limitless number of grammatical sentences. None of this, Chomsky claimed, was to be expected on a Skinnerian model. All of it, he thought, pointed to the existence of an innate language-acquisition device that comes pre-configured with vast knowledge of the space of possible linguistic principles and that is able, through experience, to "tune" itself to the specific principles being utilized in one's local community. What Chomsky was quite self-consciously advocating was a shift back toward the psychology of the rationalists. (See, e.g., Chomsky 1990.)

Whatever the status of Chomsky's hypotheses, his work clearly did much to bolster the plausibility of the view, which was already re-gaining its popularity, that there are important and complicated intermediaries between stimuli and behaviors. Skinner would, of course, attempt to accommodate everything that could be thrown at him from Chomsky or anyone else (see, for example, Skinner 1963), but in the end his cause would attract few new recruits.

1.2.3.2 Computer Science Also helping to foment the cognitive revolution was the advent of programmable electronic computing devices. The foundation for this work was laid partly by Alan Turing's conceptual work on the nature of computation in the 1930s. Up to that point, 'computation' was taken to refer to the kind of formal symbol manipulation that might be carried out by a human using only a pencil and paper and following a set of simple instructions, called an *effective* (or *mechanical*) procedure. In other words, a given task was thought to be comput*able* insofar as there was an effective procedure that a human could follow, without any reliance on insight or ingenuity, in order to complete the task. (See Copeland 1997.) One of Turing's big insights was that this rather informal way of defining "effective procedure," which relied on intuitions concerning what it means for a human to carry out a task without insight or ingenuity, could be recast in terms of simple activities that might be carried out by a hypothetical machine—what we now call a *Turing machine*.

A Turing machine is little more than an imaginary device that can carry out very simple instructions. It is the counterpart of a human carrying out such instructions, and it has the same basic components. In place of a sheet of paper, it has a long tape of paper divided into cells; in place of eyes and limbs, it has a device that can read the contents of cells (e.g., 1's and X's), erase those contents, write new contents, and move the tape one cell to the left or right. In place of a brain, it has a control unit that can be programmed to follow very simple instructions. (See figure 1.1.) The trick is that when you put lots of very simple instructions together in the right way, you can get the device to carry out the very kinds of symbol manipulations to which 'computation' was intuitively thought to refer. For example, the Turing machine in figure 1.1 is, assuming an infinite tape, capable of adding any two numbers. The machine's tape represents two numbers, 2 and 3, as sequences of 1's bordered by X's. The control unit executes the instructions in the table. The top row of the table lists the three possible contents of the cell being read, the left column lists the six possible states of the machine. The cells inside the table contain motor instructions (i.e., D—draw a '1'; X—Draw an 'X'; E—erase; R—move tape to the right; L—move tape to the left) and a specification of the subse-

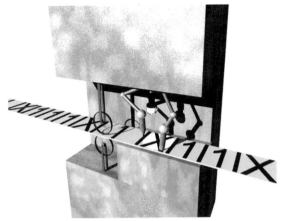

		X	1
1	D6	ER	1
2	R2	E3	?
3	R3	E4	E5
4	L4	?	R6
5	L5	?	R1
6	X6	!	R3

Figure 1.1
Left: A stylized Turing machine. Right: An instruction table for addition. Source: Adler 1961, p. 24.

quent state of the machine. The machine starts off in state 1 and reading from the cell indicated. The control table specifies (see shaded cell) that when the machine is in state 1 and reading an 'X' it should erase the contents of that cell and go to state 2. The machine will then be in state 2 and reading that there is a blank cell, and the table specifies that under those conditions the machine should move the tape one cell to the right and remain in state 2. The process continues until '!' is reached, which means the addition process has been completed.

Turing's basic proposal regarding the nature of computation was not very novel. The proposal was that a task is computable if and only if there is an effective procedure for it. His main innovation, however, was to recast effective procedures as the sorts of simple instructions that can be followed by a Turing machine (i.e., instructions like those contained in the machine table for the device in figure 1.1).

Turing later realized that the state transitions of any particular Turing machine could themselves be recorded on a tape and fed to a second machine, called a universal Turing machine, that would be capable of mimicking the first machine. A universal Turing machine, in other words, could be *programmed* to do what any simple Turing machine does.

All this work took place before the advent of electronic programmable computers. By the middle of the twentieth century, John von Neumann would propose a different sort of machine. This one was like a universal

Turing machine in that it could take as input either data or instructions and could do anything that a universal Turing machine could do, but it was considerably more complex in other respects. For instance, his machine's ability to access particular memory contents was not restricted by which contents had been accessed previously—that is, the device could be instructed to jump from one memory register to any other—and this allowed for a far more sophisticated range of basic instructions. EDVAC, built in 1951, was the first actual implementation of these architectural principles. The vast preponderance of computers in existence today are also constructed in accordance with these principles and so are known as *von Neumann devices*.

The design of the modern programmable computer was inspired at least in part by an interest in how an automaton might do what a human does, and so computers were made to have some of the same basic components as humans. They have, to start with, input devices that are analogous to sense organs, and they have output devices that are analogous to human limbs, vocal tracts, etc. Even the electronic circuitry was modeled after that found in human brains (Asaro 2005). In addition, and of great relevance to the cognitive revolution, the behavior of a computer cannot be predicted solely on the basis of knowledge of past and present stimuli. To know what a computer is going to do, one must know about the complex intermediaries between stimuli and responses. This was a fact about computers that clearly helped inspire Chomsky's work in linguistics, as is evident in the following passage from his critique of Skinner's *Verbal Behavior*:

It is important to see clearly just what it is in Skinner's program and claims that makes them appear so bold and remarkable. It is not primarily the fact that he . . . limits himself to study of 'observables,' i.e., input-output relations. What is so surprising is the particular limitations he has imposed on the way in which the observables of behavior are to be studied, and, above all, the particularly simple nature of the function which, he claims, describes the causation of behavior. One would naturally expect that prediction of the behavior of a complex organism (or machine) would require, in addition to information about external stimulation, knowledge of the internal structure of the organism, the ways in which it processes input information and organizes its own behavior. (1959, p. 27)

Nor, we shall see, was this lesson lost on the new breed of experimental psychologists.[10]

Another interesting fact about computing machines is that their operations can be understood at any of a number of independent levels of abstraction. (See also section 6.2.) For instance, if the Turing machine depicted in figure 1.1 were an actual machine, one could, in principle, explain and predict its behavior on the basis of knowledge of its physical parts and the constraints governing their interaction. Alternatively, however, if we knew that it implemented a particular machine table, we could predict and explain its behavior solely on the basis of our knowledge of its basic functional components, the current state of the machine, the table of instructions, and the contents of the cell being read. These basic properties and principles can be implemented by devices that are in many ways physically diverse (e.g., by a hard-wired Turing machine or a universal Turing machine, either of which can be made in different ways and out of different materials). At an even higher level of abstraction, we could simply view the machine as performing the operation of addition. On this approach to the machine's operations, we know that for any two numbers we put on the tape (in the right format of course) when we set the machine to running, it will somehow produce the representation of their sum. We can know this about the machine, and thus gain some predictive leverage over it, even if we do not know the lower-level instruction set it used to implement this operation. In fact, addition can be implemented by different types of computer architecture (e.g., by a von Neumann device) and, correlatively, in terms of very diverse instruction sets. It is these multiple-realization relations that mark the independence of the different levels of abstraction at which the operations such devices can be understood (Pylyshyn 1984, p. 33). This fact about computational systems turns out to be important to cognitive science for a variety of reasons, only some of which will be discussed in this book. For the moment, it is enough to note that computer operations can be understood at a very high, or abstract, level, and that among the high-level operations that computers can carry out are both mathematical operations *and* logical operations.[11] This may have been on the mind of Turing (1950) when he proposed that computers might one day be programmed to think (albeit on a specific, operationalized version of what 'thinking' means). It was, in any event, clearly on the minds of Allen Newell, J. C. Shaw, and Herbert Simon, who in 1956 devised the first artificial intelligence program, a theorem-proving device known as Logic Theorist. By the early 1970s, the project of attempting to model human thought processes using high-level implementations of (inter alia) the principles of formal logic was in full swing. The techniques varied significantly, but even today the production-system architecture developed by Newell and Simon (1972) remains one of the most popular modeling tools in AI. In order, therefore, to get a more in-depth look at the techniques employed in traditional AI research, let us take a closer look at how production systems do what they do.

To focus on a specific kind of task, a production system can harbor sentence-like representations of both the current state of its environment and a desired state. For instance, a production system can be used to represent the positions of three blocks (let us call them 'A', 'B', and 'C') relative to each other and to a table.[12] Specifically, it might represent, with the help of the following formulas, the fact that block A is on top of block B, that blocks B and C are on the table, and that nothing is atop either A or C:

Ontop <A, B>
Ontop <B, Table>
Ontop <C, Table>
Empty <A>
Empty <C>

It might also have as its goal the following state of affairs:

Ontop <C, B>

Production systems can also determine the consequences of specific alterations to the current state of the world by applying inference rules (called *operators*) to the contents of its working memory. For instance, the hypothetical production system described here might have an operator called Move <x, y> that takes two arguments, x and y, and which, when applied, updates the contents of short-term memory to reflect the fact that a block that has been moved will be on top of whatever surface it is moved to, that the surface from which it was moved will be vacant, and so on.[13]

In addition to operators, productions systems utilize a further set of rules, called *productions*, and a set of heuristics in order to determine which operator applications will bring them closer to a particular goal.[14] Whereas operators contain information about the consequences of alterations, it falls to productions, of which there are typically at least three sets, to determine which operators to apply in a given situation. The first set, the *operator proposal productions*, determine which operators contained in long-term memory *can*, given the contents of short-term memory, be applied. For instance, the Dump <x, y> operator might take as one of its arguments the name of a container and as the other argument the name of the container's contents. Thus, if there is no container represented in short-term memory, the operator proposal productions would not return the Dump <x, y> operator as one that can be applied in the situation in question. Of the (usually many) operators that can be applied, a further set of *operator-comparison productions* determines, either through random choice or on the basis of some learned or programmed preference, which of these will be likely to bring the system closer to its goal. Finally, it falls to the *operator-application productions* to execute the operator that was output by the decision process. Execution of operators can either be carried out with respect to the world itself (whether real or virtual) or "in the head of" the production system, thus enabling the system to think before it acts. Thus, for example, our hypothetical production system might determine that the above goal state can be reached by first moving block A to the table and then moving block C atop block B. Having figured this out, the model might carry out the corresponding sequence of alterations in its environment.[15]

Although the overarching goal of a production system will generally be to find a chain of inference that extends from the actual state of affairs to the desired state, production systems incorporate knowledge and strategies that can streamline this process. One important form of knowledge, gained through learning, is knowledge for which operators or sequence of operators led to the desired result under similar conditions in the past. This knowledge is incorporated into the operator-comparison productions, thus freeing the system from having to try out operators at random, and it can also be packaged into useful "chunks." The strategies, or heuristics, incorporated by production systems include the establishment of sub-goals and backwards reasoning.[16] The latter can enable a production system to consider which actions would constitute an immediate cause of the desired state, which actions would bring about this cause, and so on until (to quote someone who described just such a process centuries earlier) "some cause is reached that lies within [its] power" (Hobbes 1651/1988).

Soon after the development of production systems, it was recognized that the basic package of production-system techniques could be applied to problem-solving activities over any of variety of domains—that is, as long as the relevant constraints governing such domains could be encoded in the form of productions and operators. John Anderson's ACT* model (1983), for instance, was an adaptation of the production-system architecture in order to model language comprehension. In fact, by the late 1970s researchers were utilizing production systems and other variations on the technique of encoding knowledge in the form of sentences and inference rules for embodying the knowledge that experts bring to bear in such contexts as classification, troubleshooting, and medical diagnosis; for constructing computerized vision systems and controlling effectors; and for modeling both knowledge of typical events and our ability to override default assumptions about typical properties of objects and conglomerations thereof.[17] By the late 1970s it was also becoming clear that there were different research agendas in AI that could be individuated by the different uses to which researchers, in AI and elsewhere, thought computers could, or ought to, be put.[18]

The research agenda that has the least relevance to the study of the human mind is what might be called the *pure engineering* approach, the goal of which is merely to get computers to perform tasks that seem to require intelligence when they are performed by humans. IBM's famous chess-playing computer Deep Blue is now the standard illustration of this strategy at work. The goal set for Deep Blue was to defeat the world's greatest chess player, plain and simple. It managed to do just this by calculating the consequences of huge numbers of moves, something that no human can do. It is of little import to its designers, however, that Deep Blue happens not to play chess in a manner that precisely mimics how humans play chess, for modeling human thought processes was never their intent.

The second research strategy is distinguished by a commitment to no more and no less than what might be called *prescriptive* computationalism. On this view, many scientific theories—cognitive-scientific or otherwise, but especially the complex ones—ought to be expressed in terms of effective procedures. As we saw above, effective procedures are just the sorts of instructions that can be carried out by a Turing machine, a universal Turing machine, or (more relevantly) a von Neumann device. When theories are formulated in terms of effective procedures, computing machines can obviate the need to rely upon intuitions regarding whether or not a theory has particular implications, for the formulation of a theory in terms of effective procedures can enable those implications to be determined by purely mechanical means.[19]

Prescriptive computationalists tend not to demand that *all* theories be formulated in terms of effective procedures. However, when theories become so complex that we lose confidence in our ability to evaluate their implications, the formulation of theories in terms of effective procedures can be quite useful. "One of the clearest advantages of expressing a cognitive-process model [though the same lesson clearly applies in other cases] in the form of a computer program is, it provides a remarkable intellectual prosthetic for dealing with complexity and for exploring both the entailments of a large set of proposed principles and their interactions."

(Pylyshyn 1984, p. 75; see also Johnson-Laird 1983) An AI researcher who is committed to no more and no less than prescriptive computationalism thus sees the computer as a tool for getting clear on the tenets of, and for determining the implications of, a particular model of cognitive processing. The research strategy employed in this case is a great deal like that employed in other areas of science where computer modeling is important (e.g., plate tectonics, economics, astrophysics).

The third type of research strategy in AI is characterized by a commitment to what might be called *theoretical* computationalism. Theoretical computationalists in AI are committed to prescriptive computationalism, but they also favor a hypothesis concerning the relation between the human cognitive system and the effective procedures devised to model it. In particular, theoretical computationalists believe that the human brain implements the very rules (or perhaps close variants thereof) that are constitutive of their computational models; they consider the brain to be a similar sort of computational system. This is clearly much stronger than the commitment to no more and no less than prescriptive computationalism.[20]

Theoretical work undertaken in the 1940s by the neurophysiologist Warren McCulloch and the logician Walter Pitts did much to bolster the apparent viability of the theoretical computationalists' research agenda. As was mentioned above, McCulloch and Pitts were well aware of the basic findings regarding the functioning of neurons, and they were able to envision how networks of simple processing units that obeyed these same principles might implement certain principles of logic. They also proposed that an appropriately configured network of these processing units would, if supplied with a memory tape and a means of altering its contents, have the same computing power as a universal Turing machine (Bechtel, Abrahamsen, and Graham 1998, p. 30). Such findings naturally strengthened the pull of the view that the brain is a computer, for the high-level programs (e.g., production-system models) run on electronic computers could, in principle, also be run on neural networks.

In addition to these rather well-known research strategies in AI, there is room for a fourth in an oft-unnoticed middle ground between theoretical computationalism and mere prescriptive computationalism. This is because one can, on the one hand, reasonably claim that an AI model (e.g., a production-system model) consists of some of the same functional components and processes on which humans rely when dealing with analogous problems (e.g., heuristics such as forward and backward reasoning, a form of chunking, and the establishment of sub-goals) while, on the other hand, denying that the representations of the environment harbored in human working memory either have a language-like structure or are manipulated through the application of syntax-sensitive inference rules. Most AI models can be viewed in a similar manner—that is, it is possible to understand them as having some of the same basic functional components and processes as the brain without committing oneself in any way to the view that the brain is a computational system.

1.2.3.3 Cognitive Psychology By the 1960s, experimental psychologists were surely feeling pressure from neuroscience, linguistics, and computer science. Real change for psychology would, however, have to come from within. Experimental psychologists would have to find a way to study, in a fully scientific manner, the complicated processes mediating human interactions with the world.

Though behaviorists tended not to countenance intermediaries of the requisite sort, the importance of behaviorism to the eventual development of a legitimate experimental psychology is difficult to overstate.[21] Behaviorists recognized that the only admissible data for a respectable science of psychology are stimuli and responses. To be sure, radical behaviorists also tried to winnow down the space of plausible theories to those that concerned law-like S-R relationships, but even this failure was an important advance, for it helped to direct the attention of psychologists to precisely what it was that they were lacking—namely, models of the complicated mechanisms intervening between stimuli and behaviors. Let us turn, then, to the ingenious set of techniques developed to tackle the problem of formulating and testing competing models of these intermediaries.

Today, *cognitive* psychologists are concerned with understanding the processes by which representations are formed, manipulated, and utilized. They are, however, not (at least not in the first instance) interested in either neuroanatomy or neurophysiology. In fact, unlike neuroscientists, pure experimental psychologists never look directly at the organ whose activities they are studying. Because of this, the challenges they face are in many ways more daunting than those faced by neuroscientists. The only data they have to go on are the behaviors exhibited by subjects under various (usually well-crafted) conditions. Though there are different sorts of behavior that can be measured, the two most popular—reaction times (RTs) and recall scores—are adaptations of methods first developed in the nineteenth century. To get a good sense of how cognitive psychology works, it will help to consider some early, representative illustrations of how these measures were used in the testing of models of cognitive processing.

1.2.3.3.1 Reaction Times   Picture, if you will, a horse. By default, your imagined horse probably is facing in a particular direction and is upright. Now imagine what the horse would look like if it were upside down. Did you mentally rotate the horse 180° around a particular axis, or did the horse simply appear there? You may or may not feel that there is clear-cut answer to this question. Fortunately, your own introspective impression of the process is, from where the cognitive psychologist sits, far from decisive. Instead, the choice between these competing theories (continuous mental rotation and instantaneous transformation) might be decided, at least as a first pass, by the time that it takes for subjects to move mental images through various degrees of transformation (45°, 90°, 135°, . . .). For instance, if it were found that it takes twice as long to transform an image by 180° than it does to transform it by 90°, and similarly for 45°, then we would have some reason for thinking that the transformation takes place in a continuous fashion (i.e., like rotating a picture) rather than in a more instantaneous fashion. Of course, one can't simply ask subjects when they have completed the various transformations. Indeed, in order to minimize the influence of subject expectations, it would help if subjects had little or no idea about the purpose of the experiment at all. Thus, what one might do, and what some (e.g., Shepard and Metzler 1971) have done, is ask subjects to evaluate whether pairs of images depict the same object. For instance, a subject might be presented with one image on the left side of a page (or a computer screen) and an image to the right of it which in some cases is, apart from being rotated to some determinate degree, identical. Subjects can then be asked to evaluate, by pressing one of two buttons, whether or not the two images depict the same object. If the instantaneous-transform theory is correct, we would expect, in those cases where subjects correctly respond that a pair of images depict the same object, that their reaction times would not be systematically influenced by the degree to which the two depictions are offset relative to one another. If the continuous-rotation theory is correct, on the other hand, we would expect the reaction time to be systematically influenced by the degree to which the depictions are offset relative to one another. In Shepard and Metzler's (1971) study, it was found that there is a positive linear relationship between RTs and the degree to which images of the same object are offset relative to one another. Their results, in other words, favor the continuous-rotation model over the instantaneous-transform model and provide a nice illustration of how RTs can be used to test competing theories concerning processes that are at least plausibly considered to be introspectively impenetrable.[22]

1.2.3.3.2 Recall Scores   Recite, if you will, your phone number. Now think about all the cognitive operations that might have figured into your execution of this simple instruction. For starters, you probably had to be able to read and understand my instructions. And you probably transformed a neural representation of your phone number into an acoustic representation, and in order to do that you had to manipulate, quite precisely, the tremendous number of muscles controlling your vocal chord, tongue, lips, and so on. You also had to *remember* your phone number.

Now have a look at this number: 723-3684

Please close your book, go to your phone, and punch the number in. It seems likely that some of the same cognitive processes you brought to bear in the execution of this set of instructions were also brought to bear when simply reciting your own phone number, though some are probably different. But which ones are the same, and which are different? More specifically, how is it that you were able to remember the number after the book had been closed, and is the same kind of memory used in this case as was used to remember your own number? One final question: What kind of experiment would you devise in order to answer the last question? Devising such an experiment is no easy task, but it can be, and has been, done. To see how, try something else. Once again, I am going to present you with a number. But this time, after you have closed your book and before punching in the number, count backwards from 15 as fast as you can. Here is your number: 537-9671. Now go to it.

How did you do? If you are anything like the rest of us, you probably had a bit of trouble. At the very least, it was probably harder for you to carry out this set of instructions than the previous set. That is, the task of counting backwards probably presented something of a distraction. How do you think you would have fared had you been asked to count backwards before dialing your own phone number? Intuitively, at least, it seems likely that your performance would hardly have been affected. Now we are getting somewhere, but we haven't quite achieved scientific respectability. (We have attained roughly the same level of respectability as Ebbinghaus.)

Through the use of instructions not unlike the ones I just gave you, a far more credible set of data was generated in the 1960s (Postman and Phillips 1965; Glanzer and Cunitz 1966). Subjects in these experiments were presented with rather long lists of items (words, numbers, nonsense syllables, and so on), one item at a time, and after presentation they were asked to recall the items on the list. The results were then graphed out, and they looked something like figure 1.2. Items near the beginning and near the end of the list were recalled more readily than items in the middle, a pair of phenomena known as the *primacy effect* and the *recency effect,* respectively. The two effects happen to be separable—that is, under certain conditions the former effect remains intact while the latter is severely diminished. For instance, when subjects are asked to perform some activity (e.g., counting backwards) in the interval between list presentation and recall, the primacy effect is undiminished while the recency effect nearly disappears. The curve of serial positions ends up looking more like figure 1.3.

The length of the distraction period has a definite influence on the magnitude of the recency effect. It has been concluded on the basis of these and other results that two distinct memory mechanisms are being utilized in order to remember the list items. The first is a long-term storage mechanism. The early list items make it into this long-term store because one

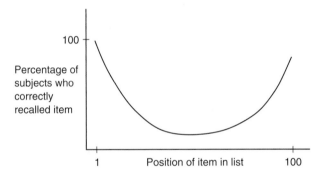

Figure 1.2
An approximation of the serial-position curve.

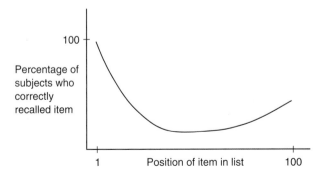

Figure 1.3
An approximation of the serial-position curve, with distraction.

is able to repeat them to oneself a few times after they have been presented. When a large number of items have been presented, however, subjects are no longer able to repeat the entire list before the next item appears. Thus, once the list has grown beyond a few items, fewer of the items make it into long-term storage. The items at the end of the list, on the other hand, are thought to be held in a short-term storage mechanism. Items seem to remain in this mechanism for only a few seconds before they fade. They can be refreshed through repetition, but when something prevents repetition they are soon forgotten. Thus, you may have difficulty dialing a strange phone number after being asked to count backwards because you were not able to repeat the number to yourself, but counting backwards has no effect on your ability to remember your own number, which is in long-term storage.

Measures of recall provide another useful way of investigating cognitive processes. Today the use of recall measures (an offshoot of Ebbinghaus' technique of learning to criterion) is one of the most popular techniques for investigating cognitive processes—in particular, those associated with learning and memory.

1.2.3.3.3 Controls and Statistics How do psychologists deal with the tremendous variability in the performance levels of individual subjects? In the case of mental rotation, for instance, the amount of time that it takes one person to make a correct judgment that two images depict the same object in the event that the depictions are offset by 90° might be less than the time it takes for another person to make such a judgment when the depictions are offset by 45°—unless, that is, the former is not well rested, or is about to attend a job interview, or is too cold, or. . . . What is needed is a way of controlling for variability, or, failing that, a way of mathematically factoring out whatever variability cannot be controlled.

One way of controlling for variability is to see to it that there are few relevant differences between the groups. That is to say, on average, each group being studied should be of about equal intelligence, equal age, equally well rested, and equal on any other metric that might affect the outcome of the experiment. One way of ensuring equality on all these dimensions is to use the same experimental subjects as both the control group and the experimental group. That is to say, sometimes it is possible to use what is called a *within-subjects design* instead of a *between-subjects design*. For instance, in the context of an experimental study of the recency effect, one might measure the behavior of the very same subjects under both normal recall and distraction conditions.

Use of this technique does, however, raise the further concern that the order in which the two conditions are examined might have some effect on the results. In order to mitigate this worry, one might *counterbalance* the presentation of the two tasks such that half of the subjects are required to perform the distractor task before the normal recall task and the other half are required to perform the tasks in the opposite order. These, then, are some of the most basic techniques that experimental psychologists utilize in order to counteract the inherent variability of human behavior.

Still, just as a perfectly normal coin can be flipped twenty times in a row and come up heads every time, the differences between two groups of behavioral measurements can turn out to be a mere anomaly. Consider, for instance, the finding that the recency effect is diminished when subjects are asked to perform a distractor task between presentation of the last list item and recall of the list. How big a difference between the slopes of the tails of the serial-position curves would be enough for you to conclude that this experimental manipulation had a definite effect? It will always be within the realm of possibility that an observed difference between the two conditions is a mere anomaly. In order to figure out whether or not the manipulation of an independent variable (in this case the presence or absence of a distractor activity) had a genuine effect on the dependent variable, one must rely on statistics.

As I have noted, Fechner was one of the first to use statistics in order to deal with uncontrollable variability. The field of mathematical statistics has advanced tremendously since Fechner's time, however, and the statistical analysis of behavioral data now constitutes a tool that is as reliable as it is indispensable. Occasional erroneous poll results and spurious correlations have, of course, caused statistics to become much maligned in popular culture, but the use of statistics in order to determine the probability that two or more sets of measurements have been taken from distinct populations—and thus whether or not manipulation of an independent variable had a real effect on a putative dependent variable—has become an exact science. An extended lesson in psychological statistics is not feasible here, but some sense can be given of the kinds of things a good statistical analysis will take into account.

Consider, for example, the reaction-time experiment discussed above. A statistical analysis of the data from this experiment will enable a quite precise determination of the probability that the difference between two groups of response-time measurements (e.g., the average response time for a 45° transformation and a 90° transformation) is just random variation.

To start with, notice that if one were to find only a moderate difference between the averages for two groups of RTs, and if the groups consisted of only three measurements apiece, these results would not lend a great deal of credence to the mental rotation theory. On the other hand, if a moderate difference were found between the averages of two groups of 10,000 measurements, this result would be more persuasive. The number of separate measurements that figure in an average measurement is thus something that must be, and is, taken into account by modern statistical techniques.

Notice also that the degree to which individual measurements vary from their group average is of some importance. For instance, if every one of 100 people took exactly half a second to determine that two images depict the same object when they are offset by 45° and exactly a second when one of the images are offset by 90°, we would have a pretty informative result. On the other hand, if the time to make such judgments varied from 0.1 to 0.8 second in the first case and from 0.25 to 0.95 second in the second case, what we should conclude becomes far less clear. Thus, an informative statistical analysis must take into account the standard deviation from the average.

With the help of equations that take into account these and other factors, one can determine quite precisely the probability that one's experimental manipulation had an effect. In general, anything greater than a 5 percent chance that the difference between two groups of measurements is just random variation is taken as a failure to provide sufficient warrant for concluding that one's manipulation had an effect. When the probability that the difference between two measurements was the result of random variation is 5 percent or less, the results are taken to be indicative that the experimental manipulation did have an effect. In such cases, the difference between the two groups of measurements is considered *statistically significant*. Researchers are, of course, happier when the probability that random variation is responsible for their results is far less than 5 percent. They also like it when their findings are replicated independently.

1.2.3.3.4 Cognitive Psychology and the Hallmarks of Science

With the help of statistics, cognitive psychologists have been able to make theirs a genuine experimental science. In fact, of the nine hallmarks of science mentioned in subsection 1.2.2, cognitive psychology exhibits all the requirements but the seventh—that is, it has not resulted in the formulation of a body of laws. Interestingly, behaviorism satisfied the seventh requirement but not the sixth (and it arguably failed to satisfy the ninth).

Cognitive psychology, on the other hand, satisfies the sixth requirement but not the seventh. This reflects the tendency of behaviorists (and most philosophers) to hold the discovery of laws to be the fundamental goal of science. The cognitive psychologist is, in contrast, interested in formulating viable models of the complex systems that mediate human interaction with the world. Cognitive psychology, it seems to me, got the better end of the deal.[23]

1.2.3.4 Inter-Disciplinary Research in Cognitive Science

In recent decades, there has been a great deal of interest in clarifying and fostering the connections that exist between research in, among other disciplines, the neurosciences, artificial intelligence, and psychology. The rationale for this is quite simple: The cognitive branches of these sciences clearly have a common subject matter, so their findings should be both mutually constraining (when it comes to the space of viable models) and enlightening.[24] As a brief illustration of how fruitful this interdisciplinary activity can be, consider just a few of the advances that have occurred since the cognitive revolution began.

1.2.3.4.1 Neuropsychology In neuropsychology, the tried-and-true method for correlating cognitive functions with anatomical structures is still the study of individuals with some form of detectable brain damage (e.g., after surgery, stroke, excessive alcohol consumption, accidents, gunshot wounds, and so on) or some other pathology (e.g., schizophrenia, Parkinson's Disease, autism, etc.). Present-day neuropsychology is thus a continuation of the research program begun by the likes of Broca and Wernicke in the nineteenth century. Present-day neuropsychologists do, however, take more care in their analyses.

One common technique employed by early neuropsychologists was to group individuals into categories of pathology according to the family of symptoms they exhibited and to see what neural structures could be associated with these pathologies. The emphasis has shifted in recent years, however, from associating cognitive deficits with neural pathologies to *dissociating* particular cognitive deficits from one another (Ellis and Young 1988). This enables researchers to reach conclusions about the independence of various cognitive functions. For instance, if it were found that an individual or a group of individuals suffered brain damage that resulted in their being unable to recognize faces while they remained fully capable of recognizing tools, we would have some basis for thinking that the two functions are carried out by separate neural mechanisms. Of course, we should also like to be sure that the problem is not due to poor visual acuity (e.g., a person with low acuity might be able to discriminate a hammer from a saw but not be able to distinguish Hillary Clinton and Tipper Gore). Had we established that the problem is not vision-based, the case for functional independence would be made even stronger were the converse deficit also observed. That is to say, the claim of functional independence would be more persuasive if some individuals had difficulty recognizing faces (and not tools) while others had difficulty recognizing tools (and not faces). Instances of *double dissociation* are generally viewed as providing compelling evidence that two cognitive functions are carried out by independent neural mechanisms. This is just one research angle, however.

In order to understand the precise nature of a functional deficit, it may also be necessary to heed a variety of subtle clues offered up by behavior. Neuropsychologists have thus devised some unique methods for making inferences about cognition from observable behavior, and they have also co-opted some of the techniques employed by cognitive psychologists. As an illustration of the former, imagine that you are studying two individuals who seem, on cursory examination, to suffer from some form of attention deficit. To study the precise nature of their respective deficits, you might employ as one of your tools the Rey-Osterrieth Complex Figure (figure 1.4). Now suppose that when you ask the two individuals to copy the figure with the aid of pencil and paper, you notice that one is able to accurately depict the fine-grained features of the diagram while erring with regard to the global arrangement of these features. The other has the

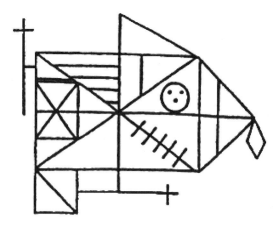

Figure 1.4
The Rey-Osterrieth Complex Figure.

opposite propensity; that is, she creates an accurate portrayal of the arrangement of some of the features while overlooking many of the details. On this basis, you might tentatively hypothesize that one of the two individuals is impaired in the ability to attend to local features of a scene while the other is impaired in the ability to attend to global features. The behavior of the latter might, however, stem from poor visual acuity, so, once again, a test of visual acuity might be administered to this individual. Likewise, for the first individual, some other deficit might account for the poor global organization of the diagram. For instance, perhaps an impairment to short-term memory or some motor deficit is responsible. Thus, for each individual, a battery of tests is administered in order to rule out alternative explanations and isolate the precise nature of their cognitive deficit. If after this battery of tests has been administered the original pair of hypotheses remains credible, one will have discovered an important double dissociation between global and local attention mechanisms.

There are clearly some major differences between this kind of behavioral analysis and the kind carried out in cognitive psychology. For instance, instead of using only a few behavioral measures to study a large group of individuals, a large number of behavioral measures are used in the study of individuals. There are, however, also situations in which neuropsychologists are able to co-opt the techniques pioneered by cognitive psychologists. These techniques are especially useful for studying large and rather well-defined populations of pathological individuals.

One way of applying these techniques is in the comparison of performance on a task or on multiple tasks by some clinical population with the performance of the population at large. For instance, a comparison of the serial-position curve for Alzheimer's patients with the serial-position curve of the rest of the population might reveal a statistically significant difference in the size of the primacy component between the two groups. Insofar as the primacy component is taken on independent grounds to be an indicator of long-term memory functioning, one thereby has some reason to believe that these individuals suffer from an impairment to long-term memory. One can, in addition, compare levels of performance between distinct clinical populations in order to doubly dissociate cognitive functions.

1.2.3.4.2 Cognitive Neuroscience   Advances in imaging technology have made it possible to study the levels of neural activity in the brains of individuals as they carry out some task. Positron emission tomography (PET), for instance, measures activity in various parts of the brain based on the rate of blood flow to those regions. In general, blood flow will increase as a particular part of the brain becomes more active. Thus, by tracking blood flow, PET allows researchers a glimpse into what parts of the brain are most active under a given set of conditions. Another imaging technique, functional magnetic resonance imaging (fMRI), tracks changes in oxygen concentration, though the rationale is much the same as in the case of PET.

One of the exciting new strategies employed by cognitive neuroscientists (who traditionally are psychologists or neuroscientists by training) involves pairing these sophisticated imaging technologies with carefully controlled behavioral measures in order to correlate anatomical structures and cognitive functions. In particular, cognitive neuroscientists have come to rely heavily upon the subtraction method developed in nineteenth century by Donders.

As I explained earlier, the essence of the subtraction method is to subtract a subject's reaction times on a simple task from that subject's reaction times on a more complex task of which the simple task is a component. When used in functional neuroimaging research, the only difference is that one instead subtracts measurements of neural activity from one another. Suppose, for instance, one were interested in determining what part (or parts) of the brain is (or are) responsible for the comprehension of linguistic stimuli. Obviously, one would utilize a task involving language comprehension. But language comprehension requires the contribution of several cognitive systems, and only some of these are of direct interest. For example, comprehension of a written sentence may come after various stages of processing involving the visual recognition of letters and words, and there might also be a separate analysis of grammatical structure. In order, therefore, to distinguish the brain activity that is involved in language comprehension from that which is associated with these other processes, one can have subjects perform a task that taps all the relevant processes *except* comprehension. One can then subtract the levels of activity that are detected under this condition from the levels of activity registered during sentence comprehension. For example, one might have subjects read sentences that are grammatically well formed but which have little or no meaning. These might include sentences that are semantically anomalous (e.g., "The broom ate the ball to the window") or sentences that contain pseudo-words (e.g., "The dwardums glipped the actiphale"). Bernard Mazoyer and colleagues (1993) carried out a study along these very lines. After subtracting brain activity (measured with PET technology) during comprehension of normal sentences from activity measured while reading either semantically anomalous sentences or sentences containing pseudo-words, Bernard Mazoyer et al. found that a particular region of the brain was more active in the former cases than in the latter. This region, named for Carl Wernicke, had, for independent reasons, long been considered to play an important role in language comprehension. Mazoyer et al. also used variations on this technique in order to identify regions associated with auditory, phonological, lexical, syntactic, and prosodic processing, essentially providing a flow chart of stages of information processing from sensory input to comprehension.

1.3 Philosophy and Cognitive Science

Gosh, the sciences of the human mind have sure come a long way since the nineteenth century. What we have in cognitive science is an interdisciplinary endeavor to understand the complicated mechanisms that mediate our interactions with the world that is truly majestic in scope. Its central disciplines range from the lowest-level sub-cellular goings-on to the highest-level organization of knowledge, and cognitive science is, at its best, characterized by the sharing of information between forward and reverse engineers at all levels of analysis. As a result, cognitive science far surpasses introspection in affording a view of the complicated mechanisms that mediate our relationship with the world. Gone, it would thus appear, are the days when philosophers of mind, language, and knowledge had to rely entirely on introspection and intuition. Clearly philosophers should start comparing notes with cognitive scientists. The basic rationale is quite simple: We share a common subject matter, and so our findings should be both mutually constraining (i.e., when it comes to the space of viable models) and enlightening. Indeed, it can only be to the embarrassment of philosophy if no determinate connections are established between claims made by philosophers about mind, knowledge, and language and what cognitive scientists say on these same topics. (It is not enough to maintain mere consistency with cognitive science. So long as there are no connections between two sets of claims, inconsistencies will be hard to find.)

Not everyone sees it this way, of course. Some claim, for instance, that there are (at the very least) areas of the philosophy of mind, knowledge, or language that are in no way answerable to cognitive science. Individuals of this sort might be heard quoting from Gottlob Frege, who famously rejected the proposal that the study of logic could be informed by psychology. Frege claimed that the rules of logic are not simply principles governing our inference processes, for specific rules are valid whether anyone thinks this is the case or not.[25] This harkens back to claims about mathematical knowledge made by the rationalists (which can themselves be traced back to Plato)—namely, that any (unimpaired) person willing to take the time and effort can come to appreciate the necessity and time-lessness of certain truths.[26] I have considerable sympathy with this line of thinking, but I also cannot help but take to heart a point made by John Dewey (another famous nineteenth-century American functionalist): "If one denies the supernatural, then one has the intellectual responsibility of indicating how the logical may be connected with the biological in a process of continuous development." (quoted in Houts and Haddock 1992, p. 376)[27] We are, as Dewey suggests, biologically evolved physical creatures. If one has reasons for thinking that we can come to know the kinds of things that rationalists and Frege claimed that we know, then it is perfectly sensible to ask how it is that a finite biological creature could come to possess this kind of knowledge. At the very least, it is sensible to ask why it is that many of us *claim* to have this kind of knowledge. There is just no reasonable way to dodge the issue.

This is, at any rate, just one sort of philosophical concern. Although it is the one that crops up most frequently when philosophers try to defend the autonomy of philosophy from science, it is not the primary focus of this book. What I wish to demonstrate here is that there are, in fact, *several* important areas of inquiry in which philosophers and scientists can help one another, and this can often be done in a way that privileges neither.[28] This is clearly not a novel suggestion, but it has gone largely unheeded outside the inward-facing circle of "naturalistic" philosophers. The blame can be placed at least partly on us naturalists, for we have failed to present truly compelling demonstrations of how philosophy and cognitive science can help one another. I hope to do my part to remedy this state of affairs. I intend to show, in particular, how it is that some traditional and recent questions in the philosophies of mind, knowledge, and science can be answered with the help of cognitive science, and, conversely, how some of the conceptual tangles into which cognitive science has found itself ensnared can be unraveled with a bit of careful armchair philosophy.

1.3.1 Common-Sense (a.k.a. Folk) Psychology

One issue that has held the attention of naturalistic philosophers for far too long has to do with the relationship between our common-sense or folk-psychological theory of the causes of human behavior on the one hand and the deliverances of cognitive science on the other. Philosophers have been focused mainly on one important facet of folk psychology: the assumption that we humans often formulate and execute plans of action on the basis of our beliefs and desires. For example, I once made it my goal to please my visiting in-laws. I also believed, on the basis of past encounters, that they derived great enjoyment from well-prepared exotic meals. I thus tried to recall all the exotic meals that I could prepare. I then eliminated from consideration the meals I had already prepared for them, and picked one of the remaining meals. I now had a plan of action that I hoped would enable me to achieve my goal. Of course, in order to pull it off I needed to obtain the right ingredients, and this required remembering (or inferring) which stores might have them, and so on and so forth. This is an unexceptional example of how we folk psychologists tend to make sense of both our own behavior and that of our fellow humans. We have been doing it this way throughout recorded history.

As I explained at the start of this chapter, just after the mechanical worldview took hold in Western culture many important new questions were raised about the mind. The vast majority of them, however, *presupposed* the correctness of folk psychology. More recently, however, with the advent of a viable, interdisciplinary *science* of the underlying causes of human behavior, philosophers have begun to ask an even deeper question. Although it is largely agreed upon that we, qua folk, ascribe hidden mental states and processes to ourselves, and to one another, for purposes of the prediction and explanation of behavior (i.e., we take behavior to be *caused* by, among other things, beliefs, desires, and reasoning), some philosophers have wondered whether or not these posited states and processes map onto any of those that cognitive science has either discovered or eventually will discover. Put in a succinct (and common) fashion, they wonder whether or not folk psychology is any more respectable than folk astronomy, folk physics, or folk biology, none of which has a particularly good track record.

A tremendous amount of time and energy has been spent, and continues to be spent, debating this issue. However, as I will explain in the next chapter, most of the philosophical arguments for and against the scientific respectability of folk psychology are premised on some deeply misguided assumptions about the predictive and explanatory practices of cognitive science. Moreover, once these mistaken assumptions are replaced with accurate ones, it becomes perfectly clear that most of what folk psychology has to say about the underpinnings for human behavior has already been amply vindicated by cognitive science.[29]

1.3.2 Intentionality

Whereas chapter 2 concerns the relationship between cognitive science and some of the most easily discernible tenets of common-sense psychology, in chapter 3 I will zoom in, as others have been doing of late, on the precise manner in which we folk psychologists classify mental states. At a coarse grain of analysis, it appears sufficiently clear that we folk psychologists commonly individuate mental states (e.g., the belief that my in-laws like well-prepared exotic meals) on the basis of both the so-called *attitudes* involved (e.g., beliefs, desires, hopes, fears, etc.) and what the states in question are about, or their *contents* (e.g., the relationship between my in-laws and well-prepared exotic meals). What many philosophers wonder about, however, is the precise manner in which the contents of mental states are commonsensically fixed and whether or not contents, so fixed, are the sorts of properties that a thoroughgoing physicalist can reasonably countenance. (This is thorny terrain, but I do my best to blaze a path through it that any motivated philosopher or cognitive scientist can follow.)

Philosophers who are interested in mental contents have tended to consider real and imaginary cases of content attribution in order to highlight the principles on which we folk psychologists rely, if only tacitly, when determining the contents of mental states. The results are now in, and they don't look good for contents. It seems that, insofar as mental contents are concerned, we folk psychologists draw the relevant category boundaries in a manner that is ill suited for a legitimate role in the scientific explanation of human behavior. It turns out, however, that a minor modification of these category boundaries yields a means of fixing the contents of mental states that is far more palatable.

1.3.3 The Structure of Mental Representations

The arguments of chapters 2 and 3 have the ultimate effect of situating folk psychology near the high end of the theoretical-accuracy continuum. This, in turn, restores a certain level of trust in intuitive and/or introspective evidence concerning the nature of human thought processes. To be sure, cognitive science has shown that introspection does not enable us to delve very deep, but that does not mean that it cannot supply some evidence over and above that generated from the objective, third-person point of view. The interplay of these two sorts of evidence seems to have been what interested Jerry Fodor when he claimed that "convergence between what's plausible a priori and what's demanded ex post facto is itself a reason for believing that the theory is probably true" (1978, p. 325). The overarching goal of chapters 4–6 is to attain this kind of convergence with regard to a particular theory about the structure of mental representations.

Over the millennia, philosophers have discovered several principles that an adequate model of mental representation ought to accommodate. In chapter 4, I will discuss two such models: the logic metaphor and the scale-model metaphor. The former inspired, and later took inspiration from, the production-system approach to the computational modeling of human thought processes.[30] Work in computer science has, unfortunately, shown that the logic metaphor cannot fit the most important bill for which it was slated—specifically, it has been shown to fall victim to the *frame problem* with regard to basic practical reasoning (McCarthy and Hayes 1969). Accordingly, I resurrect an alternative explanatory metaphor according to which humans harbor and manipulate the cognitive counterparts to scale models. This model does not suffer from the frame problem, and it clearly matches or surpasses the logic metaphor with regard to some of the most important philosophical desiderata.

Though the arguments of chapter 4 will suffice to demonstrate the plausibility of the scale-model metaphor for mental representation when it comes to mechanical reasoning, one could easily be misled into thinking that a specific sort of hybrid model is ultimately required in order to account for the full range of human thought processes. In particular, one might think that there is still a need for sentences in a special thought language of the sort posited by proponents of the logic metaphor. There are at least two sorts of arguments that might convince one of this. Arguments of the first sort are the culmination of a long tradition of philosophical inquiry into the nature of mental representation; arguments of the second sort are the product of a more recent psychological inquiry into the nature of human reasoning. In chapter 5, I will show that arguments of the first sort are based on some very unrealistic assumptions about human thought processes. (These are assumptions that, like the faulty assumptions about cognitive science I expose in chapter 2, are sure to give cognitive scientists the impression that philosophers are playing their own private games.) Moreover, once these assumptions are discarded it becomes clear that proponents of the scale-model metaphor can account for a far wider range of thought processes than is generally believed. I go on to show that arguments of the second sort derive most of *their* force from a faulty taxonomy of human reasoning processes. Once this taxonomy is put right, it becomes clear that the scale-model metaphor supplies the best account of the structure of the representations underwriting the bulk of human reasoning. The remainder can then be explained in terms of the manipulation of "external" sentences.[31]

There is, nevertheless, still one gigantic challenge facing the proposal that humans harbor and manipulate the cognitive counterparts of scale models. It is a challenge that proponents of the logic metaphor have long since met, and unless we proponents of the scale-model metaphor follow suit the advantage will go to our rivals. In particular, it must be shown that the kinds of representations and representational manipulations in question are of the sort that can in principle be implemented by the human nervous system. As we have already seen, the modern programmable computer is the crucial link between the logic metaphor and the human nervous system. It is widely believed that this route to mechanistic reformulation is not open to proponents of the view that humans harbor and manipulate the cognitive counterparts to scale models. Nor is it likely that some more direct connection to the nervous system will be found (i.e., that someone will discover literal scale models in the head). This leaves the scale-model metaphor stuck in an unpleasant metaphorical limbo. In chapter 6, however, I will supply the long-awaited key to its salvation. Along the way, I will explain how a determinate computational solution to the frame problem has unwittingly been devised by virtual-reality modelers and mechanical engineers. The end result is the formulation of the Intrinsic Cognitive Models (ICM) hypothesis, a high-level mechanical model of mental representation that inherits all the features that make the scale-model metaphor attractive.

1.3.4 The Nature of Explanation

In chapters 7–9, I turn to the nature of explanation. In chapter 7, I defend the bare proposal that cognitive science might have something to contribute to the study of explanation. I then go on to describe the many shortcomings of the Deductive-Nomological (D-N) model, which is the model of explanation that is, for a variety of reasons, endorsed by most philosophers of mind. Along the way, I clarify the very tight connection between the D-N model and the logic metaphor for mental representation. I close with a brief discussion of the shortcomings of the main alternatives to the D-N model.

In chapter 8, I offer up an alternative model of explanation: the Model model. One goal of this chapter is to show that the Model model satisfies our philosophical intuitions about explanation by correctly classifying the many problem cases described in chapter 7. In order to show this, however, we must delve, in standard cognitive-scientific fashion, below the introspectable surface of explanations and consider the states and processes that might underlie them. As it turns out, fleshing out the details of the Model

model through appeal to the ICM hypothesis described and defended in chapter 6 does just the trick. Another goal of chapter 8 is to show that the Model model satisfies our most basic intuitions, our *meta*philosophical intuitions, about what we take ourselves to have when we take ourselves to have genuine explanations for events and regularities. The other major models of explanation do not fare very well in this regard, but the proposal that we take ourselves to have an explanation for an event or a regularity only if we have an intrinsic cognitive model of what produced it seems right on target. The final goal of chapter 8 is to show that this model provides a unified framework for understanding the intimate relationship among the frame problem of artificial intelligence, the ceteris paribus and surplus-meaning problems of the philosophy of science, and the question of how it is, precisely, that people are able to hang onto their pet theories in the face of otherwise disconfirming evidence.

Although (for reasons that will be explained in chapter 2) I am concerned to supply an alternative to the Deductive-Nomological model that fits well with the predictive and explanatory endeavors of cognitive science, the many successes of the ICM-enriched Model model of explanation canvassed in chapter 8 leave me optimistic that it is an accurate model of the psychological underpinnings for explanations of events and (physical) regularities *across the board*.[32] Accordingly, in chapter 9 I push the Model model to its limits. My goals there are twofold. First, I wish to offer a mechanical explanation for the unique kind of knowledge that we have of geometrical principles. Second, I wish to show that the D-N model can be pushed out of its stronghold—namely, fundamental physics. In this regard, I am also pushing my own expertise to (and beyond) its useful limit. I therefore do not hesitate to make frequent appeals to authority. The book comes to a close with some speculations concerning how genuine, enlightening explanations might once again be had in the realm of fundamental physics.

2 | Folk Psychology and Cognitive Science

In chapter 1 we saw that the task of creating a genuine science of the mind required, among other things, finding sources of data other than introspection. Instead of one, or even a few, alternative sources of data, many have been found, and they range from measurements of the activity of single ion channels to measurements of errors made by subjects when recalling the information contained in passages of prose. Now that cognitive science has at its disposal this wide range of alternative sources of data, many wonder whether or not its deliverances will corroborate our pre-scientific (and, arguably, introspection-inspired) conception of how the mind works. What they have failed to see, however, is that cognitive science is dominated by an ongoing research program that has no serious competitors and that presupposes this common-sense ("folk") conception of how the mind works.

2.1 Introduction

As I explained in chapter 1, many consider folk psychology to be a theory that we humans wield in order to make sense of, and to anticipate, the behavior of our fellow humans. If this is an accurate characterization of folk psychology, and if folk psychology, in turn, is an accurate theory, then we humans spend a considerable amount of time trying to figure out how, in light of our beliefs, to fulfill our desires. Quite sensibly, philosophers have been consulting our best science of the underpinnings for human behavior, cognitive science, in order to determine whether or not folk psychology *is* an accurate theory. Unfortunately for folk psychology, this endeavor has led to the assembly of a rather elaborate gauntlet of irrealism for the folk-psychological ontology.

From a distance, this gauntlet looks quite forbidding. On closer inspection, however, it appears to be peopled with some rather sickly-looking foes. What I show in this chapter is that the disease inflicting many of these arguments is their acceptance of some popular, though deeply misguided, assumptions regarding the predictive and explanatory practices of cognitive science. I have no intention of addressing every argument against folk psychology, merely those that happen to be premised on the faulty assumptions to which I have just alluded. Nevertheless, those who take cognitive science to be a legitimate arbiter of the status of folk psychology's ontology should, in the final analysis, be convinced that cognitive science vindicated that ontology long ago.

2.2 The Gauntlet of Irrealism

The gauntlet begins for folk psychology with the question of whether or not we humans are truly capable of both predicting and explaining the behavior of our fellow humans, for there is a case to be made that folk psychology fails to do either on a consistent basis. There are, after all, many instances in which we are utterly incapable of predicting what our fellow humans—even those near and dear to us—will do. Likewise, when it comes to explaining behavior, we often have no idea why someone acted in the particular way he or she did. Moreover, even in cases where we *claim* to be able to explain how someone's beliefs and desires conspired to cause his behavior, it is possible that such accounts are little more than Kiplingian just-so stories (i.e., fanciful stories that have nothing to recommend them beyond the fact that they provide a way of making sense of the behavior in question). Predictive and explanatory limitations of this sort seem to be what Paul Churchland has in mind when he claims that folk psychology might provide "a positively misleading sketch of our internal kinematics and dynamics, one whose success is owed more to selective application and forced interpretation on our part than to genuine theoretical insight on folk psychology's part" (1989, p. 7). Nor, it seems, do the explanatory shortcomings of folk psychology end there. After all, folk psychology also seems to fail miserably in terms of its ability to explain such psychological phenomena as "mental illness, sleep, creativity, memory, intelligence differences, and the many forms of learning, to cite just a few" (Churchland 1998, p. 8). Because of this, Churchland claims, it is disturbing that folk psychology has remained stagnant for thousands of years (and thus offers no promise of *ever* explaining these phenomena) and has also persistently resisted integration with the rest of science—which is the only other thing that might have made it worth hanging on to. These considerations alone seem to bolster the plausibility of an eventual *elimination* of the folk-psychological ontology from scientific discourse.

Even if there are ways to address these charges of predictive and explanatory inadequacy, the gauntlet has only begun for folk psychology. Proceeding in logical, rather than chronological fashion, the next challenge facing folk psychology has to do with the question of just how, cognitively speaking, predictions and explanations of everyday behavior are effected by the folk. According to one proposal, we predict and make sense of ('explain' might be too strong a word if the proposal is accurate) the behavior of our fellow humans by, roughly speaking, taking an imaginary walk in their shoes (Gordon 1996). For example, in order to answer the question "Where will Maxi say the chocolate bar is hidden?" we might imagine what it would be like to be Maxi as she sees the bar hidden, leaves the room, and returns.[1] That is, in order to answer the question of where Maxi will say the bar is hidden, perhaps we imagine what it would be like to be Maxi and then answer the simpler question "Where is the chocolate bar hidden?" What is so "radical" about this proposal, Gordon claims, is that the procedure can be carried out without any understanding of such categories as *belief* and *desire*. The procedure therefore seems to obviate a theory regarding the hidden underpinnings of human behavior. If this Radical Simulation theory is correct, then what we wield in order to make sense of and anticipate the behavior of our fellow humans is not a *theory* at all. This, claim Stich and Ravenscroft (1994), would seem to render questions about the scientific respectability of folk psychology moot and, thereby, undermine at least some versions of eliminativism.[2] What these authors do not tell us, however, is that the theory of radical simulation is just as much a threat to *realism* with regard to the folk-psychological ontology. There are, after all, many who feel that realism with regard to this ontology will ultimately be justified through the scientific vindication of a folk-psychological theory that counts beliefs and desires as among its posits. If folk psychology is not a theory, then this avenue to realism will have been blocked.

It may be, then, that folk psychology would fare much better (i.e., insofar as its scientific standing is concerned) if there were reasons for preferring the Theory theory, according to which our proficiency at predicting and explaining the behavior of our fellow humans stems from our mastery of a body of laws which specify the relationships between, among other things, particular beliefs, particular desires, and particular behaviors. According to the Theory theory, a person might predict that Doug will walk to his refrigerator and remove a pickle by implicitly invoking a law like this one:

If (x desires a pickle and has no stronger desires whose satisfaction would preclude his/her having a pickle, and x believes that there is a pickle in his refrigerator that belongs to x and that said pickle can be obtained by walking to his refrigerator and removing it), then (ceteris paribus) x will walk to his refrigerator and remove a pickle.

If experimental findings consistently favored the Theory theory over the Radical Simulation theory, this would clearly go a long way toward justifying the claim that there is a theoretical ontology constitutive of folk psychology that might eventually be vindicated. It has, unfortunately, proven exceedingly difficult to tease apart Radical Simulation theory and Theory theory on an experimental basis.

Of course, even if there were good reasons for thinking that we humans are highly effective at predicting and explaining the behavior of our compatriots in virtue of our mastery of a set of laws (like the one above) that make reference to such theoretical posits as beliefs and desires, folk psychology *still* has a tough row to hoe. After all, folk psychology might still turn out to share the fate of Ptolemaic astronomy, which also happened to do a fine job of supplying predictions and explanations. In the case of Ptolemaic astronomy, a more compelling theory came along and eliminated such posits as epicycles, and perhaps something similar will happen in the case of such folk-psychological posits as beliefs and desires. Cognitive science might, for example, accomplish all of its predictive and explanatory goals by instead appealing to trajectories through n-dimensional state space (Churchland 1989) or through other means not friendly to folk psychology (see, e.g., Brooks 1991; van Gelder and Port 1995).

Amazingly, even if cognitive science *did* embrace folk psychology and its ontology, this, in and of itself, would not justify realism with regard to the folk-psychological ontology. After all, as Dennett (1991) points out, we still have the option of various shades of irrealism, including instrumentalism. Beliefs and desires might, for instance, turn out to be like centers of gravity. As one version of the argument goes, although there are no such *things* as centers of gravity—after all, they take up no space and engage in no causal interactions—we gain a great deal of inferential leverage by acting *as if* there were. Perhaps a similar set of claims can be supported with regard to the folk-psychological ontology.

It would, on the other hand, seem to constitute a major victory for folk psychology if a particular variant of theoretical computationalism (see subsection 1.2.3.2)—namely, Fodor's (1975) Language of Thought (LOT) hypothesis—were shown to be true. After all, if the LOT hypothesis is correct, then particular beliefs and desires are, at least in present-day humans, *token* identical[3] to brain states that, in comparison with centers of gravity, seem far better candidates for playing a genuine causal role with respect to behavior. Unfortunately for proponents of folk psychology, none of the relevant token identities has ever been established.

As an alternative, Fodor and others (e.g., Pylyshyn 1984; Devitt and Sterelny 1987) have argued that cognitive science simply cannot get by without the LOT hypothesis. This strategy has, of course, spawned great debates about just what kinds of things can and cannot be accomplished through the application of syntax-sensitive inference rules to syntactically structured representations and about whether or not other techniques (e.g., artificial neural networks that are not simply implementing the tenets of the LOT hypothesis) can do the same. Unfortunately for folk psychology, even if it could be shown that the LOT hypothesis truly is the only game in town, serious concerns about folk psychology and its attendant ontology would persist.

One such concern stems from the fact that folk psychology seems to, and the LOT hypothesis certainly does, posit states with content, for it has been argued that contents have no legitimate role to play in any science of the underpinnings for human behavior. This concern has been fleshed out in various ways because there are many theories regarding both the nature of mental contents and the factors that fix the content of a particular mental state. Let us focus on the latter set of theories for a moment.

There are, at present, two broad schools of thought regarding the factors that determine the content of a particular mental state. Crudely put, there are, on the one hand, internalist theories of content fixation according to which what is inside of an individual's head fixes the contents of their mental states. There are, on the other hand, externalist theories according to which facts about what is going on, or has gone on, outside of an individual's head determine what their thoughts are about. The arguments against the scientific legitimacy of contents (and, thereby, of folk psychology) are often directed at specific versions of one or the other of these theories of how contents are fixed.

One of the better-known argument against the legitimacy of folk psychology is directed at a specific internalist theory of content fixation according to which the assignment of content to a mental state is effected relative to the network of further mental states—what Stich (1989) calls its "doxastic surrounding"—within which it is embedded. Put simply, according to this view, the content of an individual's belief cannot be determined in isolation from the rest of what they believe. Suppose, for example, that Laurie claims to own a pair of gold earrings, but, after talking to her for a bit, you find that she denies that gold is shiny, malleable, or considered valuable by many, and that she doesn't agree that ears are used for hearing, though she does insist that inanimate objects such as rocks can own things. When you learn all of this about Laurie, you may be less inclined to attribute to Laurie the belief that she owns a pair of gold earrings. This is an extreme case, but there is, according to proponents of this brand of internalism, nothing about it that makes it qualitatively distinct from more mundane cases. In other words, even in more normal cases we take mental contents to be fixed in no small measure by their doxastic surroundings.

On the assumption that this internalist theory of content fixation is correct, two arguments have been made that contents have no legitimate role to play in cognitive science. The first, which has been voiced by Stich (1989) and Fodor (1994), is roughly as follows:

The primary goal of cognitive science—or any science, for that matter—is to formulate laws. Since doxastic surrounding varies from individual to individual, mental contents vary from individual to individual. There can thus be no laws that quantify over mental contents, and so cognitive science must eschew mental contents.

The second, also attributable to Stich (1996), looks something like this:

Cognitive science is committed to the computational theory of mind, according to which mental states are individuated on the basis of their local, syntactic properties. Yet the contents of mental states are determined by doxastic surrounding, a non-local property. Cognitive science therefore has no use for contents.

Insofar as cognitive science has veto power over folk psychology, these arguments raise concerns about folk psychology. Specifically, if folk psychology is a theory that posits mental states that are individuated on the basis of their doxastic surroundings, and if cognitive science must eschew states of this sort for either of the above reasons, then folk psychology must be mistaken. So much, then, for our illustration of an argument against folk psychology that proceeds by way of an attack on a specific, internalist theory of content fixation. (Whew!)

There are also arguments against folk psychology that are premised upon the claim that the folk take the contents of a person's mental states to be determined by factors outside of that person's head. This is because when everything inside of a person's head is held constant, the beliefs that we are inclined to attribute to them will apparently vary with variations in environmental factors, and this is so even if they are completely unaware of the environmental differences in question. I'll deal with this argument for externalism at great length in the next chapter, but here, to a first approximation, is one of the worries that this form of externalism raises about the scientific credentials of contents and, thereby, of folk psychology:

Folk psychology individuates mental states on the basis of their contents. However, contents can differ even while the causes of behavior remain unchanged, so contents do not track the causes of behavior. There is, then, no place for mental contents in cognitive science. This poses a threat to folk psychology because folk psychology adverts to properties that have no legitimate role to play in cognitive science.

These arguments against folk psychology all take a path through particular theories of content fixation. There is, however, another argument that takes a path through a theory concerning the kinds of properties contents are reputed to be in and of themselves. The argument (which will be discussed at length in the next chapter) looks something like this:

Mental contents, by widely endorsed definition, are relational properties (i.e., they involve relationships between mental states and the world). They are, however, relational properties that have no relevant causal impact on behavior. As such, there is no place for contents in cognitive science.

And, once again, what is bad for contents would seem bad for folk psychology. This, again, is just the unifying theme of this entire set of arguments against folk psychology.

To recap, popular philosophical wisdom has it that the vindication of folk psychology requires the defense of many controversial theses.[4] In particular, it must be shown that the folk really do enjoy a sufficiently high level of predictive and explanatory success with regard to the behavior of their fellow humans, that neither folk psychology's inability to explain other cognitive phenomena nor its stagnancy in this regard poses any threat to folk psychology, that the aforementioned predictive and explanatory successes stem from reliance on an ontology that includes beliefs and desires among the causal determinants of human behavior, that our adoption of this ontology is more than a useful fiction because a version of the computational theory of mind—the LOT hypothesis—is accurate, and that, in pursuit of its explanatory and predictive goals, it is permissible and advisable for cognitive science to individuate the internal, syntactically structured states posited by the LOT hypothesis on the basis of their contents. Things look quite bad for folk psychology, but appearances can be deceiving.

2.3 Archaic Presuppositions

One of the principal reasons why philosophers have failed to find their way clear of this gauntlet is that they have often assumed that the mission of cognitive science is the discovery of psychological laws of the sort that can enable the prediction and explanation of particular everyday behaviors. Given this portrayal of the mission of cognitive science, philosophers have naturally concluded that folk psychology will attain scientific respectability only if cognitive science starts coming up with gobs of laws whose antecedents invoke particular beliefs and desires and whose consequents specify activities like removing pickles from refrigerators. In other words, popular philosophical wisdom seems to have it that folk psychology will be vindicated only if cognitive science starts looking a lot like folk psychology as it is portrayed by the Theory theory! If popular philosophical wisdom is to be believed, then folk psychology really is in a great deal of trouble. After all, the primary mission of cognitive science has most assuredly not even been the search for reliable generalizations. Nor are the explananda one finds invoked in the context of cognitive scientific research particular everyday behaviors, such as going to the refrigerator for a pickle.

While many philosophers *assume* that the primary goal of cognitive science is to discover laws, only Fodor has had the decency to try defending this assumption. What he has to say on this particular matter is, unfortunately, of limited merit: "I cleave to [the idea that psychological explanation typically involves law subsumption] because it's hard to doubt that at least *some* psychological regularities are lawlike (for example: that the Moon looks largest when it's on the horizon; that the Müller-Lyer figures are seen as differing in length; that all natural languages contain nouns)." (1994, p. 3)

There are, to be sure, many regularities that cognitive scientists find deeply interesting.[5] To the above, we might add the phonological-similarity effect, the word-superiority effect, the primacy and recency effects, the STROOP effect, various semantic-priming and motor-learning phenomena, cognitive and motor deficits associated with disorders such as multiple sclerosis and Parkinson's Disease, various forms of aphasia and agnosia, and critical periods. However, it is not for their explanatory power that cognitive scientists find such regularities deeply interesting. Rather, these regularities are, one and all, precisely what cognitive scientists take to stand in need of explanation (Waskan 1997, 1999; Cummins 1999). As I will discuss in greater detail below, what we find playing the part of explanantia to these explananda are not more reliable generalizations, but models of the mechanisms giving rise to them. Fodor nearly admits as much: "An implementing mechanism is one in virtue of whose operation the satisfaction of a law's antecedent reliably brings about the satisfaction of its consequent. . . . Typically, though not invariably, the mechanisms that implement the laws of a science are specified in the vocabulary of some other, lower-level, science." (1994, p. 8) Fodor presumably thinks that if the implementing mechanisms are specified in the vocabulary of lower-level sciences, then he can hang onto both psychological laws and the autonomy of psychology.[6] This disclaimer, however, does nothing to alter the fact that the reliable generalizations that interest cognitive psychologists are the explananda of research. Moreover, if it happens to be the case that psychologists typically invoke the vocabulary of lower-level sciences in the process of formulating explanantia for these explananda — if that is what explanation in cognitive psychology consists of — then so much the worse for the autonomy thesis. The autonomy thesis is not my present target, however, and, to be fair, psychologists need not, and frequently do not, invoke lower-level vocabulary when proposing mechanisms that explain regularities. After all, a finer-grained functional breakdown of the cognitive system is very often the immediate goal of psychological investigation. For example, in order to explain the fact that visual processing causes a decline in performance on a concurrent visuospatial reasoning task while auditory processing causes no such decline, cognitive psychologists posit two independent short-term memory stores: a phonological store and a visuospatial sketchpad (Baddeley 1990). In and of itself, this model entails nothing about the locus, the structure, or the manner of operation of the implementing neural ensembles. In other words, what explains the finding is a model of the underlying mechanisms, but this model is not specified in the vocabulary of a lower-level science.

I will have quite a bit more to say on the nature of explanation in cognitive science, but before proceeding I should quickly dispense with the stronger and doubly ludicrous suggestion that cognitive science will vindicate folk psychology by supplying intentional generalizations of the sort mentioned above.[7] Whatever one's reasons are for thinking that cognitive science *should* supply explanatory intentional generalizations that quantify over states like wanting a pickle, one would be very hard pressed to find evidence that cognitive science *does* supply such generalizations. In fact, I do not think that I would be going out on much of a limb were I to claim that not one law of this kind has ever been proposed in cognitive psychology or in any of the neurosciences.[8] If we are to make any progress in our understanding of the relationship between cognitive science and folk psychology—indeed, if we are to make any progress in the philosophy of mind or the philosophy of cognitive science at all—we must cast aside these distorted theoretical lenses and see cognitive science as it truly is.

2.4 Schematic Models

At the foundation of mainstream cognitive science are some highly schematic, collectively consistent, and intuitively plausible models of the underpinnings for human behavior. One such model, the one on which I will be focusing much of my attention in this and later chapters, depicts humans as engaging in a process of planning, a process whereby one determines how to get from some actual state of affairs to some desired state. In order to make this determination, one represents the two states of affairs and manipulates the former until, crudely speaking, it comes to look like the latter. Planning, in everyday terms, simply involves thinking ahead, or looking before we leap.

As it stands, this model is highly schematic. It supplies only a very broad functional breakdown of the underpinnings for certain human behaviors. It entails no commitments regarding the structure of beliefs or desires (e.g., whether they are sentential or imagistic), nor does it provide any specifics regarding how one reasons one's way from the former to the latter. Like the model of short-term memory described above, the kind of breakdown that the model supplies is functional in roughly the weak sense suggested (to a certain extent) by Lewis (1972) and developed by Lycan (1987) and by Bechtel and Richardson (1993). That is, the model provides a highly schematic understanding of the parts of the cognitive system, of the activities or functions that they carry out, and of how they conspire to cause the phenomena of interest.[9]

The planning model obviously did not originate with today's mind sciences. It has, after all, been invoked in the works of countless poets, playwrights, and novelists throughout the centuries; it has been described in detail by Aristotle (fourth century B.C./1987), by Thomas Hobbes (1651/1988), and by G. W. Leibniz (1705/1997); and (if everyday discourse is any guide) it is a part of our intuitive understanding of how humans operate. It is, in short, an integral part of folk psychology. Of course, were common sense the only grounds we had for endorsing this model, it would fall far short of the mark of scientific respectability. It has, however, long since been adopted, refined, and vindicated by cognitive science.

The proposal that humans plan in the aforementioned manner first began to take on the appearance of a scientific hypothesis when it was invoked in order to explain a general feature of human behavior. As Köhler (1938) and Craik (1952) suggested, a capacity to think ahead would explain why humans often respond in such an unhesitating (once they get started, that is) and effective manner to even highly novel environmental conditions.[10] By the same token, this model can also explain why humans respond in such a flexible manner to even similar environmental conditions.[11] That is to say, it explains why (pace Skinner) human behavior is not stimulus driven.

Today it is considered something of a platitude among cognitive scientists that we humans enjoy an advantage over many other critters in virtue of our capacity to look before we leap. My favorite nemesis-cum-hero puts it this way: "That people . . . act out of their beliefs and desires, and that, in the course of deciding how to act, they often do a lot of thinking and planning, strikes me as maybe empirical in principle but surely not negotiable in practice." (Fodor 1994, pp. 3, 4) To drive Fodor's point a little further home and to get clearer on the precise role that this model plays in cognitive science, it is worth considering the ways in which its role in cognitive science resembles the role played by the theory of natural selection in evolutionary biology.

2.4.1 Natural Selection and Planning: Explanatory Successes and Shortcomings

Notice, to start with, that selectionist explanations of particular traits are sometimes belittled as just-so stories (Gould and Lewontin 1979). That is to say, although a particular explanation might have an air of plausibility to it, it is nevertheless often possible to construct an equally plausible alternative account by utilizing the same general explanatory apparatus (i.e., by appealing to selection pressures, variation, and heritability). For example, there are several plausible explanations for the fact that humans, unlike other primates and unlike most other land-dwelling mammals, are not covered in fur (e.g., the easy removal of parasites, cooling of the body in a savanna-like environment, and the facilitation of swimming) (Morris 1967). In this and other cases, there is, largely because a vast amount of time has elapsed, too little evidence available to suitably constrain the space of plausible hypotheses. This is hardly a problem for the theory of natural selection, however. The problem instead lies entirely with the epistemically impoverished situation of the theorist, a situation that is straightforwardly implied by the theory of natural selection itself. When it comes to explaining specific traits, then, the leverage gained through adoption of the theory of natural selection—which includes a characteristic ontology of states and processes—may be quite limited.

Be this as it may, when construed as an explanation for the more general fact that organisms tend to be well adapted to their particular environments, the theory of natural selection succeeds like no theory before or since. It is thus only when the model is viewed as an explanation for a very general fact about the relationship between organisms and their environments that its tremendous explanatory power becomes apparent.[12] In fact, even if we were—for the aforementioned epistemic reasons—incapable, save in a select few cases, of reaching definite conclusions about the various factors that conspired to yield particular traits, this model should still enjoy our favor.[13]

The proposal that humans are capable of planning has roughly the same explanatory strengths and weaknesses as the theory of natural selection. Notice, for instance, that in many instances it would not be unwarranted to belittle a particular explanation of a particular behavior as a just-so story. That is to say, although a particular explanation might have an air of plausibility, it is nevertheless often possible to construct an equally plausible alternative explanation by utilizing the same general explanatory apparatus (i.e., by appealing to beliefs, desires, and inferences). For example, you might recall that there was a fair amount of debate regarding the motivation behind President Bill Clinton's decision to launch air strikes against Iraq at a time when he also happened to be the subject of some rather harsh criticism for his personal indiscretion and related behavior. It was variously suggested that Clinton ordered the air strikes to divert attention from his troubles, that he wished to make himself appear more presidential, and that the advice of military strategists was the only relevant factor (i.e., the timing was merely coincidental). Most of us lack sufficient evidence to have real confidence in any one of these explanations. Proponents of the folk ontology should hardly despair, however. After all, our inability to satisfactorily explain Clinton's behavior is a consequence of our impoverished epistemic predicament. That is, one's access to the factors (e.g., beliefs, desires, and inferences) that conspire to give rise to particular behaviors is often quite limited. This is a situation that is straightforwardly implied by the planning model itself. When it comes to explaining specific behaviors, then, the leverage gained through adoption of this model—which includes its own characteristic ontology of states and processes—may be quite limited.

Be this as it may, when construed as an explanation for the more general fact that creatures like ourselves are able to respond so effectively to novel circumstances and so flexibly to similar ones, the planning model succeeds like no theory before or since. It is only when it is viewed as an explanation for a very general fact about the relationship between humans and the various contingencies they confront that the true explanatory power of the theory becomes apparent. In fact, even were we—for the aforementioned epistemic reasons—incapable, save in a select few cases, of reaching definite conclusions about the various factors that conspired to yield particular behaviors, this model should still enjoy our favor.

One other parallel between the two theories bears mentioning. Most people readily acknowledge the profound effects that selective breeding can have on the character of descendents. The folk, in other words, have a reasonable grasp of, and (whether they like it or not) tacitly accept, some of the basic tenets of the theory, and this was the case long before those tenets were invoked as part of an explanation for the relationship between species and their environments (Darwin 1859). So too do the folk have a reasonable grasp of, and tacitly accept, some of the basic tenets of the planning model, and this was the case long before these tenets were invoked by cognitive science as part of a scientific explanation for the fact that humans are quite adept at dealing with even very novel environmental contingencies.

2.4.2 Natural Selection and Planning: The Goal of Prediction

The analogy between the theory of natural selection and the theory of planning does break down to some extent where prediction is concerned, but the points where the analogy holds are quite illuminating. Notice, to begin with, that the predictive leverage gained through adoption of the theory of natural selection is probably quite limited, at least insofar as the natural emergence and increasing prevalence of a particular trait in a particular population are concerned. A number of factors are responsible for this limitation: The time frame undercuts the utility of offering such predictions, adoption of the theory does not enable one to predict which of potentially very many useful phenotypic variations will obtain, and it is certainly not the case that species tend to evolve with respect to an unchanging environment (i.e., the environments are themselves subject to evolutionary pressures). These factors add prohibitive complexity to the problem of predicting the natural emergence and increasing prevalence of a particular trait in a given population and quite clearly rule out the possibility that the theory of natural selection will be corroborated because of such predictions.

On the other hand, where selective breeding is the outcome of conscious human intervention, we can—insofar as we are aware of the selection criteria—advance some pretty accurate predictions concerning what a given line or breed will come to look like. In such cases, selection for reproduction is not based on natural fitness; it is comparatively insensitive to environmental changes, and there is little danger that some other set of features will be selected for. Moreover, because selection pressures are so strong, the course of evolution is greatly accelerated.[14]

Be this as it may, the theory of natural selection is most assuredly not valued for its ability to support predictions concerning the emergence of particular traits. Nor do the predictions that hold the greatest interest for evolutionary biologists have the power to either falsify or corroborate the theory of natural selection, at least not directly. The predictions that are of the greatest interest from the standpoint of evolutionary biology are those that figure in the progressive *refinement* of the theory of natural selection through the testing of competing models concerning, for example, the levels at which natural selection is operative (e.g., individuals vs. populations) and the underlying mechanisms for natural selection (e.g., the nature of environment-gene interactions or gene-gene interactions). The guiding assumption behind most of this research is that the theory of natural selection is basically correct. The work of the evolutionary biologist is generally geared toward filling in the details of this broad explanatory framework. To put it in Bechtel and Richardson's (1993) terms, the evolutionary biologist is engaged in an iterative process of decomposition and localization whereby one determines the relevant functional parts of a system and how those functions are effected by those parts, which, in turn, often involves an appeal to further, functionally individuated parts.

Predictions play a crucial role in this process because they figure in the testing of competing models, but they are not the sorts of predictions that are capable of falsifying or corroborating the broader theory, *at least not directly*. I add the disclaimer because there is a case to be made that these predictions do play an evidentiary role with regard to the truth or falsity of the broader theory. In short, the fact that the theory of natural selection has shown itself amenable to ever-greater refinement seems to be a real testament to its viability. Ongoing research has revealed mechanisms and processes fully capable of filling the various complicated functional roles, and our understanding of these mechanisms and processes has itself undergone a tremendous degree of further refinement. A related, perhaps less controversial evidentiary consideration is that the theory of natural selection happens to be consistent with, and well integrated with, the rest of science, including geology, chemistry, microbiology, and even physics. Our endorsement of the theory of natural selection is thus not warranted on Popperian grounds (i.e., by the fact that the theory has passed a series of severe tests), but it is warranted for reasons that are far more Quinean (i.e., the theory lies at the nexus of a larger network of beliefs, and abandoning it up would cause a large-scale disruption to the coherence and simplicity of this network).

Many of these same points apply to the theory of planning. For instance, although the time frame is far shorter, our ability to predict what someone will do is limited by several factors. For one thing, there are usually many ways of getting from the way things are to the way one wants them to be; as the folk say, there is more than one way to skin a cat. So even if you know what someone desires and a great deal about what he believes, you might still have a very hard time figuring out how he will go about trying to fulfill his desires. Nor should we make light of the fact that under normal circumstances we have at best only a superficial understanding of what someone believes and desires and that any of an individual's unknown beliefs or desires may well directly influence his behavior. That is to say, isotropy—the fact that anything you know might figure in the determination of what else you believe (Fodor 1983), including what you believe you ought to do—characterizes the processes of behavior guidance as surely as it does the process of belief formation. As obvious as this point is, it has gone strangely unnoticed by those philosophers—and there are lots of them—who are committed to the idea that the goal (or a central goal) of psychology is to come up with laws relating particular stimuli, particular mental states, and particular behaviors. I'll return to this. For now, suffice it to say that the sheer volume of potentially relevant causal factors seems, in and of itself, to preclude a high degree of success at predicting particular everyday behaviors.

On the other hand, there are certain cases in which much of this complexity is factored out and in which we are, as a result, able to advance some pretty accurate predictions concerning what someone will do. These are the sorts of cases to which Fodor draws our attention when he suggests that folk psychology works so well that it disappears. For example, if a friend of mine tells me that he is coming to town on a particular day, I will feel pretty confident that he will indeed arrive on that day. I need not take into account the effect that all of my friend's beliefs and desires might have on his behavior, for in telling me of his plans he has done this for me. By the same token, when I see an automobile driven by a stranger approach a red traffic light at a busy intersection, I will feel quite confident that the car will not go through the intersection while the light is red. There is a simple inductive justification for this confidence: People tend not to drive through red lights. But there is also a folk-psychological explanation for this pattern. It seems reasonable to suppose that people are aware of the dire consequences of driving through red lights. The severity of the consequences in this case suffices to render irrelevant considerations that would otherwise cause a great deal of uncertainty. For instance, in such cases it no longer matters whether or not an individual is late for an appointment, is hungry, or believes that his country has been corrupted by socialists. There are surely many cases in which complexity is effectively reduced, and these appear to be the only cases in which our predictions of behavior are justified.

Be that as it may, the planning model is most assuredly not valued by cognitive science for its ability to support predictions concerning particular behaviors. Nor do the predictions that hold the greatest interest for cognitive scientists have the power to either falsify or corroborate this model, *at least not directly*. The predictions that are of the greatest interest from the standpoint of cognitive science are those that figure in the progressive *refinement* of the planning model through the testing of competing models concerning the underlying mechanisms. In the end, this model turns out to be amenable to a high degree of refinement and, thus, well integrated with the rest of science.

These points are both important and controversial, so it is worth devoting a bit more time to their defense. Before proceeding, however, I would like to draw attention to one disanalogy between the theory of natural selection and the planning model. Whereas the theory of natural selection is arguably the fundamental starting point for mainstream evolutionary biology, the planning model is (as I noted above) just one of a collection of highly schematic, collectively consistent, intuitively plausible models of the underpinnings for human behavior that lie at the foundation of mainstream cognitive science. These models come as a package, and they have been refined and vindicated as a package.

2.4.3 Other Folk Models Endorsed by Cognitive Science

If what poets, playwrights, and novelists have written throughout the centuries is any guide, the folk have a lot more to say about what it is that makes humans tick than is encompassed by the bare planning model.

What the folk seem to endorse are (inter alia) the following interrelated proposals concerning the underpinnings for human behavior:

- People are able to plan how to get from the way things are to the way they would like them to be by thinking about the consequences of their actions.
- What people believe is sometimes based on what they perceive to be the case.
- What people believe is sometimes based on what they are informed (e.g., by understanding what others have said or written) is the case.
- What people believe is sometimes the result of what they infer, on the basis of their other beliefs, to be the case.
- People are able to express their beliefs and desires in written and spoken form.
- People are able to remember and recall their beliefs and desires.[15]

Many of the same points about the predictive and explanatory utility or disutility of the planning model apply to the rest of these models. To be brief, there is obviously a very close match between these models and the broad explanatory models advanced and refined by cognitive scientists who are investigating the processes of planning, inference, perception, language comprehension and production, and memory. Though these models do a nice job of explaining some general features of human behavior, the predictive and explanatory leverage they afford when it comes to particular everyday behaviors may be quite limited. In fact, the predictions that are of the greatest interest from the standpoint of cognitive science are those that figure in the progressive refinement of this set of models through the testing of competing hypotheses regarding how the various processes are effected.

2.4.4 Refinement and Vindication of Folk Psychology

It has been suggested elsewhere that there is a close relationship between folk psychology and cognitive science (Burge 1986; Horgan and Woodward 1995), but the details of this claim have yet to be fleshed out in a way that makes it clear that folk psychology has already been fully vindicated by cognitive science. For instance, while Horgan and Woodward draw attention to the intimate relationship between folk psychology and cognitive science, they also argue that folk psychology is an autonomous, high-level theory and that therefore the failure to find the neurological realizers of particular beliefs and desires would not undermine it. What is wrong with this strategy is that it fails to justify the jump from instrumentalism to full-blown realism. After all, one can get great predictive and explanatory mileage out of cognitive theories that invoke beliefs and desires, computations, or even intentional causation, but as long as the implementation details remain an utter mystery, the possibility remains open that the mileage is gotten merely by treating cognition *as if* it involved beliefs and desires, computations, or intentional causation.[16]

What Tyler Burge has to say regarding the relationship between folk psychology and cognitive science is also relevant and merits quoting at length:

> In taking psychology as it is, I am assuming that it seeks to refine, deepen, generalize and systematize some of the statements of informed common sense about people's mental activity. It accepts, for example, that people see objects with certain shapes, textures and hues, and in certain spatial relations, under certain specified conditions. And it attempts to explain in more depth what people do when they see such things, and how their doing it is done. Psychology accepts that people remember events and truths, that they categorize objects, that they draw inferences, that they act on beliefs and preferences. And it attempts to find deep regularities in these activities, to specify mechanisms that underly them, and to provide systematic accounts of how these activities relate to one another. (1986, p. 8).

Indeed, psychology—by which I presume Burge means cognitive psychology (see subsection 1.2.3.3)—has done more than *seek* to refine our understanding of the mechanisms underlying planning, language comprehension/production, memory, and inference. Cognitive psychology has actually provided a fine-grained functional breakdown of the cognitive system that includes a specification of the various waypoints of processing, alternate routes of processing, and what it takes to get from one to the next.

Consider the study of declarative memory, which includes memory for facts about the world of a public and often general nature (e.g., the fact that Bush defeated Gore or the fact that water is H_2O) and memory for more personal and specific facts (e.g., that you wanted a particular toy for Christmas one year). There is clearly not much difference between beliefs and desires, on the one hand, and declarative memories, on the other. Also in keeping with folk psychology, memory researchers countenance such means of acquiring declarative memories as perception, inference, and the comprehension of natural language. For the cognitive scientist, however, this is merely the jumping-off point for an investigation.

A look at even the most basic findings of cognitive psychology shows that research in this discipline has greatly refined our understanding of the myriad mechanisms and processes that are involved in the encoding, storage, and retrieval of declarative memories. There are, for instance, good reasons for thinking that there are two distinct modes of storage. One of these seems directly implicated in the process of inference, is quite transient (perhaps as a result of the overwriting of earlier memory traces by later ones), and is subdivided into multiple, independent, possibly modality-specific types. (See subsection 1.2.3.3.2.) The other is far more enduring, and such things as the conditions of encoding and what information has been stored previously dictate the facility with which information can be later retrieved.

These findings, which only scratch the surface, are paralleled by further psychological findings regarding the mechanisms and processes involved in perception, various forms of language comprehension and language production, and inference. This marks a major advance over the bare folk models described in the previous section, and it puts us well on the path toward their full vindication. In and of itself, however, research in cognitive psychology might not suffice to placate die-hard instrumentalists. What should placate these individuals, however, is a demonstration that the broad functional breakdown accepted by the folk and refined by cognitive psychology maps straightforwardly onto what is known about the brain. One of the achievements of the collaboration between cognitive psychology and the various branches of neuroscience (i.e., neuropsychology, cognitive neuroscience, neuroanatomy, and neurophysiology) has been to demonstrate precisely this. (See subsections 1.2.1 and 1.2.3.)

Admittedly, many of the models advanced by neuropsychologists are pitched in fairly abstract terms. For example, many of the models of various forms of agnosia, dyslexia, and aphasia are implementation-nonspecific flow charts. These flow charts overlap nicely with those formulated on independent grounds by cognitive psychologists, and they add to the former's depiction of the established routes of processing a specification of various "bumpy" detours.[17] However, unlike the research undertaken in cognitive psychology, neuropsychological research also does much to chip away at instrumentalism, for the diagnoses offered for the various pathologies also suggest—or at least begin to suggest—ways in which the various routes and waypoints of processing map onto specific structures. Functional neuroimaging research carried out in cognitive neuroscience is an additional, largely independent source of evidence for these function-to-structure mappings.[18] This research is giving us a clearer picture of the loci of the component mechanisms responsible for language comprehension and production, the various forms of short-term memory, encoding, storage, retrieval, perception, and so on. These findings, in turn, have been related to even the lowest-level facts of neuroanatomy and neurophysiology. To make it perfectly clear that this is so, let us continue our elementary survey of declarative memory research, and let us focus, in particular, on the long-term component.

According to a model that is very popular among cognitive neuropsychologists, the long-term storage of declarative memories involves two distinct stages. This model is motivated by the observation that damage to the inner temporal lobes (viz., the hippocampus) tends to result in permanent anterograde amnesia (i.e., no new long-term declarative memories can be formed) and retrograde amnesia (i.e., loss of memories formed before hippocampal damage) spanning up to three years. The best explanation for this regularity seems to be that the hippocampus stores long-term declarative memories for up to three years and, during that time, engages in a process of consolidation whereby the long-term memories it holds are progressively given more permanent storage at the cortical surface (viz., at or around the sensory areas where they were initially encoded). For all its merit, the consolidation hypothesis would be pretty clearly falsified if the hippocampus turned out to be wired up all wrong (e.g., if it had only afferent connections from the olfactory bulb and efferent connections to calf muscles). Neuroanatomists have shown, however, that the hippocampus is connected up in just the ways we would expect an intermediate-term storage site for declarative memories to be. Specifically, it has incoming connections from the sensory areas and outgoing connections to each of the sensory association areas. Neuroanatomists, neurophysiologists, and computational neuroscientists have, accordingly, undertaken the task of determining how the hippocampus is internally wired up (i.e., the various areas and roles they play), the synaptic basis for memories (e.g., a process known as *long-term potentiation* may be involved), and how the consolidation process might operate.

Although the science discussed here may be old news, the way it fits together—and, consequently, its relevance to folk psychology—has generally been overlooked by philosophers. Just as the predictions that are of interest to evolutionary biologists lack the power to directly corroborate or falsify the theory of natural selection, the predictions that are of interest to cognitive scientists lack the power to directly corroborate or falsify the set of models constitutive of folk psychology. Instead, such predictions are used in the testing of competing hypotheses concerning how this set of models is best refined. For this reason, such predictions do ultimately play an indirect evidentiary role with regard to the broader set of models. For starters, the fact that the attempt to refine these folk-psychological models is meeting with great success seems a real testament to their viability. What ongoing research is revealing is that there are mechanisms and processes capable of filling the relevant functional roles, and our understanding of these mechanisms and processes is, in turn, undergoing ever-greater refinement. By the same token, it has been shown that the folk models are not sui generis but are instead well integrated with various sciences. It is, in fact, no small matter that the folk models are constitutive of a much more elaborate set of interrelated proposals spanning the highest and lowest levels of cognitive scientific investigation. The fact that multiple independent forms of investigation have converged in supporting this set of models shows that they—and folk psychology along with them—have passed what may be science's most stringent test: They have shown themselves to be robust (Wimsatt 1994). Thus, like evolutionary biology, folk psychology may not have much warrant on Popperian grounds, but its warrant on roughly Quinean grounds more than makes up for this deficiency.

2.5 The Gauntlet Revisited

Popular philosophical wisdom regarding what sciences ought to look like, and what cognitive science in particular ought to look like, does not comport well with the actual predictive and explanatory practices of cognitive science. In fact, knowing what we now do about the actual goings-on in cognitive science takes much of the sting out of the arguments comprising the gauntlet of irrealism.

2.5.1 Churchland

The gauntlet began for folk psychology with the question of whether or not we are truly capable of predicting the behavior of our fellow humans. As I explained above, there are good reasons for thinking that our ability to predict and explain particular behaviors is quite limited. Be this as it may, folk psychology has been simultaneously refined and vindicated through ongoing cognitive scientific research in such a way as to render any such predictive and explanatory shortcomings irrelevant. In fact, the manner in which cognitive science has vindicated folk psychology provides a straightforward way of replying to Churchland's complaint that folk psychology does not explain such phenomena as "sleep, creativity, memory, intelligence differences, and the many forms of learning" (1998, p. 8). That was never a fair criticism to begin with. Folk psychology, after all, need not explain every facet of cognition in order to win our approval.

Churchland is all too familiar with this position and none too sympathetic: "This is an unfortunate defense, as can be seen from other uses of this same strategy. One can defend Ptolemy's ragtag astronomy (as Ptolemy *did*) by insisting that it was never supposed to address the real physics, or the actual causes, or the complete story of astronomical behavior, and by insisting that it properly serves only the narrow interest of predicting the angular positions of the planets as seen from Earth. One can defend any hangdog theory by this strategy, so long as it has some paltry success for some benighted purpose within some sheltered domain." (1998, pp. 22, 23)

Though Churchland is right to point that this strategy is easily abused, he is wrong if he thinks that it is always wrong to adopt this strategy. After all, Kepler's account of planetary motions was restricted to the same sheltered domain as Ptolemy's: It was meant to explain the peculiarities of the apparent motions of the planets relative to a fixed backdrop of stars. It thus fails to explain all sorts of phenomena that are properly viewed as the falling under the purview of astronomy. It tells us nothing about why the Sun generates light, why Mars is red, or why one side of the Moon always faces the Earth. It does, however, dispatch its limited duties quite well. Of course, while both the Ptolemaic and Keplerian models do a fine job of predicting planetary motions, Kepler's has the advantage of being well integrated with the rest of astronomy and the rest of science. Indeed, our best model of the formation of our solar system not only explains why the planets move roughly in accordance with Kepler's three laws of planetary motion; it also explains why the Sun generates light, why Mars is red, and why one side of the Moon always faces the Earth. A similar story can be told with regard to folk psychology. While folk psychology provides a fine explanation for some general facts about human behavior, it was never meant to explain sleep, creativity, memory, intelligence differences, or the many forms of learning. To its credit, however, it is (pace Churchland) well integrated with the various sciences of cognition, and these sciences have a lot to say about the phenomena for which Churchland demands explanations. For instance, the study of the encoding, storage, and retrieval of declarative memories is clearly the study of an important form of learning; according to one popular view, sleep is part and parcel of the hippocampal consolidation process described earlier (Karni et al. 1994; Wilson and McNaughton 1994); and creativity may best be explained by analogical mappings between representations of familiar and unfamiliar domains. (See Churchland 1989; Fodor 1983; Holyoak and Thagard 1995.) The charge that folk psychology has remained stagnant is refuted by these same considerations. While the theory of natural selection and the Keplerian model of planetary motions have both preserved most of their initial character since their introduction, developments in a variety of fields constitute progress for these theories. In precisely the same manner, developments in cognitive science constitute progress for folk psychology.[19]

2.5.2 Radical Simulation

Stage 2 of the gauntlet has to do with whether the predictive and explanatory successes enjoyed by the folk with regard to the behavior of their fellow humans stem from their reliance on an ontology that posits beliefs and desires as among the causal determinants of behavior. The worry, once again, is that if the folk predict and explain the behavior of their compatriots by simulating rather than theorizing, then folk psychology is atheoretical, and there is no folk-psychological ontology to vindicate. I have done little here to bolster the claim that folk *do* enjoy a good deal of predictive and explanatory success with regard to the behavior of their fellow humans. I have, in fact, taken great pains to clarify precisely why it is that they are not likely to succeed, but I have also shown why folk psychology is none the worse for wear.

Even if it happens to be the case that our attempts to predict and explain one another's behavior involve simulation, this is clearly not the whole truth of the matter regarding how it is that we understand one another. Given what has been written throughout the centuries, one would be hard pressed to deny that we humans tend to view one another as creatures that believe, desire, plan, remember, infer, pay attention, perceive, comprehend, and so on. The words 'belief' and 'desire' are clearly used by us folk on a regular basis to describe our fellow humans, and all indications are that we intend these words to refer to unobservable intentional states; no one, at any rate, has come up with a viable alternative to this analysis. The simulation argument, then, was always a bit of a red herring. Indeed, even Gordon (1996) claims that the process of simulation has the ultimate effect of "bootstrapping" our grasp of the meanings of intentional terms. In short, whether we simulate or not, the question remains: Do the various inner states and processes posited by us grown-up folk map onto the actual causes of behavior? The answer, mainstream cognitive science tells us, is that they do.

2.5.3 Churchland (Again) and Dennett

It is, of course, possible that mainstream cognitive science is mistaken. For instance, perhaps dynamical systems theory or Gibsonian anti-representationalism (each of which has been claimed to do away with the need to posit mental representations by stressing the importance of environmental factors) will win the day; perhaps descriptions of trajectories through state space exhaust what we need to know about the underpinnings for human behavior; or perhaps a new type of reinforcement learning will be discovered that resurrects behaviorism. Bear in mind, however, that if mainstream cognitive science really were so mistaken as to require the abandonment of folk psychology, this would strike at its very foundations and necessitate a revolution that spans several disciplines. It would, for instance, require that we give up on the encoding specificity hypothesis, on the idea that short-term memory is the locus of inference, on the proposal that the hippocampus consolidates declarative memories, and on the Wernicke-Geschwind model of language comprehension and production. What the eliminativist advocates, in other words, is the abandonment of decades of fruitful interdisciplinary research on the bare promise that something better is around the bend. The instrumentalist simply overlooks this research.

Philosophers have, of course, made it a common practice to exaggerate the importance of the fringe elements in cognitive science, and while predictions concerning impending "paradigm shifts" are about as common as doomsday prophesies, they are also about as warranted. Should one these prophesies chance upon the truth, so be it; I will stand corrected. In the meantime, those of us with a more sober disposition should be content to let the state of the art in cognitive science, which is far from a fledgling enterprise, continue to act as our guide. I'll have more to say on this topic, but let us first complete the dismantling of the gauntlet of irrealism.

2.5.4 The LOT Hypothesis

The strategy of showing that cognitive science cannot do without the LOT hypothesis (i.e., that there are good a priori reasons for favoring the latter) seems to have been offered up as a way to defend this particular brand of intentional realism without having to establish that particular expressions of mentalese, the putative language of thought, are token identical with particular brain states. Yet, as I suggested earlier, even if these indispensability arguments were sound, they would only suffice to undermine Churchland's brand of eliminativism, not Dennett's instrumentalism.

Some might claim that, if not the LOT hypothesis, then at least *some* version of the computational theory of mind lies at the very foundation of mainstream cognitive science in the same way that folk psychology has here been said to. Fodor and Pylyshyn claim, for instance, that "it would not be unreasonable to describe Classical Cognitive Science as an extended attempt to apply the methods of proof theory to the modeling of thought" (1988, p. 30). A look at the models advanced in such fields as cognitive psychology, neuropsychology, and cognitive neuroscience supplies little in the way of support for this contention. Indeed, virtually all that goes on in cognitive science (e.g., see section 2.4), and that includes traditional artificial intelligence (see subsection 1.2.3.2), is perfectly compatible with outright rejection of the computational theory of mind. Thus, the claim that cognitive science is committed to the computational theory of mind, accepted uncritically by many philosophers, is just another archaic presupposition that acts as a crucial premise in numerous debates but—when the actual goings-on of cognitive science are understood—is found to have little basis in fact. It is thus fortunate for folk psychology that its fate is not tied to that of the computational theory of mind, nor, a fortiori, to that of the LOT hypothesis.

2.5.5 Content

The final challenge confronting folk psychology has to do with whether or not contents have any legitimate role to play in cognitive science. As we have seen, various arguments have been leveled against the scientific credibility of contents, and they have been directed at particular theories of either content fixation or what contents are in and of themselves.

2.5.5.1 Internalism The arguments against folk psychology that presuppose an internalist account (viz., a doxastic surrounding account) of content fixation are clearly premised on the aforementioned misconceptions regarding the predictive and explanatory practices of cognitive science.

The first such argument is clearly premised on the mistaken assumption that cognitive science is primarily interested in formulating laws—specifically, laws that specify the relationships among particular stimuli, particular internal states, and particular behaviors. As we have seen, the search for such laws is no part of the ongoing activities of cognitive science.[20] In fact, if the argument under consideration shows us anything, it is that the search for such laws would be a fool's errand from the start, for it brings into sharp relief the fact that human behavior is determined by highly complex arrangements of internal states which are clearly going to diverge in fairly radical ways from individual to individual. Cutting contents out of the picture therefore does nothing to resuscitate the hope that we will be able to find laws that apply across individuals and that quantify over particular types of mental states.

All of this does, however, raise at least one sensible question: How *does* cognitive science cope with the vast differences between people? How does it cope, in other words, with the isotropic nature of the underpinnings for human behavior? The answer is that cognitive science copes with this complexity in the same way that radio engineers cope with the fact that only some radios play "The Macarena" while fewer play the score to *Carmen*, and the vast majority never play Nick Drake's "Time Of No Reply." As we have seen, cognitive science has adopted, refined, and vindicated a set of models concerning the mechanisms underwriting human behavior and is coming to understand what and where the main components are and how they work (e.g., what and where *their* components are). Thus, cognitive science offers theories that cut across vastly different belief networks. The fact that individuals have different belief networks does not belie the claim that they share mechanisms of belief formation, memory, inference, language production and comprehension, and so on. If contents are determined by doxastic surroundings, this will not impede efforts to understand how these mechanisms are connected up and how their internal workings enable them to do what they do.

The second argument against internalist accounts of content fixation is clearly premised on the groundless assumption that cognitive science is committed to the computational theory of mind. This, we have seen, is a myth that has been propagated by philosophers who have some pretty specific ideas about what cognitive science *ought* to look like but little appreciation for what it *does* look like.

2.5.5.2 Externalism and the Relational Nature of Contents While the foregoing considerations provide a simple and effective means of dismantling much of the gauntlet of irrealism, they do leave the remaining arguments against folk psychology—namely, arguments having to do with externalist theories of content fixation and the purportedly "wide" character of contents themselves—untouched. Still, it is worth pausing a moment in order to consider just how far we have already come.

While it is commonly assumed that folk psychology will be in big trouble if cognitive science is forced to eschew contents, significant portions of folk psychology have already been vindicated by cognitive science. There is, in addition, a growing awareness in the folk psychology literature of the fact that a theory can be wrong in certain respects without its ontology undergoing elimination. The contrary view was, for instance, implicit in the arguments against folk psychology offered by Stich (1989), but he has since (1996) followed Lycan (1988) in adopting a more sensible position which recognizes that common sense may direct us toward, and give us an imperfect appreciation for, natural kinds which are only later (e.g., through scientific inquiry) fully grasped. Thus, Stich claims, we may even be jumping the gun if we conclude that terms like 'phlogiston' and 'witch' fail to refer. Some of what common sense said about these putative entities was wrong, but common sense was not entirely wrong. The same, adds Crane (1998), can be said of planets, but it is far from obvious that—before Galileo for instance—the term 'planet' failed to refer. By the same token, if the various folk models happened to be accurate in every respect save for their invocation of contents, then it would not be unreasonable to conclude that there really are beliefs and desires. This would surely be far less contentious than claiming that witches and phlogiston exist. After all, theories that quantified over witches and phlogiston—not to mention planets—occupied the extreme lower end of the theoretical-accuracy continuum, whereas folk psychology, sans contents, sits somewhere along the upper half of that continuum. While these hedges should not be lost sight of, in the next chapter I will resolve the outstanding concerns about contents, which enables us to localize folk psychology to a point that is very near the high end of the theoretical-accuracy continuum.

2.6 Cognitive Science and the Landscape of Competing Research Programs

Before we tackle this difficult material, let us pause and take in the landscape of competing research programs in cognitive science. This, I think, is important, for there is general tendency among cognitive scientists (and even more so among philosophers) to treat mainstream folk-inspired cognitive science (FICS) as just one of many equally viable research programs, and this has had a major influence on how the members of both of these professions have chosen to spend their time. To gain the proper perspective, we will first have to survey some of the important progress that philosophers have made—roughly, in the past hundred years—in their attempts to understand science more generally.

2.6.1 Philosophy of Science 101
Perhaps the most important fact brought to light by the philosophical scrutiny of science is that there are seldom grounds for saying of some scientist that his or her continued support for a particular theory is, in view

of the data, irrational. A scientist can, whatever the data, generally find a rationale for maintaining belief in a particular theory, for there is almost always some other belief that can be let go of in its stead.

The mode of reasoning involved can be formalized to some extent.[21] For instance, where H is a statement describing a given explanatory hypothesis that in conjunction with a further set of auxiliary assumptions A_1 & A_2 & ... A_n implies some statement, I whose truth value can be determined through testing, we get

$$[H \ \& \ (A_1 \ \& \ A_2 \ \& \dots A_n)] \to I.$$

Should testing reveal that 'I' is false, this clearly does not entail that 'H' is false, but only that *either* 'H' *or* one of the auxiliary assumptions is false. I am painting with very broad strokes here. One important detail not represented by this formalization is that, when faced with otherwise unfavorable data, it is often possible to modify the hypothesis itself. Another strategy, and perhaps the one most commonly used in actual practice, is to deny that the test in question provides a fair assessment of the truth value of 'I.'

Attempts have been made to specify the constraints that govern when it is, and is not, permissible to "rescue" a theory through any of these methods, but such proposals have (for reasons that will be discussed below) invariably proven too restrictive—that is, they wind up classifying as irrational some of the great success stories in the history of science. The standard illustration of this point has to do with the failure of Newtonian mechanics to predict the position of Uranus. Despite the unfavorable data, some chose to hang onto Newtonian mechanics and scrap an auxiliary hypothesis—namely, the hypothesis that all the planets in our solar system had already been discovered. In contrast, there were those who urged that we instead reject Newtonian mechanics or, at the very least, restrict its domain of application to our very immediate celestial neighborhood. As it turns out, the failed predictions of Newtonian mechanics were due to the gravitational influence of the as-yet-undiscovered planet Neptune. The general lesson of which this is a case in point is roughly the following: However unlikely it may seem at the time, it is always possible that the theorist who, despite the seemingly unfavorable evidence, clings to his or her pet theory will be vindicated in the end.

Thomas Kuhn made a name for himself by grabbing this particular thread and running with it. His chief contention was that particular fields of science tend to be dominated, for finite periods of time, by scientific theories that are very broad in scope. These theories do not fall out of favor because they are falsified—again, seemingly inaccurate predictions can almost always be explained away—but rather, as more and more of the predictions generated by the theory do not come to pass and are explained away, dissatisfaction with the theory grows, becomes more widespread, and eventually gives way to a large-scale search for an alternative. Thus, while Kuhn's contemporaries were trying to discern the logic behind the exemplary mode of reasoning that undergirds the evaluation of particular theories, Kuhn took a step back and caught sight of a process of theory change that was not as cold and rational as it was commonly believed to be. What he saw, instead, were large groups of people unified by their endorsement of broad theoretical frameworks and by their commitment to a distinctive set of research activities. Theory change, as Kuhn saw it, was driven more by the old dying off than it was by any special mode of reasoning employed by scientists. Thus, these broad theories and their concomitant research techniques looked as though they merely afforded different ways of seeing and going about things, where no one way could be said to be preferable to any other.[22]

Kuhn's proposals convinced many that *science itself* is just one of countless, equally viable ways of dealing with the world—that, in other words, there is nothing about scientific thinking that makes it more rational than any other mode of thought, nor anything about scientific theories that makes them better justified than theories of any other sort. This, of course, is a bunch of hooey—reducing, as it does, everything that has transpired in the sciences since the start of the Enlightenment to a series of intellectual fads—but it does force us to ask what it is about science that makes it so special.

Imre Lakatos (1970) seems to have come very close to finding the answer. He was quick to realize that most of Kuhn's central insights could easily be co-opted in the service of a more traditional conception of science. There was, to be sure, no going back to the days where individual theories were taken to be assessed relative to particular empirical results; science, like long-term memory, has a great deal of global structure to it that must be taken into account. Accordingly, Lakatos, like Kuhn, noted that science is characterized by groups of individuals committed to particular large-scale research programs. Each such program includes sets of claims, some of which (what he called the *hard core*) its proponents are committed to protecting and some of which (the *protective belt*) can be modified or abandoned so as to protect the hard core from what would otherwise have to be counted as falsifying data. Like Kuhn, he recognized that it often takes the accumulation of many failed predictions and, ultimately, the demise of minds long ossified, before a once-dominant research program can fall from grace. So far, then, there is nothing terribly novel about Lakatos' position. What he also realized, however, was that it is actually *a very good thing* for science—and isn't this just the point of the Uranus/Neptune example—that its practitioners are often simply unwilling to give up on a particular research program despite seemingly unfavorable data. He realized, in other words, that scientific progress *requires* a certain amount of dogmatism, for dogmatism enables a scientific field as a whole to cover its bases. After all, a broad theoretic framework that appears more fit than its competitors at one point in time may, as the evidentiary environment changes, have a relatively hard time coping.

It is, according to Lakatos, within a particular research program that the real theory testing occurs. The research activities of FICS and evolutionary biology certainly fit this pattern, but even in these fields it must be admitted that the dogmatic adherence to one's pet theory is quite common and, therefore, that falsification in the Popperian sense is (pace Lakatos) not the sole force behind low-level theory change. Rather, within a given field, the best a theorist can generally hope for is to drive his competitor into a corner that few newcomers will be eager to share. That is to say, while the belief system of each competitor may well be perfectly coherent, it ultimately falls to those just starting out in a particular field, to those whose minds have not yet ossified, to decide on the relative plausibility of everything from research programs to the lowest-level theories. (See subsection 1.2.3.1.) All of this clearly places a very heavy load on those who are just starting out, but it is their load to bear all the same.[23]

2.6.2 A Sales Pitch for Newcomers

These basic facts about how science works turn out to be quite relevant to our discussion of the scientific credentials of folk psychology. In particular, the failure to understand the pride of place enjoyed by folk psychology within mainstream cognitive science and the related failure to understand the status of this mainstream research program relative to others has led to a highly distorted view of cognitive science. This, in turn, has had a very real practical effect on both cognitive science and the philosophy of mind. To see how and why, let us consider how newcomers to either of these fields might reasonably proceed if they were led to believe that FICS is just one research program among the many that happen to be competing for dominance in cognitive science.

Such individuals might, to begin with, think it wise to consider as many models of how the mind works as have been dreamt up, no matter how at odds with common-sense psychology they happen to be. That is to say, they would see no reason to restrict their focus to theories that are consistent with the claim that humans harbor beliefs and desires, recognize objects, pay attention, think ahead, have memories for facts about the world and personal events, etc. They would therefore see themselves as perfectly justified should they chose to spend a bit of time picking through the collection of extant research programs, while, at the outset at least, privileging no one over any other. Perhaps they will find it easiest to start small, searching for particular combinations of background theory and data-gathering techniques that seem to show promise in terms of their ability to make sense of some particular facet of cognition. If they should find themselves bemused by a particularly striking combination, they would, of course, surely be forgiven for wondering whether or not a similar combination might not prove useful when attempting to understand other facets of cognition—whether, that is, they might not have caught sight of the schematics for a bold new research program. Should they find themselves, perhaps with the gentle prodding of established figures, heartened by the outcome of such reflections, they might even find themselves revisiting some very big questions, such as whether or not the success of the research program they envision would strengthen or weaken the pull of our common-sense conception of the mind. Of course, the sexiest conclusion they could reach at this point would be that common sense has things all wrong.

This is how one might proceed were one under the impression that FICS is just one more entry—and, at least on the face of things, not a particularly flashy one—in the field of research programs that happen to be competing for dominance in cognitive science. In fact, it looks for all the world as though many *are* under this impression and that, as a consequence, this is precisely how they *have* chosen to proceed. Be this as it may, FICS should no more be considered just another research program among many than evolutionary biology should. By way of defending this claim, I need to first explain how, in view of everything I have said about the importance of competition, I can justify granting privileged status to FICS.

We saw above that Lakatos realized that the competition among the dogmatically committed was ultimately a good thing for science. He put it as follows: "The history of science has been and should be a history of competing research programmes (or, if you wish, 'paradigms'), but it has not been and must not become a succession of periods of normal science: the sooner competition starts, the better for progress. 'Theoretical pluralism' is better than 'theoretical monism'...." (1970, p. 155) All this is well and good, with just one caveat: The importance of pluralism at the level of research programs clearly varies with context. To see that this is so *in principle*, let us take a brief flight of fancy. Suppose, if you will, that, from where God sits, it is perfectly clear that a particular research program has chanced upon the truth. Suppose, specifically, that the hard core of the program is entirely correct, that the techniques wielded by its proponents are enabling them to fill in the remaining details, and that the only alternative research programs are fledgling enterprises that will ultimately lead nowhere. In a case such as this, Lakatos would surely be incorrect were he to claim that the near monopoly enjoyed by this program is a bad thing for the field. This is, of course, purely a metaphysical point about whether or not the competition among competing research programs is always a good thing for science, and, insofar as *we* do not have God's perspective on things, one might reasonably wonder whether or not it is relevant to the cases we have been considering. Still, haven't we, in both evolutionary biology and cognitive science, come to a point where only the deepest skeptical doubts (e.g., doubts about whether or not the way things appear to us is anything like the way they are in and of themselves) would suffice to shake our faith in the research programs by which they are dominated? In both fields, as our ability to match structure to function has increased, the viability of mere instrumentalism is correspondingly diminished. Again, only the most extreme skeptic could avoid the pull of realism. In fact, I am prepared to go on record right now: I am an unabashed realist about DNA. Indeed, I not only think that there is such a substance, I am also convinced that it plays a very important role in the process by which characteristics of parents are inherited by their offspring and in the broader process of natural selection. I would also like to go on record on another point: I am a realist about the hippocampus. In fact, I not only think that there is such a structure (unless I was dreaming or am an intelligent mist from Pluto, I have seen and touched a few of them); I am also convinced that the hippocampus plays an important role in the process by which our beliefs about the world are stored, retrieved, and ultimately archived.

Perhaps a different way of looking at the matter will help get the point across. Notice that what we have in evolutionary biology and FICS is a pair of broad research programs that are generating a coherent set of explanations for a very large body of empirical data, that are not embarrassed by an ever-growing scrap heap of empirical anomalies, and whose competition is still in the most speculative stages. Thus, it would be an undesirable state of affairs were the bulk of these professions caught up in the task of trying to coax flames from the embers of some supposed alternative research program when there is a raging pyre nearby that suits their needs very well.

There are, of course, qualifications. It is, admittedly, a good thing for cognitive science—and probably for evolutionary biology—that there are some researchers caught up in this very task. Indeed, one does find some important data being generated by die-hard opponents of FICS. However, while these fringe elements would tout their data as an embarrassment to FICS, I have never known its reach to extend any deeper into FICS than the surface of its protective belt.[24]

The qualification, then, is just that some amount of anti-establishment thought is probably necessary to keep the establishment honest. Nevertheless, it is a tremendous distortion to suggest, as many do, that FICS is just one research program among many. The failure to recognize this has adversely affected both cognitive science and philosophy, for young researchers are far too often fed this distortion and lured away from FICS when there is still much important work to be done. For scientists, this includes figuring out how the individual component processes are carried out by biological circuitry, how they all fit together, and, ultimately, how to implement these processes in non-biological systems, both on an individual basis (e.g., for prosthetic purposes) and collectively.[25] For philosophers, the important work of which I speak includes finding answers to the questions that were raised at the end of chapter 1. Admittedly, the attainment of these ends might reinforce the status quo in cognitive science; but it would also revolutionize society as we know it, and that, to me, is pretty sexy stuff.

2.7 Conclusion

Though it would be impracticable for me to address all the concerns about folk psychology that have been voiced, I believe that I have addressed many of the most troublesome. Virtually all the concerns about the scientific credentials of folk psychology dissipate once we pay closer attention to the actual predictive and explanatory practices of cognitive science. Indeed, while philosophers have been busy placing bets on how cognitive science will ultimately pan out, cognitive science has been quietly effecting a rather persuasive vindication of folk psychology and its ontology. It is, in addition, no small matter that many of the misconceptions about cognitive science are at the foundations of various ongoing debates in the philosophy of mind. As a result, philosophers of mind have spent far too much time debating the merits of fledging research programs—whether or not certain claims are compatible with the existence of psychological laws, whether or not computational theories of mind should be just about the syntax, and so on. In short, while cognitive science does not find itself in dire need of an alternative research program, it seems pretty clear that the philosophy of mind does.

2.8 Postscript: A Confession

I have neglected to mention two important facts. First, although explanation in cognitive science is not simple law subsumption, this is how explanation is portrayed by what is, for the moment, the only remotely viable model of explanation. Philosophers can therefore be forgiven, to *some* extent, for continuing to think of cognitive science in terms of laws. Second, although cognitive science as a whole neither needs to be nor is committed to either the general computational theory of mind or the more specific LOT hypothesis, there are good reasons why many individuals (mainly philosophers) are so committed. Indeed, we shall see that these two sets of issues are intimately related, and that the kind of shift in research program that I envision for the philosophy of mind will require supplanting the LOT hypothesis with a better model of truth preservation and using this model to formulate an anomological theory of explanation.

3 | Content, Supervenience, and Cognitive Science

As I have explained, folk psychology is the theory that we humans use, with somewhat limited effectiveness, to understand and anticipate the behavior of our fellow humans. Many philosophers have wondered whether cognitive science has vindicated, will vindicate, or even can vindicate this theory. Many of the concerns raised about folk psychology in this regard were addressed in chapter 2. The remaining concerns, addressed in this chapter, have to do with the fact that the mental states to which folk psychology adverts are about (among other things) the way things are and the way we would like them to be; they are, in other words, states with content. Many philosophers believe, as do I, that the manner in which the folk assign contents to mental states (i.e., folk semantics) is, from a scientific standpoint, highly suspect. It turns out, however, that some sensible modifications to folk semantics yield a new semantic framework that has a legitimate and very important role to play in cognitive science.

3.1 Introduction

With Brentano's claim that mental phenomena are unique in exhibiting "reference to a content" (1874/1995, p. 124), a debate began over where, if at all, contents might fit within the ontology of a thoroughgoing physicalist. The debate continues today, mostly along one of two research tracks. Along the first track, we find consideration of the possibility that contents might be "naturalized" by clarifying the sorts of causal and historical process that would suffice to justify the attribution of contents to certain states of a creature. Along the second track, we find discussion of the more general question of whether or not contents are the sorts of properties that can play any legitimate role in the ongoing interdisciplinary enterprise known as cognitive science.

In this chapter, I will focus mainly, but not exclusively, on the second track, where it has been shown that the manner in which the folk (implicitly) take the contents of mental states to be determined deprives mental contents of any legitimate role to play in cognitive science. There is, we shall see, an alternative to this "folk semantics"[1] that plays an essential role in our best explanation for a very important facet of human behavior. Because contents, according to this alternative, are fixed in an ahistorical manner, by the end of this chapter I will also have shown that pursuit of the first research track is not necessary for the naturalization of content.

3.2 Ramifications for Folk Psychology

How this debate over the status of contents ultimately pans out will clearly have ramifications for folk psychology. Specifically, because folk psychology is a theory whose posits include beliefs and desires, and because these mental states are almost universally taken to be about (inter alia) the way things are and the way we would like them to be, if we were to find that contents have no legitimate role to play in cognitive science, this would clearly diminish hopes that folk psychology will one day be fully vindicated by cognitive science. We should proceed cautiously, however, for a theory can be wrong in certain respects without its ontology undergoing outright elimination. Indeed, as I explained in chapter 2, it is pretty clear that the bulk of folk psychology has already been sufficiently vindicated by cognitive science. Thus, regardless of how the debate over contents pans out, folk psychology should be taken to be situated, at worst, somewhere in the upper half of the continuum of theoretical accuracy.

I will show in this chapter that aspects of folk psychology that have already been vindicated by cognitive science may, and should, be supplemented with a semantic framework that differs in certain respects from the framework implicitly adopted by the folk. This will have the effect of localizing folk psychology to a point somewhere near, but not at, the upper end of the theoretical-accuracy continuum. I have already mentioned that the semantic framework I have in mind diverges from folk semantics in that it places far less importance on historical factors. At the same time, what it shares with folk semantics is a commitment to the "wideness" of contents. Accordingly, a good place to begin our discussion is with a standard sort of argument for the wideness of contents.

3.3 An Argument for the Wideness of Contents

Ever since Burge's (1979) seminal paper on the topic, the standard strategy for defending the wideness of mental contents has been to appeal to twin cases. Imagine, for example, that there are two worlds, Earth and (somewhere out in space) Twin Earth.[2] At a certain point in the past (viz., before the modern atomic theory of matter), these two worlds were identical in every local respect save for the fact that for every molecule of H_2SO_4 on Earth, in its place on Twin Earth was a different molecule (let us call it XYZ). On both worlds, however, the local compound goes by the name oil of vitriol.

Imagine now that a particular man on Earth, $Tony_E$, honestly claims to believe that a certain sample of liquid is oil of vitriol, and that on Twin Earth his doppelganger, $Tony_{TE}$, does the same. Though the two Tonys are locally indistinguishable, they differ in one important respect: $Tony_E$'s belief is *about* H_2SO_4, but $Tony_{TE}$'s belief is about XYZ. Thus, $Tony_E$'s belief is true just in case the sample really is H_2SO_4, and $Tony_{TE}$'s belief is true just in case the sample really is XYZ. By the same token, if the two Tonys were (unbeknownst to either) suddenly switched, their (let us assume) previous true beliefs about the sample would be rendered false.

If all of this is indeed the case, the two Tonys' beliefs can be said to have different truth conditions and thus different contents. Nevertheless, they are, ex hypothesi, intrinsically indistinguishable (i.e., they have exactly the same local properties). Once we have these facts in order, the argument for the wideness of contents seems straightforward. To generalize beyond this particular case, the broader lesson is supposed to be that, because the local indistinguishability of two individuals does not entail sameness of their mental contents, mental contents cannot (at least not always) be local properties of individuals.

3.4 A Digression on Supervenience

If sameness of local properties does not entail sameness of mental contents, what does this tell us about the locus of the mental states whose contents are at issue? Many seem to think that the best way to flesh out the ramifications of the wideness of mental contents with regard to the locus of mental states is by considering what the truth of this thesis would tell us about the "supervenience base" of mental states. In this context, to say that a mental state supervenes upon some base is just to say that differences in the mental state can only occur if there is a difference in that base (Davidson 1970).

The thesis of *local* supervenience is the claim that differences in an individual's mental states are only possible if there is some local (viz., neurophysiological) difference. However, what the argument of the previous section shows is that the thesis of local supervenience is incorrect. After all, differences in mental states may result from either local or non-local (e.g., environmental) differences, and so the thesis of *non*-local supervenience is correct. Mental states supervene not just on human brains but on features of the environment as well.

This, in and of itself, is not very interesting. There is, however, another fairly widespread view among philosophers—namely, that mental states are token identical[3] with whatever they happen to supervene upon. According to Fodor (1987, p. 30), the rationale behind this assumption is that "mind/brain supervenience (and/or mind/brain identity) is . . . the best idea that anyone has had so far about how mental causation is possible." We should, however, take care not to conflate supervenience and token identity, for to say that a mental state supervenes upon some base is, once again, just to say that differences in the mental state can only occur if there is a difference in that base. At best, then, supervenience provides a means of *tracking* (i.e., by providing a reliable indicator of) token identity.

Now, if supervenience *does* track token identity, then the fact that mental states supervene both upon states of the brain and upon states of the environment implies that the mind itself extends outside of the head and into the world. This is a provocative result, but it turns out not to be an implication of non-local supervenience, for, in the end, supervenience turns out to be a very *un*reliable indicator of token identity.

In my travels and readings, it has become clear to me that a good many philosophers think that the wideness of mental states *is* an implication of non-local supervenience (see, e.g., Burge 1979; Fodor 1987; Jackson and Pettit 1988; Sosa 1993; Clark and Chalmers 1998; Stalnaker 1989). This may, again, be because the appeal to supervenience seems like the best way to make sense of mental causation. Perhaps, then, we are still owed an account of just how it is that a proponent of the wideness of contents can reasonably hold that mental states are just in the head; we are owed an account of the compatibility of wide mental-state individuation and narrow mental-state location.[4]

Donald Davidson (2001) comes very close to supplying just such an account. As he points out, the mere fact that a thought is *identified by* (i.e., picked out on the basis of) the relationship it bears to something outside of the head does not imply that the thought itself is partly outside of the head. After all, he explains, were we to adopt this line of reasoning, we would also be led to such absurd conclusions as that sunburns are not (token identical to) states of the skin. To be sure, to say of the state of, say, some patch of someone's skin that it is a sunburn is to identify it in part by the relationship that it bears to the sun. Thus, Davidson notes, if the state of an intrinsic doppelganger's skin had some other, non-solar cause, *it would not be* a sunburn. Yet this hardly shows that sunburns are not (token identical to) states of the skin.[5]

What Davidson does not (to my knowledge) make sufficiently clear is the fact that these considerations undermine the utility of supervenience as a reliable indicator of token identity. That is to say, if we reformulate Davidson's position in terms of supervenience, what we find is that the wideness of mental contents does imply non-local supervenience, but it does not imply the wideness of the mental. In other words, what we find is that even if a mental state *supervenes* on something over and above a brain state (i.e., as evidenced by the fact that the properties of the mental state can change without local changes), the mental state may itself nevertheless be *token identical* with a brain state. Thus, what Davidson's point demonstrates is that, if supervenience is supposed to allow for an explanation of mental causation by tracking token identity, it does not live up to its billing.[6] I have encountered surprising resistance to this claim, so, in order to really drive it home (and thereby reinforce the individuation/location distinction), let us consider a different example.

Imagine a case that is analogous to the earlier Twin-Earth case but that involves photographic paper instead of brains. Imagine, specifically, that there are two pieces of photographic paper that are intrinsically indistinguishable (i.e., they have the same local properties) but that have different causal histories. The intrinsic properties of one piece of paper are the way they are due to a causal interaction with a region of the Grand Canyon, while the etiology of the other traces back to a location in Valis Marineris on Mars which, when seen from a particular angle, looks exactly like the aforementioned region of the Grand Canyon when *it* is seen from a certain angle.[7] Now if we happen to know which piece of paper is which and are asked to point to the picture of the Grand Canyon, where should we point? The folk would surely advise a one-handed approach; they would, in other words, advise that we point just at the square piece of paper. A philosopher who endorses the wideness of the mental for the aforementioned reasons would, however, presumably advise a two-handed approach; they would advise that we point both at the picture and at one of the canyons. This is because a difference between doppelganger pictures can, and in this hypothetical case would, result entirely from non-local differences. In other words, since the thesis of non-local supervenience is true of pictures (for the very same reason it is true of mental states), then if one assumes that supervenience tracks token identity, one will have to conclude that a picture of the Grand Canyon just *is* (perhaps inter alia) a square piece of paper and a portion of that canyon.

Be this as it may, when asked to point at the picture of the Grand Canyon, it seems clear that we should do just as the folk advise. It is, after all, very common, and entirely unproblematic, to individuate items, states, and processes on the basis of the relationships that they bear to other items, states, or processes. The former items, states, and processes might, moreover, have to be individuated quite differently were their relationship to the latter different. Yet the mere fact that some thing, state, or process is picked out, or individuated, by appealing to one of its relational properties is no basis for concluding that the thing or state is token identical with both relata. Supervenience, in other words, is clearly a very *un*reliable indicator of token identity.

Mental states are just another case in point. Mental states stand in numerous relationships (e.g., to what is happening outside of the head), and it seems to be common practice among us folk to individuate them on the basis of certain of these relationships. The upshot is that mental-state differences can result from non-local differences, and so mental states are properly viewed as *supervening* upon both brain and environment. This, however, does not imply that mental states are token identical to states of both the brain and the environment. In other words, nothing about the wideness of mental contents entails that mental states themselves are anywhere but in the head. Anyone who thinks otherwise is probably making the mistake of assuming that states are token identical with whatever they supervene upon.

This, it turns out, is not the only problem with the argument from the wideness of contents to the wideness of the mental. Indeed, we shall now see that an even deeper problem with this view is that it mistakes the manner in which we, qua folk, attribute mental states to one another for a deep metaphysical fact about mental states themselves.

3.5 What Twin-Earth Thought Experiments Demonstrate

The argument I presented in section 3.3 is a standard piece of conceptual analysis; its goal is to satisfy our intuitions about the individuation of contentful mental states and, thereby, to elucidate certain of our metaphysical presuppositions. What the experiment reveals, in particular, is a construal of the representation-represented relationship that is presupposed by our everyday practice of attributing mental states to one another. It does this by following the same pattern of reasoning as a simple scientific experiment. In both sorts of experiment, the goal is to determine whether or not, when all relevant factors are held constant, the manipulation of an independent variable has an effect on a dependent variable. For instance, the two Tonys and the conditions surrounding them are identical in *every* respect save for the fact that there are, unbeknownst to either, differences in the microstructure of the stuff typically classed as oil of vitriol by the locals.

At first glance, one might easily suppose that changes in the value of this independent variable suffice to create a difference in the contents of the two Tonys' otherwise-indistinguishable mental states. Appearances can be deceiving, however, for mental content is clearly not the dependent variable in the experiment. This is no small matter, for were we to suppose that mental content *is* the dependent variable, we would be misled into thinking that these experiments elucidate a metaphysical fact about mental states. Quite the contrary, however, the only thing that these experiments elucidate is an empirical fact about the construal of the relationship between mental states and what they are about that is presupposed by our everyday attributive practices. That is to say, the dependent variable here is just the manner in which we (who happen to have a God's-eye view of the situation in question) are normally inclined to individuate the mental states of the doppelgangers. The conclusion to be reached on the basis of this experimental effect is that we, qua folk, individuate the mental states of individuals on the basis of factors (e.g., microstructure and, for reasons not covered here, social milieu) that are external to those individuals. While one may not readily assent to this brand of externalism before a given thought experiment, afterwards one ultimately sees that this is indeed how we normally divide things up.[8]

If the foregoing analysis accurately portrays how it is that we, qua folk, normally *do* individuate mental states, we are still left with the further, normative question of whether or not this is how we, qua cognitive scientists, *ought to* individuate mental states for purposes of scientific explanation. Later I'll argue that the answer to the normative question just posed is "No," and later still I'll offer an alternative, externalist strategy for individuating mental states that cognitive science *should* adopt. First, however, we need to dig a bit deeper into the metaphysical presuppositions elucidated by these thought experiments.

3.6 Ahistorical Determinants of Content

To recap: On the present way of viewing the matter, the usual doppelganger thought experiments do not reveal metaphysical facts about the contents of mental states; they instead reveal empirical facts about the metaphysical presuppositions of our workaday attributive practices. While one might be able to show that we, qua folk, have very good practical reasons for hanging on to these presuppositions, it turns out that certain explanatory ends can only be attained if we, qua cognitive scientists, jettison at least one of them—namely, the assumption that causal history determines of content. In order to make logical room for an alternative (i.e., for ahistorical determinants of content), it will help if we first get perfectly clear on the difference between contents and the determinants thereof.

3.6.1 Contents and the Determinants Thereof

An easy way to gain the requisite clarity is to consider a "toy" case like that of the ocean-born magnetotactic bacteria popularized by Fred Dretske (1986). These bacteria have an internal magnet, or magnetosome, which orients itself, and the bacterium along with it, along downward-oriented lines of geomagnetic force in—depending upon the hemisphere in which the bacteria live—the direction of the northern or southern geomagnetic pole. As a result, these organisms propel themselves away from toxic (because oxygen-rich) surface water. The orientation of the internal magnetosome thus provides a reliable indicator of the direction of the nearest magnetic pole which, in turn, provides a reliable indicator of the direction of oxygen-poor water. In light of these facts, it is quite reasonable to suppose that this trait was selected for because it serves a basic biological need.

While there has been some disagreement regarding precisely what it is that the orientation of the magnetosome represents—for instance, whereas Dretske (1986) claims that the magnetosome represents the orientation of the prevailing magnetic field, Millikan (1989) claims that it represents the direction of oxygen-free water—what matters for our purposes is that the long-term causal history of the species is what these authors take to determine the function of, and thereby the content of states of, the device.[9] We might reasonably suppose this causal history to include at least one chance mutation and the consequent differential selection for reproduction of the bacteria possessing the resulting trait. To get to the point at hand, while these teleological strategies for individuating the function of the magnetosome imply that what fixes the content of states of the device is a process that is complex, diachronic, and causal in nature, it seems clear that *the content itself* is some relatively simple (albeit relational), synchronic, and (hence) non-causal property; it is just a specification of an orientation or direction. Content, in other words, clearly must be distinguished from what fixes, or determines, it.

3.6.2 Non-Teleological Functions and Ahistorical Determinants of Content

While one might think that history *just is* what determines the function of the magnetosome, a gedanken variant of this toy case makes it clear that functions, and the contents they fix, can also be individuated in an ahistorical fashion.

Imagine that a group of scientists has been engaged in genetic engineering with the goal of creating bacteria that ingest ocean-borne pollutants and break them down. To make things perfectly cut and dried, imagine further that our hypothetical scientists have, in the interest of safety, engineered these bacteria in such a way as to render them incapable of reproducing. Having created the ideal pollution-eater, our hypothetical scientists manufacture tons upon tons of the little critters and dump the lot of them into the ocean. Several years later, the scientists, discouraged by the results, test the concentration of the bacteria at various points in the ocean and find the heaviest concentrations near the poles. They then place a number of the bacteria from one of these samples under a microscope and notice that they all tend to swim in the direction of magnetic north.

At this point, our scientists are faced with the following, good old-fashioned scientific "How?" question: How are the bacteria able to manifest this ability to orient and propel themselves in the direction of magnetic north? A plausible answer, they quickly realize, is that the bacteria possess an internal device whose function, relative to that ability, is to orient the magnetosome, and the bacterium along with it, in the direction of magnetic north. The problem then becomes one of figuring out whether or not there is any internal device capable of fulfilling this function. A bit of additional microscopy reveals the presence of magnetosomes similar to those found in naturally occurring bacteria, and our scientists take this as confirmation of their original hypothesis. To be sure, they still do not know exactly *why* these organisms possess magnetosomes oriented in the precise way that they are, though they strongly suspect that this is somehow the by-product of a manufacturing process that involves a growth medium containing minute quantities of magnetite. This, however, is a further question, and it demands its own distinct answer. The initial "How?" question has, in contrast, already been answered to everyone's satisfaction.

As we saw earlier, a teleological analysis of the function of a device like a magnetosome yields an historical account of what fixes the content of states of that device. It is, however, quite plain that this strategy is ruled out in the case of our engineered pollution eaters. Nevertheless, insofar is one is interested in the mechanisms that underlie a capacity (i.e., that explain *how* it does what it does), what this example illustrates is that one may, as Cummins (1975) explains, individuate the function of a device relative to its contribution to that capacity. This has obvious ramifications for the matter of whether or not the determinants of content in such cases are historical. On a teleological analysis of the naturally occurring magnetosome, the determinants of content were historical because the function of the device doing the representing was itself determined by historical factors. In the case of our engineered bacteria, however, there is no such history that can be appealed to in order to assign functions or fix contents thereby.

For a further, less hypothetical illustration of these points, consider the fact that many species of migratory fish are capable of returning to the precise body of water in which they were spawned. Just as in our thought experiment, we are faced here with a standard scientific "How?" question, and, as before, it is reasonable to answer this question through an appeal to functions that are performed by underlying component mechanisms, some of which may involve representing. A similar appeal to non-teleological functions carried out by component mechanisms has been made en route to explaining countless other capacities, biological and otherwise.[10] Those cases in which one of the functions of a device is to represent tend to involve navigation or food procurement, though we shall soon see that one of the most interesting cases of this sort does not fall neatly into either category.[11] Still, in all such cases, it is clear that the evolutionary history of the organisms in question drops out as irrelevant. Indeed, had an indistinguishable group of "swamp organisms," whether they be bacteria, fish, or humans, been created by a bolt of lightning striking a swamp, the same questions would arise and the answers given to them would be the same.

Returning to the relatively simple case of naturally occurring magnetotactic bacteria, what we find is that there are at least two senses of 'function' to which we might appeal when answering questions about them, and there is little sense to be made of the claim that one is, independent of context, better than the other. Instead, one or the other (or perhaps even a third or fourth) will be appropriate depending upon the type of question one is trying to answer. Put simply, the suggestion is that, in our discussions of function and content, we take to heart Bas van Fraassen's (1980) point that, corresponding to different questions of why [and how], there are different proper answers.

Before pushing forward, I think it bears noting that an appreciation of these points softens the border between intrinsic and derived intentionality. (See Dretske 1986.) While I would certainly not advocate going postmodern, I do think that the assignment of function, and thereby of intentionality, is driven by *our* explanatory interests (this just extends the lesson of section 3.5). At least from the standpoint of cognitive science, intentionality need not be viewed as an explanandum that holds theoretical interest in its own right or as a reward bestowed solely on those who have undergone a long process of natural selection. If intentionality is cashed out in some non-ephemeral way and makes a legitimate and valuable contribution to some well-regarded explanans, this is all that any naturalist can rightfully demand.

3.6.3 Why Consider "Toy" Cases?

The appeal to "toy" cases such as real and hypothetical magnetotactic bacteria in discussions of content bears some similarities to the early use of "toy" worlds (i.e., those consisting of just a few simple objects) in artificial intelligence. (See subsection 1.2.3.2.) In the latter context, one of the important goals was to gain a better understanding of the kinds of component processes that are required in order to carry out such activities as goal-directed reasoning and language comprehension/production. For instance, in order for a device to achieve the goals it is assigned without lots of fumbling about, AI researchers realized that it must be able, among other things, to represent the way the world is, the way it ought to be, and which of the huge number of alterations to the world will bring about the goal state. This requires the ability to manipulate representations in a truth-preserving manner which, in turn, requires knowledge of how the world works. Of course, what is achieved with regard to a "toy" world may not scale up to more complex situations, but realizing this can also be a step forward, for it can point in the direction of further processing requirements.

In the same way, the point of the foregoing analysis of magnetotactic bacteria is just to pare away most of the complexity characterizing the human case in order to elucidate some of the basic components of content attribution. To reverse the order in which the components were introduced, we found that one can start either with the question of what historical factors led to the organism having a particular trait (i.e., a magnetosome) or with the question of how the organism is able to do what it does (i.e., swim toward the north pole). Depending on the question, this leads to the assignment of either a teleological or a capacity-based representational function to a particular mechanism, and the function assigned to the mechanism determines, to some extent, the contents of states of the device. This brings into sharp relief an important distinction between contents, which are synchronic, non-causal properties, and the determinants thereof, which, depending upon the kind of function one assigns, are either synchronic or diachronic. To be sure, these are a lot of factors to invoke in the analysis of such a simple creature, but the failure to make these distinctions has created considerable confusion among those trying to figure out whether or not the attribution of representational content is a legitimate scientific practice. This, of course, is precisely what *we* are trying to figure out, so let's get back to it.

3.7 Externalism without Twins

An ahistorical construal of what determines the content of the states of magnetosomes in natural and engineered bacteria might lead one to reject the wideness of contents, at least in those cases where such an ahistorical construal is appropriate. After all, a good deal of the force behind doppelganger arguments for the wideness of contents stems from the fact that we often take the contents of representational states to be determined by the causal histories of those states—that is to say, it is largely because indistinguishable local states can be the product of distinct causal histories that we are led to attribute divergent contents to otherwise indistinguishable individuals. We need, however, to be clear on the fact that the claim that contents are "wide" rather than "narrow" properties can be understood in either of two distinct ways, neither of which requires the *backing* of doppelganger thought experiments (although such experiments are part of the definiens of both 'wide content' and 'narrow content' on the second way of understanding this distinction).

There is, first of all, the proposal that contents are wide because they are not local properties of individuals, but rather relational properties (i.e., of a non-local sort). While there is nothing inherently objectionable about the use of doppelganger thought experiments in support of this claim, it is coming to be appreciated that an appeal to doppelgangers was never actually required. (See Stich 1978; Stalnaker 1989; Davies 1991.) After all, according to just about everyone, for some thing or state to represent is for that thing or state to stand in a relationship with something else. In the absence of some such relationship, there is simply no representing going on, and consequently no content. Again, the appeal to doppelgangers was not necessary to show that contents are non-local relational properties; they are so by (widely endorsed) definition.

There is, nevertheless, still an important lesson to be drawn from doppelganger thought experiments. What they show is that even opaquely read ascriptions of propositional attitudes (PAs)[12] can be infused with natural and social presuppositions. This turns out to be important because it makes them *un*reliable indicators of the proximal causes of behavior. Specifically, the contents attributed when we make opaque PA ascriptions do not always capture exactly how things seem to the individual to whom the PAs are being ascribed (the phenomenology of their mental states, what they take words to mean, etc.).[13] Yet this seems to be what we should like to know in order to predict and explain behavior (Fodor 1980).

What we seem to stand in need of, then, is a means of individuating contents, and thereby mental states, that *does* capture how things seem to the ascribee. It is for precisely this reason that philosophers have been trying to develop a "narrow" theory of content, by which is meant a theory of content on which the mental states of doppelgangers will always have the same content. Contents of this sort, it is quite reasonably claimed, provide a better indication of what we need to know in order to predict and explain behavior.

Though the motivation behind the search for such a theory of content is sound enough, the expression 'narrow content' seems poorly chosen. It is, specifically, either oxymoronic or misleading. There are, after all, just two ways in which the search for a theory of narrow content can pan out. On the one hand, we might find a way to characterize *only* how things seem to the ascribee—that is, to classify what is in their heads in isolation from the environment. This might do just fine for purposes of explaining behavior, but to call the psychological properties in question 'narrow *contents*' would be oxymoronic (Stich 1978; Stalnaker 1989). That is to say, given the fact that contents just are non-local relational properties—which is just part and parcel of the tight relationship between representation, content, and truth conditions—it is very difficult to understand why the local properties in terms of which the mental states are being classified should be considered contents at all.[14] As I have explained, contents in this sense just are wide.

On the other hand, we might develop a semantics that enables the attribution of genuine content (i.e., the real, relational stuff) to mental states in a way that precisely parallels how things seem to the ascribee. In that case, however, the phase 'narrow content' seems misleading, for narrow content on this view is certainly not narrow in the sense of being local, it is just as wide as so-called wide content; it merely sticks more closely than the folk attributive practice with how *ascribees* cut the pie rather than how Mother Nature or society cuts it.

If someone who understands these facts still wishes to hang onto the phrase 'narrow content', so be it. They must, however, bear in mind that this mere turn of phrase will most assuredly not enable them to avoid some of the most serious charges that have been leveled against "wide" theories of content. As explained in greater detail below, proponents of such "narrow" theories of content—that is, in the second, doppelganger-relative sense of the wide/narrow distinction—have themselves (some-what unwittingly) supplied some pretty compelling arguments that contents, whether shared by doppelgangers or not, are irrelevant to the explanation of behavior.

It is time, now, to get to the main point of this chapter. By way of tying the foregoing lessons together, what I will explain here is that one of the foundational models of cognitive science explains an important human capacity by appealing to systems whose function it is to represent the way the world is and the way we would like it to be, and, because history is irrelevant to explanations of this sort, this model presupposes ahistorical determinants of contents. To break this down into pieces that are easier to swallow, let me start by clarifying the motivating "How?" question.

3.8 The Planning Model

One of the foundational models of cognitive science answers a "How?" question that is quite similar to the "How?" questions considered earlier. To illustrate the explanatory goals of this model, consider the device depicted in figure 3.1. Notice that it would be quite easy for the average human to envision any number of methods for obtaining the coin, perhaps the most entertaining of which is simply to turn on the spigot. Unlike other creatures, we humans can quickly solve countless problems of this sort. We are thus faced with yet another good old-fashioned scientific "How?" question: How is it that we humans are able to behave in such an unhesitating (i.e., after we've had a moment to mull things over) and effec-tive manner in the face of even highly novel environmental conditions? The answer, according to one very popular theory, is that we have a highly developed capacity to think ahead. (See sections 1.2., 1.3, and 2.4.) The crux of this proposal is that we represent both the way the world is and the way we would like it to be, and we are able, by manipulating our rep-resentations in a truth-preserving manner, to find a route from the former

Figure 3.1
Left: A Rube Goldberg-style device for obtaining a coin that rests atop a piston. Right:
A close-up of the coin on the piston.

to the latter. This model also supplies a natural explanation for why human behavior is so flexible in the face of similar environmental conditions.

This model has clearly been co-opted from folk psychology (one of the central tenets of which is just that, by thinking ahead, we humans are able to figure out how, in light of our beliefs, to fulfill our desires), and to describe it as I just have is considered rather banal by cognitive scientists. It is, after all, the *only* satisfactory explanation ever given for one of the most important and arguably distinctive facts about human behavior. In the present context, what is so interesting about this model is that it adverts to the same basic sorts of mental states whose individuation conditions have been the topic of heated discussion in the philosophy of mind, but, because cognitive scientists wield it to answer the above "How?" question, it presupposes a theory of content that looks considerably different from the social-historical theory of content that we, qua folk, seem normally to rely upon when attributing mental states.

3.8.1 Folk Semantics and the Planning Model
The planning model supplies an answer to a "How?" question that is very much like the questions of how salmon are able to find their way to a specific inlet, how swallows are able to find their way to Capistrano, how rats find their way to a food source, and how magnetotactic bacteria are able to orient themselves so that they face magnetic north. In attempting to answer questions of this sort, what we seek is an understanding of the mechanisms that sustain the ability in question. As I have noted, causal history is no part of these explanations; the same explanation would be applicable even if the causal history of the device were very different or

non-existent. This, in and of itself, obviously creates considerable tension between the planning model and folk semantics. If, for instance, swamp people were confronted with the device in figure 3.1, they too would obtain the coin in the very same unhesitating and effective manner, and, like the rest of us (and unlike many other critters), they would also deal effectively with an extremely wide range of further environmental contingencies.[15] We would, in other words, be left with precisely the same "How?" question, a question to which the planning model would still supply the answer.

In addition, because folk semantics leads us to classify mental states in deference to Mother Nature and society, the usual concerns about its relevance to psychological explanation seem to make it a poor adjunct to the planning model. To make the point explicit, consider the consequences of having a suitably constructed Twin-Earth scenario obtain with respect to the device in figure 3.1. Rather than taking a mental trip back in time, let us suppose that all the observations of present-day physicists and chemists on the two worlds are the same but that there are (to capitalize on the "data underdetermine theory" loophole) still-undiscovered facts about microstructure that distinguish the materials in these two parts of the universe. Thus, on Twin Earth there are twin-oxygen, twin-hydrogen, twaluminum, etc. Let us also suppose that most lay folks$_{TE}$ refer to the device with the hose attached to it as a 'spigot', but unbeknownst to them it is a spigot only if it does *not* have a hose attached to it. As any decent gardener$_{TE}$ will attest, when a hose is attached to the device it becomes a spogot. The lay folk$_{TE}$ would, of course, defer to the judgment of local professionals in such matters. I could continue adding variations that are beyond the ken of the individuals we are studying, but let me get to the point. Folk semantics would lead us to make such opaque PA ascriptions to our hypothetical Earthlings as these:

They believe that turning on the spigot will make water come out.
They believe that when the pail fills with water it will exert downward pressure on the lever.
They believe that downward pressure on the lever will cause the opposite end of the lever to rise and thus bring the gold coin within reach.

But if we have constructed our example carefully, none of these attributions would be true of their Twin-Earth doppelgangers. Nevertheless, it seems clear that they and their doppelgangers behave in an unhesitating and effective manner when faced with the device *for the exact same reasons*, and they would continue to do so even if they were to switch places. Thus, it is natural to wonder why cognitive scientists should care about the psychological distinctions made from the standpoint of folk semantics.

If the problem were isolated to science fiction, then perhaps we could be forgiven for not losing much sleep over it. But folk semantics clearly permits many cases of this sort under even the most mundane conditions, owing to the simple fact that *ascribees* are often unaware of how either Mother Nature or society cut up the pie, and yet we *ascribers* individuate ascribees' mental states relative to both schemes. In other words, it may be quite common for us folk to attribute mental states to one another on the basis of factors that are completely beyond the ken of, and that are thus no part of the proximal causation of the behavior of, the individuals to whom those states are being attributed. It might be nice, then, if we had a semantics on which facts of this sort turned out to be irrelevant. This, once again, is a large part of what motivates the desire for a characterization of content (i.e., a so-called narrow theory of content) that makes no distinctions between doppelgangers.

I should point out that it has been suggested in the face of similar concerns that the psychological distinctions made from the standpoint of folk semantics *are* relevant to the scientific explanation of behavior. In my earlier example, whereas $Tony_E$ succeeds in obtaining oil of vitriol, $Tony_{TE}$ only succeeds at getting some other substance (Burge 1986). In other words, the differences in their mental states are, it is claimed, causally relevant because they issue in different behaviors. Like many others, I am not persuaded by this reply. One of my worries is that it seems to sidestep the original concern entirely. The concern was, to be specific, that folk semantics leads us to make distinctions *in the proximal causes* of behavior because of factors that are beyond the conscious or even the unconscious ken of the individuals in question. It is because these factors are beyond their conscious or unconscious ken that they seem not to bear on the proximal causation of their behavior. The only thing the reply seems to add is that the folk semantic distinctions are paralleled by distinctions in the *effects* of behavior, but that is not what is at issue.

It also bears mentioning that the mere fact that the two hypothetical worlds reside at different points in space is enough to guarantee differences in the *effects* of the two Tonys' behaviors. We can, for instance, just as easily imagine keeping *everything* the same except for the locations of the two worlds. In that case, there is still a difference in the effects of the behaviors of the two Tonys, for while $Tony_E$ succeeds in obtaining oil of vitriol *here*, $Tony_{TE}$ only succeeds at obtaining oil of vitriol *there*. There was thus never any doubt that the effects of their behaviors would be different, but I still cannot fathom why a psychologist ought to care about *these* differences.

I also find myself imagining how an analogous line of argument would look were it offered in another scientific arena. Suppose, for instance, two biologists, B1 and B2, disagree about the best way to individuate species in biology. B1 thinks that causal history is something that matters, and B2 thinks that local structure is all that matters (cf. Hull 1987 and Mayr 1987). Thus, had a doppelganger to the Earthly species *Canis lupus* evolved in parallel on another planet, B2 would classify it as *Canis lupus* but B1 would not. Debate thus ensues about which is the more scientifically respectable way to divide the world up. While there are clearly many important considerations to bear in mind here, it would not do for B1 to try assuaging any of B2's legitimate fears about the historical scheme by reading off of the thought experiment that the imagined difference not only gives rise to differences in how he would classify the two sets of creatures but also gives rise to scientifically important facts such as the fact that, whereas *Canis lupus*$_E$ is attracted to *Canis lupus*$_E$, *Canis lupus*$_{TE}$ is attracted to *Canis lupus*$_{TE}$. I think B2 would be right to object at this point that B1 was pulling some kind of parlor trick. (Cf. Fodor 1991a.)

These, at any rate, are some of my lingering concerns about the reply on the table. I am, in short, still highly suspicious of folk semantics because it seems, quite systematically, to lead to psychological distinctions that are not paralleled by any differences in the proximal causes of behavior.

If you share my concerns about folk semantics, the following proposal may be of interest. Bear in mind, however, that even if you do not share my concerns, it has already been established that the planning model answers a legitimate scientific "How?" question in a way that demands a semantic framework that diverges significantly from folk semantics. The answers it supplies will remain the same even if there are imperceptible differences in environmental microstructure or unknown facts about social milieu, and (crucially) even if the creature in question lacks our kind of history altogether. The best that those advocating the scientific credibility of folk semantics can hope for, then, is an alternative set of questions to which folk semantics does supply an important and unproblematic part of the answer.

3.8.2 Semantics$_{PM}$ and the Determinants of Content

In chapter 2, I made a big deal out of the fact that the planning model is much like the theory of natural selection in that its true power inheres in its ability to explain a quite general fact about the creatures falling under its purview. Specifically (and yet again), in the case of the planning model, what is explained is the fact that humans are able to respond in an unhesitating (once we get started) and effective manner to even highly novel environmental conditions. The manipulation of *representations* figures prominently in the model, and those who hope to naturalize contents through an appeal to this model must provide a correspondingly general account (let us call it semantics$_{PM}$) of how the contents of these representations are fixed. This account must, of course, be compatible with the capacity-based individuation of functions. Allow me to introduce the schematics for this semantic framework via the toy case of magnetotactic bacteria:

On a capacity analysis of 'function', states of a magnetosome can be said to have the function of representing the direction of magnetic north because the relationship between states of the magnetosome and the magnetic north pole—namely, that the former points in the direction of the latter—is what enables the bacterium to swim towards the north pole; this is what fixes the content of the representation. The content—namely, that the direction of magnetic north is *that* way—is the state of affairs that would have to obtain in order for the representation to be veridical, and the magnetosome is fulfilling its function only if it is representing accurately —that is, only if it is oriented in the direction of magnetic north.

The capacity analysis of the representational function of the magnetosome gives us a schema that can be utilized to flesh out the details of semantics$_{PM}$. Let us begin, then, by filling in the easiest placeholders of this schema (in italics) and leaving the others blank:

On a capacity analysis of 'function', states of a *planning mechanism* can be said to have the function of representing ___ because the relationship between states of the *planning mechanism* and ___—namely, that the former are ___ the latter—is what enables *the organism in question* to *behave effectively in the face of the circumstances at hand*; this is what fixes the content of the representation. The content—namely, that ___—is the state of affairs that would have to obtain in order for the representation to be veridical, and the *planning mechanism* is fulfilling its function only if it is representing accurately—that is, only if ___.

The planning model is obviously far more complicated than the magnetosome model, and, as a result, so too are the fillers of the remaining placeholders. However, if we restrict ourselves merely to the way that person in question represents the world as being (i.e., to beliefs), I think that the final result will look something like the following (where, for ease of reference, only the fillers of the remaining placeholders have been italicized):

On a capacity analysis of 'function', states of a planning mechanism can be said to have the function of representing *the way the world is and the way it will be in light of alterations to it* because the relationship between states of the planning mechanism and *the way the world is or would be if particular alterations were made to it*—namely, that the former are *isomorphic with*[16] the latter—is what enables the organism in question to behave effectively in the face of the circumstances at hand; this is what fixes the content of the representation. The content—namely, that *the world is in such and such a state or will be in light of alterations to it*—is the state of affairs that would have to obtain in order for the representation to be veridical, and the *planning mechanism* is fulfilling its function only if it is representing accurately—that is, only if *the states* are *isomorphic with the way the world is or would be in light of particular alterations.*

This is not yet a complete account of content fixation. For one thing, because isomorphism is cheap, something will have to be said to answer the question of why not just any isomorphism will do. At least the beginnings of such an answer are implicit in the above analysis. The isomorphisms in question are going to have to be those that are capable of ushering in effective planned behaviors relative to some type of system. This means that (i) the isomorphic states will have to be connected up to behavior-guiding mechanisms in the appropriate way (i.e., they must be capable of playing the right causal role) and (ii) the individual in question will have to be appropriately situated relative to a system of that type. For instance, although Tony's brain may well harbor states that are isomorphic with the workings of an ice cream factory, the Boston sewer system, or a zone defense in American football, unless (i) these states are connected up to his behavior-guiding mechanisms in the appropriate way and (ii) Tony is appropriately situated relative to the type of system in question, these brain/world isomorphisms will not enable Tony to fix problems in an ice cream factory, navigate Boston's sewers, or call an effective play on offense.

Another issue that will ultimately need to be dealt with is the fuzziness of the line between accurate and inaccurate representations. In the ideal cases, which never materialize, an individual will succeed because his representations are perfectly isomorphic with what they represent and fail because his representations are not at all isomorphic. In actual cases, accuracy will come in degrees. Still, the general fact that humans succeed in the face of novel conditions is a consequence of the isomorphism between their representations and what they are representations of. Likewise, when representations are to blame for failures in this regard, this will always be a consequence of a lack of isomorphism. One could also say that a given representation of a represented system is true in some respects and false in others, but because there are just so darned many respects, at least for the purposes at hand let us allow for an analog version of truth—let us call it *veridicality*—that comes in degrees.

Notice that the general semantic framework just outlined gets precisely at the thread that runs through the various permutations of the coin-on-piston problem discussed above and illustrated in figure 3.1. To start with, because the determinants of content are not historical, facts about the behavior of swamp people can be explained in the same way that we explain facts about "normal" people. In addition, the very same explanations of success will apply in cases where particular materials have been replaced with superficially indistinguishable counterparts, where the individuals in question lack scientifically informed natural-kind beliefs altogether, and cases where the manner in which the local community of experts divides things up has been altered. That is, it cuts across the troublesome distinctions that folk semantics leads us to make.

I think this suffices for the purposes at hand. Any other minor details that need filling in will have to wait, for there is still a very pressing concern that will, if it cannot be dealt with head-on, blow the entire project of naturalizing contents out of the water. Like all *genuine* theories of content, this one construes contents as wide properties. The problems considered so far arise when the mental states of individuals are individuated on the basis of microstructural or social-historical factors of which those individuals (ex hypothesi) have no knowledge. There is however, another very-widely discussed concern that has to do with the width of content rather than the depth of an individual's knowledge. This concern was first voiced by enemies of so-called wide theories of content, but it turns out to be one with which any theory of content will have to come to grips. It is one that has not, as yet, been satisfactorily resolved.

3.9 The Problem of Causal Impotence

The most pressing concern about the legitimacy of appeals to contents in scientific contexts is, as a first approximation, something like this: Sciences, cognitive science included, are only permitted to appeal to causally potent properties, but contents are causally impotent (Fodor 1987, 1991a). There are, of course, several complications, and we have to map them before we can continue. To start with, we must get clear on the precise depth of the impotence that may characterize contents.

3.9.1 The Nature of the Problem
As Fodor explains, certain properties of an item can be causally impotent *in fact* while being causally potent *in principle* (Fodor 1987, p. 166, note 4).

These are the *causal powers* of an item. To say, for instance, that water solubility is among the causal powers of salt is to say that the property, solubility, will be efficacious if certain conditions obtain, and so the presence of this power is perfectly compatible with it never being exercised. In the case of contents, in contrast, the worry is that there are *no* conditions under which contents have effects that should be of interest to cognitive science; it is not merely that they are causally impotent in fact, but that they are causally impotent in principle.[17] Thus, as a second approximation, the worry about contents is that they are devoid of causal powers.

This worry stems in part from the fact that contents are relational properties (of the non-local variety). This, however, cannot be the whole story, for it seems that most (perhaps all) relational properties have causal powers, including contents (Fodor 1991a). So long as it is possible for there to be a detector for a given relational property, then one of the causal powers of that property will be its power to affect (or, for sticklers, to be responsible for an effect on) such detectors. Thus, as a third approximation, the worry about contents is that they are devoid of *relevant* causal powers.

The reason contents seem devoid of relevant causal powers is that they seem incapable of affecting behavior (viz., the behavior of the individual whose states are being individuated on the basis of the contents of those states). A popular way to show that this is so is to consider the kinds of cases considered earlier—namely, cases where contents and causal powers fail to keep step with one another. Consider, once again, the case of Tony$_E$ and Tony$_{TE}$. Because they are indistinguishable in terms of local properties, they would seem to have exactly the same causal powers. Drop either into a situation and you will always get the same result. However, while they are identical in causal powers, some of their mental states have, from the standpoint of folk semantics, different contents. That is, Tony$_E$ has beliefs about water, while Tony$_{TE}$ has beliefs about twater. In the face of such considerations, and without getting into the details, something like the following dialectic has ensued.

Burge (1986): Contents and causal powers are not out of phase in such cases, for although Tony$_E$ and Tony$_{TE}$ have different mental states, those states also have *different causal powers*. For instance, having water thoughts causes water-getting behavior and the like, while having twater thoughts causes twater-getting behavior.

Fodor (1991a): Be this as it may, Tyler, contents and causal powers *are* out of phase. The analysis you offer does not meet one of the conditions that must be satisfied when attempting to demonstrate differences in causal powers—namely, the differences in the effect must not be not conceptually related to the differences in the cause. In other words, it is just a conceptual truth, and not an empirical fact, that twater thoughts cause twater-getting behavior.

Fodor (1994): OK, you were right, Tyler, albeit for the wrong reasons. Contents and causal powers *are* in phase, for Mother Nature prohibits certain cases (e.g., the Twin-Earth scenario) where changes in content are not paralleled by changes in behavior and experts are just instruments.

In addition, we have seen that semantics$_{PM}$ cuts across the distinctions that give folk semantics so much trouble, and it thereby keeps contents and causal powers in phase.

This is all quite well and good, but none of it addresses the original problem: Even if contents *track* causal powers, contents themselves seem devoid of relevant causal powers; they are incapable of affecting behavior. Indeed, the only purpose the consideration of twin cases could serve *here* is to highlight this fact by showing how contents and causal powers can fall out of phase with one another. Finding a way to put them back into phase does nothing to establish that contents have relevant causal powers. It is here, therefore, that I must part ways with both Fodor and Burge.

What I do think that Fodor has established quite effectively is that in order for contents to have even the potential to have a causal impact on behavior, what seems to be required are, rather loosely speaking, "detectors" for these peculiar relational properties that are part of the local makeup of the individuals doing the representing. The problem facing both folk semantics and semantics$_{PM}$ is, to paraphrase Kant (1992), that it is very hard to understand how the representers could step outside of the representation/represented relationship in order to detect the correspondence between the two. Contents, in short, seem poorly situated to have a causal impact on behavior. (If you do not find the concern here entirely clear, you will after we consider the Autobot.)

As one might expect, even this simple proposal has to be qualified. It is, after all, surely quite possible, and probably quite common, for one sensory system to be calibrated on the basis of feedback from another. In such cases, one sensory system (e.g., proprioception) would be acting as a relational property detector for another (e.g., vision). As one of my primary goals is to demonstrate the legitimacy of semantics$_{PM}$, let me simply note that this proviso does not quite suffice to get the sorts of contents countenanced by semantics$_{PM}$ out of hot water, for the representations at issue are supposed to play—this is their very raison d'être—a far more direct role in the explanation of human behavior. The representations posited by

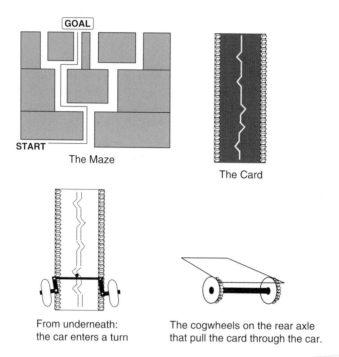

GOAL

START

The Maze

The Card

From underneath:
the car enters a turn

The cogwheels on the rear axle
that pull the card through the car.

Figure 3.2
Autobot. Source: Cummins 1996, p. 95.

the planning model are supposed to figure directly, rather than through the mediation of a calibration process, in an explanation for the human ability to respond to novel environmental contingencies in an unhesitating and effective manner. To put it a bit differently, it is not an *essential* feature of such explanations that a calibration process occurs at all. What *is* essential is that humans harbor representations that are isomorphic with what they represent in a manner that supports effective planned behaviors.

These are clearly very complicated issues. But I think we can once again reign in some of the complexity by considering another toy case. This time, the Autobot—a hypothetical vehicle described by Robert Cummins (1996) and shown here in figure 3.2—supplies precisely the kind of toy case that we need.

3.9.2 Content and the Autobot

The behavior of the Autobot is largely determined by a drive train (not pictured in figure 3.2) and by the interaction between a slotted card and a steering mechanism. As the vehicle moves forward, gears on the rear wheel push the card forward, which causes the steering pin to be manipulated by the slot in the card. The vehicle described by Cummins is one that happens to be quite successful at navigating a particular maze. It seems reasonable to explain this fact on the basis of the relationship—really a set of relationships—between the card and the maze. For instance, it seems highly relevant, insofar as the success of the car is concerned, that for each turn in the path there is a notch in the card, that the sequence of left and right turns is mirrored by the sequence of right/left notches, and that the relative distances between the notches mirrors the relative distances between the turns.

The card, in short, is appropriately isomorphic with the world in the two senses covered earlier. That is, the card is (i) connected up to behavior-guiding mechanisms in the appropriate way (i.e., it is capable of playing the right causal role), and (ii) the entire device is appropriately situated relative to the system with which the slot is isomorphic. Let us, then, treat the slot as a representation of the path through the maze and see whether or not the content of this representation has any relevant causal powers. I think, with a bit of reflection, you will see that it does not. In particular, it seems that the relationship between the shape of the slot and the shape of the maze is incapable of *causing* the Autobot to behave in the particular way that it does. To put it a bit differently, the car is incapable of detecting the relationship—Kant's worry is unmitigated—and so the behavior of the car is unaffected by it. Thus, if we continue to demand that the properties appealed to in scientific explanations are those that have relevant causal powers—which requires, in turn, that such properties have at least the potential to causally affect the behavior of the relevant system—then it is illegitimate to explain the successful navigation of the maze by the car in terms of the relationship between the slot and the maze. The content of the card will, in other words, be no part of any legitimate explanation.

I suppose that one who is resistant to this conclusion might be inclined to search for some way of showing the causal efficacy of the relationship between slot and path. One might suggest, for instance, that this relational property causes another relational property. But even if this is so, this is not the same as showing that the first relational property has relevant causal powers. To see why it is not the same, notice that there are many cases in which one pair of relata causes another pair of relata. For instance, when two watches indicate the same time at time t, they also indicate the same time at time at $t + 1$. The explanation for this is that the behavior of

Watch1 at t causes its behavior at $t + 1$ and the behavior of Watch2 at t causes its behavior at $t + 1$. The relationship they bear to one another, however, is not a property with any relevant causal powers.

A related approach would be to argue that the relational property does not affect the behavior of just the Autobot, but that it does have a causal impact on the entire individual/world system. Once again, however, while the individual relata may have causal effects, the relationship they bear (i.e., isomorphism) to one another seems causally impotent.

I don't think these points can be sensibly disputed, so we are left with one of two options. We might, on the one hand, conclude that the appeal to the content of the card is, in the case of the Autobot, illegitimate because the appeal to isomorphism is. In the case of human planning, the same conclusion will be reached in the same way by the simple fact that brain states have relevant causal powers, but the relationships they bear to states of the outside world (viz., whether or not they are isomorphic with the world) do not. The other option, which I pursue here, is to drop the stricture that sciences are only permitted to appeal to properties that have relevant causal powers. Dropping this stricture will enable us to see why it is that contents are, in fact, properties in good scientific standing.

3.9.3 Causal Impotence and Explanatory Potency

Jackson and Pettit (1988) have come pretty close to showing this already. They begin by noting that there are many legitimate explanations where relational properties play an essential role. Some of the cases they cite share structural features with the watch example. They note, for instance, that when two particles accelerate at the same rate, physicists might explain this fact by noting that the same force was applied to each particle. To be sure, the sameness of force is causally impotent (save for its effect on the scientists), but it seems perfectly legitimate for the physicists to invoke this property when supplying an explanation for the sameness of acceleration. Though Jackson and Pettit might be credited with drawing our attention to the fact that there are many such examples, they miss the mark when they attempt to elucidate precisely how it is that this dispels concerns about the explanatory relevance of contents.

Regarding the ongoing debate about contents and causal powers, what they take to be the main source of concern is that any of many distinct causal antecedents can give rise to a single mental state. In other words, Jackson and Pettit take the problem to be that the causal antecedents which they take to bestow content on a mental state are "invisible" to that state. (This, they correctly point out, would also be true in the case of so-called narrow contents, for one and the same internal state can be caused by any of a large number of further internal states.) The antecedents of behavior, in other words, contain no record of *their* causal antecedents. Without going into too much detail, the mistake in Jackson and Pettit's (1988) analysis—which is also the mistake in Jackson's (1995, 1996) analysis—is that it confuses the diachronic, and purportedly content-*fixing*, causal relationship between represented and representation with the content relationship itself, which is a synchronic and non-causal relationship.[18] (See section 2.6.1 above.) In short, because Jackson and Pettit misconstrue the nature of the concern, which is that contents have no relevant causal powers, they fail to adequately address it. What we still need to know, then, is what it is about the explanations to which Jackson and Pettit draw our attention that makes them legitimate. If we can determine this, then we ought to be able to determine whether or not explanations that appeal to contents satisfy the same conditions.

3.9.4 The Causal Impotence and the Explanatory Potency of Contents

There is, unfortunately, no agreed upon explication of 'explanation' that we can appeal to here (though I will attempt to remedy this state of affairs in chapters 7–9). Nevertheless, our present needs should be met as long as we can agree upon some sufficient conditions for explanation that cover the sorts of cases in which we are interested. It will not matter if these conditions happen to be too restrictive to cover all genuine cases of explanation; what matters is that they are restrictive enough to exclude cases of non-explanatory inference.

Notice, then, that with regard to the cases we have been considering (i.e., the watch and particle-acceleration examples) the relational property that we take to do the explaining is causally inefficacious but its presence has definite implications. That is to say, it is a necessary constituent of the explanation because, in conjunction with knowledge of other factors, knowledge of its presence is what enables us to infer the occurrence of the event in question (i.e., the sameness of time at $t + 1$ and sameness of acceleration), and, keeping everything else constant, knowing that it was absent would lead us to infer the non-occurrence of the event. Knowledge of the relational property is, in short, a crucial ingredient in the inference from explanans to explanandum.[19]

The other crucial ingredient is knowledge of some form of production, causation, or at least change, at the level of individual relata. In the cases at hand, we know that although the relational properties invoked in these explanations are themselves causally impotent, changes in the individual relata are also partly responsible for the occurrence of the event to be explained. Knowledge of these changes seems to be another crucial component of the inference from explanans to explanandum in each of these cases.

To fill in a few additional details, let us say, then, that, relative to a backdrop of explanatory interests, we have an explanation that legitimately invokes a causally impotent relational property if it is knowledge of (or hypotheses concerning) both those relational properties and changes at the level of the individual relata that enables us to infer that (ceteris paribus[20]) what stands in need of explanation is or was to be expected.

To give another, rather extreme illustration, consider how Leibniz (with whom I will presume some familiarity) would explain the case where you and I both see the table in my dining room. According to Leibniz, there is no causal commerce at all between you and me or between either of us and the table; we are all windowless monads unfolding in our own preprogrammed ways. Nevertheless, there is, says Leibniz, a legitimate explanation for this putative fact about us—namely, he claims, there is a certain pre-established harmony between my unfolding, your unfolding, and that of the table. This harmony, very much like the synchronization of watches, guarantees that my seeing you (i.e., with eyes open, etc.) and the table will be paralleled by your seeing me and the table. So even though the harmony between my unfolding and yours is a relational property that, ex hypothesi, has no causal impact on anything whatsoever, the harmony does have very real implications. In particular, it, in conjunction with change at the local level, implies that my seeing you and the table will be paralleled by your seeing me and the table; it is to be expected on this view. Just as in the watch and particle-acceleration examples, the explanation in this case necessarily, and legitimately, appeals to a property that has no relevant causal powers.

The case of the Autobot fits the same pattern. Specifically, the Autobot's capacity to successfully navigate the maze is implied, in part, by the set of relationships between the card and the maze. To be sure, these relationships do not themselves *cause* the car to behave in the particular way that it does relative to the maze; they do not cause anything whatsoever, at least insofar as the car/maze system is concerned. Nevertheless, the presence of these relational properties has real and important implications. What it implies, roughly, is a general *absence* of causal commerce between the car and the blocks that make up the walls of the maze.

The explanation for how it is that humans, unlike many other critters, are able to respond in such an unhesitating and effective manner to even highly novel environmental conditions (i.e., the answer to the question of what are the mechanisms underlying this capacity) also makes an essential, and legitimate, appeal to causally impotent relational properties (i.e., contents). The answer to this question is, once again, that we represent both the way the world is and the way we would like it to be and that we are able, by manipulating our representations in a truth-preserving manner, to find a route from the former to the latter. Without trying to beg any later questions about representational format, the general explanation on offer here is that we harbor models of the world and assess the consequences of actions via the (largely) truth-preserving manipulation of those models. The contents of the representations in question are just the conditions under which they would be veridical. Per semantics$_{PM}$, representations are veridical to the extent that they are isomorphic (i.e., given some sensible restrictions on which isomorphisms matter) with how the world is or would be in light of specific alterations. It is the entire conglomeration of claims constitutive of the planning model that enables us to infer that the ability in question was to be expected.

One of the interesting characteristics of this explanation is that the relational properties to which it adverts do not always obtain. Specifically, the explanation is that we harbor representations of both the actual state of affairs *and* of how the world *would be* were we to take specific actions with regard to it. That the latter representations are generally veridical, which requires that they be isomorphic with how things would be, is also an essential component of the overall explanation. It is because our representations of how things would be in light of specific alterations are generally veridical that we are able to avoid doing things that would be useless, counterproductive, or downright dangerous. It is, again, only when the planning model is taken as a whole that we are able to make sense of the ability in question.

The outcome of these considerations is that contents should be considered relational properties in good scientific standing. Contents are clearly not constitutive of the proximal causes of behavior, nor are they at all causally efficacious insofar as the human-plus-world system is concerned. Nevertheless, they are, in conjunction with local changes in the relata, a crucial ingredient in the explanation offered by the planning model for an important facet of human behavior; they figure centrally in the explanation for how it is that we humans are able to deal effectively with a wide array of novel environmental conditions.

3.10 Recap

Philosophers have long wondered where, if at all, contents might fit within the ontology of the thoroughgoing physicalist. What we now have in hand is a specific semantic framework and a pretty good understanding of the role it is plays in a specific, mechanistic model of the underpinnings for human behavior. If, in the final analysis, there is nothing inherently wrong with either the model or the semantics, I think we may at last rest assured that contents are properties in good scientific standing. This, of course, reflects favorably on folk psychology, although the semantics of folk psychology ultimately had to be scrapped in order to hang onto the broader theory.

We can also now see better why an appeal to causal history is not needed in order to naturalize contents. In fact, appeals to causal history turn out to be unwelcome insofar as the bulk of the explanatory endeavors undertaken in cognitive science are concerned, for the core of cognitive science is devoted to explaining a set of *abilities* such as those discussed in subsection 2.4.3. Cognitive science is, in other words, devoted to answering a set of "How?" questions like those considered here, and long-term causal history is no part of the answers to such questions. I do not mean to say, however, that there is no place in cognitive science for teleological explanations, and insofar as there is a place there might also be room for contents that are fixed by long-term causal history. Moreover, because this kind of explanatory endeavor lies at a pretty fair distance from folk psychology proper, if the conclusions reached on the basis of it should turn out to be at odds with our intuitions about content attributions we might need to be a bit forgiving.

Getting back to my own proposal, we have seen that it also satisfies the main impetus behind the search for a so-called narrow theory of content, albeit for somewhat limited explanatory ends. Attempts to develop such a theory are motivated by the intuition that, because the proximal causes of behavior are in the head, those interested in explaining behavior need only concern themselves with what is in the head. It turns out, fortunately for contents, that we can hang onto the first part of this intuition and drop the second. Although contents do not cause human behavior, they are an essential ingredient in our best explanation for a central facet thereof.

4 Dueling Metaphors

The logic metaphor for mental representation and inference has been said to account for several important properties of human thought processes. These include the capacity to represent countless distinct states of affairs and to manipulate those representations in a truth-preserving manner, the systematicity of thought, and the capacity to think about non-concrete states of affairs, genera, and specifics. However, insofar as systematicity and truth preservation are concerned, the case for the logic metaphor has been overstated, for thought happens to be far less systematic than language and the powers of truth preservation exhibited by formal systems are severely limited by their susceptible to the frame problem. The scale-model metaphor, in contrast, supplies a very elegant account of systematicity and exhibits immunity to the frame problem.

4.1 Introduction

In chapter 2 we saw that the dominant research program in cognitive science has vindicated, and has greatly refined our understanding of, the folk-psychological ontology. In chapter 3 we saw that the attribution of contents to some of the states (viz., beliefs and desires) that are constitutive of that ontology plays an essential role in our ability to explain an important facet of human behavior. Taken collectively, this supplies a good basis for thinking that human behavior is guided by the truth-preserving manipulation of representations of the world. From here, it seems only natural to turn our gaze inward and examine the precise nature of those representations and representational manipulations.

Questions about the structure, or format, of mental representations have long interested philosophers, in no small part because many have thought it sensible to gain a better understanding of the instrument by which knowledge is attained in order to determine its powers and limitations. (See section 1.1.) Philosophical discussions about the format of mental representations have historically tended to be framed in terms of two competing metaphors: the logic metaphor (Leibniz 1705/1997; Kant

1787/1998; Boole 1854/1951) and the picture or image metaphor (Aristotle fourth century B.C./1987; Locke 1690/1964; Berkeley 1710/1982). The purely metaphorical status of these proposals is suggested by the fact that until recently no one has had the slightest idea how to make sense of the claim that the brain—or any other device—might literally harbor and manipulate representations of the appropriate sort.

A number of well-known arguments, both old and new, have been offered up from the philosopher's armchair with the goal of demonstrating that the logic metaphor is the only game in town. In this chapter I will review these arguments and show that they are wanting in several respects. I will also show that a close relative of the image metaphor, the scale-model metaphor, succeeds brilliantly in precisely those places where the logic metaphor fails.

In chapter 5, I will continue my offensive against the logic metaphor with the goal of driving it to the brink. In chapter 6, however, I will show that proponents of the logic metaphor have the resources to launch their own counter-offensive because only the logic metaphor has been reformulated in more mechanistic terms. By the end of that chapter, however, the scale-model metaphor will undergo a similar mechanistic reformulation, and this should be enough to turn the tide permanently in its favor. We clearly have a long march ahead of us, and it begins with a brief discussion of how cognitive scientists typically effect the transition from explanatory metaphors to explanatory mechanisms.

4.2 Metaphors and Mechanisms in Cognitive Science

One way of effecting the transition from explanatory metaphors to explanatory mechanisms is to show that there exist, or might exist, physical systems that are similar to the system of interest (e.g., the brain), that embody the chief characteristics of the explanatory metaphor, and that, thereby, inherit that metaphor's precise virtues and limitations. Case in point: Selfridge (1959) had hoped that much of human cognition could be explained by his Pandemonium model, which amounted to a screaming match between layers of simple homunculi that he called "demons." (See Bechtel, Abrahamsen and Graham 1998.) One source of support for Selfridge's model was its ability to explain how we are able to guess the identity of letters when features of those letters are missing or obscured. To bolster the plausibility of the model still further, Selfridge created a network of simple, neuron-like processing units that embodied the central characteristics of the network-of-demons metaphor (e.g., competitive interaction) along with its attendant explanatory virtues, and in this way he can be said to have effected its mechanistic reformulation.

Cognitive science is, in fact, rich in explanatory metaphors (e.g., see Lakoff and Johnson 1980; Fernandez-Duque and Johnson 1999), and some of these metaphors lend themselves quite readily to a similar sort of mechanistic reformulation. We find, for example, much talk of information flowing, with occasional bottlenecks and alternative passages, like a raw material through various conduits and stages of processing. Only a basic knowledge of neurophysiology is required in order to appreciate how the central characteristics of this set of metaphors might be reformulated in more biologically plausible terms. There are, however, other explanatory metaphors—for example, Kahneman's (1973) pool-of-resources metaphor for the allocation of attention—that do not lend themselves quite so readily to this kind of mechanistic reformulation. Still, while their mechanistic reformulation is far more difficult to carry out, the general strategy to be pursued in the service of this goal is exactly the same. The strategy is, once again, to show that there exist physical systems that are similar to the brain in relevant respects, that embody the chief characteristics of the explanatory metaphor, and which, thereby, inherit its desirable features.

The logic metaphor has, of course, already undergone this kind of mechanistic reformulation. A good way to describe how this transition from explanatory metaphor to explanatory mechanism was effected in the case of the logic metaphor is to begin with a discussion of how the chief characteristics of this explanatory metaphor give rise to its precise virtues and limitations. We will then have an easy time understanding how there can be brain-like artifacts that embody those characteristics and, as a consequence, inherit both the virtues and the limitations of the logic metaphor. (See section 6.2.)

Introducing the hypothesis in this way is, to be sure, somewhat of an historical idealization. After all, some of its virtues and limitations came to light well after it had already been reformulated in more mechanistic terms. Nevertheless, at the expense of historical accuracy, we gain a useful template to follow when attempting the mechanistic reformulation of the scale-model metaphor. Accordingly, after I catalog the principal virtues and limitations of the logic metaphor, I will do the same for the scale-model metaphor.

4.3 The Logic Metaphor

The logic metaphor has been said to explain the human capacity to think before acting and to satisfy numerous philosophical intuitions concerning the nature of mental states (Fodor 1987). Indeed, on the surface, the hypothesis really is quite elegant, and it is no surprise that so many smart people have come to endorse it. A deeper analysis reveals, however, that the logic metaphor is beset by a variety of problems. One of these, the frame problem, is so serious as to make the search for a viable alternative appear downright mandatory.

4.3.1 Planning

It is often claimed that the cardinal virtue of the logic metaphor is that it can explain—some even contend that it is the only way to explain—the generally truth-preserving character of thought sequences (Pylyshyn 1984; Devitt and Sterelny 1987; Fodor 2000). Such sequences underlie our ability to think ahead. For this reason, they figure centrally in the broader explanation of the fact that humans often behave in such an unhesitating (once they get started) and effective manner in the face of even highly novel environmental conditions.

The claim that human behavior might be guided by forethought has been in circulation for quite some time. Aristotle states that "sometimes you calculate on the basis of images or thoughts in the soul, as if seeing, and plan what is going to happen in relation to present affairs" (fourth century B.C./1987, 431b). The philosophical naturalist Hobbes (1651/1988) attempted to *explain* forethought, ostensibly in terms of the same corpuscular (i.e., mechanistic) worldview that was affording such predictive and explanatory leverage in astronomy and physics. (See section 1.1.) Hobbes proposed a rather sophisticated associationist theory that made provisions for backward reasoning (thereby anticipating recent advances in artificial intelligence) and attempted to explain why humans' trains of thought vary from the regulated (e.g., during planning) to the unregulated (e.g., when daydreaming).

We also saw in chapter 2 that forethought began to be considered a powerful explanatory construct in its own right in the twentieth century. This is when the psychologists Wolfgang Köhler (1938) and Kenneth Craik (1952) proposed that one could, by positing a capacity for forethought, explain why human behavior is often so appropriate in the face of even novel environmental conditions. In Köhler's terms, forethought gives one "insight" into a problem.

Köhler was, of course, very interested in determining whether chimpanzees and other non-human primates might also exhibit insight. This question continues to generate controversy. At some level, it is just one facet of the more general, all-too-familiar concern that we are being too generous when we ascribe to other animals the same high-level cognitive abilities that we humans seem to possess. Daniel Povinelli (1999; 2000) has, in fact, recently provided some compelling demonstrations that we should be leery of such ascriptions, at least where forethought is concerned. In one experiment, Povinelli and his colleagues presented a chimp with a setup not unlike the one depicted in figure 4.1. To an adult human, it would be fairly obvious that, when pulled, the implement on the left (the "toothless rake") would pass over the banana, while pulling on the implement on the right (the "T-bar") would cause the banana to move within reach. Yet, on seeing Povinelli's footage of a chimp pulling ineffectively and repeatedly on a toothless rake in full view of the T-bar, one is left with the distinct impression that chimps lack the capacity for forethought that we humans seem to possess.[1] Perhaps, then, a well-developed capacity to think ahead is one of the things that distinguish humans from other terrestrial critters. (See also Gopnik 2000.)

Figure 4.1
A choice between a "toothless rake" and a "T-bar" (an inverted version of the "toothless rake") as a tool for removing bananas from an enclosure. Based on work by Povinelli (1999, 2000).

It should at least be clear that the proposed capacity to manipulate representations in a truth-preserving manner is properly viewed as a hypothesis that is constitutive of a very nice explanation for why it is that human behavior is often so appropriate in the face of novel conditions. According to this model, we represent novel situations as they arise; we then manipulate these representations in order to generate predictions concerning how alterations to the world will play out; lastly, we select the action or sequence of actions that might lead us to our goal. One of the most attractive features of the logic metaphor is that it promises to fill in important details of this process.

4.3.1.1 Phase I: Representational Productivity The planning process is said to begin with the construction of representations of whatever environmental contingency confronts us. If this characterization is correct, then we humans can be said to possess a highly productive (i.e., expressive) representational system.[2] One advantage of the logic metaphor is that many formal languages exhibit, thanks to their combinatorial and recursive syntax, tremendous representational productivity. Perhaps the easiest way to explain this point is to consider how the combinatorial and recursive syntax of *natural* languages such as English are responsible for *their* tremendous representational productivity. (If you find this overly pedantic, you may wish to skim ahead.) Let us begin with combinatorics.

Consider this simple English sentence:

(1) The boy hit the ball.

This sentence is a structurally *molecular* natural-language representation. That is to say, it is a linguistic unit made up of *atomic* constituents: 'the', 'boy', 'hit', and 'ball'. The meaning of the resulting sentence is, moreover, determined (at least to a large extent) by its constituents and the order in which they appear. The atomic constituents of (1) can, for instance, be rearranged to convey a very different message:

(2) The ball hit the boy.

There are, of course, constraints on how these parts can be combined. These constraints are, for instance, satisfied by (1) but not (as my word processor is now indicating) by

(3) Hit boy the the ball.

One of important feature of this set of constraints, the *syntax* of the language, is that it permits tokens of a specific type of constituent to appear in lots of mental formulas (e.g., 'ball' appears in both (1) and (2)).

With even a very limited syntax and a small lexicon, a language can exhibit some degree of representational productivity. Suppose, for instance, there were a language that only permitted the noun-phrase–verb-phrase–noun-phrase (NVN) construction and that it had a small lexicon consisting of 'the', 'boy', 'hit', 'ball', 'saw', and 'teacher'. Even that simple language could be used to generate all of the following sentences:

The boy hit the ball.
The ball hit the boy.
The teacher hit the boy.
The teacher hit the ball.
The ball hit the teacher.
The boy hit the teacher.
The boy saw the ball.
The teacher saw the ball.
The boy saw the teacher.
The teacher saw the boy.

This, of course, is still a far cry from full-blown representational productivity, for the number of representations that can be generated on this basis is finite and, relatively speaking, quite small.

In order for the language to exhibit true, open-ended productivity, we would first have to expand the syntax so that it had provisions for the *recursive* use of molecular types. For example, a simple way to expand the system just described would be to allow any two well-formed expressions to be combined into a single expression by connecting them with 'and'. Since any molecular expressions formed through the use of 'and' can, in the simplest case, be conjoined with itself, the addition of this kind of recursion to the syntax allows the construction of sentences of unlimited size.

While the set of syntactic principles just described does enable the construction of an infinite number of distinct representations, it can only be used to represent a finite number of distinct states of affairs. That is to say, while one can continue producing new representations, one will eventually end up constructing expressions that represent the same states of affairs in different ways. In order to approach true productivity, then, we would have to add to the repertoire of permissible syntactic forms and greatly expand the vocabulary. This is roughly what fluent users of natural languages have at their disposal. One could still argue that this only amounts to quasi-productivity, but it is still an extremely high degree of representational productivity.

Getting back to the logic metaphor for *mental* representation, one could argue that a very large lexicon and a combinatorial and recursive syntax at the level of thought would explain what needs explaining—namely, our capacity to represent environmental contingencies as they arise.

4.3.1.2 Phase II: Truth-Preserving Manipulation It is, as you are probably well aware, formal languages such as predicate calculus (PC) that supply the true inspiration for language-based models of thought. This is because, unlike natural languages, these languages are complemented by a set of syntax-sensitive inference rules that enable the truth-preserving manipulation of the representations in question.

Specifically, when it comes to planning, what proponents of the logic metaphor typically contend is that the consequences of particular alterations to the world are predicted, cognitively speaking, with the help of mental inference rules whose antecedents specify both the starting conditions and the nature of the alteration under consideration and whose consequents specify the consequences of the alteration.

Consider, for example, the set of items depicted in figure 4.2. We all know a great deal about the consequences of alterations to this system. We know, for instance, that when the ball is placed inside the bucket and the bucket is kept upright, the location of the ball will henceforth change with that of the bucket. We also know what will happen if the ball is set inside the bucket, the bucket is set atop the door, and the door is subsequently pushed. If the logic metaphor is correct, we are able to predict such consequences by relying upon the cognitive equivalent of mental inference rules that run something like this:

If
the bucket is resting atop the door, and
the ball is inside the bucket, and
the door is pushed
then
the bucket and the ball will fall to the floor.

Indeed, if the logic metaphor is correct, we can be said harbor huge numbers of these mental inference rules.

Philosophers have been greatly swayed by this model, which had its first clear statement in the early days of artificial intelligence. As we saw in chapter 1, developers of production systems have long utilized this basic framework in order to model the process of planning. The latest versions of Soar, for example, enable the representation of states of the world in

Figure 4.2
A simple physical system: a doorway, a bucket, and a ball.

terms of well-formed formulas (wff) held in a working memory system, and they enable inferences concerning the consequences of alterations to the world to be effected by applying rules ("operators") to those formulas. It is in this way that the Soar architecture permits the construction of systems that can think ahead.

4.3.1.3 Phase III: Selection of Appropriate Actions In order to guide behavior effectively, a worldly alteration (or sequence of alterations) that will bring us closer to the attainment of our goals must be selected from among the very many that can generally be envisioned with the help of our basic truth-preserving machinery. For example, for one who has the desire to move the ball in figure 4.2 from one side of the wall to the other, it is apparent that throwing the ball over the wall or using the bucket to hurl it through the door will have the desired effect. There are, of course, other alterations that will fail to bring one closer to this goal. Nevertheless, when we engage in planning we are somehow able to sift through these alternatives and settle on an alteration, or sequence of alterations, that will lead to the fulfillment of our desires.

Taking its cue, once again, from artificial intelligence, the logic metaphor promises to fill in important details of this process. The solution involves a specification of the larger set of mechanisms in which the basic truth-preserving machinery might be embedded. According to one proposal, this larger set of mechanisms enables such processes as heuristic-guided searches, backward reasoning, and learning. (See subsection 1.2.3.2.) These processes enable a fallible, but (relative to an exhaustive search of the space of possible alterations) highly efficient method for reasoning from the way things are to the way we would like them to be. Production systems have, once again, been used to model these very processes through the incorporation of further, higher-order, syntax-sensitive inference rules called *productions*. In this way, these models lend further credence to the logic metaphor for representation and inference, for they spell out in greater detail the kinds of logic-based processes that might underwrite our ability to make effective use of the basic truth-preserving machinery described above.

4.3.2 Systematicity

Many philosophers also deem it a great virtue of the logic metaphor that it offers an explanation—and as with truth preservation, some say the *only* explanation—of the putative systematicity of thought. To understand the case for this claim, it helps if one first understands why human *linguistic abilities* are systematic.[3]

To say that our linguistic abilities are systematic is to say, minimally, that any fluent speaker of a language such as English who can produce and parse a certain sentence can produce and parse a systematic variant of that sentence. Systematic variants are most frequently illustrated by switching noun phrases. For instance, one simply doesn't expect to find fluent language users who are able to produce and parse (4) while being unable to produce and parse (5):

(4) Ike hit Tina.
(5) Tina hit Ike.

Our ability to produce and parse systematic variants in this way seems to be a product of our mastery of the principles governing the well-formedness of English sentences (i.e., our implicit knowledge of the syntax). For instance, one might say that it is a rule (albeit a highly superficial one) of English that sentences of the form NVN are grammatical. Thus, anyone who can produce and parse (4) on the basis of his implicit mastery of this rule will be able to re-deploy that mastery in order to produce and parse its systematic variant (5). In short, it appears as though the linguistic abilities involved here are systematic and that the explanation for this fact is that fluent users of a language have mastered the combinatorial and recursive syntax of the language.

It has been claimed that, since thought is just as systematic as language, our ability to think thoughts must likewise be rooted in our mastery of the combinatorial and recursive syntax of the language of thought (a.k.a. Mentalese). The argument for the first part of this claim begins with the sensible proposal that fluent language users are not merely able to produce and parse sentences; rather, production and parsing are generally carried out in the service of the expression of thoughts and the comprehension of sentences, respectively. Restricting our focus to the latter, it seems that to comprehend a sentence is just to entertain the thought that the sentence expresses. Now if linguistic abilities are, so to speak, systematic *all the way down* to the semantic level, then anyone who can comprehend a sentence such as (4) will be able to comprehend its systematic variant (5). Thus, if linguistic abilities are systematic all the way down, then anyone who can think the thought expressed by (4) can think the thought expressed by (5). In other words, if linguistic abilities are systematic all the way down, then thinking abilities are just as systematic as linguistic abilities—that is, thought is just as systematic as language.

The logic metaphor promises a very simple explanation for the systematicity of thought: If mental representations have roughly the same kind of syntactic structure that characterizes natural and formal languages, then the same syntactic constraints that license one mental representation will license, through a simple rearrangement of constituents, the systematically related representation.

This seems like a very elegant explanation, a fact which is not lost on its proponents, but there is a big problem with the argument just sketched: It is not entirely clear that thought *is* just as systematic as language. The argument for the claim that it *is* assumes that linguistic abilities are systematic all the way down (i.e., down to the semantic level, the level of thought), but it is far from clear that this is so. To see why, notice that in light of the syntactic constraints governing English, the following pairs of sentences are syntactically well formed:

(6) The food coloring was rinsed from the cloth.
(7) The cloth was rinsed from the food coloring.
(8) The ball rolled down the inclined plane.
(9) The inclined plane rolled down the ball.
(10) The water balloon burst on the sidewalk.
(11) The sidewalk burst on the water balloon.

(12) Fred examined the definition.
(13) The definition examined Fred.

Although these sentences are syntactically well formed, it is not clear to me that they are semantically well formed. It seems perfectly clear that any fluent language user who can produce and parse the first in each pair can produce and parse the second, but it is far less clear that any fluent language user who can comprehend the first in each pair can comprehend the second. On the standard account of systematicity (Fodor and Pylyshyn 1988), however, there should be no doubt as to the ability of fluent language users to do this, for all that is required is a simple rearrangement of the constituents (the mental noun phrases) of the sentences in the language of thought.

One could, I suppose, come up with a story about how there are additional constraints governing the well-formedness of thought sentences that permit certain systematic variants but not others, but given the great to-do that has been made about how constraints on processing that explain semantic systematicity must not be ad hoc, but must rather follow directly from the assumptions of the hypothesized mechanism (Fodor and Pylyshyn 1988), this option seems less than desirable.[4] It sure would be a lot nicer, then, if there were a straightforward explanation for the fact that the first in each pair can be comprehended quite easily while comprehension of the second is, at the very least, far less straightforward.

4.3.3 Representing Non-Concrete Domains, Genera, and Specifics

Philosophers have also frequently drawn attention to the fact that, unlike the picture metaphor, the logic metaphor can easily account for our ability to understand words and phrases that denote entities, properties, and processes—such as 'war criminal', 'ownership', 'economic inflation', and 'electricity'—that defy straightforward depiction. In order to account for our ability to comprehend these words and phrases—which may, for lack of a decent term, be called *non-concrete*—Fodor and others (see Fodor 1975 and Fodor, Fodor, and Garrett 1975) have proposed that we harbor a set of syntax-sensitive rules, or "meaning postulates," that enable us to effect the relevant semantic inferences. It is considered a great virtue of this basic sentence-and-rule model of how semantic information is represented—which, not coincidentally, has long been modeled using traditional AI techniques (e.g., Quillian 1968), including production-system architectures (Anderson 1983)—that it is indifferent to whether the terms at issue are concrete or non-concrete. For example, a semantic entailment of 'economic inflation' might be captured with the help of a cognitive inference rule that states the following: "If economy x undergoes inflation, then the unit of currency in x will have less overall purchasing power."

It is also considered a virtue of the logic metaphor that it can explain how it is that we are able to think about genera. We humans are able to think, for instance, not only about specific triangles, but about triangles in general (Berkeley 1710/1982; Kant 1787/1998). This, I take it, is a bit different from explaining our ability to understand non-concrete terms. Genera, after all, are sometimes highly concrete (e.g., rocks), and non-concrete terms need not denote genera (e.g., 'the Enlightenment'). At any rate, because the terms of natural and artificial languages seem so well adapted to representing genera, it would be just as easy for the terms of a mental language to do likewise.

Lastly, it has been pointed out that the hypothesized sentences of Mentalese would account for our ability to think thoughts involving the assignment of specific properties to specific objects (Fodor 1975, 1981; see also Wittgenstein 1953). For instance, the thought that Fred's car is green singles out, from among a tremendous number of properties, a single property of Fred's car. Just as natural and artificial languages can be used to represent such property assignments, so too might the hypothesized mental language.

4.3.4 Levels of Description

Another important feature of the expressions of natural and artificial languages—albeit one whose true import has to do with the role it plays in the mechanistic reformulation of the logic metaphor (see section 6.2)—is that they can be understood at any of multiple, independent levels of abstraction. For present purposes, I'll restrict my focus to just two such levels.[5]

On the one hand, we can describe the physical embodiment of a natural-language expression in a certain medium such as ink and paper or sound waves. One and the same expression (i.e., one and the same combinatorial structure) can be realized in either of these media and countless others as well. Natural-language expressions are thus multiply realizable with regard to realizing media. We can, in other words, abstract away from differences in how types of expressions are realized and talk purely in terms of the properties of those types. The fact that types of expressions can be realized, or *tokened*, in any of countless distinct physical media indicates that talk of the properties of expressions is pitched at a higher, and independent, level of abstraction than talk of the properties of realizing media (Pylyshyn 1984, p. 33).

4.3.5 The Frame Problem

Although the logic metaphor has many apparent virtues, it also has at least one major shortcoming—namely, the frame problem. McCarthy and Hayes (1969) are generally credited as being the first to recognize (and name) the frame problem, which has to do with the challenge of getting a representational system to predict what will change and what will stay the same following alterations to the state of the world (Bechtel, Abrahamsen, and Graham 1998).[6] A general way to characterize the nature of the problem confronting the logic metaphor—which, mind you, first came to light following early attempts to model forethought with the help of PC-like formalisms—is to say that, although the postulation of a mental logic seems to do a reasonable job of accounting for representational productivity (i.e., the capacity to represent countless distinct states of affairs), it does not account for *inferential* productivity (i.e., the capacity to predict the consequences of countless distinct alterations).

The frame problem comprises at least two component problems. The first of these, the prediction problem (see Janlert 1996), stems from the fact that an immense number of inference rules (of the sort described in subsection 4.3.1.2), or *frame axioms*, would be required in order to effect the predictive inferences that underwrite everyday planning. Consider again the scenario depicted in figure 4.2. Now take a moment to envision the consequences of each of the myriad ways in which one might alter this simple setup. From an engineering standpoint, the problem that quickly arises is that no matter how many alteration/consequence pairs one builds into the knowledge-base of one's model, there will generally be many more that have been overlooked. Notice, moreover, that if we were to scale the scenario up even slightly (e.g., such that it also includes a board), this would have an *exponential* effect on the number of possible alteration/consequence pairs and, as such, on the number of frame axioms that one would have to incorporate into one's model (Janlert 1996). In this case, we are still dealing with a fairly simple physical system; it is far simpler, in fact, than the scenarios that humans generally confront. Where more realistic systems are concerned, the challenge of specifying the consequences of each possible alteration looks to be insurmountable. According to a recent manual on production systems, "when working on large (realistic) problems, the number of operators [i.e., frame axioms] that may be used in problem solving and the number of possible state descriptions will be very large and probably infinite" (Congdon and Laird 1997, p. 28). We have, moreover, thus far been talking about knowledge of the consequences of alterations to discrete systems containing finite numbers of objects. Our knowledge of the consequences of worldly alterations is, however, immeasurably more complex than this. In order to embody what the average human knows about the consequences of worldly alterations, a frame axiom system would have to contain rules specifying how countless objects, both familiar and novel, will behave relative to one another following each of the consequently infinite number of possible alterations. What started off as an engineering problem therefore gives way to serious a priori concerns about the viability of the logic metaphor itself, for no finite set of frame axioms would ever suffice to express what we know about the way the world will change following various alterations.

The prediction problem, which is sufficiently worrisome by itself, is compounded by another component of the frame problem, the qualification problem (McCarthy 1986). It is compounded because, in order to embody what we know about the consequences of alterations to the world, not only would an infinite number of rules be required, but each rule would also have to be qualified in a seemingly infinite number of ways. For instance, suppose the items in figure 4.2 are reconfigured such that the ball is inside the bucket and the bucket is held upright over the floor. In this case, it is true that if bucket is tipped over, then the ball will fall to the floor—provided, of course, that the ball is not wedged into the bucket, there is no glue in the bucket, and so on indefinitely. In order to capture what you and I implicitly know about the consequences of this alteration, all the relevant qualifications would have to be added to the relevant frame axiom. Once again, the magnitude of the engineering problem quickly gives rise to serious a priori concerns about the viability of the logic metaphor itself. It is time, then, to give serious consideration to alternatives.

4.4 The Scale-Model Metaphor

Images and scale models fall under the more general heading of physically isomorphic models (PIMs), which are representations that owe their powers of inference to the fact that they possess some of the very same properties as that which they represent.[7] (See Palmer 1978.) Because forethought often requires the truth-preserving manipulation of representations of three-dimensional spatial and causal relationships, the PIMs that hold the greatest interest in the present context are scale models.[8] Like the logic metaphor, the scale-model metaphor has its own distinctive set of advantages and disadvantages.

4.4.1 Planning

The idea that planning might be underwritten by the cognitive equivalent of scale models is not a new one. Craik, for instance, suggests that "if the organism carries a 'small-scale model' of external reality and of its own possible actions within its head, it is able to try out various alternatives, conclude which is the best of them, react to future situations before they arise ... and in every way to react in a much fuller, safer, and more competent manner to the emergencies which face it" (1952, p. 61). To see how this model of forethought fares, we can start by evaluating whether or not it can explain the human ability to represent novel situations as they arise, to manipulate them in a truth-preserving manner, and to determine which worldly alterations will bring us closer to the attainment of our goals.

4.4.1.1 Phase I: Representational Productivity In order to understand how the scale-model metaphor accounts for representational productivity, we need to turn our attention from models themselves to the modeling media from which they are constructed. When we do, we see that there clearly are productive (or at least quasi-productive) media for the construction of scale models. A finite supply of Lego blocks can, for instance, be utilized in order to model virtually any edifice.[9] There are, of course, many other modeling media that exhibit representational productivity (e.g., matchsticks and glue, clay, and papier-mâché)—the world is, in fact, its own modeling medium.

Notice also that the addition of elements of the same type, a kind of recursion, does far more to enhance the representational productivity of modeling media than the recursive use of constituents does to enhance the representational productivity of linguistic media. As the number of modeling elements increases, so too does the upper limit on the number of states of affairs that can be represented. As we saw earlier, the allowance for recursive use of sentential constituents does not so much increase the number of states of affairs that can be represented as it increases the number of ways in which the same state of affairs can be represented.

4.4.1.2 Phase II: Truth-Preserving Manipulation Although the scale-model metaphor for mental representation has been largely overlooked since the early days of AI, the (less impressive) picture metaphor has lately reclaimed the attention of philosophers, psychologists, and computational modelers. A big part of the reason for this is that spatial representations can be used to generate predictions in a manner that obviates rules (i.e., frame axioms) that specify the consequences of each possible alteration to a represented system (Haugeland 1987; Johnson-Laird 1988; Lindsay 1988; Janlert 1996). Notice, for example, that one can use a sheet of graph paper to represent the relative positions of Harry, Laura, and Carlene (figure 4.3). Should one wish to know what the relative locations of all these individuals would be if Harry moved to a new position, one can simply delete the mark representing Harry and insert a new mark in the square corresponding to the new position.

Two-dimensional spatial media can also be used to represent the structure of objects, and collections of such representations can be used to predict the consequences of changes in both relative location and orientation. For instance, a cardboard cutout of my coffee table (as seen from above) can be conjoined with two-dimensional representations (of equal scale) of the rest of the items in my living room and a depiction of the room itself in order to generate predictions concerning the consequences of countless changes in the relative spatial locations and orientations of these items (Haugeland 1987). This is a strategy that obviates rules which specify the myriad consequences of each of the countless possible changes to the represented system. Thus, with regard to this limited set of represented dimensions, such representations exhibit immunity to the frame

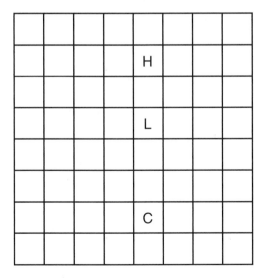

Figure 4.3
Use of a spatial matrix to represent the relative positions of objects.

problem. Moreover, they can easily be scaled up to include representations of further objects. As I noted above, systems that rely upon frame axioms have problems with this kind of scalability. It is for this reason that Janlert suggests that scalability provides an indicator of whether or not a representational system suffers from the frame problem. Janlert puts it this way: "A sign that the frame problem is under proper control is that the representation can be incrementally extended: A conservative addition to the furniture of the world would involve only a conservative addition to the representation." (1996, p. 40)

Mere images do fall a bit short of the mark when it comes to supporting the kinds of predictions that humans routinely make. A viable model of human forethought must explain the capacity to predict the consequences of spatial and causal alterations in three spatial dimensions. With the scale-model metaphor for mental representation, these demands are easily met.

Scale models have, of course, long been a mainstay of design testing. Much like the representations underwriting forethought, scale models are used to predict the behavior of countless systems, both familiar and novel (e.g., new structures, devices, manufacturing processes, etc.).[10] As compared to mere images, scale models exhibit immunity to the prediction problem with regard to a much wider range of represented dimensions. One can, for instance, use a reasonably faithful scale model of the door-bucket-ball setup in order to predict the consequences of countless alterations (e.g., what happens when the bucket with the ball in it is set atop the door and the door is pushed, what happens when the bucket with the ball in it is tipped over, what happens when the bucket is used to throw the ball at the door, and so on indefinitely) to this system. To use Haugeland's (1987) terms, the side effects of alterations to such a representation will mirror the side effects of alterations to the represented system *automatically*—that is to say, without requiring their explicit specification. Nor, once again, do incremental additions to the represented system have an exponential effect on what has to be built into the representation. The addition of a board to the system in figure 4.2, for instance, can be handled by the simple addition of a scale model of the board to the representation.

No do scale models suffer from the qualification problem. To see why, notice that much of what is true of a modeled domain will be true of a scale model of that domain. With regard to a scale model of the setup in figure 4.2, for instance, it is true that the scale model of the ball will fall out of the scale model of the bucket when it is tipped over, but only if the ball is not wedged into the bucket, there is no glue in the bucket, and so on indefinitely. Just like our own predictions, the predictions generated through the use of scale models are implicitly qualified in an open-ended number of ways; thus, these qualifications need not be made explicit.

4.4.1.3 Phase III: Selection of Appropriate Actions While it might initially appear to be a virtue of the logic metaphor that it makes the problem of selecting an appropriate course of action tractable, the way that it does so is far from desirable. This is because the problem is made tractable for the logic metaphor by the fact that the prescience of logic-driven systems is quite limited (i.e., they suffer from the frame problem). This means that the field of possible actions, and thus the search space, has been reduced to a great, and psychologically unrealistic, extent. Scale models, on the other hand, permit predictions concerning the consequences of innumerable alterations. This means that the search space cannot be explored exhaustively, but only strategically. Still, the basic explanatory approach will not diverge significantly from the set of techniques described by Hobbes (1651/1988) and settled on by designers of production systems. The basic proposal will still be that there are extra-representational mechanisms and strategies (e.g., learning, heuristics, backward reasoning, etc.) that permit effective use of the basic truth-preserving machinery.[11]

4.4.2 Systematicity
The logic metaphor seemed, at least at first glance, to offer a plausible account of the systematicity of thought. This is because the same syntactic constraints that permit one expression will also permit systematic variants. The logic metaphor is, however, most definitely not the only game in town. To see why, one merely has to take note of the fact that the world itself admits of certain systematic variations. For instance, not only can the cat be on the mat, but the mat can be on the cat; not only can Ike hit Tina, but Tina can hit Ike; not only can Venus precede the Sun, but the Sun can precede Venus; and so forth. Thus, instead of pushing the structure of language "down," so to speak, into the thought medium, a proponent of the scale-model metaphor would suggest that we instead push the structure of the world "up."[12] Moreover, as a result of making this move we find ourselves with a far more elegant account of the extent to which thought is *less* systematic than language.

As explained above, the initial plausibility of the logic-metaphoric account of systematicity was undermined to some extent by its inability to straightforwardly explain the differential ease of comprehension of sentences (6) through (13). On the other hand, at least with regard to (6)–(11), the scale-model metaphor accounts for differential ease of comprehension in an intuitively quite palatable manner. Specifically, while the construction of a scale model that is consistent with the description supplied by the first member of each pair would be quite straightforward, the construction of a scale model consistent with the description supplied by the second member of each pair would, at the very least, be far more challenging. This is because, when the meanings of terms are construed in their usual manner, the kinds of events described could not unfold in the world; as such, they could not unfold in a scale model of the world. For instance, given the usual meanings assigned to 'sidewalk', 'water balloon', and 'burst on', sidewalks cannot burst on water balloons. This makes comprehension difficult, but perhaps not impossible, for we may be able to dream up alternatives to the usual readings of these terms. To keep things brief, while it is not a straightforward implication of the logic metaphor that some well-formed, systematic variants are difficult or impossible to comprehend, it is a straightforward implication of the scale-model metaphor.

4.4.3 Representing the Non-Concrete, Genera, and Specifics

It has to be admitted that, by itself, the scale-model metaphor does not offer an obvious answer to the question of why (13) is so difficult to understand while (12) is not. But the problem in this case has nothing to do with systematicity; it is simply one illustration of a broader set of concerns that has been raised regarding the representational capacities of images and (by extension) scale models. In particular, just as has frequently pointed with regard to the image metaphor, the scale-model metaphor seems to face difficulties in terms of its ability to represent non-concrete domains, genera, and the assignment of specific properties to particular objects. Much of the next chapter will be devoted to showing that these arguments are premised on a naive picture of cognition, but for the moment let us simply take in the magnitude of what has already been achieved.

Systematicity shmystematicity!

The biggest draw of the logic metaphor has *always* been its promise of accounting for the kinds of truth-preserving representational manipulations that underwrite planning. What you just witnessed, then, was a *major* defeat for the logic metaphor and an equally major victory for the scale-model metaphor. A defeat of this magnitude ought to cause all but the most ideologically committed to at least consider switching sides or, barring that, to consider pursuing a peaceful co-existence.

4.4.4 Levels of Description

To finish up our comparison of the two explanatory metaphors, notice that another important feature of scale models—albeit one whose true import has to do with the role it plays in the mechanistic reformulation of the scale-model metaphor (see section 6.4)—is that they can be understood at any of multiple, independent levels of abstraction. To see why, notice that the same criterion of levels individuation described above (i.e., multiple realizability) can be employed in the case of scale models. Notice, for instance, that if we take a given model *type* to subsume those *token* models that respect a particular set of inter-dimensional worldly constraints, there will generally be multiple modeling media that can be used to implement a given model type. One type of model is the sort that can be used to predict the consequences of various three-dimensional spatial alterations to the items in my living room. I can make such a model out of any of a variety of materials, including clay, papier-mâché, Lego blocks, and so on. There is, in other words, a multiple-realizability relationship between model types and the various media that can be used to implement them. Thus, there are at least two levels of abstraction at which a given model can be understood: the level of modeling medium (i.e., the implementation base) and the level of the type which it instantiates.

4.5 A Diagnosis for the Frame Problem

While it is clear that scale models exhibit immunity to the frame problem, in order to accomplish the goal set for the chapter 6—namely, providing a mechanistic reformulation of the scale-model metaphor—it is important that we understand precisely why this is so.

4.5.1 Intrinsic and Extrinsic Representations

Some have said that the reason PC-style representations suffer from the frame problem while images and scale models do not is that the former are extrinsic representations while the latter are intrinsic (Palmer 1978; also see Haselager 1997; Haugeland 1987; Janlert 1996). The intrinsic/extrinsic distinction was first introduced by Palmer, who offered it as a way of distinguishing between types of representation. Representations are said to be extrinsic, according to Palmer, when they must be arbitrarily constrained in order to respect the non-arbitrary, or inherent constraints characterizing a given represented domain; while representations are intrinsic when they do not need to be arbitrarily constrained in order to respect (i.e., they inherently respect) the non-arbitrary, or inherent constraints characterizing a represented domain. According to this analysis, the use of PC to predict the behavior of physical systems generally yields extrinsic representations. This is because, as Haselager notes, "logic in itself has few isomorphies with the world" (1997, p. 64), and so constraints must be imposed in the form of additional inference rules or formulas in order for PC to support the requisite truth-preserving representational manipulations. Scale models, on this analysis, constitute intrinsic representations because they do not require the imposition of arbitrary constraints in order to preserve truth with respect to what they represent.

Although it has a certain intuitive pull to it, one of the problems with this way of distinguishing between representational formats is that it relies too heavily upon a somewhat unclear distinction between inherent and arbitrary constraints. Notice, for instance, that if one is merely interested in truth preservation with regard to the taller-than relation, one can devise a logical system (let us call it PC+) that is perfectly suitable. In other words, PC+ would not have to be arbitrarily constrained in order to preserve truth with regard to the taller-than relation, and so there will be formulas of PC+ that ought to be considered intrinsic representations of relative height. But then, if the presence of one or two simple axioms makes PC+ a medium for the construction of intrinsic representations of relative height, so much the worse for the intrinsic/extrinsic distinction. It does not enable us to clearly distinguish between logic representations and scale models, nor does it supply a diagnosis for why the former seem to suffer from the frame problem while the latter do not.[13] Nevertheless, it seems clear that there is some difference between the way frame axiom systems and scale models support truth preservation and that this difference—let us call it the *real* intrinsic/extrinsic distinction—has something to do with their relative susceptibility to the frame problem.

Rather than relying on the notion of arbitrary vs. inherent constraints, we would be better served by distinguishing between logic representations and scale models in terms of whether or not they support predictions concerning particular alteration/consequence pairs on the basis of distinct data structures or, relatedly, in terms of whether or not the consequences of each type of alteration need to made explicit. In order to generate predictions concerning the consequences of particular alterations, the traditional frame-axiom approach is to utilize inference rules whose antecedents specify the starting conditions and nature of the alteration and whose consequents specify the myriad consequences of the alterations. In other words, the frame-axiom approach mandates that the information be made explicit. This is why the frame-axiom approach suffers from the frame problem: In order to embody what the average human knows about the consequences of worldly alterations, a frame-axiom system would have to contain distinct rules specifying how each of countless objects, both familiar and novel, will behave relative to one another following each of a consequently infinite number of possible alterations.

In the case of scale models, on the other hand, no separate data structures are required in order to predict how particular objects will behave relative to other objects in light of particular alterations. With a suitable model of the relevant system in hand, the consequences of countless distinct alterations to the representation will automatically mirror the consequences of the countless alterations to the represented system. In other words, all the relevant information is implicit in the representation and thus need not be made explicit. Moreover, the reason scale models scale up so gracefully is that a scale model augmented with a new item will also implicitly contain all the information needed to predict the consequences of alterations to the new system. By the same token, the utility of the approach is not restricted to individual systems that contain finite numbers of objects. With the scale-modeling approach, there is no need for an antecedent and explicit specification of how each of countless objects, both familiar and novel, will behave relative to one another following each of a seemingly infinite number of possible alterations. There is not even a need for an antecedent specification of the furniture of the world, for the information that we require will—as the use of scale models in design testing illustrates—be implicit in the models that we construct as circumstances dictate.

4.5.2 Some Points of Detail

When it comes to predicting the behavior of physical systems (even simple ones), it will generally not suffice to utilize intrinsic representations of each property in isolation. For instance, whether there is an advantage to using a simple lever to move an object will depend not only upon the length of the lever, but also upon how this property relates to such further properties as the rigidity and strength of the materials, the placement of the fulcrum, and the mass of the object to be moved. As Palmer (1978) notes, worldly constraints are interdependent, and intrinsic representations of complex *inter-dimensional constraints* are hard to find, the obvious exception being scale models and other PIMs. For his part, Palmer tentatively suggests a hybrid account according to which the brain is said to harbor sets of intrinsic representations of particular properties and extrinsic representations that coordinate the intrinsic representations in such a way as to capture the inter-dimensional constraints of the represented system. It is, however, less than obvious that this hybrid solution is viable given that countless rules and exceptions would be required in order to capture all the ways in which the different properties interact—that is, the approach also suffers from the frame problem. An indication that this is so is the fact that this approach fails to satisfy Janlert's (1996) scalability condition for, as Palmer himself notes, "as more and more dimensions are added, higher-order structure increases dramatically" (1978, p. 274). Thus, it seems that what is required in order to avoid the frame problem when representing systems of even moderate complexity are intrinsic representations of inter-dimensional constraints.

On a related note, Zenon Pylyshyn (1984) claims that there are cases in which representations encoded on the basis of the primitive operations of an implementation base (e.g., a virtual machine) will implicitly contain information that would, given a different implementation base, have to be made explicit. For instance, instead of building separate data structures corresponding to each alteration/consequence pair, one might instead rely upon primitive operations of a virtual machine that have the same logical properties as certain relationships obtaining in the represented system. One then merely has to specify what logical type the represented relationship is, and, says Pylyshyn, the rest of the information "can be obtained 'free' as a by-product of using that particular primitive operation" (ibid., p. 100). When the various represented dimensions interact, however, one runs into the same problem described in the previous paragraph. For instance, the transitivity of a certain primitive operation might be invoked in order to infer from the facts that Tania is taller than Brandon and Anthony is taller than Tania that Anthony is taller than Brandon. Likewise, the symmetry of another primitive operation might be invoked to infer that since Anthony stands at the same elevation as Brandon and Brandon stands at the same elevation as Tania, then Anthony stands at the same elevation as Tania. Perhaps a certain amount of further information would be implicit in such a scheme, but, as it stands, it would not include the fact that the top of Anthony is at a higher elevation than the top of Brandon. The problem is, once again, that the system does not automatically represent how the properties interact. To make even this very simple inference, the relationship between elevation of the base of an object and the height of the top of an object would—unless there happened to be some further, complex primitive operation of the virtual machine that exhibited the relevant isomorphisms—have to be made explicit; and, as already explained, as further represented dimensions are considered, the amount of information that will need to be made explicit increases exponentially.

Notice also that the atomic constituents of frame axioms are traditionally viewed as standing in something very close to a one-to-one correspondence relation with the terms comprising the corresponding natural-language descriptions (Haselager 1998). In fact, the susceptibility of frame-axiom systems to the frame problem seems to be just one illustration of the limited inferential capabilities of systems that base their predictions entirely on generalizations regarding particular objects (or object types) and relationships (or relationship types). A similar problem crops up, for instance, in the case of associationistic models of forethought like those of Hobbes and later empiricists.[14] As Leibniz (1705/1997) notes in his critique of associationistic psychology, statistical generalizations might lead you to expect that one kind of event will follow another, but, since they don't tell you why, they are of little use when it comes to predicting the effects of other alterations to the same system or for anticipating exceptions to an observed regularity.

Those of you who (like me) are big fans of connectionism should bear in mind that Leibniz' critique applies to standard back-propagation networks as well. The problem, as Clark (1993) puts it, is that first-order connectionist systems seem unable to learn how to deal sensibly with what he terms structure-transforming generalizations. To put the point rather crudely, imagine that a connectionist system has learned (and can thereby predict) that a bucket containing a ball will fall from atop a pushed door. This bit of knowledge would be of little use to the system if it were asked to determine whether or not a bucket can be used to carry a ball through a door. In other words, while a set of connection weights may suffice to pick up on the fact that a bucket containing a ball will fall from atop a pushed door, this set of weights cannot be re-deployed in order to predict, for instance, what happens when an upright bucket containing a ball is transported through a doorway. In order to make this prediction, a new set of statistical regularities must be picked up on with a new, though probably overlapping, set of weights. In other words, what might reasonably be construed as a new data structure is required, for the requisite information is not implicit in the earlier set of weights. Thus, feedforward connectionist systems seem to suffer from the frame problem, at least when they are used to pick up on coarse-grained regularities concerning the consequences of alterations to items like buckets, balls, doors, etc.

The grain of analysis is, however, only part of the problem. To see why, notice that a *mere* appeal to microfeatures will not alleviate the frame problem for either frame-axiom systems or feedforward connectionist systems. For instance, mere microfeatural encodings of the parts of objects will not by themselves encode any information about the relative spatial arrangements of the parts or of the relationships that distinct objects bear to one another. (See Barsalou and Hale 1993.) While this information can be made explicit in the form of further features, the price is, once again, a lack of scalability (St. John and McClelland 1990).

I do not here supply a connectionist solution to the frame problem, but a recipe for constructing intrinsic representations of inter-dimensional constraints will be provided in chapter 6 that is general enough to suggest how such a solution might be found.

5 | Thinking in Its Entirety

My goal in chapter 4 was to bolster the plausibility of the claim that we at least sometimes reason through the manipulation of the cognitive counterparts to scale models. One could thus still claim that the domain of this particular model of cognitive processing is highly restricted and that there is still a need to posit the manipulation of representations in a special thought language. My overarching goal in this chapter is to weaken whatever remaining pull this claim might have. I start by addressing some philosophical arguments that are supposed show that insurmountable problems with the image metaphor for thought mandate an appeal to mental sentences. I then address the claim, made by some prominent psychologists, that deduction is our primary mode of reasoning.

5.1 Introduction

When I first learned of the proposal that humans unknowingly think in a common internal language known as Mentalese, I was skeptical, but my skepticism was probably more of a gut reaction than a considered stance. Now, however, I at least feel justified in my skepticism concerning the ability of this hypothesis to explain a very important subset of human thought processes—that is, our thoughts about the behaviors of mechanical systems.[1] Insofar as the principal theses defended in the following chapters are concerned, I could even afford to stand pat and simply allow that sometimes mental representations take the form of the cognitive counterparts to scale models and sometimes they take the form of sentences in a special thought language. But my gut will not let me; it keeps telling me that this special thought language is not needed at all. One of the principal goals of this chapter will thus be to justify, entirely post hoc, what my gut has been telling me all along. In particular, I will address some arguments from the philosophical and psychological sectors that are purported to show that a special thought language *is* needed.[2]

The first class, discussed in section 5.2, includes some well-known philosophical arguments. The general strategy followed in each case is to argue that we think about things that mental images would be ill equipped to represent but that mental sentences easily could represent. Many take these arguments to be quite compelling, but in fact they are based on a highly simplistic model of human thought processes. Once this is understood, the arguments lose much of their force.

The second class, discussed in section 5.3, involves the view, held by some prominent psychologists, that deduction is the form of reasoning that guides the vast preponderance of our day-to-day actions. If this is so, then it will greatly restrict the scale-model metaphor's domain of application and all but invite Mentalese back in. I argue, however, that these psychologists are working with an inadequate taxonomy of reasoning processes and that, once the proper distinctions are made, it is clear that the scale-model metaphor best accounts for the bulk of the inferences in which they are interested. I then propose that whatever remaining, purely formal reasoning capabilities we happen to have can easily be explained without recourse to the manipulation of sentences in Mentalese. They can, instead, be explained in terms of some combination of the redeployment of our non-sentential modeling medium, the reliance upon extra-representational cognitive resources described in section 5.2, and the manipulation of the sentences of "external" languages.[3]

5.2 Traditional Philosophical Objections

In terms of its ability to explain our prescience with regard to everyday environmental contingencies, the scale-model metaphor is currently without peer. Likewise, the scale-model metaphor supplies an elegant account of the differential ease with which we are able to comprehend systematically related sentences concerning such contingencies. It has, however, long been maintained that the image metaphor faces difficulties in terms of its ability to explain how it is that we are able to think about non-concrete domains (e.g., war criminals, ownership, economic inflation, and electricity), genera (e.g., trianglehood and doghood), and the assignment of specific properties to specific objects (e.g., the fact that Fred's car is green). (See subsections 4.3.3 and 4.4.3.) More recently, it has been suggested that the image metaphor is incapable of explaining our ability to understand sentences containing certain logical terms (viz., 'not' and 'or') (Pylyshyn 2002, pp. 180, 181). All these concerns apply, mutatis mutandis, to the scale-model metaphor, and, adding insult to injury, sentences in Mentalese appear well equipped for the task of explaining this entire range of thoughts. Proponents of the image and scale-model metaphors will thus need either to address or, even better, to undermine these concerns if they are to convince anyone that it is possible to have a Mentalese-free account of thought processes in their entirety.[4]

5.2.1 Abilities Brought to Bear When Thinking

Before getting into the details of precisely where it is that these objections go wrong, we first need to get a few facts straight. First, as was discussed in chapter 4, natural languages constitute productive media for the expression of thoughts. It therefore requires a creative leap of very minimal daring to imagine that corresponding to each comprehensible natural-language expression there might be a synonymous sentence in Mentalese. Indeed, before we even begin to consider the different types of thoughts that are reputed to give the image metaphor trouble, we know beforehand that the logic metaphor will have no trouble at all. After all, so long as such thoughts can be described in words, which they will have to be for argumentative purposes, we know that proponents of Mentalese will have an explanation for them. Everything thus comes quite easily for the logic metaphor. It may be, however, that they come *too* easily—that is, the logic metaphor may explain *too* much. Allow me to explain.

The logic metaphor has such an easy time of it that it leads us to expect, quite mistakenly, that mental representations ought to shoulder virtually the entire load when it comes to the task of explaining the non-attitudinal components of the propositional attitudes (PAs).[5] That is, the logic metaphor leads us to expect that whenever we have beliefs or desires about *x*, we harbor a single, and in many ways simple, representation of *x*—for example, to believe that Fred is a war criminal is to have a mental representation that means the same thing as "Fred is a war criminal" tokened in one's belief box (Fodor 1987, p. 17). Proponents of the logic metaphor never question this assumption—let us call it the *single-representation assumption* (SRA)—because their model accommodates it so easily: Replace '*x*' with its Mentalese counterpart, end of story. It turns out, however, that representations should *not* be charged with shouldering the entire burden when it comes to explaining the non-attitudinal component of the PAs.

If single representations *can* do all the work, why shouldn't we assume that they do it? The general problem is that this position rules out the very likely possibility that a variety of other cognitive abilities—and these are abilities that virtually all parties to the debate think we possess—also play an important role in thinking.

One of the most fundamental of these is our ability to recognize the relationships between the elements of distinct representations. We wield this ability for a variety of purposes, one of which is to draw, and reason on the basis of, analogies. When *drawing* an analogy, we generally compare two domains (e.g., a pair of entities, events, processes, etc.), one of which tends to be more familiar, or better understood, than the other. When *reasoning* on the basis of an analogy, we reach a conclusion regarding the latter, the "target" domain, because of its similarity to the former, the "source" domain (Holyoak and Thagard 1995). Philosophers have, as a result, long taken this kind of reasoning to be decomposable into three distinct steps.

In the first step, one looks for properties that the two domains have in common. One might, for example, notice apparent similarities between the behavior of water waves and the behavior of light: Each reflects off surfaces in such a manner that the angle of incidence equals the angle of reflection, and each refracts when entering a new medium. In the second step, we notice that, besides the similarities noted in the initial comparison, the source domain has some additional property. One might notice, for instance, that water waves are transverse waves—that is, vibration is perpendicular to, rather than (as with sound waves) parallel to, the direction of propagation. Finally, on the basis of the other similarities between the two domains we conclude that the target domain is also likely to possess this property. For instance, one might, like Thomas Young (1773–1829), conclude that light is made up of transverse waves.

While there has been some experimental research aimed at showing that analogy and metaphor run deeper than the surface structure of language (see, e.g., Gentner and Gentner 1983), most of the research on analogy simply takes for granted that this is so and instead attempts to shed light on the processes by which we draw, and reason on the basis of, analogies.[6] For instance, analogical inferences clearly range from the simple (i.e., where only a few, non-relational properties are at issue) to the highly complex (i.e., where a comparison between two domains is effected on the basis of networks of relational properties), and there seems to be a developmental progression leading up to adult competence at analogical reasoning that can be tracked by this metric (Gentner and Toupin 1986). Though much has been learned about the processes underwriting analogical thinking, about how the capacity for this kind of thinking develops, and about the factors that influence our ability to wield analogies effectively, what matters for our purposes is the bare fact that we often use analogies to think and reason about unfamiliar and poorly understood domains. In and of itself, this suggests that thinking about x will sometimes involve something more than a single representation of x. If, for instance, Young were to say "Water waves and light are similar in that each has a speed that is independent of the strength of its source," a proponent of the logic metaphor *could* propose that the thought that gave rise to this utterance consisted of a single representation (i.e., the Mentalese counterpart of Young's utterance). A far more plausible model, however, would be one that takes the non-attitudinal component of the thought process to include a comparison between distinct representations of two domains.

We also use our ability to recognize the relationships between the elements of distinct representations in order to think ahead. After all, unless I can map the elements of my representation of how things might be onto the elements of my representation of the way things are, the former representation will not be of much use to me. Suppose, for instance, I were to write a name on the face of a playing card and bury it in a small pile of shaving cream. How might you determine what name was written there? There are different ways of going about it, but whatever option you settle upon is probably going to be the result of a bit of means-end reasoning, and that sort of reasoning can, and often is, reported on; the literature on reasoning contains many such reports. A person might claim, for instance, "I could find out the name by reaching into the pile, pulling out the card, and wiping it on my trousers." What they would be reporting in this case might well be a bit of means-end reasoning, and by all accounts this kind of reasoning involves both the *manipulation* of representations and *the establishment of correspondences* between the elements of *distinct representations* of the way things are and the way they might be.[7] In short, it seems at least plausible that what it means to think the thought corresponding to such sentences involves more than an attitude (e.g., belief) and a single, simple representation (e.g., a sentence in Mentalese).

Continuing on, it is hardly open to dispute that we have the ability to selectively attend to some objects in our environments at the expense of others or to (local and relational) properties of objects at the expense of other properties of those same objects. This ability is, for instance, clearly implicated in the process whereby I look at the bulletin board over my desk and report "The board is rectangular in shape and has a single salmon-colored tack in it." I think everyone will agree that the *etiology* of my report includes the utilization of this ability to selectively attend. There are, however, no obvious grounds on which to rule out the possibility that the exercise of this ability is *constitutive* of some of my thoughts, such as the thought that the board is salmon-colored.

I'll have more to say on this count in a moment, but first let me reiterate the more general point that the ease with which the logic metaphor accounts for any expressible thought whatsoever can easily mislead us into overlooking the possibility that our thoughts might involve more than attitudes and single, simple representations. This is what I mean when I say that the logic metaphor may explain too much. In fact, so long as it remains a live possibility that the SRA is false, arguments against the image metaphor (and, by extension, the scale-model metaphor) that are premised upon the SRA should be considered highly suspect. As it turns out, all the philosophical arguments described above *are* premised upon this questionable SRA.

I believe that the foregoing considerations alone go a long way toward leveling the playing field. Still, as one who is dissatisfied with any appeal to Mentalese whatsoever, I feel obliged to say something more about how it is that one *might* appeal to plausible cognitive abilities—including, but not limited to, those noted above—in order to explain what it means to think each of the kinds of thoughts that are claimed by proponents of the logic metaphor to raise such problems for the image metaphor (and, by extension, the scale-model metaphor). Accordingly, in the remainder of this section I will speculate on what might be involved in thinking such thoughts. Throughout this discussion I continue pressing the claim that the SRA is false. As a result, what first seemed a clear windfall for proponents of Mentalese will begin to take on the appearance of ill-gotten gains.

5.2.2 Non-Concrete Domains

There are many words and phrases that denote entities, properties, and processes that defy straightforward depiction. It is difficult, for instance, to imagine how one might realistically depict (e.g., with an image or a scale model) the property of being a war criminal, the property of ownership, the process of economic inflation, or electricity. The first two examples have a heavy normative dimension to them, and this at least partly explains why they are difficult to depict. This is no recommendation for the logic metaphor, however, for it seems entirely likely that our thoughts about normative properties like these—along with our thoughts about properties such as justice, benevolence, and mercy—involve, in addition to representations, an amalgam of affective states, modal attitudes, and other-directed mental-state attributions.[8] I do not know precisely how all of this is to be worked out, but neither does the competition. What we all do know, I think, is that single, simple representations are not enough.

On the other hand, perhaps we can make some quick headway when it comes to understanding the processes that are involved in the comprehension and production of sentences containing terms such as 'economic inflation' and 'electricity'. For us layfolk, at least, it seems likely that our thoughts about such processes and entities involve some reliance upon analogies and metaphors that are rooted in domains that we *can* represent with images and models.[9] Discourse about non-concrete and poorly understood domains is, after all, positively shot through with analogy and metaphor (Lakoff and Johnson 1980; Lakoff 1987, 1989). For instance, the very phrase 'economic *inflation*' suggests that our thoughts about this domain may be infused with metaphors. And while the word 'electricity' may not similarly betray an underlying reliance upon analogy or metaphor, discourse *about* electricity does. Gentner and Gentner (1983), for instance, found that when subjects are asked about electrical circuitry, they commonly talk in terms of water moving through pipes or crowds moving through corridors. Each source domain is, moreover, very useful for making inferences about the 'flow' of electrical current under various configurations of electrical components (figure 5.1), and Gentner and Gentner found that, at least to a large extent, subject performance reflected this fact. It thus seems at least plausible that our thoughts about non-normative properties that are (if only because they are poorly understood) difficult to depict might involve such processes as metaphorical pretense and analogical mapping.

Prinz (2002) has argued that this approach will not work. His concern is that when we think metaphorically about some domain, we are aware of both the similarities *and* the differences between the domain of interest and the domain from which the metaphor issues. For this reason, he claims, there must be aspects of the former domain that we represent to ourselves in a non-metaphorical way. Before evaluating this argument we should set aside the question of whether or not our thoughts about normative properties can be explained in this way; as already noted, they probably cannot. Once our focus is properly restricted, we find that there is less of a problem here than Prinz might think. Consider, for example, the flow of electricity through a particular set of circuits. In this case, electricity is —*at least* for the layperson—something understood largely in terms of where it comes from, where it goes, and the kinds of effects that it has along the way. These are things that can often be understood in a non-metaphorical way (e.g., with the help of circuit diagrams, thoughts about a light turning on, a switch closing, etc.). There is, however, a lacuna in our understanding, for we do not know how to visualize the 'thing' itself, and it is this lacuna that must be filled with analogy and metaphor.

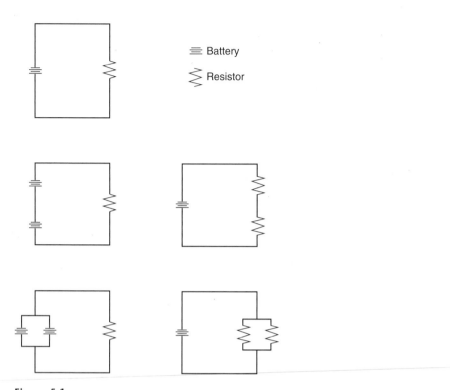

Figure 5.1
Batteries and resistors in series and in parallel. Based on a description in Gentner and Gentner 1983.

To take another example, notice that there was a great deal that Young knew about the behavior of light from what he and others had observed and inferred. What Young and other physicists did not know—though they desperately wanted to—was what kind of "thing" could give rise to these observable events and behave in the ways in which they had been able to infer that light behaves, and it was, once again, only this lacuna that needed to be filled with analogy and metaphor.[10]

5.2.3 Assigning Specific Properties to Specific Objects

It has been pointed out that sentential representations are particularly well suited to the task of representing the assignment of specific properties to specific objects. For instance, just as we can think that Fred's car is green —thereby singling out, from among a tremendous number of properties, a single property of Fred's car—we can represent this property assignment with a sentence:

(1) Fred's car is green.

As usual, the logic metaphor has a very easy time of things because any thought that can be expressed in natural language can just as easily be represented in the hypothetical thought language. At the same time, it is perfectly clear that neither pictures nor scale models can, *by themselves*, do what we do in thought—namely, single out particular properties of particular objects. A scale model of Fred's car, for instance, will represent a good deal more than just its color; it may also represent the number of doors, the body type, the shape of the headlights, and so on. Still, as with the earlier concerns, this one quickly dissolves once we give up the unrealistic stricture that thinking the thought corresponding to a sentence such as (1) involves nothing more than an attitude and a single representation. As already noted, we have the ability to selectively attend to some objects in our environments at the expense of others or to certain (local and relational) properties of objects at the expense of other properties of those same objects,[11] and it is entirely plausible that this ability is heavily implicated in the production of certain statements. We also have the ability to attend to particular objects and properties in external pictures and scale models.[12] The proposal that we might re-deploy the same attentional mechanisms with regard to inner (which are really just off-line) representations is thus entirely plausible; once this is recognized, the argument falls apart and the SRA on which it is based once again looks unjustifiably restrictive.

5.2.4 Genera

At first glance, the image and scale-model metaphors seem to run into insurmountable problems when it comes to accounting for our ability to think about genera, or to "grasp" universals. There are, however, several considerations that help to temper this concern. To start with, we must not lose sight of the fact that the debate over universals is as old as philosophy itself, and two of the most famous positions regarding the ontological status of universals themselves (i.e., nominalism and Platonism)—positions which lie at opposite ends of the anti-realism to realism continuum—deny that finite human thought processes are constituted by representations of universals.[13] Proponents of the logic metaphor never question whether or not our minds *are* fit for conceiving of universals because, once again, things seem to come so easily for their model. After all, they figure, the words of natural and artificial languages are capable of representing genera, so the terms of Mentalese can do this as well.

One may reasonably wonder, however, whether this position is truly tenable. Do thoughts about genera merely amount to the bearing of attitudes toward the contents of single mental representations whose constituents represent the genera in question?

5.2.4.1 Reasoning about Genera

If we take a mental trip back to a time before the invention of analytic geometry, we find reasons for thinking that there is more to this story than the SRA lets on and that the scale-model metaphor is able to pick up at least some of the slack. In that era, geometers were able to reach conclusions about all members of a particular geometric category (e.g., the class of right triangles), but only by reasoning about some particular member (e.g., some particular right triangle).

As an illustration, let us consider one of the many spatial proofs of the Pythagorean theorem. Before getting on with the proof, however, it is worth emphasizing that while *we* typically represent this theorem to ourselves in algebraic terms (i.e., as "$a^2 + b^2 = c^2$"), philosophers of Pythagoras' day were, for obvious reasons, forced to think of them in other terms. The square of the hypotenuse was thought of as the four-sided equiangular figure—that is, the literal square—whose sides had the same length as the hypotenuse of a particular right triangle. When we think of the meaning of "the square of the hypotenuse" in these terms, we find that the Pythagorean theorem amounts to the claim that such a square will have an area that is equal to the sum of areas of the squares formed from the other two sides of that triangle (figure 5.2). That is what the present proof demonstrates. The proof that follows is, in fact, just one of a great many such spatial, or *synthetic*, proofs, and we shall see that its success depends upon the inferential productivity of both the external *and internal* representations that are utilized along the way.

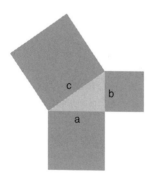

Figure 5.2
Squares of sides of a right triangle.

Getting on with the proof, one first draws a pair of squares, one with sides of length a and the other with sides of length b (figure 5.3a). What we now need to show is that the combined area of the two squares is exactly the same as the area of a square whose sides are equal to the hypotenuse of a right triangle whose two shortest sides are of lengths a and b. Fortunately, superimposing such a triangle on the two squares is very easy (figure 5.3b). Now imagine if we were to slide this triangle to the right, so that its shortest side aligns with the right side of the smaller square. In this case, the area of the entire figure does not change, and the length of the bottom edge of the figure remains $a + b$ (figure 5.3c). We can now easily envision a congruent triangle being inscribed within the left side of the figure. (See figure 5.3d.) Now we can start mentally cutting and rotating parts of the two squares. First, then, let us imagine that the top vertex of the leftmost triangle is a fixed point and let us mentally rotate the triangle around this point so that the side of length a is aligned with the top edge of the square, which is also of length a. Since both are of length a, there will be no overlap. Also, when two right angles are placed adjacent to one another in this way they will form a straight line. Once again, the total area of the figure will have remained unchanged (figure 5.3e). Finally, let us imagine that the top vertex of the other triangle is fixed and rotate the triangle so that the side of length b aligns with the

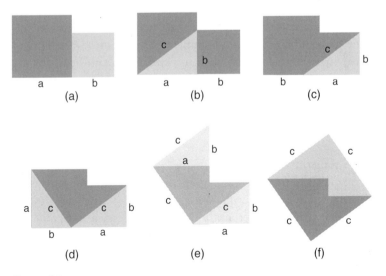

Figure 5.3
A spatial proof of the Pythagorean theorem.

top edge of the smaller square, which edge is also of length b. The side of length a will also be a perfect fit since the height of the previous figure was just the height of the left square (i.e., a) plus the length of the shortest side of the left triangle (i.e., b). Subtracting the length of the left side of the smaller square from this total leaves us with an edge of length a. The end result of this second move is therefore a square whose sides are of length c and whose area is exactly the same as the sum of the areas of the original two squares (figure 5.3f).

I think we can agree that we know the consequences of each particular manipulation—for instance, consider again the consequences of the first manipulation—before we draw the results out. The external diagrams merely help us to keep track of these consequences. An important question raised by this proof is thus whether the logic metaphor or the scale-model metaphor better accounts for *how* it is that we know about these consequences. A complete answer to this question requires delving into a number of complicated issues, and I will do just that in the next chapter. Still, a quick and easy answer is forthcoming if we restrict ourselves to the version of the logic metaphor that its proponents seem to have in mind —namely, the one according to which our thinking and reasoning about the meanings of terms like 'right triangle' is underwritten by Mentalese counterparts of these terms that are embedded within a larger network of Mentalese sentences and inference rules (i.e., the account that is directly inspired by production systems; see subsection 1.2.3.2).

We saw chapter 4 that this approach to representation and inference is beset by the frame problem, and this simple fact undercuts the viability of the proposal that the logic metaphor can explain our knowledge of the consequences of the above manipulations. Notice, for instance, that the above proof depends upon our ability to predict the consequences of some very unusual alterations. It is, in other words, a pretty compelling illustration of the inferential productivity of human thought processes (see subsection 4.3.5), and inferential productivity is, to say the least, not the logic metaphor's strong suit. One could, of course, provide a post hoc specification of the kinds of sentences and axioms that might underlie this proof (e.g., one could posit a mental inference rule stating "If two squares are placed adjacent to one another and a triangle is inscribed in one of the squares such that . . ."), but one must bear in mind that no finite set of such rules is going to account for the geometric knowledge that we are able to draw upon when constructing spatial proofs of geometrical theorems. If you are not convinced, you should bear in mind that this is just one of a large number of spatial proofs for the Pythagorean theorem that have already been devised; there are countless others that have not yet been "discovered"; and this is just *one* theorem!

In contrast, as was explained in chapter 4, the kind of inferential productivity at work in this kind of spatial reasoning is easily accounted for by the scale-model metaphor. This is a nice result for proponents of the scale-model metaphor, because understanding this proof amounts to understanding a fact about all right triangles. Thus, we have here an account of what it means to think (viz., to reason) about universals by manipulating representations that are only of particulars. (See Waskan 1999.)

I doubt that any reasonable person who has followed this proof would object that the representational manipulations just performed only demonstrate the truth of the Pythagorean theorem for this particular pair of squares and that a true proof would require, per impossibile, a repetition of this process for all possible pairs of squares. What our finite minds are somehow able to "grasp" is that the size that we chose for the original squares had no bearing on the success of the proof.[14] Insofar as we recognize that the sizes chosen have no bearing on the proof, we understand that the theorem is true no matter the sizes of the squares and, hence, no matter the lengths of the sides of the right triangle. To understand all of this is just to understand that the proof is true of all right triangles.

A reasonable person *might* object, however, that the belief *that the sizes chosen had no effect on the success of the proof* cannot be accounted for on the scale-model metaphor. This, however, is very different from the objection that no representation of a specific right triangle could do justice to all right triangles. The new objection is that a representation of a specific right triangle can do justice to all right triangles only if paired with the knowledge that the inference about all right triangles did not depend upon the specifics so represented. It is, moreover, a lot less difficult to explain *this* knowledge than it might seem at first glance. This knowledge seems to be the combined effect of knowing that each individual manipulation made over the course of the proof would have had the qualitatively identical outcome no matter the initial lengths of the right triangle's three sides. If you quickly review the manipulations made above, I think you will agree that the scale-model metaphor has little difficulty in accounting for these individual pieces of knowledge.

The account I have offered of what it means to know, on the basis of the above proof, that the Pythagorean Theorem is true of all right triangles actually has its roots in the philosophy of antiquity. For instance, on the heels of Plato's theory of geometrical knowledge came Aristotle's: "[I]t is not possible to think without an image. For the same effect occurs in thinking as in drawing a diagram. For in the latter case, *though we do not make any use of the fact that the size of the triangle is determinate, we none the less draw it with a determinate size.* And similarly someone who is thinking, even if he is not thinking of something with a size, places something with a size before his eyes, but thinks of it not as having a size. If its nature is that of things which have a size, but not a determinate one, he places before his eyes something with a determinate size, but thinks of it simply as having size." (fourth century B.C./1987, pp. 449b and 450a; emphasis added)

This, in fact, is the account of geometrical thinking that was preferred up until, and even for a while after, the development of analytic geometry (more on which below). Moreover, as Aristotle surmised long ago, the utility of the kind of thought process just described is not restricted to geometrical reasoning. Notice, for instance, that the subjects in Gentner and Gentner's (1983) study were asked to reach some general conclusions about the properties of electrical circuits—for instance, to determine whether or not there will be more current flowing through a circuit with two parallel resistors than a circuit with a single resistor—but they often reasoned their way to such conclusions by constructing external depictions. Obviously, the diagrams they created were unavoidably specific in many respects, but subjects were somehow able to grasp that these specifics had no bearing on the conclusions that they reached.

This kind of reasoning is similar in many respects both to reasoning by analogy and to means-end reasoning. Specifically, to know whatever it is that the reasoning process reveals is to have engaged in an oftentimes complicated thought process. Thus, to report that one knows that x may well be more than to simply have a representation that means 'x' tokened in one's belief box.

5.2.4.2 Other Kinds of Thoughts about Genera
Reasoning about genera on the basis of instances is, I believe, a very important part of what it means to think about genera, but it is, alas, very far from being the entire story. Among the important questions that remain are the following:

(i) What does it mean to think the bare thought that some individual is a member of a category?

(ii) What does it mean to think thoughts about the category-independent properties of some category member?

(iii) What does it mean to think thoughts about what it takes fall into a particular category?

The first question follows directly on the heels of the above considerations. Though we did see how one might account for our ability to reach conclusions about all members of a category by manipulating a representation of a particular member of that category, this leads to the further question of what it means to think that the particular individual being reasoned about is a member of that category in the first place. In the present context, an important question is whether or not the bare thought that some individual is a member of a category can be explained in terms of the representations of particulars to which the scale-model metaphor is restricted. Just as in the other cases, if one demands adherence to the SRA here, things do look quite bad for the scale-model metaphor. An external scale model of an item cannot by itself represent the fact that the item is a member of a category, and so the internal counterpart to such a model will not by itself fare any better in this regard. There is, however, no more reason to demand adherence to the SRA in this case as there was in the others.

Even so, it is a formidable task to devise even a speculative account of how the cognitive counterparts to scale models might, in conjunction with other plausible processes, underwrite the thought that some individual is a member of a particular category. But then, despite what you may have heard, it is a formidable task to explain this *no matter which* model of the format of mental representations you happen to be working with. To see why, we first need to get clear on the fact that use of the word 'concept' in contexts such as these generates more confusion than enlightenment.

In order to answer question i, what we require is an explanation for both the manner and extent to which we bring to bear, when classifying a particular individual as a member of a specific category, our long-term declarative knowledge of—or, in philosophical parlance, our dispositional beliefs concerning—that category.[15] That is, we need an explanation for the manner and extent to which we bring to bear the kind of knowledge at issue in question iii, and so a full answer to i presupposes an answer to iii. A full answer to ii also presupposes an answer to iii, for what we need to know in that case is the manner and extent to which our long-term declarative knowledge of multiple categories is utilized when, for instance, we have a belief that an object of a particular type has a property of a particular type.

Still, even before we begin answering iii, we can be reasonably sure that when we think the thoughts at issue in questions i and ii, we do not always bring to bear our long-term declarative knowledge of the relevant category (or categories) *in its* (or their) *entirety*. When, for instance, someone explains to me that some unusual looking paper is foreign currency, it is doubtful that I will be caused to think about everything that being foreign currency implies, connotes, or suggests. This is not to deny holism. (See sections 2.2 and 2.5.) Perhaps it is true that in order for me to be counted, at least by folk-psychological standards, as someone who has the *occurrent* belief that a particular piece of paper is foreign currency, I might also need to have lots of further *dispositional* beliefs. That is, in psych-speak, I might need to have lots of different facts stored in long-term semantic memory. All I am claiming here is that the limitations of attention and short-term memory make it highly unlikely that this knowledge is accessed in its entirety when I think the thought in question. Likewise, when I briefly revel in the fact that the money I just got from the ATM is crisp and new, I am not likely to be thinking any thoughts whatsoever about the fact that money is an arbitrary, but socially accepted medium for the exchange of goods and services; nor, a fortiori, am I likely to be thinking about what goods or services are.[16]

These simple considerations call into question the wisdom behind continued use of the word 'concept' when posing answers to questions i–iii. Concepts are very widely assumed to be the building blocks of thoughts. More specifically, these putative building blocks are claimed to have a coarseness of structure and content that parallels that of natural-language terms. (See subsection 4.5.2.) For instance, corresponding to the word 'dog', there is claimed to be a concept *dog* that is an actual *part* of one's thoughts about dogs. It is, at the same time, also widely assumed that concepts embody the kind of knowledge of categories that we have been discussing. There is a real tension between these two assumptions, however. After all, if we take the concept *dog* to be constituted by the sum (or even a significant part) of my knowledge concerning what membership in the category entails, connotes, or what-have-you, and if this knowledge is not (in its entirety) usually a simple constituent of my thoughts about dogs—for instance, my thought that Fido is a good dog—then concepts cannot be discrete parts of thoughts. Faced with such facts, we can deny the building-block view and hang onto the claim that a concept is that which embodies our knowledge of a particular category; we can cling to the building-block view and deny that a concept is that which embodies our knowledge of a particular category; or, to avoid confusion and senseless debate about who gets to use the word 'concept', we can avoid using the word altogether. The last option may be the most sensible.

These considerations also point up the simplistic nature of the logic metaphor. What proponents of this view claim—though it is worth noting that they tend to claim this only in the context of criticisms of the image metaphor—is that what makes the thought that Fido is a dog a thought about the category of dogs is the fact that one has in one's belief box a sentence, one of whose constituents is the Mentalese counterpart of 'dog'. As explained above, because the words of natural and artificial languages seem capable of representing genera, proponents of Mentalese think that the terms of their hypothesized thought language can do this as well. But thinking thoughts about genera is clearly a far more complicated process than having the right arrangement of symbols in one's belief box. For instance, the kinds of thoughts at issue in questions i and ii surely involve (inter alia) some limited form of access to our long-term declarative knowledge of categories, and positing a single term in a hypothetical thought language can hardly do justice to the complexities of this process. Thus, when one thinks that Fido is a dog, one is utilizing, in some unknown manner and to some unknown extent, one's extensive declarative knowledge of the category of dogs.

Things are complicated enough as they stand, but they appear more complicated still once we consider the nature of the declarative knowledge that is being accessed. There are, after all, different kinds of beliefs that we can, and intuitively seem to, have about particular categories. For instance, it seems plausible that some of us are psychological essentialists[17] when it comes to certain categories (e.g., the category of dogs), that some of us believe that there are sufficient (or at least necessary) conditions for being members of other categories (e.g., the category of bachelors), that some of us explicitly stipulate necessary and sufficient conditions for membership in still other categories (e.g., as is common when formulating operational definitions), that some of us defer to expert beliefs about the conditions for membership in particular categories (e.g., the category of crystals), that in some cases category membership is a matter of degree (e.g., the category of furry things), and that in some cases we simply know a member when we see one (e.g., the category of blue things). Nor are these options mutually exclusive. For example, one might believe that there is some microscopic essence, known by the experts, that is common to all crystals and is responsible for whatever superficial properties they have a tendency to share. Complicating matters further is the fact the character of these beliefs may be dependent upon the kind of category in question, of which there are many. There are, for instance, artifact categories, biological categories, substance categories, texture categories, social categories, activity categories, grammatical categories, mathematical categories, direction categories, ideological categories, category categories, and so on. The upshot is this: In order to offer an adequate defense of a model of the kinds of thoughts implicated in question iii—and thus before we can even begin to think about formulating a complete explanation for the thoughts implicated in questions i and ii—one would have to show that one's model of declarative knowledge of categories covers at least a wide range of categories and a wide range of types of belief about the nature of category membership.

I have no intention of defending such a model here. I simply wish to draw attention both to the tremendous difficulties involved in accounting for the various kinds of thoughts we have about genera and to fact that the appeal to Mentalese provides a false sense of security. A viable account of our thoughts about genera will need to answer questions i–iii, but none of these questions can be answered simply by positing terms in Mentalese with the appropriate content (e.g., the Mentalese counterpart of 'dog'). At the same time, if we unburden ourselves of the onerous SRA, the space of possible answers to these questions opens up before us. Knowing this, I find it far easier to embrace the possibility of a life without Mentalese.

Finally, to engage in a bit of further speculation regarding what this life could be like, I would like to suggest that the search for answers to questions i–iii could be expedited if we pay particular attention to the language that we use when we voice the kinds of thoughts at issue in question iii. Notice, specifically, that discourse of this kind is heavily laden with a recurring set of metaphors. It is, for instance, common to talk of categories as though they were social groups with their own membership conditions (e.g., an individual can be said to "belong to" or "be a member of" a particular category).[18] It is also common to talk of categories as though they were containers (e.g., an individual is sometimes said to "fall into" a category) (Lakoff 1993). In other cases the "boundaries" are said to be "fuzzy" rather than "sharp." None of this matters, of course, if these are just façons de parler. But perhaps they are not. (See subsection 5.2.2.) Perhaps they are indicative of the way we understand the world. That is to say, we may think of the world as though it were "divided up" in certain ways, as though it were made up of entities that "belong to" or "fall into" certain categories. At the very least, all of this fits with the sensible proposal that our inborn cognitive abilities are restricted to just those that natural selection favored, eons ago, because they enabled humans to do things like plant, build, hunt, and fight competitors on a collective basis.

5.2.5 Negation and Disjunction

The previous objections to the image metaphor (and, by extension, the scale-model metaphor) have been in circulation for quite some time. It has, more recently, been objected that these models are non-starters because negations and disjunctions are impossible to depict (Pylyshyn 2002, pp. 180, 181). As with the other objections, however, this one clearly rests upon the overly restrictive SRA, and as soon as this assumption is abandoned it becomes far easier to imagine the possibility of a Mentalese-free account of the kinds of thoughts at issue here.

Starting with negation, it seems (at the very least) plausible that our ability to map between the elements of distinct representations figures centrally in our ability to produce and comprehend at least certain sentences containing negations. One apparent proponent of the scale-model metaphor has, in fact, already come up with what amounts to a plausible account of this ability. According to Josef Perner, very early in development children acquire the ability to model entities and relations in the world and to manipulate these models. Perner illustrates with a simple scenario involving a park and, some distance away, an ice cream truck that is parked adjacent to a church. A developmental transition occurs, according to Perner, when young children are first able to represent counterfactual situations, such as a situation in which the ice cream truck is at the park rather than at the church. Perner explains: "There are clear indications that the infant's mind begins to transcend the constraints of reality and branch into the hypothetical and counterfactual. . . . If this is to be possible without utter confusion about reality an adequate mechanism of mental representation has to be available. My suggestion is that this mechanism consists of manipulable models. The infant transports the mental elements of his knowledge base [i.e., of his representation of the actual state of the world] into another model where he can rearrange these elements in different ways." (1988, pp. 145, 146)

Perner's account supplies a simple explanation for the thought processes that give rise to the child's utterance of "That's wrong" when told, for instance, that the ice cream truck is at the park (ibid., p. 148). In order to reach this conclusion, says Perner, the child must first represent the meaning of the (counterfactual) description he or she is given and then compare, and attend to the differences between, this representation and his/her representation of the way the world really is. (See also Langacker 1991; Fauconnier 1985; Goldberg 1995.) This is a very intuitive account of the cognitive processes involved thinking the thoughts corresponding to sentences that deny the correctness of other sentences, and it is also nearly an account of what it means to think thoughts corresponding to at least certain sentences containing negations. After all, "That's wrong" is just shorthand for "What you just said is *not* correct."

To take a different sort of case, imagine comparing your declarative memories for the past and present contents of a particular room and noticing that they differ in that only the former represents the room as containing a sofa. One could report the outcome of this comparison by claiming "The sofa is no longer in the room." It seems at least plausible (if not obvious) that the kind of comparison and recognition of a difference just described accounts for what it means to think the thought corresponding to this sentence, and yet, on this plausible account, the meaning of 'not' is nowhere explicitly represented (e.g., with a term in Mentalese). All of this is, of course, in direct violation of the SRA, which at this point I take to be indication that we are on the right track. To be sure, the logic metaphor is able to account for negation in a way that respects the SRA ('not' is just another word in Mentalese), but a claim of victory here would be a lot like a child claiming that he is superior because his index finger bends all the way back. Sure, he can do it, but why would anyone want to?

There are, admittedly, other thoughts involving negations, such as those involving denials of category membership, that are more difficult to explain, but the difficulties here stem from the fact that thoughts involving *affirmations* of category membership are not well understood. Still, the speculative proposal offered at the end of subsection 5.2.4.2 might provide some guidance. For example, perhaps to think the thought corresponding to "the Batmobile is not an SUV" is to think that there is a container-like category of things known by us English speakers as SUVs and that the Batmobile falls outside that category. This model has it both that the representations we wield are concrete and specific throughout and that the meaning of 'not' is nowhere explicitly represented. Moreover, because the choice of the Batmobile and SUVs was entirely arbitrary, this *synthetic* model (cf. Lakoff 1993, and see subsection 5.2.4.1 above) of thoughts about denials of category membership could account equally well for *all* cases in which we are thinking that an object is not a member of some category.

What it means to think disjunctive thoughts can be accounted for in much the same way. In particular, there is no need to assume that disjunctive thoughts have parts that mean the same thing as 'or'. After all, as just about everyone agrees, we are capable of thinking about multiple, possible states of affairs. In light of this simple fact, it seems quite plausible that we can think thoughts corresponding to sentences containing 'or' without wielding a Mentalese counterparts of this term. That is, it seems plausible that our thoughts about disjunctions involve bearing the appropriate modal attitude toward multiple representations. These could be representations of the states of affairs consistent with a given sentence, or even representations of the states of affairs ruled out by a sentence (Johnson-Laird 1983, p. 36).[19]

While I am not convinced that these accounts of what it means to think thoughts about negations and disjunctions is correct, I do think that they, like the other speculative proposals offered above, illustrate an important point: As soon as we abandon the needlessly restrictive SRA, what once appeared inconceivable become conceivable. The philosophical objections all depend, of course, on the *in*conceivability of a life with only images and models—that is, without Mentalese.

5.2.6 Final Thoughts on the Philosophical Objections

Here I have attempted to undermine philosophical arguments that are purported to show that the image metaphor (and, by extension, the scale-model metaphor) fails, on a priori grounds, as an alternative to the logic metaphor (viz., as an alternative to the logic metaphor's appeal to the special thought sentences of Mentalese). I have shown that these arguments are based on the questionable assumption that single representations should bear the entire load when it comes to explaining the non-attitudinal component of thoughts. I have also shown that, as soon as this assumption is discarded, dissipating soon thereafter is the air of inconceivability that first surrounded the proposal that the scale-model metaphor might, without any reliance upon Mentalese, account for the various kinds of thoughts at issue. In closing, and at the risk of getting repetitive, let me pose one last question: Does it not seem suspicious that the logic metaphor promises to explain any expressible thought whatsoever without ever having to mention reasoning, attention, emotions, interrepresentational mapping abilities, semantic memory, or much of anything else that one would expect out of a model of human thought processes? If only things were so simple!

5.3 Reasoning and Representation

I have already discussed how one might, through a sensible appeal to extrarepresentational cognitive resources, offer a Mentalese-free explanation for our ability to think the thoughts corresponding to sentences containing terms such as 'or' and 'not'. Explaining such thoughts is just one facet of the broader problem of explaining how it is that we engage in deductive reasoning. The importance assigned to the problem of explaining untrained competence at deduction depends on which cognitive scientist you ask. There are many in cognitive science who view deductive reasoning as our go-to, everyday mode of reasoning, but there are also many who think that it is instead non-monotonic reasoning that is most important.

Lance Rips claim that an understanding of deductive competence is required if we are to give "an account of how the inferences people draw manage to be truth preserving in a sufficiently large number of cases to make both science and practical affairs possible" (1990, p. 293). Likewise, Philip Johnson-Laird and Ruth Byrne suggest that "a world without deduction would be a world without science, technology, laws, social conventions, and culture" (1993, p. 323) and that the capacity for deductive reasoning is what underwrites the truth-preserving representational manipulations implicated in planning (1991, pp. 2, 3). As we shall see, Rips and Johnson-Laird and Byrne (henceforth cited as J-L&B) part ways when it comes to precisely how it is that they would explain deductive reasoning, but they ultimately have more in common with each other than they do with others in cognitive science. For example, a well-known antagonist of theirs is Nick Chater, who champions the view that non-monotonic, rather than deductive, reasoning is fundamental. Chater claims, for instance, that "an account of deductive reasoning casts light on a fascinating if rather arcane human ability; an account of nonmonotonic inference in general would be little short of a theory of thinking" (1993, p. 340). The debate between these camps is, unfortunately, muddled by conflations and oversights. By way of setting things straight, we should first get clear on the fact that there are multiple forms of non-monotonic reasoning, and champions of the claim that non-monotonic reasoning is fundamental typically have only one of these in mind.

5.3.1 Varieties of Reasoning

Starting with the basics, when we reason, we reach conclusions on the basis of one or more beliefs or assumptions—in other words, we reach conclusions on the basis of premises, very broadly construed. In a deductively valid argument, the truth of the premises *guarantees* the truth of the conclusion. For example, if (2) and (3) are true, (4) must be true also:

(2) If dogs are mammals, then dogs are warm blooded.
(3) Dogs are mammals.
(4) Dogs are warm blooded.

In other words, so long as (2) and (3) are true, no further evidence can be brought to light that will undermine the truth of (4). Moreover, if (4) were shown to be false, then one of the premises would have to be false as well.

The latter fact is really the crux of monotonicity as it is normally understood. (See Chater 1993, p. 340.)

Now consider the following scenario: One afternoon, an automated teller machine refuses to give me any cash. I know that I have plenty of money in the account, so I conclude that there is a problem with the machine. A few moments later, however, I notice that someone else is having no trouble at all getting cash from the ATM. In this case, from my belief that (a) there is plenty of money in my account and the fact that (b) the machine will not give me access to it, I conclude that (c) there is a problem with the ATM. This conclusion is, however, overridden (albeit fallibly itself) by the additional fact that someone else had no trouble at all getting cash from the machine. In this case, then, the truth of premises a and b fails to guarantee the truth of the conclusion, (c). By the same token, when I come to believe that c is false, I do not take this to imply that either premise a or premise b is false. This kind of *defeasibility* (i.e., where conclusions can be defeated while leaving the truth of the premises intact) is the hallmark of *non*-monotonic reasoning.

What is too often overlooked is that each of the aforementioned forms of reasoning can be divided into multiple sub-types. Non-monotonic reasoning can be divided into at least three: abductive, inductive, and analogical. I have already discussed analogical reasoning in subsection 5.2.1, so let me turn briefly to inductive reasoning.

When one reasons inductively (as I am using 'inductive'), one reaches a conclusion about an entire class (a.k.a. 'population') on the basis of what one knows about a subset (sample) of that class. For example, I might make an inference from (5) to (6):

(5) Every cow that I've ever seen or heard of has chewed cud.
(6) All cows chew cud.

This is a reasonable inference, but (6) can be false even if (5) is true. It is, for instance, within the realm of possibility that, unbeknownst to me, a horse-to-cow transplant operation has been performed by some brilliant scientist so as to yield a cow with a stomach that can fully digest grass in one pass.

Now consider the inference from (7)–(9) to (10).

(7) The car will not start.
(8) The fuel gauge reads 'empty'.
(9) The electrical system appears to be functioning properly.
(10) The car will not start, because it is out of fuel.

This is also a reasonable inference, and it is another clear-cut case in which the truth of the premises fails to guarantee the truth of the conclusion, (10); the inference is once again defeasible. Like the example of the ATM, this is an illustration of what is known as abductive reasoning, or "inference to the best explanation." In the case of abduction, one (crudely put) reasons from the facts to an explanation for them.

Abduction not only plays an important role in our day-to-day lives, it is one of the main forms of reasoning employed in scientific investigation—including, of course, cognitive scientific investigation. It is this form of reasoning that Chater clearly has in mind when he claims that an account of "non-monotonic reasoning" would be "a theory of thinking" (1993, p. 340), for he later claims that this form of "commonsense reasoning may be conceived of as a species of inference to the best explanation" (ibid.).

It bears noting that some have attempted, though with little success, to model the abduction process computationally (ibid., p. 341). In particular, research efforts have recently been directed toward the creation of abductive formalisms with the hopes of being able to capture the rules by which we reason from facts to hypotheses. While Chater attributes the shortcomings of this line of research to the frame problem (ibid.), it is hard to image there being much success in this endeavor unless researchers get clear on the fact that monotonic reasoning is *constitutive of* abductive reasoning.[20]

To see why one might think that this is true, consider again the abductive inference from (7)–(9) to (10).[21] In this case, it is true that, *temporally* speaking, one begins with the facts and goes on to formulate an explanation for those facts. Nevertheless, when we consider what makes something an explanation in the first place, it appears as though monotonic reasoning plays an ineliminable role. For instance, it seems plausible that the reason the car's being out of fuel explains one's inability to start the car is that the absence of fuel (in conjunction with some further assumptions) indefeasibly implies that the car will not start. Thus, if after one last try the car did finally start, we would be forced to revise our belief that the car is out of fuel (or one of the background assumptions).[22] Likewise, in all the explanations that we have considered thus far (e.g., cognitive scientific explanations, biological explanations, intentional explanations, explanations for why cars fail to start, why ATMs fail to deliver money, etc.), there is a specific relationship between what does the explaining and what is being explained. Specifically, in every case the former indefeasibly implies the latter.[23] What makes abductive reasoning defeasible is the simple fact that there can be more than one explanation for a given event or regularity, and new facts sometimes come to light that lead us to believe that the old explanation is at least partially incorrect or that a different one is even better.

In light of these basic facts about reasoning, Chater's claim that our go-to mode of reasoning is non-monotonic rather than monotonic looks like a category mistake. After all, the form of non-monotonic reasoning that he has in mind—namely, abduction—is actually constituted by at least one form of monotonic reasoning.

5.3.2 Deduction vs. Exduction

Rips and J-L&B might take this to constitute a victory for their proposal that deduction is of paramount importance. The role played by deduction in abduction, they might argue, is just one of the many uses to which our deductive reasoning capacity is put; it is also used in the service of making predictions, fleshing out the implications of sets of claims, evaluating their consistency, etc. They do not seem to realize, however, that deduction is only one of (at least) two distinct forms of monotonic reasoning.

5.3.2.1 Deduction Deduction is a formal and monotonic reasoning process. It is monotonic because it is (when valid) indefeasible. It is widely regarded as formal in that its indefeasibility has everything to do with the semantics of logical terms (e.g., 'and', 'or', 'not', 'all', etc.) and, in an important sense, nothing to do with the semantics of the more contentful terms. That is to say, it does not matter what the connectives (consistently) connect or what the quantifiers (consistently) quantify over. In deductive reasoning, we abstract away from this content and pay attention to logical form.[24]

Deductive reasoning at least sometimes involves the rule-governed manipulation of 'external' representations, and the preferred choice seems to be the manipulation of the well-formed formula of some artificial language. Proponents of the primacy of deduction maintain that thinking is carried out through a similar, internal process of formal symbol manipulation—though, we shall see, J-L&B are not entirely consistent on this point.

5.3.2.2 Exduction In chapter 4, I pointed out that external images and scale models can be wielded in the service of monotonic reasoning. This form of reasoning is monotonic because (as with a valid deduction) *if* the world is the way we represent it to be, then certain other things *must* be true of it. By the same token, if those other things are not true of it, then the way we represent the world to be *must* be inaccurate in one or more respects.

The manipulation of scale models is, however, clearly not a *formal* reasoning process. In other words, the derivation of conclusions does require that all facts be represented in terms of, and all inferences effected in a manner that is sensitive solely to, the meanings of the standard set of logical operators. This non-formal mode of monotonic reasoning has not yet found a clear place in standard taxonomies, so let us call it *exductive* reasoning.[25] While exduction can clearly be carried out externally through the manipulation of, for instance, scale models, what I have been contending is that it can also be carried out internally through the mental manipulation of the cognitive counterparts of scale models.

With this distinction in hand, we can now make better sense of what it is, precisely, that each of the aforementioned, self-declared proponents of the primacy of deduction is actually claiming.

5.3.2.3 Rips' Predicate-Calculus-Inspired Mental Deduction Model Rips does indeed think that deduction is our go-to mode of reasoning. His proposal really just amounts to the claim that cognitive underpinnings for the monotonic reasoning amount to a system of syntactic constraints and syntax-sensitive inference rules very much like those constitutive of a formal deduction system such as predicate calculus. His production-system model of this process (see subsection 1.2.3.2), which he calls A Natural Deduction System (ANDS), embodies the core of his approach. Says Rips: "ANDS's central assumption . . . is that deductive reasoning consists in the application of mental inference rules to the premises and conclusion of an argument. The sequence of applied rules forms a mental proof or derivation of the conclusion from the premises, where these implicit proofs are analogous to the explicit proofs of elementary logic." (1983, p. 40) Rips' aptly named Mental Logic hypothesis, then, clearly does amount to the claim that deduction is of paramount importance.

5.3.2.4 Johnson-Laird and Byrne's Mental Tables and Mental Models
What Johnson-Laird and Byrne advocate is far less clear. They claim, for instance, that we reason monotonically by constructing and manipulating "mental models" that have "a structure that is remote from verbal assertions, but close to the structure of the world as humans conceive it" (1991, p. 207). Thus, despite their stated interest in deduction—it is the eponymous topic of their book—what they are really suggesting, here and elsewhere, is that our primary mode of reasoning *ex*duction. They are,

unfortunately, not consistent on this point. Consider, for instance, how J-L&B (1991) would account for our ability to reason about conditionals such as

(11) If the door is pushed, then the bucket will fall.

According to their mental models hypothesis, we make inferences from (11) by mentally representing at least some of the possible states of affairs that are consistent with this conditional. The possibilities consistent with (11) can be represented as follows[26]:

door pushed   bucket falls
¬ door pushed   bucket falls
¬ door pushed   ¬ bucket falls

A deduction, on their view, might involve the utilization of additional information in order to rule out some of these possibilities. Thus, if we also know that the bucket did not fall, we can rule out the first two possibilities. Because the only possibility remaining is one in which the door was not pushed, we may conclude that the door was not pushed.

Johnson-Laird and Byrne thus seem to believe that thinking the thought corresponding to a sentence like (11) involves representing possible states of affairs in a manner that is quite similar to how possible states of affairs are represented in the rows in the above table.[27] It is far from clear, however, that this set of "models" has a structure that is closer to the world than to (11). Notice also that it is the semantics of the logical terminology that bears the entire load on this view. It thus makes no difference whether or not the antecedent and consequent are in any way related. Thus, their proposal works the same for conditionals like

(12) If the apple can fly, then the donuts are stale.

Nor does it matter how the antecedent and consequent are (consistently) represented. In addition, thoughts involving negations are taken to be underwritten by arbitrary mental symbols that mean the same thing as "it is not the case that." All of this, in fact, comes dangerously close to the claim that mental representations take the form of terms in Mentalese! Claiming as much would not, at the very least, contradict the proposal just outlined.

Thus far, then, J-L&B's account makes monotonic reasoning look like a purely formal process: It has everything to do with the semantics of logical terms (e.g., 'and', 'or', 'not', 'all', etc.) and, in an important sense, nothing to do with the semantics of non-logical terms; it does not matter what the connectives (consistently) connect or what the quantifiers (consistently) quantify over. Indeed, as J-L&B acknowledge, their proposal bears important similarities to the purely formal method of truth-table analysis (1991, pp. 41–43). Clearly, however, engaging in monotonic inference through the use of either truth tables or the closely related sorts of spatial matrices that J-L&B use to describe the tenets of their model is a very far cry from the utilization of the cognitive counterparts of scale models. Thus, despite the suggestive name, the mental models hypothesis looks for all the world like the proposal that our everyday mode of reasoning is *de*ductive rather than *ex*ductive.

As I have already mentioned, however, J-L&B are not entirely consistent on this point. It is, for instance, *ex*duction that they seem to have in mind when they tout the affects of content on monotonic reasoning performance (1993, p. 324), when they explain the varying truth conditions of different sorts of conditionals (pp. 326, 327), and in the explanation that they offer for our ability to reason about spatial relationships (pp. 327, 328). What they appear to be searching for is *a single, unified account* of both this set of facts and our ability to reason monotonically in abstraction from specific, familiar contents (i.e., purely on the basis of the semantics of logical terms) (p. 324). Their mental models hypothesis supplies, they contend, just such an account.

Unfortunately, to the extent that they are correct, it is only because they equivocate over the word 'model'. That is, in order to account for our ability to reason solely on the basis of the semantics logical terms (e.g., 'and', 'or', 'not', 'all', etc.), they propose that we use mental models, by which they mean something akin to a spatial matrices whose rows represent (in some manner or other) possible states of affairs. At the same time, in order to account for the manner in which so-called factual knowledge affects monotonic reasoning performance, they propose that we utilize mental models, by which they mean the cognitive equivalents of scale models.

Their equivocation is clearly facilitated by the widespread, mistaken assumption that 'deductive' is synonymous with 'monotonic'. Since both of the forms of reasoning for which they are trying to account are monotonic, they, in accordance with fairly widespread psychological and philosophical practice, call both 'deductive', which gives the impression that a single, unified framework is being offered. However, once we distinguish between deduction and exduction, we see that J-L&B's model is not the single, unified model they claim it to be. Indeed, so long as they wish to maintain that the specific nature of the material being reasoned about can have a qualitative effect on monotonic reasoning, they will *need* to maintain that monotonic reasoning is bipartite. After all, deductive reasoning is formal and thus, by its very nature, is not sensitive (in the relevant ways) to the nature of the material being reasoned about.[28]

5.3.2.5 Exduction Is Fundamental

As was explained in chapter 4, deduction techniques inspired by predicate calculus are poorly suited to the task of explaining our knowledge of the consequences of alterations to the world. The mental models account of *deductive* reasoning sketched above fares no better. Specifically, in order to embody what we know about the consequences of various worldly alterations, a mental-model-driven deduction system would need to be in possession of countless sets of models (one set per possible alteration), and each set would have to include an explicit specification (perhaps as a *very* long conjunction in the left column of each row) of the innumerable conditions under which the connection between antecedent and consequent might fail to obtain. The point here is quite general: Deductive-reasoning-based accounts of our knowledge of the consequences of worldly alterations fall victim frame problem because they posit extrinsic representations of the consequences of worldly alterations (section 4.5). To put the point in a more pithy form, by abstracting from content at the outset that content has to be built back in later on.

Clearly, then, of the two forms of monotonic reasoning, it is a capacity for *ex*ductive, rather than *de*ductive reasoning, that would (pace Rips) best explain "how the inferences people draw manage to be truth preserving in a sufficiently large number of cases to make both science and practical affairs possible." Still, it has to be admitted that we do have some proficiency at purely deductive reasoning. For instance, most people probably can deduce (14) from (12) and (13).

(13) The apples can fly.
(14) The donuts are stale.

One would, therefore, like to know whether or not it is possible for this proficiency, however limited in importance it may be, to be explained without invoking sentences in a special thought language.

The problem here largely reduces to one of explaining what it means to think thoughts corresponding to sentences containing various connectives and quantifiers without claiming that those thoughts have sentential constituents corresponding to the logical terms in question. As you will recall, however, what proponents of Mentalese take to be the two most difficult cases in this regard are thoughts involving disjunctions and negations, and we have already seen that a Mentalese-free account of such thoughts is not very hard to imagine.

Even so, I think there is a great deal more to the story of monotonic reasoning than I have so far let on. In particular, I think that it is hardly open to dispute that we sometimes make deductions from particular sentences without ever thinking the corresponding thoughts. That is, sometimes we engage in deductive reasoning purely through the manipulation of "external" linguistic representations. There are, moreover, still other forms of monotonic reasoning altogether—most obviously, those involving the manipulations of expressions in mathematical notations.

5.3.3 Artificial Languages

There are, in fact, already many who criticize purely *internalistic* accounts of deductive reasoning such as those of Rips and J-L&B on the grounds that deductive reasoning is sometimes carried out on the basis of the form of externally represented premises (Bechtel and Abrahamsen 1991; Falmagne 1993; Green 1993; Savion 1993; Stevenson 1993). Savion suggests, for instance, that "there is no way of accounting, within the [mental model] theory's framework, for immediate 'automatic' inferences people generally make from formally stated premises" (Savion 1993, p. 364). Similarly, Bechtel and Abrahamsen argue that "the ability to manipulate *external* symbols in accordance with the principles of logic need not depend upon a mental mechanism that itself manipulates *internal* symbols" (1991, p. 173). They even back their proposal with a pair of connectionist models that learn, by developing the requisite pattern-recognition skills, to evaluate the validity of arguments and to supply missing information (e.g. premises).

All of this just reinforces what many of us already believe: that efficient formal symbol manipulation requires the detection of purely syntactic patterns. In sentential logic, for instance, it helps to know (and good teachers convey this fact to their students) that expressions of the form $\sim(p \lor q)$ can be quite useful, for they can easily be transformed into conjunctions of negations, and conjunctions are themselves easily "broken up" into their simpler constituents. After a good bit of practice, one tends to engage in this kind of heuristic thinking without ever considering what the symbol manipulations mean. Indeed, we saw in subsection 1.2.3.2 that before Turing 'computation' was defined in precisely this way—that is, as the sort of formal symbol manipulation that might be carried out by a human using only a pencil and paper and without any reliance on insight or ingenuity. Nor was 'computation', in this sense of the term, considered a mere abstract possibility. Turing himself directed a program during World War II in which multiple individuals were, unbeknownst to them, charged with implementing his decryption programs (Hauser 2002, p. 131). Thus, while the task of *learning* to carry out formal symbol manipulations may well be facilitated by an understanding of what the symbol manipulations mean, it is clear that (if used at all) this semantic ladder can be kicked away entirely once competence is attained.

Lending further support to this proposal, which hardly needs it, is De Renzi, Liotti, and Nichelli's (1987) examination of L.P., a 44-year-old Italian woman who had survived a bout of encephalitis. L.P. appeared to have intact grammatical abilities; she performed at normal levels when asked to detect grammatical errors, to read, to make lexical decisions, to write words and sentences to dictation, and even to disambiguate homophones. She did, however, show some semantic deficits: She had difficulty detecting sentences with semantic errors, naming objects, and pointing to named objects. L.P. did not present like a standard aphasic, however, for she had related, non-verbal semantic problems as well. For instance, she had trouble associating line-drawings of simple objects like tangerines with the appropriate colors, estimating relative weights of animals presented in line-drawings, and classifying animals according to whether they normally live in Italy. She also had a severe, and apparently quite unusual, form of retrograde amnesia that appeared to affect long-term semantic memory while leaving long-term episodic memory intact.[29] Even extensive cueing was, for example, insufficient to awaken in her any knowledge of Hitler or any facts at all concerning World War II. Nor did she have any recollection of the location or nature of the Chernobyl disaster, but she did remember that it had caused her plants to suffer.

Before her illness, and directly relevant to the point at hand, L.P. also happened to have been fairly knowledgeable about mathematics. Although she retained her high proficiency at purely formal, mathematical reasoning, L.P. seemed to have lost, or lost the ability to access, her knowledge of what the various symbol manipulations mean. De Renzi, Liotti, and Nichelli explain: "She correctly carried out not only the four mathematical operations with three and four numbers (e.g., 928×746 and $8,694/69$), but also percentage computations, sums of fractions, ranking of fractions, sums, divisions and multiplications of powers, and simple and quadratic equations. She remembered the rules for computing the area of a square, a triangle, a circle, a cylinder. It is noteworthy that although able to recognize powers and to operate upon them, she failed to answer even in vague terms the question of what a power or an exponent is, and was unable to draw a diamond, a cylinder, a trapezium." (1987, p. 579) The point, again, is just that once we have mastered the techniques of symbol manipulation, we can begin relying upon them with no thought whatsoever to what the manipulations mean.

The fact that formal systems can be dissociated from their underlying semantics in this way also means that these systems can be altered in ways that contravene the (at least somewhat) rigid constraints governing human thought processes. This is a fact that has been exploited a number of times in recent centuries, and the expert reaction to it has, not surprisingly, always been one of great ambivalence.

The developments that came just after the invention of analytic geometry provide what is perhaps the earliest illustration of this point (Detlefsen 2005). One thing that algebraists quickly discovered was that geometry proofs are often shorter and easier to construct than those that rely upon the old "synthetic" methods (e.g., the sort illustrated by the above spatial proof). At the same time, they also often require one to utilize negations and other expressions, such as $\sqrt{-1}$, that are difficult or impossible to comprehend. While these expressions might eventually be canceled out or squared, that they should be invoked over the course of a proof at all was considered objectionable by some. This was largely due to the fact that the incomprehensibility of such expressions made it difficult to determine whether or not trafficking in them was invariably truth preserving. It was for this reason that some upheld the view that geometrical reasoning should be considered suspect unless it is based on some form of imagery (ibid.). Playfair (1778), for instance, argued as follows:

The propositions of geometry have never given rise to controversy, nor needed the support of metaphysical discussions. In algebra, on the other hand, the doctrine of negative quantity and its consequences have often perplexed the analyst, and involved him in the most intricate disputations. The cause of this diversity in sciences which have the same object must no doubt be sought for in the different modes which they employ to express our ideas. In geometry every magnitude is represented by one of the same kind; lines are represented by lines, and angles by an angle, the genus is always signified by the individual, and a general idea by one of the particulars which fall under it. By this means all contradiction is avoided, and the geometry is never permitted to reason about the relations of things which do not exist, or cannot be exhibited. In algebra again every magnitude being denoted by an artificial symbol, to which it has no resemblance, is liable, on some occasions, to be neglected, while the symbol may become the sole object of attention. It is not perhaps observed where the connection between them ceases to exist, and the analyst continues to reason about the characters after nothing is left which they can possibly express; if then, in the end, the conclusions which hold only of the characters be transferred to the quantities themselves, obscurity and paradox must of necessity ensue. (Playfair, quoted in Detlefsen 2005, p. 265)[30]

Fortunately for the Western world, not everyone agreed. Berkeley, for instance, felt that when reasoning one's way from one comprehensible expression to another one need not wield comprehensible expressions throughout, and that even if one does that one need not attend to their meanings (Detlefsen 2005, pp. 267, 268).[31] Others took things even further. JohnWallis, for instance, recognized that symbols are in some sense more abstract than images, and argued on this basis that they *better* represent the invariant properties of the objects reasoned about than images, the latter of which necessarily included representations of contingent properties (ibid., p. 258).[32]

Remarkably, this highly charged debate still centered on whether it is permissible to use purely syntactic methods in order to reach conclusions about that which ultimately *could be imagined*; again, the debate was about the relative merits of synthetic and analytic techniques for doing *Euclidean* geometry. It would not be long, however, before it became clear that the syntax of analytic geometry can leave the nest of its parent semantics altogether and start a completely new life of its own. This is because, unlike the constraints governing our thought processes, the constraints governing the formation and manipulation of syntactic structures can be altered at will (though one does typically try to retain such properties as consistency). It seems that, until very recently, each time that this fact about formal systems has been fruitfully exploited, the incomprehensible nature of many of the resulting expressions has led, at the outset, to sharp resistance (in some cases, from the formal system's own inventor!), but later, when the practical benefits could no longer be ignored, reliance upon the resulting system would become accepted practice. [This, understandably, has generated many volumes of philosophical discussion.] The most recent (and, I would bet, final) illustration of this progression—namely, the advent, and reaction to, relativistic and quantum "mechanics"—will be discussed in chapter 9.

Clearly the manipulation of representations encoded in "external" languages constitutes its own unique method of engaging in monotonic reasoning. This method is used in the service of deduction, but it has also become the preferred method for mathematical reasoning. One naturally wonders (and many obviously have already) where formal mathematical reasoning fits in the taxonomy of reasoning presented here. It clearly belongs to the genus *monotonic*, but beyond that it may be sui generis. Be this as it may, I will show in chapter 6 that mathematical formalisms can, in conjunction with deductive formalisms, be used in the service of realizing *ex*ductive reasoning processes. This, it seems to me, is a profound result, and it is one that has the power to reshape a good deal of the landscape in mainstream cognitive science.

5.4 Conclusion

My goal in this chapter has been to convince you that, contrary to what you might have heard, it is possible, at least in principle, for cognitive science to do without Mentalese. This is because there is a great deal more to thinking than proponents of Mentalese have allowed. Mental representations surely play an important role in our thought processes, but they cannot go it alone. In fact, as we have just seen, sometimes they hold us back!

6 | From Metaphor to Mechanism

With the advent of modern programmable computers, proponents of the logic metaphor for mental representation and inference were at last able to provide a more literal, more mechanistic reading of their hypothesis. Proponents of the image and scale-model metaphors have, on the other hand, hitherto been unable to follow suit. Here I demonstrate, once and for all, that the image and scale-model metaphors can be reformulated in more literal, mechanistic terms. Specifically, I will show that desktop computers can, and that many of them do, harbor non-sentential images and models, and thus that brains may do the same. Along the way, I'll explain how the frame problem of artificial intelligence was ultimately solved.

6.1 Introduction

As I showed in chapters 4 and 5, the scale-model metaphor of representation and inference has a great deal to recommend it. It supplies an account of the representational productivity and the truth preservation that underlie our ability to behave in an unhesitating (once we get started) and effective manner in the face of countless environmental contingencies, and (unlike the logic metaphor) it is immune to the frame problem. It also surpasses the logic metaphor in its ability to account for the degree to which thought is, and is not, systematic. To be sure, the representations to which it adverts are unable to bear the entire burden of accounting for the non-attitudinal component of our thoughts about non-concrete domains, genera, and specifics, but on closer inspection it appears that no mere theory of mental representation should, for there is often a good deal more to thinking the thought that a sentence expresses than bearing an attitude toward a single representation. Any model of thinking ought to take into account, among other things, inter-representational mappings, representational manipulations, selective attention, and affect. Once these other processes are appealed to, the scale-model metaphor is far better able to bear its share of the explanatory load.

Despite the scale-model metaphor's many virtues, it is absolutely crucial that the metaphor be reformulated in more mechanistic terms, for, whatever other successes it might enjoy, this proposal will continue to be viewed with suspicion (and rightly so) until sense is made of the claim that brains might harbor representations of the appropriate sort. As we shall see, some think that basic facts about the brain and/or the nature of computation simply preclude the possibility of such a mechanistic reformulation. If these nay-sayers are right, then the preceding two chapters were entirely for naught. Also in jeopardy is the relevance of a vast collection of empirical results that have drawn upon, or been cited in support of, the hypothesis that humans harbor and manipulate non-sentential images and models. (See Brooks 1968; Segal and Fusella 1970; Shepard and Chipman 1970; Huttenlocher, Higgins and Clark 1971; Shepard and Metzler 1971; Kosslyn 1980; De Kleer and Brown 1983; DiSessa 1983; Gentner and Gentner 1983; Norman 1983; Johnson-Laird 1983; Fauconnier 1985; Marschark 1985; Garnham 1987; Farah 1988; Lindsay 1988; Perner 1988; Talmy 1988; Johnson-Laird and Byrne 1991; Langacker 1991; Glasgow and Papadias 1992; Hegarty 1992; Kosslyn 1994; Goldberg 1995; Janlert 1996; Barsalou, Solomon and Wu 1999; Schwartz 1999). That is to say, if it is true that the human brain cannot harbor such representations, then it would seem that, insofar as these good people have been trying to show, or assuming, that it does, they have been wasting their time. In light of these concerns, and because the logic metaphor has, in contrast, long since been reformulated in mechanistic terms, the wide following enjoyed by the resulting Mental Logic (ML) hypothesis (a.k.a. LOT hypothesis; see section 2.2) begins to make more sense.

In this chapter, I demonstrate, once and for all, that brains are the sorts of systems that are as capable of quite literally harboring and manipulating non-sentential images and models as sentences in Mentalese. I will show, moreover, that this claim is perfectly consistent with the further claim that the brain is, at some level, a computational system. In other words, and contrary to popular wisdom (see Block 1981; Pylyshyn 1984; Block 1990; Sterelny 1990; Fodor 2000), computational systems can, and many do, harbor non-sentential images and models. I will also show that such systems exhibit immunity to the frame problem and thus supply what is by far the best mechanistic model of the truth-preserving representational manipulations that underwrite everyday forethought in humans. In order to accomplish these lofty goals, I must take a few pointers from proponents of the ML hypothesis.

6.2 From Logic Metaphor to Logic Mechanism

A watershed in the history of the ML hypothesis was its maturation—thanks mainly to the advent of the modern programmable computer—from an explanatory metaphor into an explanatory mechanism. Once there existed other mechanisms whose activities could be explained, quite literally, in terms of syntactically structured representations and syntax-sensitive inference rules, it was relatively straightforward to advance beyond the mere logic metaphor to the much stronger claim that thought is *literally* effected by a mental logic.

The first step in this process was to appeal to multiple-realizability relationships as a means of distinguishing between the various levels of abstraction at which one might understand the operations of the human brain (subsection 4.3.4). This manner of distinguishing between levels of abstraction was borrowed, intact, from computer scientists who recognized that there are several distinct and independent levels at which the operations of a given computer can be understood (subsection 1.2.3). The highest, or most abstract, level is the level of the *algorithm*.[1] (See Bach 1993; Pylyshyn 1984.) A computer might, for example, output some statement of the form 'q' whenever it is given a pair of inputs of the form 'if p then q' and 'p'; it might, in other words, implement the rule of deductive inference known by logicians as modus ponens. However, knowing that this is the algorithm that a given computer computes does not tell us much about *how* it does so, for, corresponding to any given algorithm, there will generally be many different *effective procedures*—often thought of as recipes—that might be followed in order to attain the desired result. For instance, the input statements might be sent to a memory buffer, and the presence in the buffer of representations with these syntactic properties might trigger the activation of a syntax-sensitive inference rule which adds to the buffer new statements of the form 'not p or q' and 'not (not p)'. The presence of this new pair of representations might cause the activation of another rule which adds a statement of the form 'q' to the buffer and also causes this statement to be displayed on the computer monitor. This, however, is just one of the many effective procedures that can be followed in order to attain the same input/output function (i.e., to implement the algorithm). The usual way of putting this point is to say that algorithms are multiply realizable with respect to effective procedures.

The implementation of a given effective procedure in a programming language yields a *program*, and there often many different programming languages (e.g., C++, Basic, Lisp) that can be utilized in order to implement a given effective procedure. Effective procedures, in other words, are themselves multiply realizable with respect to programs. Likewise, programs can be implemented by many different sorts of computer architecture (e.g., there are different ways of configuring how information is entered into, and accessed from, memory). A particular architecture can, in turn, be instantiated through the use of many different materials (e.g., vacuum tubes, transistors, microchips).[2]

One important implication of the fact that the operations of a computer can be understood at any of multiple, independent levels of abstraction is that the properties characterizing the system when it is understood at a relatively low level of abstraction are often absent when what the system is doing is understood at a higher level, and vice versa. This is reflected in the language that we use to describe the goings-on at each level. For instance, although a given program might be described in terms of a distinctive set of function calls and executable statements, it may well be the case that neither the effective procedure that it implements nor the architecture by which is implemented ought to be described in this way. The mechanistic reformulation of the logic metaphor depends on this fact about the level-relativity of such properties. After all, when you look at the "brains" of a computer, you will not find any visible evidence that sentences are being manipulated in accordance with syntax-sensitive inference rules. Nevertheless, understanding what the computer is doing at the abstract level of effective procedures and programs requires knowledge of the syntactically structured representations it harbors and the syntax-sensitive inference rules it uses to manipulate them.

In addition to supplying an existence proof that the very general kind of processing proposed by proponents of the logic metaphor (i.e., the application of syntax-sensitive inference rules to syntactically structured representations) is mechanically realizable, early computer scientists showed how computational systems can be programmed to implement the very tenets of the logic metaphor that make it so desirable from an explanatory standpoint. Specifically, logic-based computational models of such cognitive processes as planning, semantic memory, and language comprehension (subsection 1.2.3.2) embody the characteristics of the logic metaphor that enable it to account for representational productivity, truth preservation, systematicity, and the representation of genera, specifics, and non-concrete domains. All of this lends considerable support to the claim that the principal tenets of the logic metaphor are mechanically realizable. Even further support is lent to this claim—though it doesn't help the larger cause—by the fact that logic-based models of planning are beset by the frame problem.

Over and above the fact that these computational systems supply existence proofs that the tenets of the logic metaphor are mechanically realizable, they form the basis for a powerful argument by analogy whose conclusion is that these tenets of the logic metaphor are also *neurally* realizable. As I noted in section 4.2, a good way of effecting the transition from explanatory metaphor to explanatory mechanism is to show that there are physical systems that are similar to the system of interest, that embody the chief characteristics of the explanatory metaphor, and that thereby inherit its precise virtues and limitations. Once again, at a very low level of abstraction, computers are not properly characterized as manipulating syntactically structured representations through the application of syntax-sensitive inference rules, but at the level of effective procedures and programs they *are* properly characterized that way. In other words, while their "brains"—which are best characterized at a low level in terms of a highly complicated circuitry—do not outwardly evidence the syntax-sensitive manipulation of sentential representations, this, as any programmer will tell you, is precisely what they do. Likewise, human brains—which are best characterized at a low level in terms of a highly complicated circuitry—do not outwardly evidence the manipulation of sentential representations, but it is nevertheless entirely possible that this is precisely what *they* do. Indeed, it seems possible, at least in principle, that brains implement effective procedures that are quite similar to those that constitute extant computational models of planning, deduction, semantic memory, language comprehension, and language production.[3,4]

6.3 A Dilemma

Although the logic metaphor is beset by the frame problem, its mechanistic reformulation is a major achievement. This achievement is, moreover, one that proponents of the image and scale-model metaphors have, despite their best efforts, been unable to match. In particular, no past or present attempt to effect such a mechanistic reformulation of either the image metaphor or the scale-model metaphor has managed to simultaneously (i) maintain consistency with basic brain facts and (ii) support a distinction between sentential and imagistic representations.

6.3.1 Competing Demands

The mere proposal that cognitive images and models are isomorphic with what they represent—which is essentially what Craik (1952) proposed—clearly fails to satisfy criterion ii. If the manipulation of representations —sentential or otherwise—is what enables us to plan out a course of attack in the face of various and often novel environmental contingencies, then there will *have* to be isomorphisms between the representations and what they represent.[5,6] (See also subsection 3.8.2.) For this reason, researchers have tried to find a more restrictive notion of isomorphism that might help to distinguish images and models from sentential representations.

A stronger sort of isomorphism, termed *structural* (Shepard and Chipman 1970) or *physical* (Palmer 1978), seems to fit the bill. As I explained in section 4.4, one thing that is distinctive about images and scale models is that their utility stems from their embodiment of many of the very same properties and relations as—and this is all that physical isomorphism comes to—what they represent. It is this strong kind of isomorphism that Stephen Kosslyn seems to have had in mind when he proposed, on the basis of the retinotopic organization of certain areas of visual cortex,[7] that "these areas represent depictively in the most literal sense" (1994, p. 13). The postulation of such physically isomorphic representations is, however, highly suspect for several reasons. To start with, the kind of retinotopy that we find in areas such as V1 is highly distorted because of the disproportionate amount of cortex devoted to the central portion of the retina (i.e., the fovea).[8] A square in the visual field is therefore not represented in the cortex by sets of neurons that lie in straight lines, nor, a fortiori, in parallel lines. Moreover, visual representation seems not to be effected through the activity of a single retinotopically organized neural ensemble. Rather, it involves the combined activity of a variety of systems that are, to a considerable extent, functionally distinct (Zeki 1976; Mishkin, Ungerleider and Macko 1983; DeYoe and Van Essen 1988).[9] Finally, the kind of retinotopy pointed out by Kosslyn is restricted to two spatial dimensions, and a two-dimensional representational medium will be incapable of harboring representations that are physically isomorphic in three dimensions (e.g., that are literally cubical). Nor, a fortiori, will it be capable of harboring representations that are physically isomorphic in both three-dimensional *and* causal respects. Crudely put, there are no literal buckets, balls, and doors in the brain.

The problem with the appeal to physical isomorphism is thus that it fails to satisfy criterion i. This problem has actually long been appreciated. For instance, as Shepard and Chipman note, "with about as much logic, one might as well argue that the neurons that signal that the square is green should themselves be green!" (1970, p. 2). Accordingly, they proposed the following notion of isomorphism that is a bit weaker than physical isomorphism, but also stronger than *mere* isomorphism: ". . . isomorphism should be sought-not in the first-order relation between (*a*) an individual object, and (*b*) its corresponding internal representation-but in the second-order relation between (*a*) the relations among alternative external objects, and (*b*) the relations among their corresponding internal representations. Thus, although the internal representation for a square need not itself be square, it should . . . at least have a closer functional relation to the internal representation for a rectangle than to that, say, for a green flash or the taste of persimmon." (ibid.) An appeal to second-order isomorphisms (also termed 'functional' isomorphisms (Palmer 1978)) would, Shepard and Chipman hoped, provide an alternative to physical isomorphism that both satisfies criterion i and is distinct enough from sentential accounts of representation and inference that each model will make different predictions, thus satisfying criterion ii.

A similar moderate account of isomorphism was discussed by Huttenlocher, Higgins, and Clark (1971). They had a particular interest in how subjects make ordering inferences (viz., those involving the ordering of three items along such dimensions as size, weight, and height) like this one:

Bill is taller than Chris.
<u>Chris is taller than Del.</u>
∴ Bill is taller than Del.

Huttenlocher et al. suggested that subjects might use representations that "are isomorphic with the physically realized representations they use in solving analogous problems (graphs, maps, etc.)" (ibid., p. 499). The essence of their proposal was that the mental representations that subjects form in order to solve such problems might function more like spatial arrays rather than like sentences. For instance, what seems distinctive about *external* sentential representations of three-term ordering syllogisms like the one above is that, because each premise is represented in terms of a distinct expression, terms that denote individuals must be repeated. On the other hand, when such inferences are made with the aid of external spatial arrays, the terms need not be repeated. For instance, one can make inferences about the taller-than relation on the basis of the left-of relation with the help of marks like

B   C   D

on a piece of paper. The introspective reports obtained by Huttenlocher et al. did suggest that subjects were constructing the functional equivalent of such a spatial array—subjects reported, for example, that terms were not repeated. Accordingly, Huttenlocher et al. suggested that subjects might be carrying out three-term ordering inferences on the basis of cognitive representations that function like actual spatial arrays and unlike lists of sentences.

Shepard and Chipman (1970) and Huttenlocher et al. (1971) were clearly after a notion of isomorphism that satisfies criterion i. Unfortunately, the solution they offered fails to satisfy criterion ii—that is, the problem with the appeal to functional isomorphism is that it does not clearly distinguish between sentential and imagistic representations. Huttenlocher et al. were among the first to suspect this: "It is not obvious at present whether any theory which postulates imagery as a mechanism for solving problems can or cannot, in general, be reformulated in an abstract logical fashion that, nevertheless makes the same behavioral predictions." (1971, p. 499) John Anderson is generally credited with confirming this suspicion by taking note of the possible tradeoffs that can be made between assumptions about representational structure and those concerning the processes that operate over the representations. He showed that the possible structure-process tradeoffs render sentential accounts flexible enough to handle virtually any behavioral finding. Most have since endorsed Anderson's thesis that it is, at least after the fact, always possible to "generate a propositional [i.e., sentential] model to mimic an imaginal model" (1978, p. 270). In other words, claims Palmer (1978), if you create the right sentential model it will be functionally isomorphic to what it represents in just the sense that a non-sentential model is supposed to be.

What might be considered another early attempt to supply a non-metaphorical reading of the proposal that humans harbor imagistic representations failed for similar reasons. Lee Brooks (1968) and Sydney Segal and Vincent Fusella (1970) investigated whether or not imagistic reasoning taps visual processing resources. The discovery of interference between visual imagery and visual perception, but not between imagery and auditory perception, was taken to indicate that imagery does depend upon visual processing resources. However, insofar as such findings are taken to support an alternative to syntactically structured cognitive representations, the claim that visual imagery depends upon the activity of visual processing resources suffers the same shortcomings as the notion of functional isomorphism. As Ned Block notes, because perceptual processing can, in principle, also be explained in terms of syntactically structured representations, "the claim that the representations of imagery and perception are of the same kind is irrelevant to the controversy over pictorialist vs. descriptionalist interpretation of experiments like the image scanning and rotation experiments" (1990, p. 583). (See also Anderson 1978; Fodor and Pylyshyn 1981.) In short, the claim that imagery utilizes visual processing resources fails to satisfy criterion ii.

Much of this controversy has centered on the proposal that humans harbor non-sentential mental images, but the very same set of challenges also face those who wish to supply a more literal reading of the scale-model metaphor. The crux of the problem is that it has proven exceedingly difficult to formulate these proposals in a way that is consistent with basic brain facts while at the same time distinguishing them from sentential accounts. These seemingly irreconcilable constraints continue to stymie those wishing to defend the existence of non-sentential cognitive images and models.

6.3.2 Are Computational Representations Sentential and Extrinsic?

In section 6.2, I explained how a more literal reading of the logic metaphor was supplied by showing that there exist other, non-biological (viz., computational) mechanisms that embody the central characteristics of that metaphor and which, for this reason, inherit its unique virtues and limitations. It seems worth considering, then, whether or not there are computational systems that can serve the same end for the image and scale-model metaphors. In other words, what we should like to find are computational systems that embody the unique characteristics of these metaphors and, thereby, inherit their unique virtues. It has been argued, however, that this way of attempting a mechanistic reformulation of the image and scale-model metaphors is a non-starter. The worry, in short, is that this approach fails to satisfy criterion ii. To see why, it is worth considering some of the arguments that have been leveled against Kosslyn's (1980) computational model of mental imagery and against similar models.

Kosslyn's model has several components. One is a long-term store that contains sentential representations of the shape and orientation of objects. These descriptions are utilized for the construction of representations in another component, the visual buffer, which encodes the same information in terms of the filled and empty cells of a computation matrix. The cells of the matrix are indexed by x,y coordinates, and the descriptions in long-term memory take the form of polar coordinate specifications (i.e., specifications of the angle and distance from a point of origin) of the locations of filled cells. Control processes operate over the coordinate specifications in order to perform such functions as panning in and out, scanning across, and mental rotation.

As I noted in section 4.4, one distinctive feature of "real" spatial matrix representations is that they embody some of the very same properties and relationships (viz., spatial ones) as things they represent. However, Kosslyn's computational matrix representations (CMRs) are not physically isomorphic with what they represent. Moreover, there is an argument to be made for the claim that CMRs are sentential representations. The crux of this argument is simple: Kosslyn's (1980) visual buffer representations are not "real" matrix representations, but *computational* matrix representations. To be sure, what modelers working with these representations typically see on the computer monitor are literal pictures, but the true representations of interest are located in the central processing unit (viz., in the random-access memory) of the computer running the model (Thomas 1999). Accordingly, the control operations responsible for executing representational transformations like rotation do not operate over the pictures that are displayed, but over the coordinate specifications that are stored in the computer's memory. Details aside, at a certain level of description, the computer is simply implementing a set of syntax-sensitive rules for manipulating syntactically structured representations; this is what computers *do*. It would seem, then, that the strongest claim be made regarding CMRs is that they *function* like images, and so this attempt (and all attempts) to effect a mechanistic reformulation of either the image or scale-model metaphor through an appeal to such computational models will apparently fail to satisfy criterion ii. Even worse, these systems implement rules which, at least in the case of rotation, might be construed as explicit specifications of the consequences of alterations (though it does bear mentioning that the alteration-consequence pairs in this case concern changes in the coordinates of particular cell contents). In other words, they seem to rely upon *extrinsic* representations, and one of the most important characteristics of the image and scale-model metaphors was the fact that "real" images and scale models are *intrinsic representations*. (See section 4.5.) It was, after all, this fact about images and scale models that accounted for their immunity to the frame problem.

The concerns raised in this section are very widely taken to preclude the possibility of a mechanistic reformulation of the image and scale-model metaphors that parallels the mechanistic reformulation effected on behalf of the logic metaphor. What is even more worrisome is that if, as some believe, the brain is itself a computational system in the strict, syntax-driven sense, then this would appear to place an insurmountable barrier in the way *any* attempt to effect a mechanistic reformulation of the image and scale-model metaphors, for, Fodor claims, "if ... you propose to co-opt Turing's account of the nature of computation for use in a cognitive psychology of thought, you will have to assume that *thoughts themselves have syntactic structure*" (2000, p. 13). Appearances can, however, be deceiving.

6.4 Intrinsic Computational Representations

Despite its intuitive appeal, there are seriously flaws in the line of argument just described. Indeed, even if the brain *is* a computational system in the strict sense, this will no more warrant the claim that thoughts are sentential than does the binary nature of the processes typically used to implement frame axioms entail that frame axioms are binary. In fact, and contrary to popular wisdom, there are good reasons for thinking that, at a high level of description, computational systems such as Kosslyn's (1980) really do harbor non-sentential, imagistic representations.

6.4.1 Models and Levels of Abstraction

To make good on the claim that computational systems can, and do, harbor such representations, one simply has to co-opt some of the conceptual apparatus long wielded by proponents of the ML hypothesis. In particular, one thing that all proponents of this hypothesis agree upon is that the descriptions of cognitive processing they offer are pitched at a very high level of abstraction. Earlier it was explained that the case for the mechanistic reformulation of the ML hypothesis hinges on the fact that, when a system can be understood at any of multiple, independent levels of abstraction, there can be properties characteristic of the lower levels that are absent at the higher levels, and vice versa (section 6.2). It has also been explained that the level that most interests ML theorists is, as one of its proponents puts it, "distinguished" by the fact that one finds, at that level, factual and counterfactual representations of the environment (Pylyshyn 1984, p. 95; see also sections 1.2 and 4.3).[10] At the next level down, what one might find instead are primitive constraints characterizing the implementation base for the relevant rules and representations.

Proponents of the image and scale-model metaphors can make use of a parallel set of considerations in order to effect a mechanistic reformulation of these hypotheses. To see how, recall, for starters, that the same criterion of levels individuation (i.e., multiple realizability) can be employed in order to individuate the distinct levels of abstraction at which the properties and behaviors of "real" images and scale models can be understood (section 4.4). Most relevant in the present context are the level of the representational medium (i.e., the implementation base for the images and models) and the level of the representations themselves. At the higher level, what one finds are factual and counter-factual representations of the environment (i.e., representations of various objects, properties, and relationships), while, at the next level down, one finds a different set of properties (e.g., a set of constraints governing the manner in which Lego blocks can be conjoined). This is just another case in point for the contention that the properties characterizing the system when it is understood at a relatively low level of abstraction are often absent when what the system is doing is understood at a higher level, and vice versa. All these lessons carry over quite directly into the computational realm.

6.4.2 Could Computational Images Be Non-Sentential and Intrinsic?

The distinction between real images and the media used to construct them is clearly paralleled in the case of computational images by a distinction between the images themselves and the media used to construct them, for the representation types are multiply realizable with respect to representational media. In other words, representation types (e.g., a computational image of the surface of my coffee table) transcend any particular set of sentences found at the implementation level. They are, for starters, multiply realizable by the *same* medium, because coordinates can and do change (as in rotation) without changing the non-relational properties of the representation itself. In addition, they can be realized by *different* media. For instance, instead of the filled and empty cells of a computational matrix, a representational medium might be used in which the representations are implemented by coordinate specifications of the vertices of a set of polygons.

Likewise, as with "real" images, the higher level is "distinguished" by the fact that one finds, at that level, factual and counterfactual representations of objects, properties, and relationships, while the implementation level is instead characterized by a set of primitive constraints governing the representational medium. For instance, in the case of Kosslyn's model, the medium is a set of memory registers which, in the simplest case, can be either filled or empty, that are indexed in terms of an x,y coordinate system, and whose contents can be altered in various ways. To be sure, this medium is best characterized in terms of the syntax-sensitive manipulation of extrinsic, syntactically structured representations.[11] Nevertheless, when a system is understood at a (relatively speaking) low level of abstraction, one often finds properties that are absent when the system is understood at a higher level of abstraction, and this leaves open at least the bare possibility that the representations constructed from a syntax-driven medium like the one just described are themselves not only non-sentential, but also intrinsic.[12] Let us see now why this is more than a bare possibility.

6.4.3 Why Computational Matrix Representations Are Really Non-Sentential and Intrinsic

Although the implementation base for CMRs is arguably sentential and extrinsic, CMRs themselves constitute intrinsic representations of inter-dimensional worldly constraints. (See section 4.5.) Notice, for instance, that once a medium for the construction and manipulation of CMRs has been created by imposing the relevant processing constraints, we find that the representations constructed from the "materials" supplied by this medium exhibit immunity to the frame problem, at least with regard to certain two-dimensional spatial relationships. As Pylyshyn is well aware, when it comes to predicting the consequences of alterations in two-dimensional spatial relationships "a matrix data structure seems to make available certain consequences with no apparent need for certain deductive steps involving reference to a knowledge of geometry. . . . Further, when a particular object is moved to a new place, its spatial relationship to other places need not be recomputed. . . ." (1984, p. 103) In other words, with regard to two-dimensional spatial relationships, the consequences of alterations to the representation *automatically* mirror the consequences of the corresponding alteration to the represented system. As it turns out, this effect is not restricted either to two spatial dimensions or to simple changes in relative location. For instance, media have been created—again, arguably through a reliance upon extrinsic representations—which supply an implementation base for representations that exhibit immunity to the frame problem with respect to three-dimensional alterations in both the location and orientation of a seemingly endless number of objects.[13] Glasgow and Papadias' (1992) model of mental imagery provides one case in point. Theirs, in fact, seems to be very close to the sort of system that Janlert (1996) had in mind when he suggested that the solution to the frame problem might be a kind of "mental clay." Though they hesitate to claim that their CMRs are non-sentential, Glasgow and Papadias note, much like Pylyshyn, that "although information in the spatial representation can be expressed as propositions [i.e., sentences], the representations are not computationally equivalent, that is, the efficiency of the inference mechanisms is not the same." They continue: "The spatial structure of images has properties not possessed by deductive sentential representations . . . spatial image representations . . . support *nondeductive* [see subsection 5.3.2 above] inference using built-in constraints on the processes that construct and access them." (1992, pp. 373, 374; emphasis added)

What Pylyshyn and Glasgow and Papadias are all pointing out is that, in the case of CMRs, there is no need to incorporate distinct data structures specifying how each of countless distinct objects will behave relative to one another following each of the consequently infinite number of possible alterations to their relative location and/or orientation. In other words, in the case of CMRs, the information is implicit in the representations that are created and so need not be made explicit; the consequences of alterations to the representations automatically mirror the consequences of the corresponding alterations to the world. Thus, although a description of the medium would involve talk of the extrinsic, rule-governed imposition of processing constraints (e.g., constraints on the use of memory registers), the representations implemented by that medium are, like the scale model of my living room described in subsection 4.4.1.2), intrinsic representations of the complex, inter-dimensional constraints concerning the relative shape, size, orientation, and location of objects.

Pylyshyn seems happy to concede that the relevant information is "implicit in the data structure" (1984, p. 103). He is, however, reticent to call CMRs *intrinsic*, reserving that term for the primitive constraints governing a representation's implementation base (i.e., properties of the functional architecture of some real or virtual machine or the primitive properties of some formal notation). Yet, Sterelny admonishes, "it obviously does *not* follow from the fact that a representational system is primitive that it is intrinsic: English could be hard-wired into my brain, but it is a paradigm of a non-intrinsic system" (1990, p. 623). In fact, a given functional architecture may itself be nothing more than a program (e.g., a Java virtual machine) run on some other kind of machine. It is, therefore, hard to imagine what useful notion of 'intrinsic' Pylyshyn might have in mind when he claims that the primitive properties of a notation or virtual machine are intrinsic.

It is not at the level of the primitive operations of an implementation base that we find intrinsic representations, but at the level of the representations *realized by* a given, primitively constrained implementation base. Part of what justifies this claim is the fact that certain constraints will be inviolable *at the representation level*—and, relatedly, the fact that a great deal of information will be implicit—given that the representations have been implemented by a particular kind of medium. As Pylyshyn notes, given that certain constraints have been imposed in order to implement a particular type of representational medium (e.g., a computational matrix), "a variety of spatial and metrical properties can be represented and changed and the logical consequences of the changes inferred without the need for symbolically encoded rules to characterize properties of space or other quantities (for example, Euclidean or metrical axioms)" (1984, p. 101). Pylyshyn goes on to explain: ". . . the greater number of formal properties built into a notation in advance, the weaker the notational system's expressive power (though the system may be more efficient for cases to which it is applicable). This follows from the possibility that *the system may no longer be capable of expressing certain states of affairs that violate assumptions built into the notation*. For example, if Euclidean assumptions are built into a notation, the notation cannot be used to describe non-Euclidean properties. . . ." (p. 105; emphasis added) Again, given that the representations have been realized through the use of a primitively constrained medium, certain constraints will be inviolable and a great deal of information will be implicit. Or, as Mark Bickhard (in correspondence) puts the same point, "properties and regularities are only going to be "intrinsic" at one level of description if they are built-in in the realizing level—or else they are ontologically 'built-in' as in the case of strictly spatial relationships in physical scale models." Scale models are intrinsic for the latter reason; CMRs are intrinsic for the former. Building certain constraints in at the implementation level—the level of the medium—has, in the case of CMRs, the effect of guaranteeing that the representations realized by that medium will respect complex, inter-dimensional, worldly constraints. Thus, the consequences of many types of alteration follow automatically and so need not be specified explicitly.

To recap: Just as in the case of production systems and scale models, we find that there are at least two levels of abstraction at which CMRs can be understood—that is, the level of CMRs themselves and the level of their implementation base. Moreover, not only do we find intrinsic representations at the former level and (arguably) extrinsic representations at the latter, but, just as frame axioms "are intended to represent something quite different from the expressions at the implementation . . . level" (Pylyshyn 1984, p. 94), so too are CMRs intended to represent something quite different from the expressions at *their* implementation level. That is to say, the former are "distinguished" by the fact that they are representations of objects and their relationships, while if the latter represent anything it is the numerical coordinates of filled and empty cells and the constraints governing the manner in which the coordinates of cells' contents are permitted to change.

6.4.4 Intrinsic Computational Models

Those who are interested in modeling forethought should consider the model of Glasgow and Papadias (1992) a major step in the right direction. It does, after all, harbor intrinsic representations of the complex, inter-dimensional constraints imposed by shape, size, orientation, and location, and thereby exhibits immunity to the frame problem with regard to this set of represented dimensions. However, a full-scale solution to the frame problem—that is, one that can account for the kind of inferential pro-ductivity that underlies the effective behavior exhibited by humans in the face of various environmental contingencies—requires intrinsic representations of interacting three-dimensional spatial *and* causal con-straints. There are, in turns out, computational systems that harbor such representations.

Such systems can be found in sectors of computer science that seem, as yet, a bit far removed from cognitive science proper. Specifically, virtual-reality models (VRMs), devised primarily for entertainment purposes, and finite-element models (FEMs), devised for engineering purposes, constitute intrinsic computational representations of interacting three-dimensional spatial *and* causal constraints.

6.4.4.1 Virtual-Reality Models: Ray Dream 5.02   Much like computa-tional matrix representations, virtual-reality models generally involve coor-dinate specifications (viz., in an *x,y,z* coordinate system) of modeling elements. Rather than the filled and empty cells of a matrix, however, the coins of the realm in virtual-reality modeling are two-dimensional poly-gons. Coordinate specifications are given for the vertices of polygons, and the surfaces of objects are represented in terms of the collective arrange-ment of (usually) many polygons, forming what is known as a *polymesh* (Watt 1993) or, more commonly, *wire-frame* representation (figure 6.1). As with matrices (whether spatial or computational) and scale-modeling media, the productivity of the polymesh medium varies with the number of basic modeling elements—in this case, with the number of polygons. In other words, the more polygons you have, the more different things you can represent.

While much VR modeling research has been focused on the interac-tions among the surface features of objects and various sorts of illumi-nation, VR modeling media have also been created that support the creation of representations in such a way as to enable predictions to be made concerning how countless objects, both familiar and novel, will behave relative to one another following each of a seemingly infinite

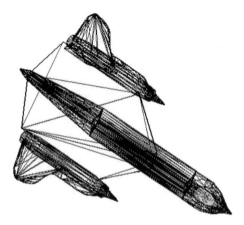

Figure 6.1
A polymesh representation of the SR-71 aircraft from the object library of Ray Dream Studio 5.0.2.

number of possible alterations. In other words, VR modeling media have been created that can be used to generate representations that exhibit immunity to the frame problem with regard to three-dimensional spatial alterations and a wide range of causal interactions. To illustrate this point, a set of models was created using an off-the-shelf program called Ray Dream Studio 5.02.

6.4.4.1.1 Representational and Inferential Productivity   Figure 4.1 depicted a problem that most intact humans would have little trouble solving. The goal is to pick the implement that, when pulled, will bring the banana within reach. If the scale-model metaphor for forethought is correct, humans construct the cognitive equivalent of a scale model of the problem and use this model to predict the consequences of pulling on each of the implements.[14] To show that, like scale models, VRMs exhibit the requisite powers of truth preservation, a model of the setup depicted in figure 4.1 was created. Having created the model, the location of each implement was made to change over time—that is, each was moved from the back of the table to the front. One would hope to find that the difference between moving the toothless rake and moving the T-bar (inverted rake) is that, in the latter case but not the former, the banana will come along for the ride. This, in fact, is precisely what transpired (figure 6.2).

The outcomes of these alterations to the representation mirrored what would happen in light of the corresponding alterations to the represented

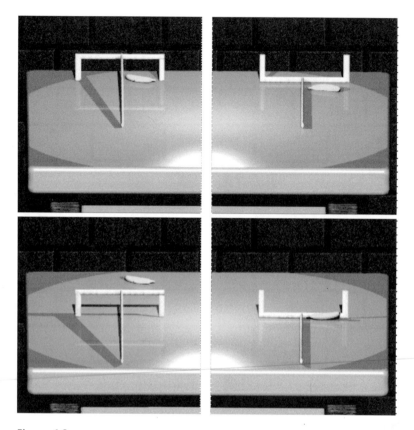

Figure 6.2
Truth preservation: effects of moving a virtual rake (top left: before; bottom left: after) and a virtual inverted rake (top right: before; bottom right: after).

system quite automatically, and thus without requiring any rules framed with respect to the properties of bananas, toothless rakes, or T-bars. In this case at least, the VRM exhibited powers of truth preservation similar to those exhibited by scale models. Of course, if VRMs truly have the same predictive powers as scale models, they will also exhibit immunity to the frame problem.

As I explained in subsection 4.3.5, one facet of the frame problem is the qualification problem. Unlike the representations implicated in frame-axiom systems, scale models do not suffer from the qualification problem because the predictions they license are implicitly qualified in countless ways. For instance, pulling on a scale model of the T-bar will cause a scale model of the banana to move within reach, provided that, among other

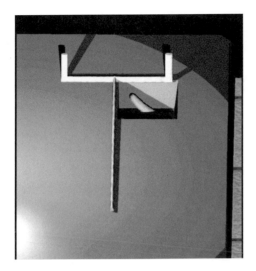

Figure 6.3
Qualified predictions: a banana falls through a hole in the table.

things, there is not a hole in the scale model of the table. VRMs also implicitly admit of such qualifications. To demonstrate that this is so, the model just described was altered in one simple respect: A hole was put in the table between the T-bar and the opening to the enclosure. Once again, the results were highly promising. Instead of the banana being carried along to the edge of the container, it fell through the hole (figure 6.3). Like our own predictions and the predictions generated through the use of scale models, predictions generated on the basis of VRMs are implicitly qualified.

The other main facet of the frame problem is the prediction problem. Scale models are also immune to this affliction, as are CMRs (at least when it comes to predicting the consequences of changes in spatial relationships). VRMs mark a major advance over the CMRs considered above in that they exhibit immunity to the prediction problem with regard to both three-dimensional spatial *and* causal relationships. To show this, a model of the setup depicted in figure 3.2 was constructed and altered in various ways.

The starting condition for the first alteration has the bucket resting atop the door and the ball positioned over the bucket. The only direct manipulation to the ensuing chain of events is that the door is opened rather abruptly. What we should like to find in this case is that the bucket and the ball fall to the floor, and this is exactly what transpired (figure 6.4). As

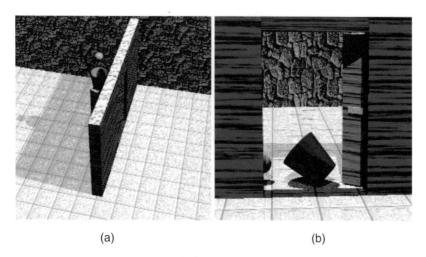

(a)   (b)

Figure 6.4
Predicting alterations: "shoving" a door that has a bucket and a ball resting atop it.
(a) Before. (b) After.

in the case of the previous model, we find that the side effects followed automatically, and without requiring any rules framed with respect to the properties of doors, buckets, and balls.

In a new scenario, the bucket is turned upside-down and placed over the ball. The bucket is then moved through the doorway and is subsequently raised. Were this alteration carried out with respect to either the actual door-bucket-ball setup or a scale model of this setup, we should expect to find the ball (or the scale model of the ball) underneath the bucket. This is also what we find in the case of the VRM (figure 6.5).

While it would be a straightforward matter to show that this same model is capable of predicting the consequences of any number of additional alterations, another way to demonstrate that VRMs are immune to the frame problem is to show that they satisfy the scalability criterion. As I have noted, Janlert (1996) suggested that a system not beset by the frame problem admits of incremental additions to the represented system without having an exponential effect in terms of what must be added to the representation. Scale models (not to mention CMRs) satisfy this scalability criterion, and so do VRMs. As a simple demonstration of scalability, a board was added to the door-bucket-ball model. To ensure that its presence was relevant, the board was placed broadside across the doorway (on the same side of the wall as the ball and bucket) and the bucket was used

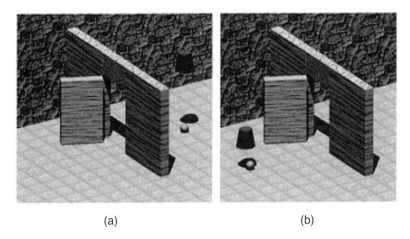

(a)   (b)

Figure 6.5
Predicting alterations: using a bucket to move a ball through a doorway. (a) Before.
(b) After.

to throw the ball on a relatively low trajectory through the doorway. Once again, what we would expect to happen in both the world and a scale model thereof took place in the VRM—that is, the ball bounced off the board instead of rolling through the door (figure 6.6).

Ray Dream models exhibit an impressive degree of immunity to the frame problem. Just as in the case of scale models, a VRM that represents the structure of the objects that make up some system, the basic properties of the materials from which they are constructed, and their relative sizes can be used to predict the consequences of countless alterations to that system. And just as in the case of scale models, there is no need to incorporate separate data structures corresponding to each alteration-consequence pair. These models do not, for instance, rely upon rules specifying that a ball inside an upright bucket will tend to move wherever the bucket moves, that a bucket set atop a pushed door will tend to fall to the floor, that T-bars can be used to drag bananas, and so forth. Instead, like scale models, the side effects of alterations to the VRM automatically mirror the side effects of alterations to the represented system. VRMs implicitly contain all the relevant information, so it need not be made explicit. In other words, while there is a case to be made that the medium used to implement VRMs involves extrinsic representations, the VRMs themselves constitute intrinsic representations of complex, inter-dimensional constraints.

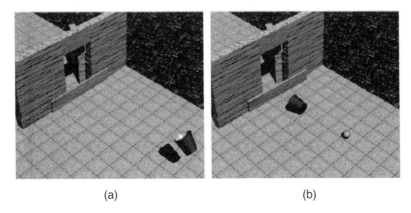

(a)   (b)

Figure 6.6
Satisfying Janlert's (1996) scalability criterion. A board is added to the model and the bucket is used to throw ball toward doorway. (a) Before. (b) After.

6.4.4.1.2 Psychological Plausibility   A viable model of forethought should be able to explain the ability to represent novel situations as they arise and the subsequent truth-preserving manipulation of those representations. For this reason, it is not unreasonable to construe Ray Dream 5.0.2 as model of forethought that enjoys a major advantage over models that rely upon frame axioms. The Ray Dream medium not only exhibits representational productivity, but the models constructed from this medium exhibit *inferential* productivity (see subsection 4.3.5) with regard to three-dimensional spatial alterations and a wide range of causal interactions. There are, however, a few complications worth mentioning.

To start with, one expects that two objects stacked in a positive-gravity environment will eventually come to rest. With Ray Dream models, however, when objects are placed atop one another they never settle entirely.[15] Instead there is always a small degree of oscillation. This was particularly apparent when the ball containing the bucket was set atop the door. The two objects never quite settled, and when they interacted on the way to the floor their motions sometimes appeared a bit jerky and artificial. It should be borne in mind, however, that in every trial the outcome of pushing the door open was basically the same: Both the ball and the bucket fell to the floor.

Another worry about the Ray Dream models (one that partly explains the previous concern) is that the outcomes of collisions are not determined by such factors as mass, momentum, or degree of rigidity/springiness. For instance, the simple bouncing behavior of the ball in the second model was not a consequence of a specification of such underlying factors as the storage and release of energy due to compression. Instead, there is a primitive rebound setting that determines how bouncy the ball is. Although this may seem like a shortcoming, there is (somewhat surprisingly) a case to be made that something similar occurs when physics-naive individuals predict the outcomes of collisions.[16] For instance, in a seminal study conducted by Chi et al. (1982), novices and experts were asked to categorize a set of physics problems. Novices were found to categorize problems on the basis of their surface features, while experts categorized them on the basis of the underlying physical principles they exemplified. Even more to the point, DiSessa (1983) examined the manner in which physics-naive individuals understand the nature of bouncing behavior, and the results were similar. DiSessa discovered, for instance, that one physics-naive individual, M, lacked an accurate understanding of the underlying basis for bouncing behavior. This property seemed, for M, to be a primitive that she discovered through experience and in terms of which she subsequently explained and predicted the behavior of objects in the world. In fact, even physics experts were found in certain cases to rely upon high-level primitives that effectively simulate the consequences of low-level principles. This, again, is not entirely unlike how the Ray Dream modeling medium supports predictions regarding physical interactions. For instance, while objects in the model do not undergo compression, the primitive constraints of the medium guarantee that they behave in many ways as if they did. As a result, these models (like those harbored by physics-naive individuals) do a reasonable job of generating the kinds of predictions required in order to respond appropriately in the face of various environmental contingencies—for example, those that include T-bars, bananas, buckets, doors, and balls.[17]

Construed as a model of human forethought, then, the workings of Ray Dream 5.02 seem consistent with some important empirical findings regarding how it is that humans predict the behavior of physical systems. Indeed, according to the picture of forethought painted by naive physics researchers, individuals create cognitive models of the world and "run" these models in order to predict and explain the behavior of various physical systems. (See Chi et al. 1982; De Kleer and Brown 1983; DiSessa 1983; Larkin 1983; Norman 1983; Schwartz 1999.) There is, moreover, widespread support among such researchers for the claim that these internal models of the world are non-sentential.

On the other hand, although the VRMs implemented by the Ray Dream modeling medium do enjoy a certain amount of psychological plausibility, the fact that objects are invariably represented as rigid means that the predictive powers of these VRMs are limited in ways that are psychologically *im*plausible. To be sure, many behaviors that result from the deformable nature of certain bodies (e.g., when balls bounce, fly off on a particular trajectory when struck, or are wedged in the bottom of the bucket) can be simulated with Ray Dream, but many others (e.g., what happens when an inflatable ball is stabbed with a knife) cannot be. There are, however, other computational modeling media that harbor representations—*finite-element models* (FEMs)—of the appropriate sort.

6.4.4.2 Mechanical Engineering and Finite-Element Models For decades, the methods of finite-element modeling have been under development for use in the engineering disciplines (for an overview, see Adams and Askenazi 1999). Like VRMs, FEMs are constructed from polymesh—that is, objects are represented in terms of a number of polygons (called *elements*) whose vertices (called *nodes*) are specified in terms of their coordinates. One major difference between FEMs and Ray Dream models is that the relative positions of the nodes constituting an object are not fixed in the former, but can change in ways that enable one to model the behavior of deformable bodies.

To provide a simple illustration of finite-element modeling, a two-dimensional finite-element model of a sheet of material (which is fixed in place by four supports at its base) was constructed with a program called PlastFEM (figure 6.7). As with other FEMs, how the material behaves under various conditions can be modeled by specifying the manner in which nodal coordinates can change, simulating the application of forces to specific nodes, and then running the model in order to see how the consequences play out. For example, how the sheet behaves in light of a causal interaction with a sharp object was modeled by applying a force to a single

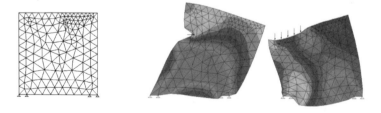

Figure 6.7
Modeling the effects of loads applied to a sheet of material. Shading indicates stress levels.

node. Likewise, how the sheet holds up in the face of a collision, of equal total magnitude, with a blunt object (in this case from a different direction) was determined by distributing the same total force across a larger set of nodes.

While the models created with PlastFEM exhibit inferential productivity with regard to the effects of loads applied to two-dimensional deformable bodies (of any shape), the same basic techniques can be scaled up in order to model the effects of collisions between, and numerous other factors affecting the behavior of, three-dimensional deformable bodies. For instance, acceleration and rotation can be modeled by distributing forces, in the appropriate directions, to some or all of the nodes constituting a model; ambient pressure can be modeled in terms of a load applied to the entire surface of an object; and the effects of thermal expansion and contraction can also be modeled by applying forces to nodes (Barton and Rajan 2000). Nor does the power of finite-element modeling method end there. As Barton and Rajan (2000) explain, this method "can solve a wide variety of problems, including problems in solid mechanics, fluid mechanics, heat transfer and acoustics, to name a few." Moreover, the techniques for modeling each sort of problem have been integrated into general-purpose modeling systems such as MSC.visualNastran and LS-DYNA. Not surprisingly, such systems are widely used in the testing of prototypes for air bags, circuit breakers, pyrotechnic devices, and countless other novel mechanisms.[18] They are also used in order to determine whether or not particular theories—concerning, among other things, spinal cords, neurons, and tectonic plates—actually explain observed phenomena (i.e., they function as the kind of intellectual prosthetic, described in chapter 1) and implement the tenets of the Model model of explanation first introduced in chapter 3 and discussed at length in chapter 8. FEMs can be used, in short, in order to make inferences concerning the consequences of countless alterations to countless novel systems.

As with scale models and VRMs, there is no need in the case of FEMs to incorporate separate data structures that represent the consequences of each possible alteration to a set of items. Instead, like scale models, the side effects of alterations to the FEM will automatically mirror the side effects of alterations to the represented system. Because all the relevant information is implicit in the FEMs that we construct, it need not be made explicit. FEMs, in other words, constitute intrinsic representations of the complex, inter-dimensional constraints imposed by size, shape, location, orientation, velocity, and numerous physical forces. FEMs, in short, exhibit full-blown immunity to the frame problem.

One big difference between FEMs and the representations underwriting human forethought is that—due in part to what amounts to a tremendous short-term memory capacity and in part to the fact that the principles built into their realization bases are inspired by our best scientific characterizations of the principles underlying the behavior of macroscopic objects—the predictions generated through the use of FEMs are generally far more accurate than those made "in the head" by humans. From a psychological modeling standpoint, then, it may be an advantage of Ray Dream models that they rely upon inaccurate, though oftentimes useful, characterizations of the physical principles underlying the behavior of everyday objects.[19] An advantage of FEMs, on the other hand, is that they support predictions concerning the behavior of deformable bodies. The truth with regard to human forethought may, therefore, ultimately lay somewhere in-between Ray Dream models and finite-element models.

6.5   The Intrinsic-Cognitive-Models Hypothesis

As I noted in section 6.2, a mechanistic reformulation of the logic metaphor was supplied by showing that there exist computational systems that embody, at a high level of abstraction, the central characteristics of the metaphor and, thereby, inherit its explanatory virtues and limitations. A similar set of claims can now be made with regard to the image and scale-model metaphors.

6.5.1   The Solution to the Frame Problem

We have already seen that the ML approach to modeling forethought is not just computationally expensive, it is computationally intractable. At a high, "distinguished" level of abstraction, models of cognition such as those constructed using production-system architectures utilize syntactically structured representations and syntax-sensitive inference rules whose constituents represent everyday objects such as balls, buckets, and doors, as well as their myriad properties and relationships. This approach does, of course, accord nicely with the tenets of the ML hypothesis, which also posits, at a high, "distinguished" level of abstraction, representations of this very sort. Unfortunately, this approach to modeling forethought necessitates rules specifying how each of countless objects, both familiar and novel, will behave relative to one another following each of the (consequently) infinite number of possible alterations. Because these separate data structures are required in order to predict the consequences of each possible alteration—in other words, because the information has to be made explicit—the approach is beset by the frame problem.

In contrast, the methods of virtual-reality modeling and finite-element modeling provide a computationally tractable means of modeling human forethought. This is because, instead of requiring a specification of how each of countless objects will behave relative to one another in light of countless possible alterations, the ontology is reduced to a very simple set of building block types and permissible building block behaviors. The representational medium that results can be used to construct representations of countless objects such that the consequences of alterations to these representations will automatically mirror the consequences of the corresponding alterations to the represented system. In other words, *just like scale models*, these representations implicitly contain all the information needed to predict the consequences of countless alterations to their represented systems. Thus, the information need not be represented explicitly with the help of countless, distinct data structures, and it is for this very reason that the approach satisfies Janlert's (1996) scalability criterion. Just as in the case of scale models, a modest addition to the represented system requires only a modest addition—that is, a finite set of additional building blocks—to the representation. This new representation will also implicitly contain all the information needed to predict the consequences of countless alterations to the new system.

6.5.2 Intrinsic Representations at a High, "Distinguished" Level

Another very important similarity between computational models and scale models is that, in each case, a distinction can be made between the models themselves and the media from which they are constructed such that talk of the former is pitched at a higher level of abstraction than talk of the latter. To be sure, the medium used to implement a given computational model might best be understood in terms of the application of syntax-sensitive inference rules to syntactically structured representations. Such rules and representations specify the coordinates of polygon vertices and constrain the manner in which they are permitted to change. It may, therefore, be appropriate to describe these media as relying upon extrinsic, sentential representations—although it does bear emphasizing that the representations at issue are mathematical formalisms whose variables take on continuous numerical values and which thus bear only a superficial resemblance to traditional frame axioms. Be this as it may, it is only at the high level of the models implemented by such media—a level that is "distinguished" by the fact that one finds, at that level, representations of various objects, properties, and relationships—that we find intrinsic representations of complex, inter-dimensional constraints. This is just another case in point of how, when a system is understood at a low level of abstraction, one often finds properties that are absent when the system is understood at a higher level of abstraction, and vice versa.

6.5.3 Systematicity and the Need for Extra-Representational Resources

Just like scale models and the world itself, computational representations such as VRMs and FEMs admit of certain systematic variations. For instance, an FEM can represent not only that the cat is on the mat, but that the mat is on the cat, and so forth. According to ML theorists, systematicity is to be accounted for by the fact that the systematically related thoughts are made of the same parts and that these parts can be rearranged in accordance with the syntactic constraints of Mentalese. While the systematicity exhibited by VRMs and FEMs can also be explained in terms of the rearrangement of parts, the manner of their rearrangement is about as sentential as the rearrangement of the parts of a scale model is. More importantly, if humans use representations that are like VRMs and FEMs and unlike sentences and frame axioms, we can make sense of the fact that language is *more* systematic than thought. (Recall section 4.4.)

We also saw (in section 5.2) that the representations adverted to by the scale-model metaphor are, *in and of themselves*, unable to bear the entire load when it comes to explaining the human ability to think about non-concrete domains, genera, and specifics. Nor, and for the exact same reasons, can the computational images and models that we have been considering in this chapter bear this entire load. For instance, although the term 'triangle' represents all triangles, a CRM of a triangle is just like a picture of a triangle in that it is too specific to represent all triangles, whether right-angled, obtuse, or acute. Likewise, while humans are able, in thought, to single out specific properties of specific objects, neither scale models, VRMs, or FEMs are, by themselves, capable of doing this. For instance, while I can express my belief that Glenn's SUV is green in words, it is not obvious how either a scale model or an intrinsic computational model could convey that same message, for the same model will generally convey lots of other information.[20]

Proponents of the ML hypothesis have been fond of pointing out that a distinguishing feature of sentential representations (i.e., relative to images and scale models) is that they face no such limitations. Interestingly enough, however, these are the same individuals who so often claim that computational systems are only capable of harboring sentential representations (Fodor 1981; Fodor 2000; Pylyshyn 1984; Sterelny 1990). This, I think, presents a very uncomfortable dilemma for these individuals: They cannot, on the one hand, contend that these different representational profiles distinguish non-sentential images and models from sentential representations and, on the other hand, contend that computational models that have the exact same representational profiles as the former are nevertheless sentential. One of these two claims is going to have to be abandoned. As the intuitions behind the former are difficult to counteract, and the intuitions behind the latter have here been undermined, it seems that the appropriate course of action is to abandon the claim that computational systems are only capable of harboring sentential representations.

One mustn't forget, however, the important conclusion reached in chapter 5: *No* mere theory of mental representation should be charged with bearing the entire explanatory load when it comes to accounting for our ability to think about non-concrete domains, genera, and specifics, for there is often a good deal more to thinking the thought that a sentence expresses than bearing an attitude toward a single, simple representation. Any plausible model of these kinds of thoughts will need to take into consideration the possible roles played by a variety of extra-representational cognitive abilities.

6.5.4 The ICM Hypothesis

The foregoing considerations converge on the hypothesis that humans harbor and manipulate specific, intrinsic cognitive models of complex, inter-dimensional, worldly constraints—or, for the sake of brevity, the ICM hypothesis. The hypothesis has been sufficiently distinguished from the ML hypothesis, and it is also compatible—for the same reasons that the ML hypothesis is compatible—with basic brain facts (i.e., criteria i and ii in section 6.3 have been satisfied). It is, moreover, robust enough to withstand the possibility, however remote, that the brain is a computational system in the strictest sense. To parallel the arguments made by proponents of the ML hypothesis, we may now say that while brains are characterized by a complex circuitry and fail to outwardly evidence the harboring or manipulation of non-sentential, intrinsic models of complex, inter-dimensional, worldly constraints, perhaps, at a high and "distinguished" level of abstraction, they quite literally do harbor and manipulate such representations. This mechanistic reformulation of the image and scale-model metaphors clearly has favorable ramifications for behavioral research mentioned at the outset of this chapter that either assumes, or purports to show, that humans harbor and manipulate non-sentential cognitive representations.

6.5.5 Sundry Psychological Considerations

There are, admittedly, some properties that have, not unlike the demonic homunculi of Selfridge's (1959) Pandemonium model (section 4.2), been lost in the transition from explanatory metaphor to explanatory mechanism. One is physical isomorphism (section 4.4). This is clearly a good thing given that the brain no more harbors physically isomorphic models (PIMs) of doors, buckets, and balls than it (at least generally speaking) harbors demons.

Another difference between PIMs and such computational models as CMRs, VRMs, and FEMs has to do with the nature of constraints governing the behavior of their primitive modeling elements. While the constraints governing the behavior of physical building blocks are fixed by the laws of physics, the constraints governing the behavior of computational building blocks are primitive but not nomological. In some ways the difference is irrelevant. After all, *given* that the representations have been realized through the use of a particular, primitively constrained modeling medium, there will be certain constraints on the behavior of the representations that are (as I explained in subsection 6.4.3) inviolable and, relatedly, a great deal of information will be implicit. On the other hand, in the case of PIMs, if one wishes to know how an object would behave were it made from a different material, one will (generally) need to construct an entirely new model using that other material. In the case of computational models, however, there are certain properties of the building blocks that can be modified simply by changing the values of variables in the equations describing how those building blocks behave. One can, in effect, change what an object is made of without having to construct that object anew, though the option of constructing the object anew does remain open. Presuming, then, that the ICM hypothesis is correct, it is still an open question whether or not humans create representations of the world anew when, for instance, they discover that their default assumptions were incorrect.

One outstanding worry about non-sentential representations that bears further scrutiny has to do with Pylyshyn's (1981, 1984) cognitive penetrability criterion. Pylyshyn claims that if our cognitive representations of spatial and causal properties are influenced by our beliefs in logically coherent ways, then this will provide sufficient warrant for concluding that the representations involved are sentential in character—for logical coherence, Pylyshyn argues, can be explained only through the postulation of a mental logic. For instance, suppose it turns out that our predictions concerning the behavior of the system depicted in figure 6.4 differ—and they almost certainly will—depending upon whether we are told that the ball is a volleyball (scenario 1) or a bowling ball (scenario 2). If we adopt the cognitive penetrability criterion, we will be forced to conclude that this difference can only be accounted for by sententially structured cognitive representations. Adopting this criterion, however, also commits us to the absurd claim that scale models are sentential. After all, if I construct a different scale model of the setup depicted in figure 6.4 depending upon whether I believe scenario 1 or 2, the predictions generated by those models will clearly be sensitive to my beliefs in logically coherent ways. This consideration—not to mention the fact that we have already seen how monotonic reasoning can be accounted for without postulating a mental logic—suffices to rid us of the dubious cognitive penetrability criterion once and for all.

On a related note, although the present hypothesis clearly derives great strength from the fact that it can lay claim to the idea that ICMs contain a tremendous amount of implicit information, these same representations would also be fully capable of representing information *explicitly*. For instance, the very proposal that we make alterations to our ICMs in order to see how they will play out makes reference to the *explicit* representation of those alterations.[21] In other words, these explicit representations of alterations are not demanded by the models but are imposed upon them. Understanding this helps us to see how the present account also leaves room for the explicit representation of two other forms of information—namely, derived principles and induced principles.

A study by Daniel Schwartz and John Black (1996) provides a nice illustration of the former. Their subjects were able to represent—arguably on the basis of what I have been calling *exduction* and what they call *simulation*—the fact that when one gear is rotated, a connecting gear will always rotate in the opposite direction. Their subjects were, however, also able to utilize their explicit knowledge of this principle rather than relying upon the more cognitively demanding exduction process from which it was derived. In other words, they were able to image *that*, without imagining *why*, the second gear in a series rotates in the opposite direction to that of the drive gear. This kind of explicit representation of derived principles will clearly have some costs associated with it (i.e., it will diminish the overall inferential productivity of the ICM), but it might also be very useful (e.g., if one wishes to know with little time or effort what would happen in the larger system affected, via the turning of the second gear, by the turning of the first). The explicit representation of *induced* principles is permitted by ICMs (and by scale models for that matter) in the same manner as the explicit representation of alterations and derived principles.

6.5.6 Cognitive Models and Non-Computational Implementation

I have provided (in sections 6.4 and 6.5) a mechanistic reformulation of the scale-model metaphor that parallels the one effected on behalf of the logic metaphor. The appeal to computational systems not only provides an existence proof that the kind of processing at issue is mechanically realizable, but, given the superficial similarities between computers and brains, supports an argument by analogy whose conclusion is that brains too might literally engage in this very sort of processing. One nice thing about basing these arguments on what we know about extant computational systems is that it renders the ICM hypothesis robust enough to withstand the eventual discovery that the brain is, at some level, a computational system in the strict (i.e., syntax driven) sense. I don't think we will ever discover this. The ICM hypothesis is, fortunately, also robust enough to withstand this eventuality. What this chapter provides is a recipe for implementing intrinsic representations of complex, inter-dimensional, worldly constraints through lower-level, extrinsic means. I suspect that this recipe has been followed in the human case but with the following departure from the computational case: The representational medium is, in the case of the former, best understood in terms of the kinds of parallel constraint-satisfaction processes at which neural networks excel rather than in terms of sentences and inference rules. This is, however, a story for another day.

6.6 Conclusion

It should come as no surprise that some insight into the workings of the human mind should come from the consideration of virtual-reality and finite-element models. After all, the point of creating scale models (and, more recently, computational models) has always been to generate predictions concerning the behavior of some target system, and a similar capacity for predictive inference may well be one of the most distinctive features of human cognition. Indeed, if the ICM hypothesis is correct, then, at a suitably high level of abstraction, there are few differences among scale models, computational models, and cognitive models.

7 | Models of Explanation

In this chapter, I first defend the proposal that cognitive science might have something to contribute to the study of explanation. I then go on to describe the many shortcomings of the Deductive-Nomological model, the model of explanation endorsed by most philosophers of mind. I close with a brief discussion of the shortcomings of the two main alternatives to the D-N model.

7.1 Introduction

At the end of chapter 2, I claimed the following:

First, although explanation in cognitive science is not simple law subsumption, this is how explanation is portrayed by what is, for the moment, the only remotely viable model of explanation. Philosophers can therefore be forgiven, to *some* extent, for continuing to think of cognitive science in terms of laws. Second, although cognitive science as a whole neither needs to be nor is committed to either the general computational theory of mind or the more specific LOT hypothesis, there are good reasons why many individuals (mainly philosophers) are so committed. Indeed, we shall see that these two sets of issues are intimately related, and that the kind of shift in research program that I envision for the philosophy of mind will require (i) supplanting the LOT hypothesis with a better model of truth preservation and (ii) using this model to formulate an anomological theory of explanation.

Having completed the first part of this project, I now turn to the second. By the end of the next chapter I will have offered up a compelling defense of a model of the sorts of explanations formulated both in the special sciences (e.g., cognitive science) and in everyday, non-scientific contexts.

7.2 Cognitive Science and the Philosophy of Science

The central pillar of the Enlightenment, and the very antithesis of Scholasticism, was the idea that we humans have it within ourselves to discover new facts about the world. The appearance of science (as we now know it) was among the developments that allowed the former to overthrow the latter. (See section 1.1.) Recognizing this, Enlightenment thinkers spent a good deal of time trying to understand from whence the special powers of science issue. So began the philosophy of science, though it would not be until the twentieth century that we would begin to get things right. (See section 2.6.)

In a more recent development, some psychologists and sociologists have also begun to investigate science. To its detriment, I think, recent work along these lines—in particular, research in the psychology of science, the sociology of science, and science studies—has been almost exclusively concerned with topics such as creativity, discovery, conceptual change, and collaboration. In contrast, philosophers of science (at least, those who have not been overly swayed by Kuhn) have traditionally been more interested in answering questions that have a clearer normative dimension to them. These include questions about how scientists ought to reason, about what makes some explanations better than others, and about the difference between scientific and pseudo-scientific explanations.

The normative character of these questions has led some to believe that science cannot itself—save, that is, by supplying case studies—aid us in answering them. Science, after all, can only tell us how things are, not how they ought to be. (See section 1.3.) Even so, a cognitive science of science can take the justificatory activities of scientists as its object of investigation just as easily as it can the non-justificatory ones. More specifically, each of the normative questions raised above has, either directly or indirectly, to do with the nature of scientific reasoning, and reasoning is the epitome of a cognitive process. Thus, philosophers of science must take the deliverances of cognitive science seriously; it would be foolhardy for philosophers to ignore what cognitive science has to say about a topic (i.e., reasoning) that sits at the very center of their inquiry. This is not to say that cognitive science can, or should, *replace* the philosophy of science. As we shall see, an appreciation for the kinds of models and constraints that issue from both cognitive science and from "armchair" philosophy facilitates an unprecedented degree of progress regarding explanation—a topic that philosophers of science of *all* persuasions take to be of prime importance.

There are also those who flatly deny that there is anything psychological about explanations. Wesley Salmon (1984), for instance, claims that explanations involve relationships between objective facts (viz., the facts to be explained and the facts that explain them). He contrasts his own view with one according to which explanations consist in the overcoming of "psychological uneasiness" caused by some event. His concern about the latter view is that "not only is there danger that people will feel satisfied with scientifically defective explanations; there is also the risk that they will be unsatisfied with legitimate scientific explanations" (ibid., p. 13). For example, if we accepted that explanations consist in the overcoming of psychological uneasiness, then we would also have to accept that someone has a legitimate explanation if they happen to be intellectually satisfied with the claim that a particular storm was caused by the sinking barometric reading that preceded it. Likewise, if we accepted the overcoming-uneasiness account, we would also have to allow that it is perfectly legitimate for one who is intellectually ill at ease with all non-animistic explanations to summarily reject them. Considerations such as these lead Salmon to conclude that the only genuine explanations are not subjective, but rather involve relationships between objective facts.

One reason I am not willing to go along with Salmon on these points is that, on his view, it makes no sense to say that there can be good and bad explanations, or that there can ever be multiple, competing explanations for a given event. There is, on Salmon's view, always just one explanation; it is *the* explanation. Nor, therefore, does it make sense on his view to say that we sometimes engage in a process of figuring out which, of the multiple explanations on table, constitutes the *best* explanation for an event.[1] This is a process, however, that clearly lies at the very heart of the scientific enterprise. What is science, after all, if not one great big abductive melee? (See sections 2.6 and 5.3.) Indeed, rather than leaving room for this basic fact about the scientific enterprise, Salmon's view instead commits one to such absurdities as the claim that a "defective explanation" is not an explanation.

Despite these concerns, I believe that Salmon's anti-psychologistic stance does reflect *one* common manner of speaking. We do often talk of *the* explanation for some event or regularity, and when we do the kinds of metaphysical commitments that Salmon makes explicit may be in play. There is, however, clearly another manner of speaking—in particular, we often talk of *explaining* events and regularities, of *having* explanations, of defective explanations, and of the assessment of multiple, competing explanations. Suffice it to say, then, that it is these latter senses of the term that most interest me. In particular, what I will be seeking is an answer to the question: What is going on, cognitively speaking, when one *has* an explanation. This project is in many ways akin to the search for an answer to the question: What is involved, cognitively speaking, when one *has* a belief. If you are inclined to think that this is, from the standpoint of the philosophy of science, an uninteresting pursuit, perhaps a bit of fore-shadowing will pique your curiosity: The end result of this line of inquiry is a unified solution to both the ceteris paribus and surplus-meaning problems that at the same time explains just how it is that scientists are able to hang onto their pet theories in the face of otherwise countervailing evidence.

Salmon may have been pushed into his anti-psychologistic position by his misplaced assumption that the overcoming-uneasiness account of explanation is the *only* psychological account of explanation.[2] A far more sensible proposal would, however, be one that takes the intellectual satisfaction in question, the "Aha!" moment, to be the (at least frequent) *consequence* of another psychological process: *explaining* an event (Gopnik 2000). The question then becomes "What process enables us to overcome the psychological uneasiness caused by some event?" A simple and intu-itive answer is that our uneasiness is overcome when we understand, or think we understand, why or how the event in question occurred. This, of course, brings us right back into the cognitive realm, for what we really want to know is what this kind of understanding might amount to.

Salmon ought to have recognized that there are alternative psychologi-cal accounts of explanation, for the Deductive-Nomological (D-N) model that he spends so much time critiquing is an account of this very sort. To be sure, in one of the best-known descriptions of the tenets of the D-N model, Carl Hempel and Paul Oppenheim (1948, pp. 136, 137) try to resist this way of understanding the model by claiming that explanations are sets of external sentences that stand in certain relationships. Their resis-tance cannot, however, be reasonably sustained for a variety of reasons.

First, Hempel and Oppenheim, like Karl Popper, claim that to explain is *to deduce*. Popper describes the model they all favor as follows: "To give a causal explanation of an event means to *deduce* a statement which describes it, using as premises of the deduction one or more universal laws, together with certain singular statements, the initial conditions." (1959, p. 59; emphasis added) Clearly these D-N theorists are proposing that to explain is to deduce explanandum from explanans, and if there is deduc-ing going on, there is presumably someone doing the deducing. Deduc-ing, and reasoning more generally, are (again) paradigmatic cognitive activities.

Second, as Scriven (1962, p. 64) notes, there is no sensible way to main-tain that explanations are relationships between *external* sentences, for one can clearly be in possession of an explanation without ever telling anyone about it. A nice illustration of this point comes from the movie *Castaway*, in which the protagonist and the audience along with him, figures out that the disturbing noises that he had been hearing throughout the night were caused by falling coconuts. We all, at that moment, had that wonderful "Aha!" feeling referred to earlier. No explicit verbiage was required; we all got it. (In point of fact no *hidden* verbiage was required either, but that's an argument for the next chapter.)

Third, I think we can all agree that there were explanations long before the existence of formal logic. Since natural languages are notoriously lacking the kind of structure that would be required in order to effect the formal inference processes that Hempel and Oppenheim have in mind, the deductions that they take to be necessary for explanation would have to involve a competence at deduction that does not require an external language.

Finally, and relatedly, Hempel and Oppenheim also think (for reasons explained below) that many explanations involve only a *tacit* reference to laws (1948, p. 139). Once again, the only way to make sense of this claim is by appealing to a covert deduction process.

7.3   The Deductive-Nomological Model

Construed in this way, as a model of the psychological underpinnings for explanation, the D-N model has been shown to have more to recommend it than any other model yet proposed. It is also the received view in the philosophy of mind, and it is the standard against which the viability of alternative models of explanation are generally measured in the philosophy of science. (See, for example, Salmon 1998, pp. 302–319; van Fraassen 1980; Kitcher 1989; Churchland 1989, pp. 197–230.) The forthcoming defense of my own model of explanation will follow this pattern as well, and so, as with the closely related Mental Logic hypothesis, it is important to catalog the precise respects in which the D-N model succeeds and fails. As I promised in the previous section, this will be a two-part process. On the one hand, we will need to consider what our philosophical intuitions reveal about the nature of explanation. On the other, we will need to consider what constraints on theories of explanation arise when we look at the issue from the standpoint of cognitive science.

7.3.1   Satisfying Intuitions
Most of the aforementioned philosophical intuitions stem from our judgments about whether or not particular cases constitute genuine

explanations. In order for a model to succeed, it must not be too liberal—that is, it must not lead us to classify as an explanation something that clearly is not an explanation. Nor must it be too conservative—that is, it must not lead us to classify as a non-explanation something that clearly is a genuine explanation. If one's model of explanation does imply that certain cases fall on what seems, at first glance, to be the wrong side of the explanation/non-explanation divide, one must specify why, in the final analysis, it is perfectly fine that those cases fall on the side that they do. This, of course, is one of the most common modes of reasoning in analytic philosophy, and it is, I gather, about what Rawls (1971) has in mind with his theory of reflective equilibrium. Speaking metaphorically, the general strategy is to construct a machine such that, when we input the various cases and turn the crank, those cases will drop out the bottom and fall out into the correct basket—in the present case, the baskets are labeled 'explanation' and 'non-explanation'.[3] Similar machines have, of course, been constructed in virtually every area of analytic philosophy.

There are, however, other, *meta*philosophical intuitions that a model of explanation ought to satisfy. That is to say, it simply will not do for a model of explanation to correctly classify the various cases but, at the same time, fly in the face of our basic intuitions concerning what explanations are or the role that they play in our lives. For its part, the D-N model, unlike its chief competitors, at least manages not to fly in the face of basic intuitions of this sort, some of which I discuss in subsection 7.3.1.1.

7.3.1.1 Metaphilosophical Merits of the Deductive-Nomological Model
On the face of things, the D-N model seems to do a wonderful job of satisfying the intuition that we are able to explain, in roughly the same fashion, both particular events and laws. The following roughly exemplifies the pattern of reasoning that proponents of the D-N model take to underlie explanations for laws:

Liquids of type A are less dense than liquids of type B. L_1
When mixed, the less dense of two liquids will float to the top. L_2
∴ Liquids of type A float to the top when mixed with liquids of type B. L_3

In this case, statements describing two laws (L_1 and L_2) formed the explanans for a third (L_3). Statements of laws can, according to the D-N model, also be conjoined with statements describing specific conditions in order to deduce, and thereby explain, particular events. For instance, L_3, from the previous example, is here conjoined with a further statement to effect just such a deduction:

Liquids of type A float to the top when mixed with liquids of type B. L_3
<u>Some liquid of type A is mixed with some liquid of type B.</u> C_1
∴ The liquid of type A floats to the top. E_1

In addition to offering a unified account of our ability to explain laws and particular events, the D-N model offers a promising means of satisfying the intuition that explanation and (a certain sort of) prediction are two sides of a single coin. According to this view, the main difference between explanation and prediction is the temporal order in which phenomena and theory are introduced. In the former case, one begins with a statement describing an event or regularity to be explained and shows that it *was* to be expected by showing that statements describing it are entailed by statements describing laws and (if need be) specific conditions. In the latter case, one begins with statements describing laws and (if need be) specific conditions and shows that a given event or regularity *is* to be expected by showing that those statements entail a further statement that describes the event or regularity in question. While the temporal flow clearly differs, the D-N model does justice to the fact (see also subsection 5.3.1) that there is a shared *logical* flow at the core of both processes and, thereby, to the inferential character of both prediction and explanation. On the D-N model, both sorts of process involve the deduction of statements describing the phenomena of interest from statements describing laws and (if need be) specific conditions.

We need to be clear on the fact that Hempel and Oppenheim's claim that there is a symmetry between prediction and explanation is not the claim, as Scriven (1962) takes it to be, that *any* explanation could, before the fact, have been used to predict the event or regularity in question. Hempel and Oppenheim's claim is rather that any "fully adequate" explanation could have been used in this way (1948, p. 138). An explanation may, for instance, not be of much use in generating predictions if it is partial or incomplete because, for example, it only clarifies some, but not all, of the conditions that would, only when taken together, suffice for the occurrence of the event described by the explanandum. To take one of Scriven's (1962) examples, imagine that one were to explain the fact that Dan has paresis on the basis of the fact that he also has syphilis, since only those with syphilis contract paresis. Yet, for ex hypothesi unknown reasons, only 25 percent of syphilitics contract paresis. Thus, this explanation would, before the fact, have constituted a poor basis for predicting that Dan would contract paresis. While Scriven would argue that this indicates that there is no symmetry between prediction and explanation,

Hempel and Oppenheim (H&O) would simply point out that the explanation in this case is not fully adequate, for we still have no idea *why* only 25 percent of syphilitics contract paresis and the rest do not. If we knew this, we would know the conditions that suffice for developing paresis, our explanation would be fully adequate explanation, and it *would*, before the fact, have (in principle anyway) constituted a good basis for predicting that Dan would contract paresis.

Nor, contra Scriven (1962, p. 54), is the idea behind the symmetry thesis that any basis for prediction would, after the fact, serve equally well as a basis for explanation. What H&O claim is that those predictions that are based on deductive inferences of the aforementioned sort can be used, after the fact, to supply reasonable explanations. If, on the other hand, a predictive inference is based on some form of non-monotonic reasoning (e.g., inductive or analogical; see subsection 5.3.1), all bets are clearly off.

If one keeps these simple caveats in mind, the relationship between prediction and explanation looks far tighter than how it is very often portrayed. (More must be said on the topic, but I will get to it all by the end of the next chapter.) Remarkably, many philosophers of science, rather than address Scriven's objections, have simply given up on the idea that there is an important relationship between prediction and explanation. Proponents of the D-N model, in contrast, have acknowledged this relationship and have offered a straightforward account of it.

While I am on the topic of ill-conceived objections, let me digress a moment and consider one final objection that is taken far too seriously by far too many. This one also originates with Scriven (1962). The concern, as he explains it, is that there are many legitimate cases where an explanation is offered (e.g., when someone explains why an ink bottle fell to the floor by noting that someone bumped it) but in which an individual does not cite any laws. Scriven seems confident that, when pressed, such individuals will not be able to cite any such laws. I doubt that this is true, but even if it were a savvy proponent of the D-N model might still argue that the relevant law is implicit in our workaday inferential apparatus. In fact, H&O already explicitly claim as much when they state that explanations must involve "at least *tacit* reference to general laws" (1948, p. 139; emphasis added).

My confidence in the obviousness of this reply may stem from my familiarity with more recent formulations of the Mental Logic hypothesis. Virtually none of the proponents of the ML hypothesis think that thought and reasoning are carried out in natural language.[4] As we saw, their proposal is rather that we rely upon the mental counterpart of a formal deduction system, one that comes replete with a set of frame axioms (e.g., see subsections 1.2.3.2 and 4.3.1.2). On this view, individuals are relying, in cases like the ink bottle example, upon their tacit knowledge, embodied by the relevant axioms, of how the world will change in light of alterations to it. In the very same way, many take us to be relying upon our tacit knowledge of syntactic principles when we pass judgment on the grammaticality of sentences. Nothing about either proposal entails that we have the kind of explicit knowledge of the principles upon which we are relying that Scriven seems to demand.

Another of the great virtues of the D-N model is that it acknowledges the central role played by inference in the explanatory process. It casts explanation as a process of inference from that which does the explaining to that which stands in need of explanation. It is, I strongly suspect, this inferential connection between explanans and explanandum that gives rise to the feeling of intellectual satisfaction, the "Aha!" that accompanies (at least many) viable explanations.

So much, then, for what I like about the D-N model.

7.3.1.2 Well-Known Problems for the D-N Model As I have noted, one's model of explanation must correctly classify those cases where explanation is, and is not, taking place. From the philosopher's armchair, what looks to be wrong with the D-N model is that it classifies some cases improperly.

7.3.1.2.1 Sufficient Conditions Concerns about the D-N model are raised by cases in which seemingly genuine explanations would have to be classified as non-explanations because the putative explanans does not specify what conditions would suffice for the occurrence of the event. Without a statement describing those sufficient conditions, there is no way to deduce the explanandum from the explanans.

It is in this respect that Scriven's syphilis-paresis case may (but see subsections 7.3.1, 8.3.4, and 8.3.5) raise concerns about the D-N model. In this case, there is no way to deduce the explanandum from the explanans, but knowledge that the individual in question has syphilis might be claimed to be the basis for what Scriven would call a "useful and enlightening partial account" of why he also has paresis (1959, p. 480). As we saw, D-N theorists would be right to point out that the explanation in this case is not fully adequate; however, insofar as it is an explanation *of some sort*, the D-N model offers no insight into why this is so. Unless we have knowledge of, or a hypothesis concerning, the sufficient conditions for the occurrence of paresis, we will be unable to deduce the explanandum from the explanans. Thus, a partial explanation like this one is, as the objection goes, misclassified by the D-N model as a non-explanation.

Another worry—one that is related to the worry just described but is, in the final analysis, far more serious—concerns what have been variously termed *provisos* (Hempel 1988), *ceteris paribus conditions* (Schiffer 1991), and *hedges* (Fodor 1987, 1991b) that characterize certain laws. The root of the worry is that many putative laws admit of exceptions. One might, for instance, wish to count it a law of geology that stalactites form when mineral-laden water leaks through the ceiling of a cavern or some other rocky enclosure. There are, however, countless exceptions to this regularity. Stalactites will presumably not form, for instance, if a cavern is prone to periodic violent floods that erode the ceiling, if the inside of the cavern is too cold or too hot, if the cavern lies directly in the path of a future expressway, if the cavern is known to contain deposits of gold, if the cavern contains a nuclear weapon that is moments from detonating, if the laws of physics suddenly change, and so on. For workaday purposes, the special scientist might wish to say that the regularity holds under ideal conditions. Such an analysis stumbles toward the abyss of vacuity, however, for these conditions end up being just those conditions under which regularity holds (Fodor 1987, p. 5).

The concern that this raises in regard to the D-N model stems once again from the fact that in order to deduce explanandum from explanan, the latter must contain a law that specifies the sufficient conditions for the occurrence of the event. It will not do, however, to simply omit all reference to the conditions that must not obtain. It will not, for example, do to say that explanations of stalactite formation involve a law like this one:

If water leaks through the ceiling of a cavern or other rocky enclosure, then stalactites will form.

Such an approach to the problem would commit D-N theorists to the claim that many (arguably the vast preponderance of) genuine explanations are deductions from premises that one knows to be false—i.e., that explanation involves deductions that are clearly unsound.

Nor will it do simply to include a placeholder for the various conditions that must not obtain. It will not do, for instance, to say that explanations of stalactite formation are based on a statement like the following:

If water leaks through the ceiling of a cavern or other rocky enclosure *and conditions are ideal*, then stalactites will form.

As we saw, simply claiming that normal or ideal conditions obtain renders such statements vacuous. What is required is that "ideal conditions" be given some reading apart from "the conditions under which the regularity holds." What is required, in other words, is a way of representing what those ideal conditions are. For the D-N model, this requires an explicit specification of the countless conditions that must, and must not, obtain. But there are just *so many* conditions, and so there is no realistic way to specify them all.

One of the more popular responses to this problem is to claim that there are no genuine laws in the special sciences, and that, for this reason, there are no genuine *explanations* in the special sciences. Only the "hard" sciences, on this view, are able to come up with truly exceptionless regularities, and, thereby, to come up with genuine explanations. My discussion of Mink's (1996) model in subsection 7.3.2.1 should convince you that this is ludicrous. For present purposes, suffice it to say that this way of dealing with the problem also implies that there are no genuine *non*-scientific explanations (e.g., there are no genuine explanations for why a car will not start, for why it took so long for someone to get from Los Angeles International Airport to Simi Valley, or for how my wind-up frog is able to hop across my table). This strikes me as a pretty obvious case of misclassification. At the very least, I think we can agree that a model of explanation that allows for the possibility of special-scientific and non-scientific explanations is, all else being equal, clearly to be preferred to one that does not.

Another flaw in this response is that there are very good reasons for thinking that even the practitioners of the so-called hard sciences rely heavily upon their tacit knowledge of countless provisos. The simplest way to see this is to consider the fact that, at *every* level of science, theorists are able to find ways of hanging onto their pet theories in the face of seemingly countervailing evidence. This would not be possible were it not for the fact that there are various provisos built into the inferences in question.[5] This does not, mind you, imply that there are provisos internal to, for instance, the laws of physics. The laws of physics are, I am inclined to think, at least *supposed to be* exceptionless. When exceptions of any sort come to light, physicists tend to become a bit disenchanted. On the contrary, the ability of theorists to hang on to their pet theories come what may simply implies that provisos are present somewhere in the often long inferential chain from laws to worldly implications to observable implications. This entire chain is invoked in experimental contexts in order to make predictions, and it is likewise invoked after the data have been gathered in order to explain them. The first part of this chain was schematized as follows in subsection 2.6.1:

$$[H \; \& \; (A_1 \; \& \; A_2 \; \& \ldots A_n)] \rightarrow I.$$

The A's here are just the innumerable "auxiliary assumptions" that one could reject in order to avoid having to reject the hypothesis in question. Call them what you will; provisos by any other name are still provisos. And if not for our knowledge of these provisos, falsification would be commonplace and science would look very different (for one thing, it would be prone to getting trapped in local minima). In other words, our tacit knowledge of provisos *plays an essential role at all levels of scientific investigation.* The problem for the D-N model is that it demands the impossible—namely, that this knowledge be spelled out explicitly and exhaustively.

7.3.1.2.2 The Flagpole Problem and the Problem of Causation   One of the clearest illustrations of how the D-N model can lead us to misclassify (as explanatory) cases where no explanation has taken place is Sylvain Bromberger's flagpole example (1966). A useful variant of that example goes as follows: It seems clear that the length of the shadow cast by a flagpole can be explained by the position of the sun and the height and orientation of the flagpole. A D-N theorist might argue that this is a legitimate explanation because the length of the shadow can be deduced from these other factors. Yet the position of the sun can just as easily be deduced from the length of the shadow and the height and orientation of the flagpole. Clearly, however, these things do not explain the position of the sun.[6]

On the face of things, it would seem perfectly sensible for a D-N theorist to shore up the model by adding the simple stricture that genuine explanations are causal. On this view, the reason we can explain the length of the shadow in terms of the position of the sun and the height and orientation of the flagpole is that these factors are what *cause* the shadow to be cast as it is. On the other hand, the facts about the flagpole and the shadow do not cause the sun to be where it is. Unfortunately, this sensible modification gives way to a more serious difficulty: that of specifying what causation is. For this reason, proponents of the D-N model have been very reluctant to add this stricture to their model.

It is also worth noting that, although very few people could perform the relevant deduction, we all understand the explanation for the length of the shadow; we even take it to be a particularly good explanation. Thus, it seems, once again, that the only recourse for proponents of the D-N model is to enlist the aid of covert deduction processes and tacit knowledge of laws.

7.3.1.3 The Explanatory-Import Problem In addition to the well-known flaws described above, there are other flaws, no less serious, that have gotten far less attention. One of these has, like the flagpole problem, to do with the fact the criteria for genuine explanation supplied by the D-N model would lead us to classify as explanatory clear-cut cases where, at least to my way of thinking, no explanation has taken place. To make the defect perfectly obvious, it will help to control for the influence of background knowledge by using a fictitious example such as the following:

All glubice emits heat.	L_4
The object is made of glubice.	C_2
∴ The object emits heat.	E_2

If the D-N model is correct, then this is a legitimate explanation for the fact that a particular object emits heat. Be this as it may, the only thing that this so-called explanation tells us is that the object emits heat because it is a member of the category of things that emit heat. I, for one, find that my intellectual curiosity has not been satisfied one whit. Telling me that the object is a member of the category of things that emit heat does not enable me to understand *why* it emits heat. There must be something more to explanation than the D-N model lets on.

Salmon claims as much. He notes that, because some regularities cry out for explanation, subsuming events under generalizations cannot be all there is to explanation (1998, p. 128). He also claims that (as with the flagpole example) one of the missing ingredients is causation. Causation cannot, however, be the *only* missing ingredient, for even causal regularities cry out for explanation. L_4 seems, in fact, to be an unexceptional instance of just such a regularity. For another example, consider L_5 in the following deduction:

Yelling at glubice causes it to glow.	L_5
The glubice is yelled at.	C_3
∴ The glubice glows.	E_3

This looks like a standard D-N-style deduction, but it is (nearly, at least) as devoid of explanatory import as the previous one. I, for one, do not feel as though I understand, on this basis, *why* the glubice glows. I have to admit, however, that the claim that the one event causes the other does constrain the space of possible answers more than, say, the mere claim that the two types of event regularly co-occur. Still, until I come to have further beliefs about the connection between the yelling and the glowing, I will consider the glowing of the glubice to be a very mysterious phenomenon.[7] Although these examples reveal flaws in the D-N model (i.e., because not just any D-N-style deduction is an explanation), they lead me to believe that the earlier objection to the model that was based on the syphilis-paresis case was not very persuasive. Scriven would wish to say that knowing that Dan has syphilis and that 25 percent of untreated syphilitics contract paresis forms the basis for a "useful and enlightening partial account" of the fact that Dan has paresis. It may be useful, but it hardly seems enlightening. Indeed, such an account would be very much like, though perhaps even less enlightening than, an account of why the glubice glows that is based on the knowledge that the yelling and the glowing reliably co-occur. In the syphilis-paresis case, all we are being told is that the reason Dan contracted paresis is that having untreated syphilis is *occasionally* accompanied by the development of paresis. We still have no idea what the connection between the two types of event might be. As Salmon might put it (see Salmon 1998, p. 312), what we are being given in these cases is simply an indication of where we can look for a genuine, enlightening explanation.[8] Now let us return to the principal claim of this section. With regard to the first glubice scenario, I think all will at least agree that (all else being equal) there is a clear difference between how much enlightenment can be derived from an account of the heat generated by a particular rock that appeals to (say) underlying chemical processes and how much enlightenment can be derived from the putative account conveyed by statements L_4 and C_2 above. Likewise, with regard to the second glubice scenario, I think all will agree that (all else being equal) there is a clear difference between how much enlightenment can be derived from an account of the glowing that appeals to (say) the manner in which the chemical constituents of glubice behave in the presence of sound waves of sufficiently high amplitude and how much can be derived from an account like the one conveyed by statements L_5 and C_3 above. Thus, even if the D-N model were up to the task of *characterizing* the first in each pair (and I will argue in a moment that it is not), it gives us no means of distinguishing, on the basis of the degree of understanding afforded, between the first in each pair and the second. Any model of explanation that can do better is, all else being equal, to be preferred.

7.3.2 Psychological Plausibility

Also frequently overlooked is the fact that the D-N model is psychologically implausible in multiple respects. Perhaps the reason for this oversight is that proponents of the D-N model have, as we saw in section 7.2, maintained that explanations involve relations between external sentences. However, for the reasons described in section 7.2 and in subsection 7.3.1.2.2, this position cannot be sustained.

Paul Churchland is one of the few to have acknowledged explicitly that psychological considerations must enter into a proper assessment of the D-N model: "While much attention has been paid to the *logical* virtues and vices of this model, relatively little has been paid to its shortcomings when evaluated from a *psychological* point of view." (1989, p. 199) Unfortunately, Churchland's arguments against the psychological plausibility of the D-N model are not very persuasive. In particular, he argues (a) that the D-N model does not account for the fact that people are often unable to voice laws and boundary conditions, (b) that deduction, as a serial process, is too slow to be psychologically realistic, and (c) that animals achieve explanatory understanding and presumably lack any external or internal language capabilities.

Objection a is just a re-statement of the earlier concern raised by Scriven (1962). As we saw, D-N theorists have proposed that explanations at least sometimes involve tacit reference to laws. Objection b is premised on the mistaken idea that symbol manipulation can only be effected in serial fashion. As Fodor and Pylyshyn (1988) explain, formal symbol manipulation can, and often is, carried out in parallel. Finally, with regard to objection c, it is far from obvious that animals *are* capable of explaining anything. But even if they are, as proponents of the ML hypothesis have argued, it may be that animal thought is also effected on the basis of a mental logic (Fodor 1978). If this sounds implausible, it is probably because animals do not seem to possess the same high-level cognitive abilities that we humans possess. (See subsection 4.3.1.) But this is just a stone's throw from admitting that this particular objection to the D-N model was ill conceived.

While Churchland misses the mark with his critique of the psychological plausibility of the D-N model, he was right to point out that the D-N model is to be assessed not merely in terms of its ability to properly classify explanations and non-explanations (i.e., in terms of its "logical" virtues and vices).[9] Because it is an ineluctably psychological thesis, considerations of psychological plausibility must also come into play.

In this regard, the D-N model must ultimately share the same, unpleasant fate as the ML hypothesis. This is because at the core of each proposal lies the claim that we deduce how the world will change in light of alterations to it. Yet, as was shown in chapters 4–6, as a model of how we make inferences (viz., monotonic ones) concerning the consequences of alterations to the world, all deductivist approaches are beset by the prediction and qualification problems. This is because deduction, in whatever format, is a formal process. (See subsection 5.3.2.) It involves inferences based solely upon the meanings of logical terminology; it abstracts away from specific contents. Thus, in order to deduce—whether on the basis of a mental logic, so-called mental models, or what-have-you —facts about how the world will change in light of alterations to it, that content must be built back in as explicit specifications of the conditions under which an alteration will, and will not, have a particular consequence.

7.3.2.1 The Oversimplification Problem In view of the close affinity between the D-N model and the ML hypothesis, it should come as no surprise that the problem of provisos is just a manifestation, discovered on independent grounds, of the qualification problem. In each case, researchers were searching for a model that would be capable of doing justice to the knowledge that we bring to bear when making inferences about how the world will change in light of alterations to it. The problem with both the ML hypothesis and the D-N model is that, in order for a particular law-statement, frame axiom, or other statement or inference rule to embody that knowledge, there would have to be an explicit specification, in the antecedent of that statement or rule,[10] of the conditions that we know would suffice for the occurrence of an event. These proposals require the impossible, however, for we have tacit knowledge of *countless* conditions that would prevent a particular alteration from having a particular consequence.

Now, given that the qualification problem has a clear counterpart in the independently discovered problem of provisos, one might expect that a counterpart to the prediction problem also besets the D-N model. In point of fact, just such a problem does exist. It has been called the problem of accounting for surplus meaning (MacCorquodale and Meehl 1948; Greenwood 1999, p. 5). I will call it *the oversimplification problem*.

To understand the nature of the problem, notice, to begin with, that the inferential productivity of thought (subsection 4.3.5) plays a prominent role in our ability to evaluate the kinds of explanations we generate in everyday, non-scientific contexts. For example, suppose that a mechanic thinks that the explanation for the loss of power exhibited by my car is that it has bad rings. If the D-N model were correct, the mechanic's inference process would run something like this:

If an engine has bad rings, then pressure in one or more cylinders is L_6 low.

If pressure in one or more cylinders is low, then the engine exhibits L_7 loss of power.

The engine has bad rings. C_4

∴ The engine exhibits loss of power. E_4

There must, however, be a great deal more to the theory than is expressed by L_6–C_4. These statements, in other words, *greatly* oversimplify the theory, which can be used to generate countless predictions. That is, in addition to implying E_4, the theory also implies the following:

When the engine runs, oil leaks into the combustion chamber.

The end of tailpipe is, or will become, oily.

The exhaust looks smoky.

The ends of the spark plugs are dark instead of gray.

Changing the rings will rectify the problem, but changing the wires will not.

When tracer is added to the oil, a tracer-detecting device will register the presence of tracer in the exhaust.

A compression test will reveal low compression.

And so on, and on.

Now, the D-N model was supposed to characterize the relationship between explanans and explanandum. In this case, at least, it falls far short of the mark in terms of its ability to characterize the explanans, which has countless implications besides the event to be explained, some of which were just described and *none of which* can be deduced from L_6–C_4. The explanation in this case—and, I'll wager, in most others—is inferentially productive, and the D-N model is no more able to account for this fact than the ML hypothesis is. This is no small matter: Were it not the case the explanations have many implications aside from the event to be explained, we would not be able to test them in the way that we do. If, for instance, the mechanic's explanation for my car's loss of power were exhausted by the information contained in L_6–C_4, she would not be able to evaluate the strength of her explanation by checking the end of tailpipe, examining the exhaust, etc.

All of this carries directly over into the scientific realm. Consider, for instance, the following explanation for relationship between Parkinson's Disease and Huntington's Disease. According to Mink (1996), these diseases are caused by two different types of malfunction that occur in a single set of underlying mechanisms (figure 7.1). The function of these mechanisms is to select and execute particular patterns of behavior. Crudely put, the decision to move is made by the cerebral cortex. When the decision is made, the cortex sends a signal to the subthalamic nucleus (STN). The subthalamic nucleus causes widespread excitation of GPi and SNpr, and these systems project inhibitory outputs to the many motor-pattern generators. At the same time, the cortex sends more specific signals to the striatum (caudate/putamen). Certain neurons in this region have the function, relative to the capacity they underlie, of selecting a particular motor pattern for execution by focally inhibiting regions of the GPi and SNpr. When these regions are turned off, the motor patterns they had been inhibiting

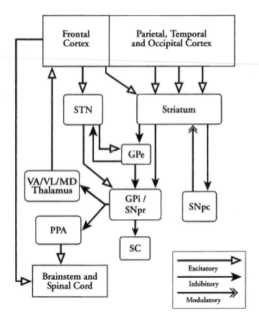

Figure 7.1
Some of the functional components underlying the selection and execution of motor patterns. Reprinted from Mink 2001 with permission from Elsevier.

turn on (i.e., are disinhibited). The end result is the execution of just one of a great many motor patterns. This is what typically occurs in healthy individuals.

Parkinson's Disease, or at least one variant of it, is known to involve the degeneration of dopaminergic (and hence inhibitory) neurons in SNpr. As I just explained, a very important function of these neurons is to prevent the simultaneous activity of competing motor patterns by inhibiting them all. Thus, when this global inhibition breaks down, multiple inconsistent patterns become active at the same time, and the body begins to lock up. Huntington's Disease, on the other hand, is known to involve loss of neurons in the striatum. Certain of these neurons have the function of selectively inhibiting areas of GPi and SNpr. Thus, if the global "brake" that these latter regions apply is not selectively turned off, movement will become very difficult. Instead of the simultaneous-contraction of muscles characteristic of Parkinson's Disease, we find—specifically, later in the course of the disease when the particular neurons discussed here are lost —failure, or slowness, in initiating movement that is characteristic of Huntington's Disease.

This is a somewhat superficial sketch of the model, and we can already see that it has countless implications. It has implications concerning the effects of focal stimulation of particular regions, the effects of increasing the quantity of dopamine precursors (which are metabolized into dopamine, and cause greater quantities to be released into the synaptic cleft), the effects of selective lesions to (or freezing of) these different areas in non-human primates, and the different observed patterns of activation that should be expected when performing functional neuroimaging on unimpaired and (both types of) impaired individuals. And once we get to know the model in its true detail, we see that these implications only scratch the surface.

The simple fact is that it is impossible to represent, using the kinds of statements and rules to which the ML hypothesis and D-N model advert, the extent of our knowledge of the consequences of alterations to even simple mechanical systems, let alone one as complicated as the one that Mink has in mind. Our representations of mechanisms, whether those mechanisms are right before our eyes or are simply hypothesized, are inferentially productive. In science, this inferential productivity plays an essential role: It enables scientists to determine the implications of theories and, eventually, the observable implications of these implications; it allows the testing of theories.[11]

7.3.3 Recap

I began this section by pointing out what I take to be the strengths of the D-N model. Among these strengths are that it satisfies important metaphilosophical intuitions by offering a unified account of explanations for both particular events and regularities, by accounting for the symmetry between prediction and explanation, and by doing justice to the sensible intuition that to have an explanation is to be able to infer what is to be explained from what is purported to explain it. I then described cases in which adherence to the tenets of the D-N model would lead us to classify genuine explanations as non-explanations and vice versa—that is, I explained the problem of provisos, the flagpole problem, and the problem of explanatory import. Finally, I explained that the D-N model is psychologically implausible for the very reasons that the ML hypothesis is psychologically implausible; this led into a discussion of the oversimplification problem. These are what I consider to be the principal virtues and limitations of the D-N model.

In chapter 8, I will show that there is an alternative model of explanation that has the same benefits but none of the drawbacks. First, however, let me briefly discuss the three best-known alternatives to the D-N model.

7.4 Proposed Alternatives to the D-N Model

A careful critique of the other models of explanation would have to be at least as thorough as the above critique of the D-N model, including, at the very least, a discussion of how they handle the various counter-examples to the D-N model. Because my main goal is to provide my own alternative, I will forgo such a detailed analysis. I will, however, suggest what it is about them that I find them unsatisfactory.

7.4.1 The Covering-Law Model

Hempel (1965) attempted to supplement the original D-N model with a closely related variant, the Inductive-Statistical (I-S) model, in order to account for explanations of particular events that are based on statistical laws.[12] In either case, explanations were to be accounted for in terms of inferences, whether deductive or probabilistic, from statements describing laws and (if need be) specific conditions. This more inclusive Covering-Law Model could, it was hoped, make sense of explanations that involve probabilistic laws. It was, for example, supposed to make sense of an explanation for why George quickly recovered from his strep infection that appeals to the fact that George took penicillin (C_5) and the fact that most patients with strep infections who are treated with penicillin recover quickly (L_8). On the I-S model, the strength of such explanations is a function of the strength of the laws invoked, with a cut-off probability of >0.5.

What many take to decisively refute this view are cases like the syphilis-paresis example, in which it is reputed that the fact that Dan has syphilis explains his paresis even though the probability that an untreated syphilitic will develop paresis is closer to 0.25. I have already noted that we should be a bit more conservative as to what we call a "genuine explanation," or even a "useful and enlightening partial explanation." Once again, the only thing that the so-called explanation supplied by the law subsumption tells us in this case is that Dan has contracted paresis because he is a member of the category of people who occasionally contract paresis. The question "Why did Dan contract paresis (rather than not contract it)?" has hardly been given a satisfactory answer. As I have promised, I'll have more to say on this topic in chapter 8.

The I-S model of statistical explanation is also beset by many of the same problems that plague the D-N model. It was established above, for instance, that many statements describing putative deterministic laws are, in the absence of a full complement of provisos, obviously false. Statistical laws, Hempel explains (1988, p. 153), fare no better in this regard, because in order to determine the correct probabilities we would have to determine how often extraneous factors interfere with the regularity in question. And, Hempel notes, even if we could provisionally describe *these* probabilities, such descriptions would themselves quickly be revealed to be subject to countless provisos.[13] Nor does the I-S model fare any better with regard to the explanatory-import problem or the oversimplification problem.

7.4.2 The Unification Gambit

According to Philip Kitcher (1989), to explain is to unify. More specifically, we have an explanation when we have an argument that (a) has as its conclusion one of our beliefs and (b) instantiates an argument pattern taken from that set of patterns that allows the derivation of the maximum number of beliefs with the minimum number of patterns.

Kitcher tests his model against the standard barrage of cases that pose problems for the D-N model, and he finds that it sorts the cases correctly. Be this as it may, it does suffer some serious limitations. First of all, just as on Salmon's view (section 7.2), on Kitcher's view it is hard to see how there could be multiple, competing explanations for a given event. Notice, for example, that there are many ways to explain why a "meow" sound happens to be emanating from my closet. In the absence of any further background knowledge, the most obvious explanation is that my cat somehow got trapped in the closet and is meowing because it wants to get out. There are, however, clearly, many other explanations. For instance, it could be that someone is playing a trick on me with a tape recorder, that my wife has learned ventriloquism, or that my brain has malfunctioned. It seems clear that in this case, and in virtually any other case that one can think of, there are *multiple* ways of explaining the event in question. Though Kitcher's framework may be of some use when it comes to helping us to determine why one of these explanations seems better than the rest, his approach does not tell us what it is about each of them that makes it a genuine explanation in the first place. In fact, on Kitcher's view, *only* one of these is a genuine explanation—namely, the one that satisfies his criteria a and b. Thus, no matter how it handles the standard barrage of cases, it appears far too conservative in that it classifies the vast majority of genuine explanations (insofar as there are generally multiple ways of explaining a given event) as non-explanations. Kitcher's model also incorporates a variant of the claim that to explain is to deduce. Although on his view this is only part of the story, it is still subject to the problem of provisos and to the oversimplification problem.

7.4.3 Salmon

Salmon's early position regarding explanation was that explanations of particular events are collections of *statistically relevant* facts—roughly, facts in the presence or absence of which the probability of the occurrence of the event under consideration will (all else being equal) vary. There is, for instance, a difference between the probability that someone will get paresis if he has untreated syphilis and the probability that he will get paresis if he does not have untreated syphilis. Having untreated syphilis is thus statistically relevant to having paresis. Salmon's method of discerning statistically relevant facts was just an extension of Mill's methods for inferring a causal relationship, and it is subject to the same limitations—for instance, instead of pointing to the cause of an event, the method sometimes points to an effect of that event or to an effect of a common cause of both events. For this reason, Salmon came to think that the real work of explaining is done by the causal factors that are indicated, albeit fallibly, by these differences in probability. Accordingly, he later claimed that "causal or theoretical explanation of a statistical correlation between distinct types of events is an exhibition of the way in which those regularities fit into the causal structure of the world—an exhibition of the causal connections between them that give rise to the statistical relevance relations" (1998, p. 123). Thus, on this view, although the search for an explanation of paresis might begin with the recognition that untreated syphilis is statistically relevant to paresis, we do not have an explanation for paresis until the causal connections between untreated syphilis and paresis are (to use Salmon's term) *exhibited*. This, of course, gives way to the difficult task (see subsection 7.3.1.2.2) of specifying, in a non-circular manner, what causation amounts to, and much of Salmon's later career was devoted to searching for a solution to this problem.

Salmon's analysis of cases like the syphilis/paresis case is certainly consistent with my own view, expressed in subsection 7.3.1.1—namely, that merely knowing that Dan is a member of the class of people who occasionally contract paresis hardly suffices to explain why Dan contracted paresis rather than not contracting it). Salmon's view is (or at least ought to be, in view of statements like the one above) that the missing ingredient is an "exhibition" of the causal connections between syphilis and paresis that give rise to the statistical-relevance relation. Though I am sympathetic with this view, I am, for the reasons I described in section 7.2, unsympathetic with Salmon's view that explanations are not psychological in nature. Nor am I sympathetic with Salmon's whole-hearted rejection of the proposal that explanations are inferences (which is just a corollary of the view that explanations are not psychological). As I noted in section 7.2, it is perfectly clear that we are often aware of, and are thus forced to weigh the merits of, multiple competing explanations for a given event. Each such explanation supplies us with a possible way of understanding why a certain event occurred. When the explanations are fully adequate, they imply the occurrence of the event in question is such a way that, had the order of events been reversed, they would (at least in principle) have served equally well as a basis for predicting the event. In order to test competing explanations, we often determine what implications they have (aside from the event of interest), and in order to hang onto them in the face of seemingly countervailing evidence we rely on our knowledge of the countless ways in which these implications are qualified. All of this suggests that explanations are rich wellsprings of inference that play a very active role in our cognitive lives. Any viable model of explanation should do justice to this fact. One should like to understand, specifically, just what the specific kind of understanding that explanations supply us with amounts to and how explanations are able to perform the various inferential functions that they do.

In point of fact, Salmon could, despite his protestations, no more consistently deny that explanations are psychological in nature than proponents of the D-N model could. For all his stated antipathy toward psychological models of explanation, he also makes claims like this one: "It is my view that *knowledge* of the mechanisms of production and propagation of structure in the world yields scientific *understanding*, and that *this is what we seek* when we pose explanation-seeking answers to why-questions." (1998, p. 139; emphasis added) And this one: "An explanation of an event involves *exhibiting that event* as it is embedded in its causal network and/or *displaying its internal causal structure*." (ibid., p. 325; emphasis added) On these points, I could not agree more. What we seek is to understanding of events through, if not knowledge of, at least beliefs about the mechanisms that produce them. But what, one wonders, could having knowledge of or beliefs about these mechanisms amount to if not, at least in part, having representations of them? And what, if not making inferences on the basis of these representations, could underlie our knowledge of how those mechanisms might produce the events or regularities in question? By the same token, given that explanations *need not be voiced*, what could an "exhibition of causal connections" or "displaying its internal causal structure" amount to if not representing causal relations *to oneself*?

From what I gather from Salmon's writings, it seems likely that his claim that explanations are not inferential in nature had do with his recognition that the sorts of inferences to which the D-N model adverts are not up to the task of "exhibiting" the mechanisms responsible for the event. His anti-inferentialism about explanation may thus have been a consequence of his inability to imagine what other form of inference could be up to the task. He was thus forced to reject the inferential view, all the while being irresistibly, and inconsistently, drawn to the idea that explanations involve *knowledge of how mechanisms produce events and regularities*.

Others have run up against this problem of specifying, without resorting to an appeal to inference, what it is about knowledge of or beliefs concerning mechanisms that provides understanding and enlightenment. Machamer, Darden, and Craver, for instance, equate explanations with descriptions of mechanisms and suggest: "The understanding provided by a mechanistic explanation may be correct or incorrect. Either way, the explanation renders a phenomenon intelligible. Mechanism descriptions show *how possibly*, *how plausibly*, or *how actually* things work. Intelligibility arises not from an explanation's correctness, but rather from an elucidative relation between the explanans (the set-up conditions and intermediate entities and activities) and the explanandum (the termination condition or the phenomenon to be explained). . . ." (2000, p. 21) I certainly agree with the proposal that explanations involve mechanisms and (pace Salmon) can be incorrect.[14] But, like Salmon's "exhibition of causal connections," this "elucidative relation" is rather arcane unless we take it to involve mental representations (toward which one can bear any of the attitudes that Machamer et al. mention) of how mechanisms produce events and regularities.

At this point you should have at least a good inkling of where I am going with all of this. It can be put succinctly as follows: We can reject the D-N model without rejecting the inferential view of explanation. What it means to exhibit or display mechanisms is, in the first instance, to harbor intrinsic cognitive models of those mechanisms. In chapter 8, to demonstrate the plausibility of this proposal, I will (among other things) evaluate its performance with respect to the cases and the problems considered above.

8 | The Model Model

In this chapter, I propose a model of explanation whose core, distinguishing thesis is that explanations for events and physical regularities are constituted by intrinsic cognitive models of the mechanisms that produce them. In essence, what I am proposing is akin to starting with Hempel and Oppenheim's stated account, replacing natural-language representations with their semantic counterparts, and replacing deduction with exduction. By way of defending this model, I show that it can address all the issues that were shown in chapter 7 to give the Deductive-Nomological model such trouble.

8.1 Introduction

There is a story about how the Deductive-Nomological model came to enjoy widespread acceptance that I find particularly compelling and illuminating. It runs roughly as follows: Science as we know it began with work in astronomical and terrestrial physics by Galileo, Kepler, and others, and it made a giant leap forward with Newton. As these sciences seemed to be paragons of explanatory success and predictive precision, many were immediately inspired to try duplicating these achievements in other fields. Everyone believed, however, that physics was science in its Platonic purity, and a proper understanding of science would therefore be most easily and accurately achieved through an analysis of this, its most perfect exemplar. What philosophers of science eventually discovered was that physics involves the proposal and testing of networks of laws whose logical structure could be represented by universally quantified conditionals. The antecedents of these conditionals specify the properties of objects, and the consequents contain mathematical equations that specify how systems with those properties behave. (See Giere 1988.) Newton's law of universal gravitation can, for instance, be expressed in terms of logical and mathematical formalisms as follows[1]:

$$(x)(y)((Mxs \ \& \ Myt) \rightarrow (F_{xy} = Gst/d^2)).$$

Latter-day physicists arguably have an even more exclusive interest in mathematical laws. However, as one climbs the ladder of levels of abstraction, one finds oneself confronted by poorer and poorer reflections of this ideal Form. For this reason, it is not uncommon for philosophers of science to maintain that the only fields that are truly worthy of the moniker 'science' are those that have discovered networks of genuine laws. (The common reaction to the problem of provisos discussed in subsection 3.1.2.1 is just one illustration of this tendency.) Science, on this view, consists of only a few fields. This has, not surprisingly, sometimes generated feelings of inadequacy and law-envy among practitioners of the so-called special sciences.

Some would have us believe that there are other lessons to be gleaned from the example of physics. If, for instance, physicists are instrumentalists, then we should *all* be instrumentalists; if physicists deny that science brings us closer to the truth, so should we all; if physics is only about prediction (not explanation), then so is the rest of science; and so on ad nauseam. One of the aims of the present chapter is to begin the process of dispelling the well-entrenched myth that as the philosophy of physics goes, so must go the philosophy of every other science. By the end of the next chapter, I will show that insofar as their power to grant genuine enlightenment is concerned—that is, to supply answers to our questions of *why* and *how*—the explanations proffered in the special sciences and in everyday life constitute the true ideal toward which latter-day physics can strive only in vain. To begin this process of turning the tables, I will first propose and defend a particular model of the source of this enlightenment, a model of explanation that I call the *Model model*. The primary goal of this chapter is to show that the Model model can satisfy our philosophical and metaphilosophical intuitions about explanations in everyday life and in the special sciences.

8.2 Basic Tenets of the Model Model

The central thesis of the Model model is that, relative to a backdrop of interests, one has an explanation for an event or (physical) regularity if and only if one possesses an intrinsic cognitive model of the mechanisms that might be responsible for producing that event or regularity.[2] As I noted in chapter 3, what counts as an explanation for a particular event or regularity does depend upon one's interests. If, for instance, one is wishes to know why, from an evolutionary perspective, a particular tree has the kind of leaves that it does, a model of the mechanisms that link that tree's DNA to the shapes of its leaves will not by itself suffice to answer the question. (If the claims made in subsections 8.3.4 and 8.3.5 are correct, such a model is not even necessary.) Only a model of specific, long-term evolutionary processes will do. Thus, while the DNA account is enlightening in its own way, it does not provide the kind of enlightenment that we are looking for. Here I will not offer any theory of how interests are represented.[3] I will, rather, focus on the central process of making an inference from that which does the explaining to that which it explains.

If the Model model is correct, such inferences take the form of ICMs of how particular mechanisms might produce the event or regularity in question. The *typical* strategy is, as naive physics researchers put it, for individuals to create cognitive models of the world and to "run" these models in order to explain the behavior of various physical systems. (See Chi et al. 1982; De Kleer and Brown 1983; DiSessa 1983; Larkin 1983; Norman 1983; Schwartz 1999; Hegarty 2004.)

There are some outlying cases that raise minor complications. For instance, I call this the *typical* strategy because there may be cases (e.g., certain mereological explanations for static properties[4]) in which one can explain merely by creating an ICM of how the static properties of the parts of an item produce a higher-level static property (i.e., one need not "run" the model). It also bears noting that 'produce', both here and in certain other contexts, does not connote a causal relation. Accordingly, I will, in what follows, take the verb 'produce' to have a wider scope than the verb 'cause'.[5] If you feel yourself getting anxious at this talk of causation, it might calm your nerves to know that later in this chapter I will discuss the important matter of what the representation of *causal* production relations amounts to.

It is with these caveats in mind that I propose that explanations for events and (physical) regularities are constituted by intrinsic cognitive models of how particular mechanisms might produce them. This, I submit, is the only way to make sense of Salmon's claim that "an explanation of an event involves *exhibiting* that event as it is embedded in its causal network and/or *displaying* its internal causal structure" (1998, p. 325; emphasis added) and of Machamer, Darden, and Craver's claim that explanations involve an "*elucidative relation* between the explanans (the set-up conditions and intermediate entities and activities) and the explanandum (the termination condition or the phenomenon to be explained). . . . " (2000, p. 21; emphasis added) Insofar as understanding *why* or *how* is concerned, without an intrinsic cognitive model of how a mechanism could produce the event or regularity in question, we are completely blind.

8.2.1 Metaphilosophical Merits of the Model Model

The Model model has the same metaphilosophical merits as the D-N model (subsection 7.3.1.1). To begin with, it provides a unified account of the explanation of both regularities and particular events. To see how the Model model accounts for our ability to explain particular events, consider how one might explain the fact that turning the knob of a particular gumball machine results in a gumball appearing behind its door.[6] One sensible although tellingly hard-to-describe proposal runs as follows: There is a shaft connecting the knob to a disk that has a gumball-size notch in it; since the gumballs in the container atop the device are funneled to an opening that terminates at the disk, when the crank is turned the notch aligns with the opening and a single gumball is forced into the notch; and as the handle continues to turn the gumball is then carried from the top of the disk to the bottom via a semi-circular arc until it reaches an opening onto a chute, into which it falls and rolls until it reaches the door. A proponent of the D-N model would claim that we explain the appearance of the gumball by deducing a statement that describes the event in question from a further set of statements that describe a variety of laws and specific conditions. My contention, in contrast, is that we explain the appearance of the gumball by constructing an intrinsic cognitive model of the hypothesized inner-workings of the machine and by altering that model (viz., mentally rotating the knob) until we find ourselves in possession of a representation of the event we wish to explain.

The Model model provides an equally straightforward account of how we explain regularities. Suppose, for example, what stands in need of explanation is the fact that a gumball has appeared every time the crank was turned just one-half of a revolution. In this case, we could modify our initial model so that there are two notches on opposite sides of the disk. This new model implies[7] that on every half turn a new gumball will appear, and this is just the regularity that we seek to explain.[8] Likewise, had the container been filled with a relatively homogeneous mixture of green, red, and blue gumballs, one would expect that after many turns of the crank roughly one-third of the gumballs obtained would be blue.[9]

The Model model also satisfies the intuition that there is a certain form of prediction that is just the flipside of explanation and that the difference between the two is just the temporal order in which phenomena and fact/theory are introduced. In the case of the above explanation for the appearance of the gumball, we are able, on the basis of our intrinsic cognitive model of its internal workings, to understand why that event *was to be* expected. Thus, had we confronted the gumball machine pre-armed with that same model, we could just as readily have predicted that turning the crank would result in the appearance of a gumball. Like the D-N model, the Model model accounts for the relationship between prediction and explanation in terms of a shared monotonic flow at the core of both processes. The symmetry obtains, of course, provided we keep in mind the sensible caveats described in chapter 7: An explanation only suffices as a basis for predicting an event or regularity if it is fully adequate (i.e., the explanation must represent the conditions that would suffice for the event's occurrence), and the symmetry obtains only in the case of predictions stemming from monotonic (viz. exductive; see subsection 5.3.2) inferences concerning how the conditions in question could produced the event or regularity.

Finally, the Model model acknowledges the central role played by inference in the explanatory process. It satisfies the intuition that we get that "Aha!" sensation, the feeling of genuine understanding and enlightenment, only when we are able to infer that the event or regularity in question was to be expected given the other things that we know or believe about the system in question, and, like the D-N model, it leaves room for the possibility of multiple, competing explanations.

8.3 Solving the Difficult Problems

There are, it turns out, many other advantages to the Model model. To start with, it easily handles all the *real* problems besetting the D-N model that were discussed in chapter 7. More specifically, and to reverse the order in which these problems were introduced, it is both psychologically plausible and supplies a sensible way of classifying the cases that gave the D-N model so much trouble.

8.3.1 Psychological Plausibility

Explanations are constituted by inferences concerning the behavior of mechanical systems. It would, to say the least, be desirable if one's model of explanation were grounded in a credible model of the cognitive underpinnings for inferences of this sort. We have seen that deductive models fare quite poorly in this regard, adverting as they do to explicit specifications of the principles governing the spatial and dynamical properties of objects and, thereby, falling victim to the notorious frame problem. We also now know that the proposal that mechanical inferences are effected through the harboring and manipulation of the cognitive equivalents of scale models is no mere explanatory metaphor, for the proposal has been given a non-metaphorical reading that distinguishes it from the ML hypothesis while at the same time maintaining compatibility with basic facts about the brain (e.g., the fact that there are no literal scale models in the head) (chapter 6). The resulting ICM hypothesis is, in fact, the only account of mechanical inferences that exhibits immunity to the frame problem. Because explanations are constituted by mechanical inferences, the only psychologically plausible account of explanation is thus that explanations for events and (physical) regularities are constituted by intrinsic cognitive models of the mechanisms that might be responsible for producing them. The only model of explanation that makes any kind of sense is, in other words, the Model model. The Model model is lent additional support by the fact that the immunity of intrinsic cognitive models to the prediction and qualification problems provides a unified solution to the much-discussed problem of provisos and the less-discussed oversimplification problem.

8.3.1.1 The Problem of Provisos The problem of provisos stems from the fact that there is a kind of knowledge that we possess—namely, tacit knowledge of the countless conditions that would prevent the consequence of a particular type of alteration from obtaining—and that we rely upon when making predictions and explanations, but which deduction-based schemes of monotonic inference are unable to represent. When confronted with examples like the putative regularity concerning stalactite formation in subsection 7.3.1.2.1, the initial, and ultimately proper, reaction had by many is to say that the regularity holds under "normal" or "ideal" conditions. As we saw, however, this response will not help the D-N model, for there is no non-vacuous way to describe what those conditions are. An explicit description of such ideal conditions must, per impossible, include a description of the innumerable conditions that must and must not obtain in order for a particular regularity to hold.

If explanations are instead constituted by ICM-based exductions, then we can easily make sense of the fact that we have this kind of open-ended knowledge (i.e., knowledge of the conditions under which an alteration will have a particular effect and those under which it will not). Consider, for instance, our earlier explanation for the appearance of a gumball after turning the crank. The Model model is the proposal that we know that the event was to be expected because of an ICM-based exductive inference. Specifically, we know, based upon our manipulation of an ICM of the internal workings of the machine, that if the knob is turned then, *if certain pro-*

visos are satisfied, a gumball will appear behind the chute. The proviso clause is added because all bets are off if any of innumerable conditions obtain. We can *begin* describing these provisos as follows:

It is not the case that the temperature inside the machine is so hot that the gumballs have become extremely gooey.

It is not the case that the shaft connecting the knob to the disk cannot bear the load (e.g., because it has rusted through, is made of licorice, etc.).

It is not the case that there is a jagged edge in the disk casing upon which the notch will get caught.

And so on indefinitely.

The provisos need not be represented explicitly, however. If our inferences are based on the manipulation of intrinsic cognitive models, then they are, like inferences based on the manipulation of external scale models, implicitly qualified in each of these innumerable ways. (See subsection 6.4.4.1.1.) That is to say, as with external scale models, were we to alter the ICM of the workings of the gumball machine in any of the respects listed above, the regularity would (with certain further provisos!) no longer obtain.

The Model model is thus able to explain our *tacit* knowledge of countless provisos.[10] Because of the inferential productivity of ICMs and their consequent ability to embody tacit knowledge of countless provisos without having to represent them all explicitly, we can, with ICMs, represent ideal conditions without having to exhaustively describe all the conditions that must and must not obtain in order for a particular regularity to hold.[11] Having such an idealized ICM of the mechanisms that sustain a regularity endows one with tacit knowledge of that regularity's countless defeaters.

What we know about the regularity concerning stalactite formation can be accounted for in this way as well. Our knowledge of the conditions under which this regularity will and will not hold is too extensive to be explicitly described, yet we have it just the same.[12] If the Model model is correct, then our knowledge of the conditions under which the regularity will and will not obtain is underwritten by an internal ICM of the process of stalactite formation—for instance, one whereby an at least somewhat volatile, mineral-laden liquid leaks through to the ceiling of an enclosure, evaporates, leaves minute quantities of mineral behind, etc. Knowledge of the conditions that would undermine the regularity can be generated from this model on demand simply by altering one's ICM (e.g., by altering it in any of the respects described in subsection 7.3.1.2.1).

This is a *very* important result, for, as we have seen, provisos are not idle bystanders in the scientific enterprise. The fact that scientists have tacit knowledge of the countless provisos characterizing the inferences that they make is what enables them to hang onto their pet theories in the face of otherwise disconfirming evidence. Metaphorically speaking, the scientific enterprise depends upon this process in order to sustain multiple decent-trajectories through explanation space and, thereby, to avoid getting trapped in local minima. (See section 2.6.) Indeed, provisos are no less active in our day-to-day lives; so-called "explaining away" otherwise falsifying evidence is a common phenomenon. A viable model of explanatory inference must therefore not reject, but embrace, the importance of provisos. To my knowledge, the Model model is the only model of explanation that does so.

These findings also help to undermine the suspicion that sciences must generate stores of exceptionless generalizations and that the special sciences are therefore sciences in name only. Moreover, if there is, as seems to be the case, but one possible solution to the frame problem, then the Model model can stake a claim to being the *only possible* account of our tacit, but nevertheless essential, knowledge of countless provisos. Given that any model of explanation must account for this knowledge, we find ourselves on the cusp of a sound transcendental argument whose conclusion is that the Model model is the only possible account of explanation. At the very least, until someone in cognitive science finds another (non-deflationary) way to solve the qualification problem, the Model model is surely the only current model of explanation worth taking seriously.

8.3.1.2 The Oversimplification Problem

We saw in subsection 7.3.2 that the apparatus supplied by the D-N model is not up to the task of representing the extent of our knowledge of the consequences of alterations to even simple mechanical systems, let alone the complicated systems that often hold the interest of scientists. We saw, for instance, that there is a great deal more to my mechanic's theory concerning the loss of power exhibited by my car than is expressed by L_6–C_4, as was evidenced by the countless predictions that could not be validly deduced from those statements. Similarly, the above theory concerning the mechanisms responsible for the appearance of a gumball has countless implications (e.g., concerning the effects of replacing the gumballs with gravel or with gumballs larger than the notch, the effects of shoving the end of a thin metal rod into the bottom of the container and turning the crank, etc.). For the same reason that the ML hypothesis is beset by the prediction problem, the D-N model is beset by the oversimplification problem. Explanations often have countless implications (and each is, of course, subject to countless provisos). The D-N model requires the impossible; it requires that these implications be spelled out explicitly. The Model model, in contrast, provides a very simple solution to the oversimplification problem. Because explanations are constituted by ICMs, they are inferentially productive (see sections 4.3 and 6.5); thus, any of these countless implications can be gotten on demand, and "for free," simply by manipulating the model.

Just like our tacit knowledge of countless provisos, our tacit knowledge of an explanation's countless implications plays an obvious and active role in the scientific enterprise. It is the wellspring of testable predictions. An adequate model of explanation must therefore not only capture the inferential connection between explanans and explanandum; it must also capture the inferential connection between explanans and the countless implications in terms of which it can be tested. Once again, the Model model is the only model of explanation that is able to do this, and it is thus (again, at least until someone in cognitive science comes up with a different solution to the prediction problem) the only one worth taking seriously.

8.3.2 The Explanatory-Import Problem

If the D-N model is correct, then the mere subsumption of an event under a nomological regularity suffices to explain that event. We can, however, deduce a statement describing an event from statements describing laws and specific conditions while still having no idea *why* the event in question occurred. We would not, for instance, understand why an object emits heat (rather than not doing so) on the basis of our knowledge that it is made of glubice if all we know about glubice is that it is a kind of substance that emits heat.

Salmon has claimed that, just as in the flagpole case, the most important thing missing in cases such as this is causation (1998, p. 129). We have already seen, however, that causation cannot be the *only* missing ingredient, for causal regularities can be equally devoid of explanatory import (subsection 7.3.1.3). Nor is this a peculiarity of the explanations proffered in everyday life. It is, to start with, also clearly true of the explanations proffered in the special sciences. For instance, an explanation for the presence of a stalactite must involve more than an appeal to the putative fact that water seeping through rocks into cavernous spaces causes stalactites to form, for this does not yet tell us *why* stalactites form. The same something more is required of the explanations proffered in physics. Hempel and Oppenheim, in fact, suspected as much from the beginning. For instance, regarding the expansion of a gas under rising temperature and constant pressure, they first note that this event can be explained by appeal to either the Gas Law or the kinetic theory of heat (1948, p. 147). Shortly thereafter, however, they point out that "it is often felt that only the discovery of a micro-theory affords real scientific understanding of any type of phenomenon, because only it gives us *insight into the inner mechanism* of the phenomenon, so to speak" (p. 147; emphasis added). Fodor comes to this conclusion as well (see section 2.3), and I concur. To have an explanation is to have "insight . . . so to speak" into the mechanisms that might produce the event or regularity. One of the great virtues of the Model model is that it enables us to dispense with vagaries of this sort (and the sort quoted in section 8.2), for it provides a clear way of understanding what this kind of insight amounts to; it gives us explanatory insight into explanatory insight.

8.3.3 The Flagpole Problem and Causation

From the height and orientation of a flagpole and the length of its shadow one can deduce the position of the sun, and so the D-N model leads us to classify such deductions as explanations for the position of the sun. The Model model, in contrast, supplies a straightforward way of satisfying the intuition that, in point of fact, this is *not* a legitimate explanation. Notice, to start with, that almost anyone, including those who have never been taught mathematics, can explain the length of the shadow in terms of the height and orientation of the flagpole and the position of the sun. If the Model model is correct, this is because we are able to construct an ICM of how the position of the sun and orientation of the flagpole produce a shadow of the observed length and orientation.[13] Insofar as we are unable to construct an ICM whereby the shadow and flagpole produce the position of the sun, we are unable to explain the latter in terms of the former.

That is the short answer to the flagpole problem. There is, however, still the matter of clarifying what it means to say that we model how mechanisms *produce* events and (physical) regularities. To get a good sense for what it means, on my view, to have an intrinsic *cognitive* model of how a mechanism produces some event or regularity, simply consider what it means to have an (external) intrinsic *computational* model of how a mechanism produces some event or regularity. As we have seen, intrinsic computational models such as finite-element models are constructed from media that consist of very simple modeling elements that are constrained to behave in a limited number of mathematically specifiable ways.[14] (See section 6.4.) From such media can be constructed models of physical systems that are like scale models in that the side effects of alterations to the representation will automatically mirror the side effects of alterations to the represented system. It is, again, for this reason that the consequences of countless alterations need not be specified explicitly. Most relevant to the purposes at hand, however, is the nature of the constraints governing the dynamics of the primitive modeling elements. A representation of the system being modeled will bottom out at (and perhaps before) the specification of the primitive constraints governing the building blocks, for there are typically not (if for no other reason than computational tractability) any deeper representations of why these principles are the way they are (i.e., representations of the underlying mechanisms that produce *them*).[15]

An unexceptional illustration of this fact about finite-element models is the model of the development of supertwisters (i.e., F4 and F5 tornadoes) created by atmospheric researchers at my home institution, the University of Illinois at Urbana-Champaign, in collaboration with the nearby National Center for Supercomputing Applications. The question confronting these researchers is very much like the question, confronting medical researchers, of why 25 percent of those with untreated syphilis contract paresis but the rest do not: "Scientists know that the strongest tornadoes are generated by a particular type of rotating thunderstorm called a supercell. The swirling winds of a supercell can produce tornadoes. But not all supercells lead to tornadoes, and not all tornadoes become supertwisters. In fact, only about 20 percent to 25 percent of supercells produce tornadoes. Why some storms spawn tornadoes while others don't—and why some tornadoes become extraordinarily strong supertwisters—is not yet well understood."[16] Like virtually every other computational model of the processes that produce some event or regularity (the exception may be traditional AI, but see subsection 1.2.3.2), this one is a finite-element model of a specific state of affairs that is constructed from a large number of simple modeling elements that are constrained to behave in a limited number of mathematically specifiable ways: "The simulation begins with data describing the pre-tornado weather conditions—wind speed, atmospheric pressure, humidity, etc.—at discrete points separated by distances ranging from 20 meters to three kilometers. Starting with these initial variables, partial differential equations that describe changes in the atmospheric flow are solved. The numerical solution of these equations proceeds in small time intervals for two to three storm hours as the supercell forms and produces a tornado. A virtual storm is born."[17]

If the Model model is correct, then the basic principles of computational modeling are just recapitulations—albeit in a way that overcomes many of our limitations—of what goes on when humans explain events and (physical) regularities.[18] Like finite-element models, intrinsic cognitive models of how mechanisms produce events and regularities rest on a foundation of—which is to say that they are implemented in terms of—unexplained regularities.

Before going any further, I should point out that this in no way implies that the Model model is just the D-N model in disguise. The major lesson of chapter 6 was that even if a modeling medium is implemented entirely in terms of deductive relations between extrinsic, sentential representations, it may nevertheless be the case that such a medium can be used in the service of implementing intrinsic, non-sentential representations and exductive inference processes. This is a very important result for the philosophy of science because there are those, like myself, who feel that explanations are, *at least* in the special sciences, somehow rooted in mechanisms rather than in laws (Salmon 1984; Bechtel and Richardson 1993; Glennan 1996; Machamer, Darden, and Craver 2000). There has, however, been a lingering, and (in the absence of a persuasive reply) legitimate, concern that this view might just be the D-N model in disguise,[19] for not long after one begins describing what the mechanism are and how they work, one winds up talking in terms of laws or, at the very least, regularities.[20] On the present account of mechanistic explanation we are able, at last, to make sense of its distinctive character while at the same time satisfying the intuition that even mechanistic explanations rest on a foundation of laws or, at the very least, regularities.

To illustrate, and by way of introducing an important fact about the somewhat diverse manner in which regularities are represented if the Model model is correct, let us once again consider Mink's model (subsection 7.3.2.1) of why it is that certain alterations to the mechanisms that underlie the selection and execution of motor patterns gives rise to the behaviors associated with Parkinson's Disease and Huntington's Disease. It has, for example, been established that the degeneration of domaminergic neurons in SNpr is accompanied by—and, for the aforementioned reasons, some believe it to be a cause of—the symptoms of Parkinson's Disease. Mink's model marks a major advance in our ability to understand *why* this regularity holds. However, in order to understand Mink's model one must be able to mentally represent a variety of principles. Understanding the model requires, specifically, an ability to represent basic geometrical and dynamical principles and also some principles (e.g., that activity in the subthalamic nucleus causes widespread excitation of GPi and SNpr) that have been either *induced* from laboratory experience or *derived* from knowledge of the mechanisms (e.g., knowledge of connectivity, neurotransmitters, etc.) that sustain them.

If the Model model is correct, then, as I explained in subsection 6.5.5, the first sort of knowledge is incorporated into an intrinsic cognitive model of how the mechanisms produce the regularity in virtue of the primitive constraints governing the virtual materials from which it is constructed, and the latter sort of knowledge is represented explicitly (i.e., in just the same way that alterations to ICMs are). Mink, for instance, might have derived knowledge of the fact that activity in the subthalamic nucleus causes widespread excitation of GPi and SNpr.[21] Nevertheless, in order to make an inference from the basic principles of his model to the behavioral consequences of the degeneration of dopaminergic neurons in SNpr, he (and we along with him) can (and we would all be very well advised to) take a mental short-cut and represent this regularity explicitly (i.e., rather than thinking about how the low-level mechanisms sustain it). Importantly, these claims no more imply that the Model model is just the D-N model in disguise than the fact that we can alter external scale models in light of our beliefs about the systems they represent implies that scale models are sentential in character (subsection 6.5.5). The appeal to intrinsic cognitive models thus enables us to make sense of what is distinctive about the Model model without denying the sensible intuition that all explanations rest on a foundation of laws or, at the very least, regularities.[22]

Let us return now to the important question of what it means to say that we harbor intrinsic cognitive models of how mechanisms *produce* events and (physical) regularities, and let us focus, specifically, on cases (e.g. the flagpole example) in which 'production' seems to have a causal connotation. (See also section 8.2.) Let us also temporarily bracket the question of how induced and derived principles are represented. If the Model model is correct, then representations of how one event causes another are constituted by intrinsic cognitive models that work in such a way that representing (i.e., as an alteration to, or as the starting condition of, the ICM) the event that occurs first (e.g., turning the crank of a gumball machine) is necessary and sufficient[23] for the occurrence of a representation of the second event (e.g., the appearance of a gumball in the chute). To invoke a colloquialism with which you are by now familiar, the ICM makes representation of the second event an "automatic" outcome of the representation of the first; it is gotten "for free" simply by constructing the model, altering it in the manner under consideration, and letting the consequences play out.

To allow for the role played by extrinsic representations of induced or derived principles (or even extrinsic representations of particular events), we might say that representations of how one event causes another are constituted by intrinsic cognitive models that work in such a way that, in conjunction with the extrinsic representation by the ICMs of certain induced or derived principles, representing (i.e., as an alteration to, or starting condition of, the ICM) the event that occurs first (e.g., degeneration of dopaminergic neurons in SNpr) is necessary and sufficient for the representation of the second event (e.g., development of the symptoms of Parkinson's Disease).[24] Of course, roughly speaking, the more one's explanation depends upon the incorporation into an ICM of extrinsic representations of principles and events that cannot be derived from one's knowledge of the mechanisms producing them, the shallower the explanation will be. I'll have a lot more to say about this below, but let me complete the present line of inquiry first.

This formulation at least comes very close to satisfying our intuitions about what it means to represent how turning a crank causes a gumball to appear behind a door or how the degeneration of dopaminergic neurons in SNpr causes the symptoms of Parkinson's Disease.[25] What matters most, for present purposes, is that we are able to make sense of what it means to harbor an ICM of causal relations through an appeal to representations of mere regularities. This is important because the problem we are trying to solve here is a close analog to one that exercised Salmon. While he was trying to effect a non-circular analysis of the metaphysics of causation, what we require here is a non-circular analysis of the psychology of causation. Because intrinsic cognitive models are hypothesized to function in much the same way that finite-element models do, this is, notwithstanding the fact that we needed to take into account our frequent reliance upon principles that are often far removed from fundamental physics, ultimately a pretty easy task.

We have just seen what it means to mentally represent how one event causes another, but one can *believe* that one event causes another without being able to represent *how* it occurs. I would argue that to believe that one event causes another is just to believe that there is a mechanism by which the former produces the latter[26] and, correspondingly, that the feeling that one event causes another dissipates the moment we no longer believe that such a mechanism exists.[27] For instance, if the glubice glows every time I yell at it, I may come to believe that there is a mechanism by which my yelling produces the glowing. If, however, a friend shows me that wires are connected to the bottom of the glubice and explains to me that the correlation is just an accidental result of his father opening and closing a circuit in the laboratory several floors down, my belief that there is a mechanism whereby my yelling produces the glowing will surely begin to dissipate. And as my belief in such a mechanism dissipates, so, in direct proportion, does my belief that my yelling causes the glowing.

8.3.3.1 Hume's Psychological Reduction These results are superficially similar to, but ultimately very different from, Hume's thesis that our thoughts about causal relations reduce to habits of expecting, on the basis of our experiences, that certain phenomena will be followed by others (1748/1993, pp. 54, 55). The defect in Hume's analysis is that it gives far too little credence to the role played by our exductive inference capacities. To see that this is so, notice that a corollary of his view, one which he appears to embrace, is the claim that no *new* predictions can ever be generated because all predictions are based on past encounters with the events in question. Hume puts it this way: "From causes which appear *similar*, we expect similar effects. This is the sum of all our experimental conclusions" (p. 23). Leibniz (1705/1997) had, in fact, already identified the weaknesses of this view in his critique of Locke's associationism. (See section 1.1 above.) As he explains, it is by probing into the reasons for what happens that we humans can determine when exceptions to a regularity will and will not occur. One of the big differences between Leibniz and Hume in this regard was the extent to which they thought discovery of "hidden springs and principles" was possible. Hume was quite pessimistic: "It must certainly be allowed, that nature has kept us at a great distance from all her secrets and has afforded us only the knowledge of a few superficial qualities of objects; while she conceals from us those powers and principles, on which the influence of these objects entirely depends. Our senses inform us of the colour, weight, and consistence of bread; but neither sense nor reason can ever inform us of those qualities, which fit it for the nourishment and support of a human body." (1748/1993, p. 21) Hume failed, however, to give proper weight to the fact that, even in his time, there were many everyday instances where regularities were discovered to be the consequence of underlying springs and principles.[28] For instance, I can believe, on the basis of induction, that the clock atop a particular tower will ring a dozen times whenever it strikes noon it. Indeed, if induction is the sole basis for my belief, then Hume would surely be right to say that my predictive ability is quite limited and that the regularity may even be a mere accident. If, on the other hand, we "probe into the reason for what happens" by entering the tower observing the mechanisms by which the clock striking noon produces the tolling, our predictive ability will undergo a manifold increase and we will have good reason to believe that the connection between the two events is no *mere* accident.[29]

This is an everyday sort of explanation, but we have seen that the same strategy has been taken up in the sciences. The difference just mentioned is, for instance, closely analogous to the difference between observing the regular connection between the degeneration of dopaminergic neurons and the symptoms of Parkinson's Disease, on the one hand, and having an explanation for why the regularity obtains, on the other. Hume would, of course, be right to point out that in all such cases our knowledge of the mechanisms connecting the two kinds of event bottoms out at unexplained regularities. We now know, however, that representations of regularities can be used to implement representations of mechanisms and that the latter representations have important properties (e.g., inferential productivity) that the former lack.

8.3.4 The Shallow-to-Deep Explanatory Continuum

Imagine being confronted with a chunk of rock-like material that feels warm to the touch and asking its owner why it is warm. (Let us call this C1.) While you have never heard of glubice, the owner nevertheless replies "It is made of glubice, which emits heat." (A1) In this case you might, at best, derive a minuscule (though hardly explanation-constituting) degree of enlightenment from this answer; at worst (and in all likelihood) you could derive none at all. On the other hand, the answer may serve your pragmatic ends quite well—for instance, maybe what you need to know is whether or not the object will cool down before the candle you placed beside it melts. If, on the other hand, the owner claims that it is made of glubice and that glubice has a very short half-life (A2), the degree to which you are enlightened (and alarmed) by this reply will surely be proportional to the depth of your knowledge concerning the (theoretical) process of radioactive decay. Still, so long as you can at least infer from this answer that it feels warm because it is made of stuff that emits heat (e.g., rather than having just been taken out of the oven), you may think that your pragmatic ends have been sufficiently served.

Perhaps Bas van Fraassen (1980) would wish to say that, in the right context, A1 can be just as enlightening as A2 (i.e., plus knowledge of radioactivity)—for instance, perhaps the item that feels warm is the only one of five, otherwise indistinguishable items that feels this way (C2). In this context, the question "Why is this object warm?" would (perhaps because 'this' is stressed) have an implicit "and none of the rest is warm" built into it. In such a context, the answer "Because it is made of glubice, which emits heat" might be a source of enlightenment. But then, in this context, the answer would also have to have an implicit "and the rest, despite looking the same, are made of stuff that does not emit heat," or some such clause, built into it; otherwise, the reply would be unenlightening, and even confusing. This, however, constitutes a different answer altogether (A3) and is thus no proof that the degree of enlightenment derived from a "Why" question can vary merely with variances in context.

Still, perhaps I am now obliged to say something about whether or not —and if so why—A3, which goes no deeper than A1, is a greater source of enlightenment. (If you think the intuitions here are so flimsy as to obviate further analysis, save your neurotransmitters and skip ahead to the next paragraph.) Notice, then, that if the owner of the rocks were instead to claim that the warm object is made of glubice, which has a short half-life, and that the other objects are made of a substance that has a very long half-life (A4), the degree to which one is enlightened by this reply will once again be proportional to the depth of one's knowledge concerning (the theory of) radioactive decay. If one's knowledge is extensive, then one will be able to formulate an explanation on the basis of A4 that runs quite deep, and certainly far deeper than if one lacks any such knowledge. Indeed, if one *does* lack any such knowledge, then if one can at least infer that the answer means that glubice emits heat, one will be in the very same position—in terms of the degree of enlightenment thereby obtained—as had the reply been A3.[30] Thus, compared to the level of enlightenment derived from A4 in conjunction with extensive knowledge of (the theory of) radioactive decay, the level of enlightenment derived from A3—which is just the same as the level derived from A4 in conjunction with no knowledge of (the theory of) radioactive decay—is terribly small. So, what we need here is an account of the difference between the absence of explanatory enlightenment—or, perhaps, the minuscule, hardly explanation-constituting degree of enlightenment—supplied by A1 in context C1 and the terribly small degree of explanatory enlightenment to be had on the basis of A3 in context C2. (Do you still wish to continue?) If the Model model is correct, then one could (were one so inclined) argue that the inference in the first case is based almost entirely upon the extrinsic representation of a regularity (i.e., one represents the object as warm for no other reason than that one has been told to). In the second case, one is making an ever-so-slightly greater use—which, mind you, is a degree of contrast that nicely fits the purposes at hand—of the intrinsic properties of one's representation of the scenario. That is to say, in the second case one has to represent the fact that there are five objects that are distinct—because they occupy distinct regions of space; one then incorporates into this ICM extrinsic representations of a pair of regularities.

But let us get back to the original point of this section. If we accept the D-N model, then we also have to accept that A1 is a fine explanation for the event in question. This is because the D-N model includes no provisions for distinguishing between, on the one hand, exceedingly shallow explanations (arguably non-explanations) such as the one conveyed (or not) by A1 above and, on the other hand, deep explanations such as the sort that might be constructed on the basis of A2 by one who has extensive knowledge of (the theory of) radioactive decay.[31] Such differences are, on the other hand, naturally accommodated by the Model model.

Let me illustrate this point with the help of a familiar and realistic example. Imagine that you wish to know why Fred has developed symptoms of Parkinson's Disease. If Fred's doctor were merely to tell you that Fred was in a high risk category, you would surely not feel very enlightened. (This is akin to the level of enlightenment you could derive from A1.) If, on the other hand, Fred's doctor were to tell you that Fred's symptoms are caused by the degeneration of inhibitory neurons in a certain part of his brain, to the extent that you derive some minuscule degree of enlightenment from this account, it is probably because you have been led to believe that there is some mechanism by which the latter produces the former. (This is akin to the level of enlightenment concerning E_3—see subsection 7.3.1.3—that might be derived from L_5 and C_3.) Now if the doctor were to convey to you some of the details of Mink's model (e.g., in the somewhat superficial manner that I have), you would surely feel that you had gained significant insight into the mechanisms that produce the symptoms. (This is akin to the degree of enlightenment you might derive from A2 if you had some, not too deep knowledge of (the theory of) radioactivity.[32]) The purposes of Fred's doctor might often be served by thinking of the mechanisms responsible in a correspondingly shallow way. (See subsection 8.3.3.) Still, if the doctor is worth his salt he will be at least capable of deriving many of the principles that he described to you from his beliefs concerning the mechanisms that produce them. He will also be able to bring this knowledge to bear, as needed, in order to anticipate exceptions to the high-level principles, generate predictions that could not be generated solely on the basis of a superficial understanding of the model, and so forth. (This is akin to the degree of enlightenment you might derive from A2 if you happened to have some pretty deep knowledge of the theory of radioactivity.) For the most part, this is just a re-statement of the tenets of the Model model that were discussed above, but the present point is that the Model model makes easy work of the fact that explanations can run the gamut from the terribly shallow to the very deep.

8.3.5 Probabilistic Explanations

Having broached the topic of radioactivity, we might as well discuss Salmon's claim that the manner in which quantum indeterminacies can affect macro-level goings on means that the special and applied sciences cannot "dispense with nondeductive statistical explanations" (1988, p. 118). If Salmon is right, then a monotonic-inference based model of explanation such as the Model model will have, at best, a limited range of applicability in the special sciences. It is therefore worth examining one of his examples in detail:

When Legionnaires' Disease was first diagnosed in 1976, it was found that every victim had attended an American Legion convention in Philadelphia, and that all of them had stayed at one particular hotel. In the population of individuals attending that convention, residence at that hotel was a necessary but by no means sufficient condition for contracting the disease. [3] Later, after the bacillus responsible for the disease had been isolated and identified, it was found that cooling towers for air conditioning systems in large buildings sometimes provide both a favorable environment for their growth and a mechanism to distribute them inside of the building. In this case, as well as in subsequent outbreaks in other places, only a small percentage of the occupants of the building contracted the disease. Since quantum fluctuations may lead to large uncertainties in the future trajectories of molecules in the air, and to those of small particles suspended in the atmosphere, [1] I believe it quite possible that there is, even in principle, no strictly deterministic explanation of which bacteria entered which rooms and no strictly deterministic explanation of which people occupying rooms infested with the bacteria contracted the disease. [2] Nevertheless, for purposes of assigning responsibility and taking preventive steps in the future, we have an adequate explanation of the disease in this very limited sample of the population of Americans in the summer of 1976. It is a nondeductive statistical explanation that, admittedly, may be incomplete. There is, however, no good reason to suppose that it can, even in principle, be transformed by the addition of further relevant information into a D-N explanation of the phenomenon with which we are concerned. . . . (Salmon 1988, p. 119; numerical indices added)

To reformulate Salmon's concern with a bit more precision, the worry is that any explanation for why some individual, say Fred, contracted the disease will, because of quantum fluctuations, be statistical in character, hence non-*monotonic*, hence non-deductive. It is the claim that some fully adequate explanations are not monotonic with which I will mainly take issue. All reference to deduction can, of course, be dispensed with as far as I am concerned.

To start with, we should be clear on what it means to say, as Salmon does at [2], that the explanation formulated by these researchers is "adequate." It cannot merely mean that the researchers' pragmatic ends have been served, for (per subsection 8.3.4 above) the degree to which one's pragmatic ends are served does not track the degree to which one has a genuine explanation. As Salmon himself famously claimed, one can come to know statistically relevant facts—which obviously have pragmatic value—while still standing far from the threshold of enlightenment. By the same token, one can take statistically relevant facts to be indicative of a causal relation and *still* have a long way to go (subsections 7.4.3, 8.3.3, 8.3.4). That is to say, merely believing that one event caused another is just to believe that there is some mechanism by which the former produces the latter. Unless we have knowledge of (or, at the very least, a hypothesis concerning) the "*mechanisms* of production," we cannot take ourselves to have "scientific understanding," which is "what we seek when we pose explanation-seeking answers to why-questions" (Salmon 1998, p. 139; emphasis added). Salmon must therefore mean that the researchers have an explanation because they have knowledge of (or, I would add, a hypothesis concerning) such mechanisms. This squares with his claims following [3]. He must, however, also believe that such knowledge [or such a hypothesis] does not amount to a representation of the sufficient conditions for the occurrence of the event. If it did, the example would pose no threat to the claim that explanations are based upon monotonic inferences.[33]

On a related note, we should also be clear on the fact that as Hempel and Oppenheim (1948) use the term 'fully adequate', to claim that an explanation is fully adequate is not to claim that the explanation touches on every detail, down to the "rock-bottom" minutiae (if such a place as Rock Bottom even exists) (Scriven 1962, p. 70); it simply means that the explanation adverts to the sufficient conditions for an event or regularity. These conditions might be describable entirely in the terms of a higher-level vocabulary even if one has no idea how these terms relate to those of some lower-level vocabulary. Let us, then, reserve 'fully adequate' for any case in which sufficient conditions for the event to be explained are known or hypothesized, even if the explanation does not hit rock bottom. Let us also call any explanation that *does* hit rock bottom an 'exhaustive' explanation. What I disagree with, then, is Salmon's claim that there are genuine explanations that are not fully adequate in the aforementioned sense.

Before this point can be elaborated further, it must be recognized that fully adequate explanations often have parts—i.e., that it is often the case that multiple, partial explanations make up a fully adequate explanation.[34] A partial explanation enables one to understand the conditions that sufficed for some necessary part of the total story to unfold. For instance, a fully adequate explanation for why Fred contracted Legionnaires' Disease would (in view of the interests of the medical investigators) involve beliefs about where the bacteria came from, how they got from their point of origin to Fred, how the particular manner in which Fred was exposed to the bacteria led him to become infected, and how infection led to the development of symptoms of the disease. Insofar as a part of a fully adequate explanation tells us the sufficient conditions for that part of the story to unfold, it is itself a fully adequate (partial) explanation. A fully adequate partial explanation might, of course, also involve multiple, fully adequate partial explanations. It may, on the other hand, quickly bottom out at unexplained or "brute" events and regularities. In light of these facts, it is clear that an explanation can be fully adequate while being deep in certain respects and shallow in others. To put the distinction metaphorically: Whether a certain part of a fully adequate explanation is deep or shallow is a vertical affair; that a fully adequate explanation must at least specify conditions that would suffice for the occurrence of the event is a horizontal affair.

If we keep these distinctions in mind, we see that what Salmon is denying, quite specifically, is that there can be a fully adequate explanation for that part of the story whereby bacteria made their way from their point of origin (that is, the cooling tower, which happened to contain a reservoir of warm stagnant water, the preferred growth medium for the bacterium *Legionella pneumophila*[35]) into the lungs of a particular individual (say, Fred). This, it seems to me, is a mistake. There is, to be sure, no way to render the explanation for this part of the story both exhaustive and fully adequate, but that is a much stronger requirement, and (fortunately) not one that must be satisfied in order for one to have a genuine explanation. A fully adequate explanation can, we have seen, bottom out at events or regularities that themselves go unexplained, most of which will be one or more steps removed from fundamental physics. To see how these lessons apply to the case at hand, allow me to make reference a bit of popular culture, of which I am an unapologetic connoisseur.

The makers of TV shows such as *CSI* and *House, M.D.*, who obviously have no stake in this particular dispute, make frequent use of virtual-reality models and other special effects in order to represent the various explanations entertained—many of which turn out to be grossly inaccurate—by crime-scene investigators and doctors interested in answering pressing questions of why and how. The representations of these thought processes often include depictions of microscopic happenings, but they all bottom out at a level far higher than quantum physics. A bullet may, for instance, be represented as tearing through flesh until it ruptures an artery at which point a massive hemorrhage occurs—this being just one *part* of a fully adequate explanation for why the person in question died. We are, in such cases, realistically led to believe that the crime-scene investigator does not think about why a fast-moving bullet tears through flesh (i.e., the crime-scene investigator does not represent the underlying mechanisms to himself). By the same token, at some point we may see a representation of an explanation entertained by an investigator in which a bacterium is discharged from some source, floats haphazardly through the air, is inhaled by an unwitting host, makes its way into the victim's lungs, gets trapped in a moist alveolus, begins to feed off the victim's lung, and multiplies (this still being just a part, albeit a big part, of a fully adequate explanation for why the person in question developed the symptoms of, let's say, Legionnaires' Disease).

Such depictions are the product of how special effects artists, in consult with actual crime-scene investigators and medical doctors, envision the thought processes of the fictitious scientists in question. I believe, however, that in so doing they have hit the nail precisely on the head. A fully adequate explanation for a particular event will often have parts, in the precise manner described above, and those partial explanations will sometimes run fairly deep while at other times they will be rather shallow. In his analysis of the case of Legionnaires' Disease, Salmon does not recognize these sensible distinctions, but once they are made we see that investigators in this case may have formulated fully adequate explanations (in the aforementioned sense) for why particular individuals, such as Fred, contracted the disease.

The parts of the explanation they may have formulated for why a particular individual such as Fred contracted the disease can be described roughly as follows: Bacteria were aspirated in large numbers from the cooling reservoir; they were carried through the ductwork into a particular room occupied by Fred; Fred inhaled the bacteria; at least one of them found a place within Fred where it could live, feed, and multiply; and this caused Fred to develop pneumonia-like symptoms. Investigators surely had a deep understanding of some, though perhaps not all, of these parts. Still, even if their explanation was rather shallow from start to finish, it would still constitute a fully adequate explanation for why Fred developed symptoms of the disease. After all, had investigators known beforehand that events would unfold in the way that they envisioned, they would have been able to predict that Fred would contract the disease. They *couldn't* have known this, of course, but that is entirely beside the point. The in-principle predictability of the event merely shows that they were able to represent to themselves the *conditions that would have sufficed* for Fred to contract the disease. Before you get your hackles up, let us focus on precisely why Salmon thinks that knowledge of sufficient conditions is impossible in this case.

Salmon claims that investigators could not have had a fully adequate explanation for that part of the story whereby bacteria made their way from their point of origin into Fred's lungs. What I am claiming, in contrast, is that investigators did have a fully adequate explanation for this part of the story. It bottomed out at a level far higher than quantum physics, but it went far deeper than the mere positing of a brute event — that is, it did not simply represent the fact that bacteria got from point A to point B without representing how this occurred.[36] To be specific, the fully adequate partial explanation in this case was constituted by beliefs about the presence of ductwork connecting the cooling tower to Fred's locale and about air being pushed from the former to the latter. A particular researcher's explanation for how Fred contracted the disease may even, one supposes, have run so deep as to specify how one particular bacterium in the larger swarm was aspirated from the reservoir, buffeted about, and carried, by air currents through the ductwork into Fred's lungs (i.e., in the style of *CSI* and *House, M.D.*). But surely the researcher's explanation bottomed out at a brute representation of the air currents involved. Nevertheless, this part of the explanation, though far from exhaustive, would have been fully adequate in the sense that it was constituted by a representation of the conditions that were sufficient for the bacterium to get from the point of aspiration to Fred.

It is quite doubtful that investigators entertained any thoughts about how quantum fluctuations affected particular atoms. A proper analysis of the explanations they possessed therefore need not, and probably should not, make any reference to quantum uncertainties. Nevertheless, let us imagine, for the sake of argument, that an investigator did consider the fact that inherently uncertain quantum fluctuation may have affected the trajectory of a particular air molecule and was, ultimately, responsible for the fact that the one bacterium responsible for Fred contracting the disease ended up in his lungs. Even in this case, the explanation would bottom out at a brute event. To be sure, the investigator could not have known beforehand which way the quantum event would turn out. Nevertheless, had the investigator known beforehand that events would unfold in the way that he envisioned (i.e., had he, per impossibile, known that the quantum event would occur in the way envisioned), he would be able to predict that Fred would contract the disease. The only qualitative difference between this case and the case where an investigator's explanation does not run so deep is just that the investigator in this case posits a brute event for which, we can assume, he believes there is no deeper explanation.

Many putative counter-examples to the D-N model have to do with the fact that explanations can be fully adequate while the partial explanations of which they are composed have varying degrees of depth. What philosophers of science seem to have overlooked is that a fully adequate, genuinely enlightening explanation can be constituted by a partial explanation that is quite shallow, or even by a part that itself has no explanatory power whatsoever (e.g., it might represent that the bacterium got from A to B, without representing how). In terms of their overall capacity to enlighten, however, there is obviously a very big difference between, on the one hand, the mere subsumption of the event to be explained under a brute regularity (e.g., A1 above) and an explanation that runs deep in certain parts but that has other parts in which one merely posits a brute event or subsumes a particular event under a brute regularity.

Evolutionary explanations can often be characterized in this way—for instance, "random" (a.k.a. "unexplained") mutations are typical brute posits of evolutionary explanations.[37] Still, the positing of one brute event does not render the explanation of which it is a part inadequate or unenlightening.[38] Notice, for instance, that the typical evolutionary explanation for how a particular trait came to be ubiquitous in a particular population is such that had one known beforehand that the story would unfold in the precise manner that one envisions, one could, in principle, have predicted that the trait would become ubiquitous.

Historical explanations of the actions of particular individuals are stories of a similar sort, though they often involve the representation of multiple brute happenings and have a heavy intentional component to them. Making sense of intentional explanations is, however, a problem unto itself, and it is one to which we turn presently.

8.3.6 Intentional Explanations

As I explained in section 2.2, one popular model of the human ability to predict and make sense of the behavior of our fellow humans is that we have tacit knowledge of a set of laws—specifically, the very sort of tacit knowledge of laws discussed in section 7.3—which specify the relationships between, among other things, particular beliefs, particular desires, and particular behaviors. This proposal, known as the Theory theory, is itself just an offshoot of the D-N model of explanation. It should also come as no surprise that proponents of the ML hypothesis also typically (perhaps invariably) embrace the Theory theory. It is, after all, a natural fit with their proposal that inference is effected through the application of syntax-sensitive inference rules to syntactically structured mental representations —that is, the data structures they posit are ideally suited to the task of effecting deductive inferences on the basis of representations of laws. We have already seen, however, that we rely heavily upon our capacity to make countless, endlessly qualified inferences with regard to the behaviors of simple machines and that deductive mechanisms are incapable of accounting for this fact. It thus seems unrealistic in the extreme to expect that a deductive model would fare any better when it comes to explaining our ability to make inferences about the behaviors of human beings. The argument here does not rely upon the assumption that we actually enjoy a great deal of predictive and explanatory *success* with regard to the behavior of our fellow humans—which is a good thing for the argument given that we are probably not very successful in this regard (section 2.4). Our mere ability to devise and communicate the kinds of post hoc, just-so stories that we encounter everyday supplies ample evidence of the tremendous productivity of the underlying inference mechanisms. If you do not think this point patently obvious, perhaps an example will help.

Suppose, then, that I hear my friend Chris, who happens to be a divorced man, making up an excuse to his daughter about why he cannot go ice skating with her. Knowing a bit about Chris, I concoct the following explanation for his behavior: Chris does not want to go to the ice rink with his daughter because he never learned to skate, and, having been passed over by his daughter in favor of his ex-wife at the custody proceedings, he is still extremely sensitive about her perception of him. This explanation can be used to generate lots of predictions. For instance, on the basis of it I can

—albeit at the risk of overlooking additional reasons for Chris' refusal—predict that if his daughter learns the actual reason for his refusal to go skating, and if she subsequently explains to him that the only reason she chose her mother was that her mother seemed far more fragile and in need of support, then he will—that is, provided certain provisos are satisfied that go beyond the additional reasons just mentioned—change his mind and agree to go skating with her. Any of the countless provisos in terms of which this prediction is qualified can, of course, be invoked should my prediction fail. Likewise, I can predict that if, after the skating event has come and gone, Chris comes to think that his daughter was merely testing to see whether or not he forgave her for choosing her mother, then, on the basis of my belief that Chris does not bear any ill will toward his daughter, Chris would find some way to convey to his daughter that he does not think she stands in need of any forgiveness. And so on and so forth, ad infinitum. And this is just a single example.

To be sure, these explanations and predictions may miss the mark entirely. For instance, maybe Chris refused to go because he was going to the doctor to be checked for syphilis. (In fact, in my case there are always good inductive grounds for supposing that I *have* missed the mark entirely.) Regardless, we are clearly able to generate and comprehend an unlimited store of explanations like this one, explanations that are complicated, laden with affective nuances (Gordon 1996), and have countless further implications (each of which is qualified in endless ways) apart from the event to be explained. This is enough to convince me that the D-N model will fare no better with regard to intentional explanation than it did with regard to mechanical explanation. What we require, once again, is an account that adverts to mechanisms that exhibit tremendous inferential productivity.

A natural first inclination might be to think that the ICM hypothesis will fare far better. It is, unfortunately, also pretty clear that the foregoing inferences concerning Chris' behavior are not based on a highly sophisticated mechanical model of the cognitive underpinnings for his behavior. We, as folk, *do* endorse a set of interrelated models of the mechanisms underwriting human behavior (subsection 2.4.3), but these models are far *too* schematic to be of any use when it comes to making detailed predictions and explanations of the sort just described.

In light of these facts, one very sensible proposal is that our intentional inferences are much like those made on the basis of alterations to model organisms in biological and medical circles. When researchers lack a detailed understanding of the mechanisms underlying some physiological phenomenon but wish to know the consequences of certain alterations (e.g., the effects of administering a certain drug, the effects of sensory deprivation on axonal connectivity, the effects of an overabundance of K+, etc.), they often subject model organisms to the same alterations. In this way, predictions (albeit highly fallible ones) can be generated, and explanations can even be formulated, though the explanations generated in this way are often quite shallow.

Suppose, for instance, that we wish to know why Brandon developed a cough and a rash, and we suspect that it has to do with a substance that he (and only he) inhaled. In this case, we could expose a model organism to similar conditions and see what happens. If the organism develops similar symptoms, we will feel more confident that inhaling the substance caused some kind of change in Brandon's physiology that led, in turn, to these symptoms. This result would, of course, have some real practical utility (e.g., we would now know to instruct Brandon to avoid further exposure to the substance), but if our knowledge of physiology were very limited it would afford only a very shallow degree of explanatory insight.

In just the same way, one can make inferences on the basis of a manipulation to a scale model of some system with great predictive and practical import, even though the degree of insight afforded in this way is quite limited. For example, if one has a full-scale model of a complicated machine such as a Mars rover, one might find that subjecting it to conditions that are similar to those on Mars causes (or at least appears to) the same response—namely, going into safe mode—exhibited by the actual rover. However useful this information may be, if this were the extent of one's knowledge of why the rover went into safe mode, one would have (at best) a very shallow explanation for that response. One should still like to know why the conditions produced the response, and understanding this requires knowledge of the intervening mechanisms.[39]

A slightly deeper level of understanding might, on the other hand, be had by someone who has knowledge of the gross functional breakdown of the rover. Such individuals might, for instance, be able to envision the manner in which the effects of the conditions in question propagated through various subsystems until reaching the one responsible for executing the instruction to enter safe mode. Hypothetical technicians of this sort are, I believe, in a position closely analogous to the position that we folk are in with regard to one another's behavior. Like these technicians, we have some knowledge of (or at least hypotheses concerning) the mechanisms that collectively conspire to cause human behavior. Still, our understanding of these mechanisms is not so deep as to enable the kinds of predictions and explanations of particular behaviors that we generate and convey on a daily basis.[40] Our only recourse, then, insofar as we wish to predict and (to a limited extent) explain human behavior, is to use *ourselves* as a model organism. We have, it seems, no choice but to imaginatively subject ourselves to counterfactual conditions.[41] We have, in other words, no choice but to take an imaginary walk in our compatriots' shoes, or to simulate (Gordon 1996; for some important refinements, see Perner 1996). To be sure, the predictions we generate in this way will be highly fallible, and the explanations we generate will be somewhat shallow. The latter will, however, at least be framed by the collection of schematic models in terms of which we understand one another's behavior.

This way of viewing the matter fits nicely with the fact that we folk ultimately have precious little understanding of the actual mechanisms by which certain beliefs and desires conspire to cause particular behaviors. For instance, I may hypothesize that Chris did not want his daughter to know the real reason he did not want to go skating and that this is what led him to make up an excuse. In a certain sense, this is as deep as the explanation can possibly go, for I do not have any understanding of the mechanisms whereby the first event produced the second.[42]

8.4 The D-N Model: A Parting Shot

In this chapter I have shown that the Model model is a mechanistic model of the psychological underpinnings for explanation and, thereby, for our philosophical and metaphilosophical intuitions concerning the nature of explanation.[43] As we saw in chapter 7, the D-N model can itself only be understood as a mechanistic model of the psychological underpinnings for explanation. Indeed, if it is not that, then it is mysterious what the D-N model could possibly be a model *of*. Construed, however, as a psychological model of explanation, it is perfectly intelligible. We can make sense of the proposal that humans harbor and deductively manipulate representations of laws and specific conditions through an appeal to a mechanistic model of the process of deduction such as the ML hypothesis.

But then one wonders whether the ML hypothesis is itself composed of a body of laws. If it is, what are they? Perhaps, with Herculean effort, an inveterate proponent of both the D-N and ML hypotheses could supply some answers. Still, we saw (in chapter 2) that the goal of cognitive science is to formulate accurate models of the mechanisms underwriting human behavior. We also saw (in chapter 6) that a great milestone in the history of ML hypothesis was its maturation from an explanatory metaphor into an explanatory mechanism, and this was based principally upon our understanding of how other mechanisms that share a relevantly similar structure can quite literally engage in the application of syntax-sensitive inference rules to syntactically structured representations.[44] While the D-N model flounders on such facts, they are explained quite easily by the Model model. The Model model makes it far easier to understand why both the Model model and the D-N model are models at all!

In this chapter, I try to push the D-N model out of its stronghold of fundamental physics by showing that the deductions from laws that occur there do not count as explanations. I also show that my ICM hypothesis explains, and largely vindicates, the intuitions behind Kant's theory of geometrical knowledge. I close with some speculation about the possibility of hyper-dimensional cognition.

9.1 Introduction

The most important objectives set for this book have now been accomplished. One major, and quite general, objective has been to show how philosophy and cognitive science (cognitive science) can inform one another without either lording it over the another. I have, of course, had a variety of far more specific objectives in mind as well. Here is a bit of background.

I started off years ago with the feeling that philosophers of mind really just don't get what cognitive science is all about. Countless discussions in the philosophy of mind have been presupposed that something very close to the D-N model supplies the correct account of scientific explanation. This, in turn, seems to have aided promulgation of the view that the computational theory of mind lies at the foundation of research in mainstream cognitive science. After all, the D-N model demands formal statements of the laws of cognition. At the same time, cognitive science cannot go without positing complicated intermediaries between stimuli and behaviors. Thus, if the D-N model is correct, what cognitive science must supply is a set of laws relating stimuli to internal states and internal states to one another and behavior. cognitive science must, in other words, specify the program being run by the nervous system, and that is precisely what theoretical computationalism is all about (Putnam 1990; see also subsection 1.2.3).

These views have, moreover, framed the debate about the scientific credentials of folk psychology. In order to be vindicated or refuted by cognitive science, folk psychology would herself have to be a theory, which, under the above assumptions, means that it would have to be composed of a body of laws. Thus, the question seemed to be whether or not cognitive science would supply a body of laws much like those supposedly constitutive of folk psychology.

All this hogwash has blinded philosophers to, among other things, the fact that the collection of schematic models constitutive of folk psychology has already been amply vindicated by cognitive science. *It is these models*, and *not* the computational theory of mind, that lie at the foundation of research in mainstream cognitive science.

Perhaps the one thing required in order for this proposal to gain general acceptance is a compelling alternative to the D-N model that might do justice to the explanatory activities of cognitive science. And in order to formulate a compelling alternative to the D-N model, what is required is a compelling alternative to the Mental Logic (ML) model (a.k.a. the Language of Thought hypothesis) of the truth-preserving manipulation of mental representations, for if the ML model of truth preservation (viz., the monotonic variety that lies at the heart of explanation and certain predictions; see sections 5.3 and 7.3) were correct, then the D-N model would also be correct. In addition, it is no small matter for philosophers of mind who are in the grips of the D-N illusion that the D-N model itself *requires* formal manipulations in Mentalese (i.e., it requires something like either the ML hypothesis or Johnson-Laird and Byrne's mental tables; see section 5.3) in order to account for what it means to *have* an explanation—that is, to account for *tacit* law subsumption (section 7.3) and the fact that explanations provide *understanding* the whys and hows of the events and regularities of interest (sections 7.2 and 7.4).

Accordingly, I set out to show that there *is* an alternative to the ML account of monotonic reasoning in the form of the ICM hypothesis (chapters 4 and 6). I then showed how this, in turn, might undergird a compelling alternative to the D-N model. (Indeed, the fates of these two alternative models are linked in just about the same manner as the fates of the D-N and ML models.) Much of this book has thus been devoted to defending these alternatives to the D-N and ML models so as to do justice, at last, to the explanatory activities of cognitive science. Whatever minor missteps I may have made along the way, I am confident that my overarching mission has been accomplished. And this, I believe, is just the first step in a major restructuring of the philosophy of mind.

Still, I find myself so impressed by how the ICM-enriched Model model of explanation has performed and so disturbed by how readily philosophers and scientists follow the example set by fundamental physics (see section 8.1) that I wish to take matters a step further. I wish to make it clear that the Model model is not restricted in scope to some subset of explanations for physical events and regularities (e.g., those formulated in everyday life and in the special sciences). I wish to show that it is the correct model of explanation for physical events and regularities of all kinds.

For this reason, I will turn to my attention the bastion of the D-N model: fundamental physics. I will show that although fundamental physics involves deductions of the very sort that D-N theorists have in mind (again, see section 8.1), it systematically fails to exhibit a fundamental hallmark of science (see section 1.2)—specifically, it habitually, and inescapably, fails to supply genuine explanations for the phenomena it investigates. I will also show that the reason these deductions are not explanations is that they are not tied to comprehensible models of underlying mechanisms.

The reasons for approaching the problem in this way are as follows. On the one hand, if the deductions of events and regularities from laws that one finds in fundamental physics are counted as genuine explanations, then the D-N model can lay claim to being the correct model of explanation for (at least part of) physics, and physics will at the same time be able to retain its exalted status. On the other hand, if even *these* deductions are not explanations, then (i) we will have some reason to believe that *no* mere deductions of statements describing phenomena to be explained from statements of laws count as explanations, (ii) the D-N model will have been driven from its stronghold, and (iii) physics—viz., the branch that uses what Einstein, quoted below, calls *analytic methods* (as opposed to synthetic methods)—will no longer seem so high and mighty.

My claim that fundamental physics does not supply explanations is, we shall see, in no way novel; it is one to which quantum and relativistic physicists readily assent. I do think, however, that we can gain a fairly deep understanding of just why this is so—that is, we can understand something about *why* fundamental physics fails to supply explanations—if we pick up where we left off in our discussion of seventeenth- and eighteenth-century philosophy (section 1.1). This will also provide answers to some age-old philosophical questions and thereby lend further support to my earlier contention (section 1.3) that there is a naturalistic explanation for *whatever kind of knowledge* we apparently possess.

Before reading on, you should heed the following disclaimers:

• What I propose here does lack the same rigor as the material presented in earlier chapters. I am delving into issues that are direct offshoots of the foregoing considerations but that do fall outside my area of specialization. I am forced, therefore, to make frequent appeals to authority.

• It is terribly difficult, when discussing issues such as these, to avoid getting sucked into the deepest problems of metaphysics. I therefore simply assume a broadly realist metaphysics. I believe, however, that this is an appropriate, and eminently sensible, assumption for philosophers of mind and cognitive scientists to make. Indeed, our work *already* assumes a basically realist metaphysics.

• Many of the arguments in this chapter are premised upon the claim that the same systems that are responsible for our immediate experiences of the world are also the ones that we use to think about it. I will not offer a sustained argument for this claim; others have already done so. (See Brooks 1968; Segal and Fusella 1970; Kosslyn 1994; Barsalou and Prinz 1997; Prinz 2002. For a novel proposal, see Cruse 2003.) However, this claim does fit very well with both the ICM hypothesis and with the character of our experiences of the world. We experience a world that is composed of objects that persist through time and that have local and relational geometrical and dynamical properties (e.g., the lid on my laptop computer is something that can be folded down, the computer is supported by a flat surface, it is within my reach, and I can feel my fingers pressing on its keys and hear the resulting clicking sound). What we experience are objects that appear to be subject to many interacting inter-dimensional constraints.[1] This is clearly the combined effect of advanced stages of processing in multiple sensory modalities (see sections 1.1 and 6.3), and it is also precisely the sort of thing that ICMs are meant to explain. All of this, incidentally, also accords nicely with what is known about the consolidation of declarative knowledge discussed in section 2.4.

Think of this chapter, then, as a bit of speculative dessert earned by your efforts up to this point.

9.2 Kant and Synthetic A Priori Knowledge of Geometry

At the start of chapter 1, I explained that philosophers of the seventeenth and eighteenth centuries witnessed the ascendancy of the mechanistic worldview and that these philosophers wondered whether or not this worldview could accommodate important facts about the mind. One feature of our mental lives that proved particularly difficult to accommodate was our seeming ability to acquire knowledge of the necessary and timeless truths of geometry. Accordingly, each of the major figures of this period undertook to solve the mystery of how such knowledge was possible. More specifically, they set out to either explain, or explain away, this kind of knowledge through an appeal to its psychological underpinnings, whether physical or non-physical.

Toward the end of chapter 1, I explained that many have since come to view this project, or similar ones undertaken with regard to logic, as misguided. On one version of this worry, the attempt to understand the psychological processes involved in the acquisition of this kind of knowledge can only yield descriptions of *contingent* facts regarding how we *happen* to think rather than descriptions of *necessary* facts concerning how we *ought* to think. The worry, then, is that what seemed most interesting and important about this kind of knowledge will fall by the wayside. While I agree that there is some basis to these concerns, I also believe that we are evolved, biological creatures. For this reason, I feel an obligation to investigate how it is that physical creatures such as ourselves could either come to have the kind of knowledge in question or come to think that we have this kind of knowledge. As it turns out, a naturalist can retain much of what is interesting and important about our knowledge of geometry, and that which cannot be retained makes room for bold new possibilities for human and non-human cognition.

Let us turn, then, to the investigation into the nature of geometrical knowledge that began early in the seventeenth century and that reached its high point late in the eighteenth century in the form of a section of Kant's (1787) *Critique of Pure Reason* titled "Transcendental Aesthetic" (TA). In this section, Kant proposed a model of the psychological underpinnings for geometrical knowledge that overcame, in a quite elegant manner, what he perceived to be the shortcomings of every major position that had come before. To be sure, concerns have since been raised about Kant's own model, and we will discuss these in due course. But before we consider these, let us first get a handle on what Kant must have found so compelling about his model. In the spirit of this exercise, let us take an imaginary walk in Kant's shoes and attempt to see the developments leading up to the TA as Kant might have seen them. In the next section, then, I give my best rendition of how Kant might have understood these developments, though I will avoid his abstruse verbiage wherever possible and throw in anachronisms wherever they prove useful. As point of reference I will call upon your knowledge of the spatial proof of the Pythagorean Theorem presented in section 5.2, for it was knowledge generated through the use of this "synthetic" method (see section 5.3) that Kant seemed most concerned to explain.

9.2.1 Kant's Desiderata for a Theory of Geometrical Knowledge: A Historical Reenactment

Any theory of how geometrical knowledge is possible must satisfy several desiderata. While various recent theories have satisfied some, none has yet satisfied all. There is, in fact, only one theory that can *possibly* satisfy all, and this provides sufficient assurance that it is correct.

A theory of geometrical knowledge must, in particular, account for the following features of the first principles (axioms) of geometry and of the additional facts (theorems) that can be indefeasibly derived from them:

i They are necessary—They are, in principle, exceptionless.

[Example: The Pythagorean Theorem does not express a fact that happens to hold of one, or of many, right triangles; it expresses a fact that *must* hold of *all* right triangles.]

ii They are synthetic—They cannot be known simply by analyzing the meanings of terms or their associated concepts.

[Example: The proof of the Pythagorean Theorem in chapter 5 was not based upon a simple analysis of what one means by the term 'right triangle.' It required, among other things, the mental 'cutting' and 'rotation' of figures.]

Kant seems to have taken *ii* to be obvious, but let me fall out of character for a moment in order to give a better sense for why Kant might have felt this way. Consider, if you will, the apparent differences between, on the one hand, the spatial proof of the Pythagorean Theorem carried out in chapter 5 and, on the other hand, an inference to the effect that all (non-pathological) lions have bones (e.g., because lions are mammals, which have vertebra, which are bones). Does not the spatial proof of the Pythagorean Theorem seem obviously different in kind? At the very least, the latter chain of reasoning is clearly far simpler to follow, and the conclusion is far simpler to 'discover' than the Pythagorean Theorem. Getting back into character. . . .]

iii They are about objects—They express truths regarding the properties of the objects that we experience.

[Example: The Pythagorean Theorem is true of any right triangle we might encounter.]

iv Theorems take effort to discover—Self-explanatory.

[Example: spatial proof of the Pythagorean Theorem in chapter 5.]

v They are universal—They can be grasped by any (unimpaired) human being who is willing to put in the time and effort.

[Example: Anyone willing to devote the requisite time and attention can understand the demonstration of the Pythagorean Theorem in chapter 5.]

vi They are known a priori—They are justified in such a manner that we are able to be certain that no possible experience could contradict them (i.e., that they are necessary).

[Example: We know that the proof would unfold in exactly the same manner for any pair of squares (and hence any right triangle) whatsoever because the lengths of the sides had no bearing on the proof; there is thus no possibility that we could encounter a counter-example.]

They are infinite in number—Self-explanatory.

§1 Hobbes

Hobbes thought that geometrical reasoning was simply the addition and subtraction of the consequences of the names that we use to signify our thoughts. While he claimed that the axioms were carefully chosen in geometry, he never did give a clear account of why one set should be chosen over another. His proposal thus:

Satisfied *i* for theorems, but not axioms. For Hobbes, *given* the axioms, specific conclusions can be indefeasibly inferred, but the axioms themselves are arbitrary.

Failed to satisfy *ii*. On Hobbes' view, geometrical reasoning is analytic.

Failed to satisfy *iii*. For Hobbes, geometrical reasoning is but reckoning (a kind of arithmetic) concerning names.

Did not fully satisfy *iv*. Analytic reasoning does take some effort, but it is far simpler than utilization of the synthetic method in geometry.

Failed to satisfy *v*. To be sure, if the axioms are settled on, anyone should be able to deduce the consequences. But Hobbes gave no account of why the axioms cannot vary from culture to culture, or person to person.

Satisfied *vi*. An implication of Hobbes' view is that the objects of experience are well-nigh irrelevant to the process of geometrical reasoning, so no experience could refute the deductions in question.

Failed to satisfy *vii*. The tree of analytic (i.e., super-ordinate and sub-ordinate) relationships is finite.

§2 Locke

Locke's work was a significant advance over Hobbes'. On Locke's view, while it may well be that the world is configured in some particular manner (e.g., it may be that there are many *real* essences out there), we epistemically impoverished creatures can obviously never attain certainty with regard to what that manner is. It does, however, sometimes prove quite useful to mark out boundaries of our own devising (cf. subsection 5.2.4.2). Says Locke (1690/1964): '[T]he *ideas* themselves are considered as the archetypes, and things no otherwise regarded but as they are conformable to them. So that we cannot but be infallibly certain that all the knowledge we attain concerning these *ideas* is real, and reaches things themselves, because in all our thoughts, reasonings, and discourses of this kind, we intend things no further than as they are conformable to our *ideas*' (p. 356). Thus, for example, if we stipulate that 'water' signifies any liquid that is, at room temperature, transparent, colorless, potable, and flavorless, then we can never be wrong in claiming that water has no flavor. Locke takes this to be no less true in the case of mathematical reasoning. Here also we impose our own classification scheme on nature and deduce consequences from that scheme, and here also our conclusions hold sway not just over ideas, but over reality as well. Locke (1690/1964) explains, 'The mathematician considers the truth and properties belonging to a rectangle or circle only as they are *in* his own mind. For it is possible he never found either of them existing mathematically, i.e., precisely true, in his life. But yet the knowledge he has of any truths or properties belonging to a circle or any other mathematical figure is nevertheless true and certain, even of real things existing, because real things are no further concerned, nor intended to be meant by any such propositions, than as things really agree to those *archetypes* in his mind. Is it true of the *idea* of a *triangle* that its three angles are equal to two right ones? It is true also of a *triangle*, wherever it really exists' (pp. 356–367).

While Locke's account of analytic a priori knowledge is entirely correct, and his account of geometrical knowledge satisfies an important additional desideratum, it does ultimately fall short of the mark. In particular, Locke's proposal is an advance over Hobbes' in that it satisfies *iii*. For this reason, it satisfies *vi* in a slightly different, but far better, manner than Hobbes' proposal. On Locke's view, if we stipulate that to be a right triangle is to have certain properties and certain consequences of these stipulations can be deduced, we can be certain that we will never encounter a falsifier. In all other respects, Locke's view is like Hobbes'. Thus, we still need a theory that satifies *i*, *ii*, *iv*, *v*, and *vii*.

§3 Leibniz

Leibniz realized that a major short-coming of Locke's account was its failure to satisfy condition *v*. His proposed remedy echoed that of earlier thinkers who claimed that mathematical knowledge is an innate, divine endowment. This strategy also enabled the satisfaction of *i* and *vi*. At the same time, however, Leibniz recognized that this view fared even worse than the analytic approach when it came to condition *iv*. As a remedy, he offered the beautiful analogy between innate knowledge and the veins in a block of marble that require effort to discover but that naturally lead to the creation of a particular sculpture (e.g., of Hercules). Still, the approach is ruled out by its opulent metaphysics and its clear failure to satisfy conditions *ii* and *vii*.

§3 Transcendental Aesthetic for Dummies

My own model meets all of the above criteria in the most elegant, and intuitive manner imaginable. Allow me to explain.

There is obviously a distinction between how objects appear to us and how they are in-and-of-themselves. Appearances are but representations of the world, and representations require a representational medium. The properties of a representational medium will, moreover, impose inviolable constraints on the properties of the representations constructed in that medium [see subsections 6.4.3 and 6.5.1]. As a case in point, notice that the use of chalk marks on a blackboard to construct representations imposes inviolable constraints on the properties of the representations so constructed. For example, if a given closed planar figure, *x*, is drawn entirely inside of another closed planar figure, y, and y is drawn entirely inside of a third closed planar figure, z, then figure x simply *must* be inside of z.

Clearly the mind's representational medium is a great deal more productive [see subsections 4.3.1.1 and 4.1.1] than a blackboard, but it too imposes constraints that no representation constructed in this medium can violate. Geometrical reasoning is simply reasoning about the constraints imposed upon the various things that might appear to us by the medium in which they appear; it is reasoning about how things must appear if they are to appear at all.

To keep things brief, my proposal satisfies the seven desiderata regarding geometrical axioms and theorems as follows:

i They are necessary—They are, in principle, exceptionless.

They are necessitated by the constraints imposed upon the structure of representations by the very medium in which they are created.

ii They are synthetic—They cannot be known simply by analyzing the meanings of terms or their associated concepts.

They are known through the construction of mental images of figures and their manipulation—for instance, through mental 'cutting' and 'rotation.'

iii They are about objects—They express truths regarding the properties of the objects that we experience.

The objects we encounter, the objects of experience, are but representations.

iv Theorems take effort to discover—Self-explanatory.

The manipulation of mental images of figures is required.

v They are universal—They can be grasped by any (unimpaired) human being who is willing to put in the time and effort.

The present proposal is a variant on rationalist nativism. It is not that we all share a store of ideas that await discovery; rather, we all share a representational medium.

vi They are known a priori—They are justified in such a manner that we are able to be certain that no possible experience could contradict them (i.e., that they are necessary).

Nothing could appear in a way that is not permitted by our representational medium; there can be no counter-examples.

vii They are infinite in number—Self-explanatory.

The medium of representation is capable of representing countless objects and alterations thereto.

A word of caution is in order here. Because the synthetic a priori knowledge supplied by geometry merely concerns the manner in which objects must appear to us, it would be a grave mistake to think that this knowledge extends to things as they are in themselves. We are in no way permitted to make the leap from properties of our representational medium to the properties of the things in themselves. That would be somewhat like inferring from a chalk depiction of a lion that lions are erasable. The certainty that characterizes geometrical knowledge only extends as far as the objects of experience.

Thanks, Immanuel. I'll take it from here.

9.2.2 Kant and the ICM Hypothesis

Where did Kant go wrong?

Popular lore has it that Kant was *proven* wrong by the advent of non-Euclidean geometries and by their eventual, and irrevocable, employment in fundamental physics which began with Einstein's "account" of gravitational attraction and has since led to the popular theory that the universe contains roughly ten spatial dimensions. There is some fact in this, but also some fiction. I will get to both in a moment, but first let us consider the relationship between Kant's views on the nature of geometrical knowledge and the ICM hypothesis advanced in chapter 6.

Put succinctly, to the extent that one shares Kant's intuitions about the nature of geometrical reasoning, the ICM hypothesis explains why. Kant, as you probably know, would have denied that the representational medium of which he spoke could *truly* be understood in mechanical terms; he claimed that it is transcendent. This may be because he was searching for a way to psychologize the knowledge at issue while hanging onto its apparent necessity and universality. There is, unfortunately, no way to do this; not really. There is, however, a way to account for, without completely deflating, our intuitions that geometrical axioms and theorems are necessarily true. Locke, in fact, came quite close to doing just that:

... knowledge is the consequence of the *ideas* (be they what they will) that are in our minds producing there general certain propositions. Many of these are called *eternal truths* (*aeternae veritates*), and all of them indeed are so, not from being written all or any of them in the minds of all men, or that they were any of them propositions in anyone's mind, until he, having gotten the abstract *ideas*, joined or separated them by affirmation or negation. But wherever we can suppose such a creature as *man* is endowed such faculties, and by this means furnished with such *ideas* as we have, we must conclude, he must necessarily, when he applies his thoughts to the consideration of his *ideas*, know the truth of certain propositions that will arise from the agreement or disagreement which he will perceive in his own *ideas*. Such propositions are therefore called *eternal truths* ... because being once made about abstract *ideas*, so as to be true, they will, whenever they can be supposed to be made again at any time past or to come, by a mind having those *ideas*, always actually be true. (1690/1964, p. 367)

This is a mouthful, but the core of the proposal is simple and accurate. In the context of the spatial proof of the Pythagorean Theorem, it amounts to something like this: Anyone whose mind works the way that mine does and who puts in the time and effort can be certain that the theorem is true of any right triangle that they may (i.e., so long as the facts about their minds remain constant) encounter.

If we replace Locke's appeal to the analysis of stipulated ideas with a basically Kantian appeal to the constraints imposed on appearances by the medium of representation, we can take matters one step further. We can take the axioms and theorems of Euclidean geometry to be derived from consideration of, and to express truths about, how things *must* appear to any creature that has a medium for representing the world that works in the way that our own does. This is a point that was hinted at in subsection 6.4.3. To reiterate, with a shift of emphasis:

> It is not at the level of the primitive operations of an implementation base that we find intrinsic representations, but at the level of the representations realized by a given, primitively constrained implementation base. Part of what justifies this claim is the fact that *certain constraints will be inviolable at the representation level . . . given that the representations have been implemented by a particular kind of medium.*

As an illustration of how this point applies to geometrical reasoning, and to quote myself again (this time from subsection 5.2.4, with emphasis added), let us revisit a bit of spatial rotation performed in our proof of the Pythagorean Theorem:

> . . . let us imagine that the top vertex of the leftmost triangle is a fixed point and let us mentally rotate the triangle around this point so that the side of length *a* is aligned with the top edge of the square, which is also of length *a*. Since both are of length *a, there will be no overlap. Also, when two right angles are placed adjacent to one another in this way they will form a straight line.* Once again, *the total area of the figure will have remained unchanged.*

It is utterly inconceivable to me, and to you as well, that alterations like the ones in question might, in either imagination or outward experience, not have the consequences described here (in italics). Kant gave us a reasonable, albeit ultimately just metaphorical, explanation for why this is so. What the ICM hypothesis provides is a more naturalistic explanation for why we feel, and are (i.e., so long as our minds continue to function in their present manner) correct in so feeling, that it is, in principle, impossible for the course of experience to unfold in any other way.

Where *did* Kant go wrong?

9.2.3   How Physics Corroborates Kant's TA and the Model Model

For starters, we cannot have any certitude that every creature works as we do, or even that *we* will continue to work in the way that we currently do —that is, we have to give up any claim to certitude when it comes to criterion *v*. Kant did not offer up any compelling arguments to the contrary, nor, from where this naturalist sits, could he have. This may, we will see later, ultimately turn out to be a good thing.

So what of the developments in mathematics and physics? Do they not straightforwardly falsify Kant's claims about the nature of geometrical knowledge? As I will explain, in point of fact they only corroborate those claims, but they do undermine Kant's position on the subject matter of physics.

9.2.3.1 Knowledge of Things in Themselves   Kant, like many others of his day, was concerned to discover the extent and limits of our capacity for a priori knowledge and, ultimately, to provide a secure foundation for the sciences by claiming that the fundamental principles of nature can be known a priori, rather than inductively as the empiricists thought. He employed the same basic explanatory strategy that worked so well for geometrical knowledge. In particular, he proposed that there are not only spatial, but also *kinematical* and *dynamical* constraints imposed upon the objects that we experience in virtue of the properties of the medium of representation through which they are experienced.[2] Moreover, he took *nature*, the subject matter of science, to be restricted to the realm of experience. Thus, on his view, fundamental physics amounted to the study of what he considered to be the fundamental spatial, kinematical, and dynamical properties of the objects of experience, and the rest of the sciences, the empirical ones, involved the study of the many properties of the many different types of things that we encounter in experience (subsection 6.4.4). These properties were, of course, taken to be *ultimately* determined by the fundamental constraints governing the medium of representation through which they are experienced which, he claimed, could be known a priori. Thus, Kant thought, the epistemological buck stops right where it should—namely, with a priori knowledge of the fundamental principles of nature.

When it comes down to the details, which I will not discuss here (but see note 3 to chapter 1), Kant's supposed proof of the necessity of specific kinematical and dynamical principles was less than compelling. What matters here, however, is that Kant thought he could supply foundations for the sciences in the form of a priori knowledge of the fundamental determinants of the behavior of the objects of experience and that he considered the subject matter of the sciences to be these very objects. Given this solution to this problem and his demand for certainty, it made sense for him to claim that no knowledge is possible regarding the fundamental properties of whatever realm might lie beyond appearances. Kant did, however, clearly overstep his bounds when it came to certain claims that he made regarding this realm, and considering just how he did so provides a nice way of highlighting the tensions between his position with regard to the subject matter of fundamental physics and the facts of the matter.

To see, then, just how Kant overstepped his bounds, consider again the chalkboard analogy.[3] In the case of the chalkboard, there are clearly some constraints governing the representations constructed with the chalkboard medium (e.g., erasability) that do not (generally) correspond to the constraints operative in the represented world, but there are also some that do correspond. For instance, if one represents the ears of a creature as being above the level of the neck and the neck as being above the level of the feet, then this will necessitate representing the ears as being above the level of the feet. Unlike erasability, there is (just as with the *contained-in* relation discussed earlier) a counterpart to the transitive *above* relation that is operative in the world.

Now, Kant (1787/1998) viewed the truths of geometry as being like erasability, as being mere artifacts of the medium that we use to represent the world. For this reason, he made claims such as the following: "Space does not represent any property of things in themselves, nor does it represent them in their relations to one another. That is to say, space does not represent any determination that attaches to the objects themselves, and which remains when abstraction has been made of all the subjective conditions of intuition . . . if we depart from the subjective condition under which alone we can have outer intuition . . . the representation of space stands for nothing whatsoever" (A 26/B42-3). Kant's apologists will contort themselves in their search for a more charitable reading. However, he is clearly claiming here that space is *not* a property of things in themselves, when what he *should* have been claiming is that we simply do not know for certain whether the truths of geometry hold in the realm of things in themselves. In other words, we do not know for certain whether they are more like erasability or more like the *above* and *contained-in* relations.

As it turns out, the truth probably lies somewhere in between, and this is where the tension between Kant's view of physics and the facts of the matter become clear. In particular, there are at least important isomorphisms between the geometry of appearances and the geometry of nature as it is in itself. These, we are told, are due to the fact that many of the ten (at last count) spatial dimensions are "curled up" in such a way that they are rendered largely inert insofar as the everyday interests of middle-sized creatures such as ourselves are concerned. Claims such as this are, of course, anathema to the Kant's position on the subject matter of physics. To be sure, Kant was correct in asserting that the certitude that we are capable of attaining with regard to how things must appear to us can never be carried over to the realm of things in themselves. But what he failed to recognize, in his admirable pursuit of certainty, is that we are able to formulate and test hypotheses regarding this realm and that *this* is what physics and the rest of the sciences are all about. Einstein would later put it this way: "The belief in an external world independent of the perceiving subject is the basis of all natural science. Since, however, sense perception only gives information of this external world or of 'physical reality' indirectly, we can only grasp the latter by speculative means. It follows from this that our notions of physical reality can never be final. We must always be ready to change these notions—that is to say, the axiomatic structure of physics—in order to do justice to perceived facts in the most logically perfect way." (quoted in Margenau, 1949, p. 248) In other words, with regard to things in themselves, we can pursue inferences to the best explanation or, failing that, to the best mathematical fit. As it turned out, pursuit of the latter was the only way to go when it came to the fundamental principles of nature.

By way of elaboration, let me pick up where I left off in my discussion of formal vs. synthetic methods in geometry in subsection 5.3.3. In my very brief survey of the history of analytic geometries, I noted that even some of the most able mathematicians objected early on to the new analytic methods on the grounds that that they required trafficking in expressions that were incomprehensible, by which I meant expressions whose meanings could not be visualized. Eventually, however, the economy and utility of analytic methods won out over the synthetic methods. This, of course, paved the way for the development of non-Euclidean geometries, for the constraints governing the formation and manipulation of syntactic structures could, unlike the constraints governing mental representations, be altered at will.

The history dissatisfaction, followed by acceptance, of relativity theory and (even more so) quantum mechanics recapitulates the closely related history of analytic geometry. In both sorts of cases, there were those who believed that the comprehensibility of mathematical expressions, in the form of the imaginability of spatial structures and (in the case of physics) mechanisms, was indispensable. Thus, for instance, we find Erwin Schrödinger claiming the following about Werner Heisenberg's quantum mechanics: "I . . . felt discouraged not to say repelled, by [Heisenberg's] methods of transcendental algebra, which appeared very difficult to me and by the lack of visualizability" (quoted in Miller 1984, p. 143). We find Albert Einstein and Hendrik Lorenz backing Schrödinger for similar reasons (ibid., p. 144). At the same time, however, there were those who, much like John Wallis (see subsection 5.3.3), thought that images and models *had* to be dispensed with. Wolfgang Pauli, for instance, admonished that "even though the demand of these children for [visualizability] is in part legitimate and healthy, still this demand should never count in physics as an argument for retaining systems of concepts" (quoted in Miller 1984, p. 137). Likewise, Heisenberg claimed that quantum mechanics can only be held back by intuitive models and pictures and that "the new theory ought above all to give up totally on visualizability" (ibid., p. 148). While physicists did not dispense with imaginability lightly, when it came to studying the fundamental structure of the universe, they realized in the end that it *had* to be dispensed with.

Just to reinforce this point, here are a few more quotes. First, we have a passage from Einstein (and note the scare quotes): ". . . the electrodynamics of Faraday and Maxwell . . . and its confirmation by Hertz's experiments showed that there are electromagnetic phenomena which by their very nature are *detached from every ponderable matter*—namely the waves in empty space which consist of electromagnetic 'fields'" (1949, p. 25; emphasis added). More recently, Richard Feynman asked: "How do *I* imagine the electric and magnetic field? What do *I* actually see? . . . I have no picture of this electromagnetic field that is in any sense accurate. I have known about the electromagnetic field a long time. . . . When I start describing the magnetic field moving through space, I speak of the E- and B fields and wave my arms and you may imagine that I can see them . . . I cannot really make a picture that is even nearly like true waves." (quoted in Brewer, unpublished manuscript, p. 9)[4] And Rick Groleau, writing for the Public Broadcasting System, gave the following synopsis of the new "string" theory:

For most of us, or perhaps all of us, it's impossible to imagine a world consisting of more than three spatial dimensions. Are we correct when we intuit that such a world couldn't exist? Or is it that our brains are simply incapable of imagining additional dimensions—dimensions that may turn out to be as real as other things we can't detect?

String theorists are betting that extra dimensions do indeed exist; in fact, the equations that describe superstring theory require a universe with no fewer than 10 dimensions. But even physicists who spend all day thinking about extra spatial dimensions have a hard time describing what they might look like or how we apparently feeble-minded humans might approach an understanding of them. That's always been the case, and perhaps always will be.[5]

This does not mean that *all* of physics must give up on images and models. As Einstein claimed, the synthetic methods are still useful for building models of complex, middle-sized objects. It is just in the realm of fundamental principles that the freedom granted by formalisms is required:

> We can distinguish various kinds of theories in physics. Most of them are constructive. They attempt to build up a picture of the more complex phenomena out of the materials of a relatively simple formal scheme from which they start out. . . . When we say we have succeeded in understanding a group of natural processes, we invariably mean that a constructive theory has been found which covers the processes in question.
>
> Along with this most important class of theories there exists a second, which I will call "principle theories". These employ the analytic, not the synthetic, method. (quoted in Cushing 1991, pp. 341, 342).

The fact that physics has followed this course contradicts Kant's claims about its subject matter. At the same time, however, the intellectual disputes surrounding the nascent non-classical physics that had to do with the impossibility of forming mental images and models of the processes in question corroborates Kant's (and my own) basic claim that the properties of the medium by which we represent the world imposes inviolable constraints on the properties of that which can be represented by that medium.

This, then, is where Kant went wrong: He was clearly wrong to lay claim to criterion *v*, and he was wrong to claim that the subject matter of fundamental physics is simply the objects of experience. Nevertheless, his model of geometrical knowledge was close to perfect, and he was at least onto something with his claim that there are, in addition to spatial principles, also fundamental kinematical and dynamical principles governing our experiences of the world.

9.2.3.2 The Model Model and Fundamental Physics

How does any of this bear on the topic broached at the start of the chapter? Here's how, and this part is not so speculative.

To start with, the advent of non-Euclidean geometries and associated formalisms and their successful employment in physics undermines formalistic models of explanation such as the D-N model. (If I were forced to choose a successor to physics, it would be something like biology.) After all, if mathematical law subsumption sufficed for explanation, by which I mean *understanding* the possible whys or hows of an event or regularity, then there should be no question that fundamental physics is a storehouse of explanations. Nothing, however, could be further from the truth; in fact, precisely the opposite sentiment appears to prevail in physics. Cushing, who appears representative in this regard, claims that "*understanding* of physical processes must involve picturable physical mechanisms and processes that can be pictured" (1991, p. 341) and this, he claims, is something that fundamental physics cannot supply. Likewise, as Glennan puts it, "it is often said that the quantum theory, while extraordinarily successful as a predictive instrument, cannot be said to explain the phenomena it predicts" (1996, p. 66). And Brewer—who is a psychologist, not a physicist, but who has amassed an impressive array of relevant quotes from leading figures throughout the history of physics—surmises: "There is strong agreement [among physicists] that model-based approaches exemplify what it means to explain a physical phenomenon. There is also moderate agreement that many formal approaches and theories of certain domains of modern physics do not provide explanations." (unpublished manuscript, p. 13) Here, as I promised at the outset of this chapter, we see a clear dissociation of explanatory insight and understanding from formalistic law subsumption.[6] All of this, of course, is just as predicted by the ICM-enriched Model model of explanation, and it denies the D-N model (or any other formalistic model) any purchase in fundamental physics.

These considerations should also cause us to hesitate before lauding fundamental physics as the paragon of science. Unlike (at least) the vast preponderance of the other sciences, fundamental physics systematically, and by necessity, fails to supply understanding of the phenomena it investigates. Thus, rather than blithely follow physics wherever it may lead, we should exercise a bit of caution.

9.3   A Return to Models?

We have seen, then, that there are constraints on the properties of representations that are inviolable *given* that the representations have been realized through the use of a particular, *primitively* constrained modeling medium. Synthetic geometry may just be an investigation of inviolable spatial properties of appearances in a way that capitalizes on the representational productivity of the medium of mental representation and the inferential productivity of the representations constructed in that medium.

Analytic geometry offered an alternative to the synthetic methods that involved the manipulation of mathematical formalisms (i.e., through the application of syntax-sensitive inference rules to syntactically structured representations). This alternative was considered suspect at first, for it involved trafficking in mathematical representations that defied human comprehension, but its utility could not in the end be denied. The sciences have, of course, come to rely heavily upon these analytic methods and the ancestors thereto.

We have also seen that one of the very nice things about the manipulation of mathematical formalisms is that this kind of process can, as Turing and von Neumann showed (section 1.2), be automated with the aid of programmable computers. This has turned out to be very useful, for one sometimes wishes to predict how some physical system will behave on the basis of lower-level, explicit (whether induced or derived; see sections 6.5 and 8.3) knowledge of the properties of the materials from which the system is constructed. Insofar as extrinsic, mathematical specifications of these properties can be had, one can use those specifications to create media for the construction of intrinsic computational models of the systems in question. This is basically what goes on with ICMs in thought, but there are severe restrictions on the amount of complexity that can be kept track of in thought. Thus, the intrinsic computational models just described are used as an "intellectual prosthetic" (Pylyshyn 1984, p. 75). In other words, the development of mathematical formalisms as an alternative to the non-formal, intrinsic representations of thought has thus led back to the creation of non-formal, intrinsic representations. We have, in other words, come full circle, and there is a truly sublime beauty in this.

But things get better still.

To start with, because the point of these intrinsic computational models is just to exhibit inferential productivity, and because inferentially productive representations of the world are what any robot will need before it can hope to match wits with a human when it comes to dealing with novelty in its environment, we can hope that representations of this sort will be utilized in the not-too-distant future in the service of constructing intelligent machines (Waskan 2000). This is why the solution to the frame problem is so important to AI.

We also saw that formalism can liberate us from our basically Euclidean-Newtonian (E-N) limitations, and this is very important because, as it turns out, the world that lies beyond appearances almost certainly does not obey the same constraints as our thought processes. What this means for researchers today is that they can utilize non-E-N formalisms in the service of constructing media for the creation of non-formal, intrinsic representations of specific hyper-dimensional objects (e.g., objects in ten spatial dimensions plus one temporal dimension). This, of course, is already a common practice, as the use of intrinsic computational models is as much a part of the far reaches of physics as it is a part of the special sciences. Scientists have thus used their formalisms in order to create non-sentential representations (i.e., representations they are specific and intrinsic) of entities and processes that are inconceivable to us. This, of course, is very useful in that it is provides a wellspring of predictions in the way that intrinsic models are supposed to (section 8.3). It may even give us some insight, by inspiring useful metaphors and analogies, into such systems, though these systems will ultimately remain beyond our grasp.

But can we not hope that, perhaps in 100 years or so, there will be artificial devices that really live, and feel perfectly at home, in what to humans is the (presumably still unintelligible) realm described by the physics of their day? They may live in a virtual world, or even a real one experienced through an array of sensors utterly unlike our own. Perhaps such creatures will be able to truly understand the behavior of objects in their full hyper-dimensional glory in the way that we understand (or at least feel that we do) what happens to old coffee when it is poured down the sink. Think of what awesome power that will give them! Their day-to-day activities will be, in a word, supernatural.

Depending upon how one ranks the level of morality exhibited by actual humans against that exhibited by robots of human devising (clearly a complicated issue), this may not be the best way to go. But there is another option, and it is one that might be realized even sooner.

To see how, we must quickly pull together a few of the ideas presented in this book. First, we saw above that the naturalistic approach to the problem of explaining geometrical knowledge required giving up on criterion *v* above. That is to say, we have no guarantee that the experiences and thought processes of all humans will be constrained in the ways that our thought processes are constrained today. Second, we have also seen that the inviolable constraints that one finds at the representation level are just a product of primitive, but *not nomological*, constraints found at the level of the representational medium. Third, while we have a good notion how to characterize the representational medium in the case of computers, it is still an open question how the representational medium is best characterized in the case of humans. I did confess, however, that it is my conviction that the medium of representation will be best understood in terms of the kinds of simultaneous constraint satisfaction activities exhibited by neural networks (subsection 6.5.6).

Let me also take a moment to point out that while I have been talking a good deal about the *geometry* of experience versus the geometry of nature (in, of course, the non-Kantian sense of the term 'nature'), the same basic considerations are likely to apply in the case of certain kinematical and dynamical principles as well. We seem, in our early years, to learn a variety of such principles. It is, one can easily imagine, for this reason that we find it inconceivable for something to happen without a cause (subsection 8.3.3). It may also be for this reason that we find it incomprehensible that something should come from nothing or for there to be action at a distance. Consider also that according to a highly regarded mathematical framework for understanding the subatomic realm it is quite common for two subatomic "particles" to behave in different ways even when they are subjected to exactly the same conditions and are intrinsically utterly indistinguishable. Apparently, and for reasons that are beyond my ken, the proposal that there are underlying, hidden variables at work in such cases has been ruled out. This seems utterly incomprehensible. But then, if the foregoing is correct, the fault may lie with us rather than with the formalisms. We also learn, perhaps to only a shallow, but sufficiently useful, degree of depth, the properties of a variety of materials (subsection 6.4.4). In fact, next to seeing the world in three dimensions—which, mind you, may itself be akin to learning the properties of materials to a shallow, but useful, degree of depth—this may be the most important thing we learn.

In any event, whatever spatial, kinematical, and dynamical principles that we come under the spell of early in our lives, they are probably learned by a vertically and horizontally inter-connected hierarchy of cortical neural networks of a self-organizing, broadly Kohonen-net variety.[7] These "maps," as they are called, may even come pre-configured to a certain extent so as to prepare them to learn what needs learning. Just which principles are learned first is, of course, just the sort of thing that is commonly investigated by cognitive psychologists interested in early development. The question as to which principles are least easily *un*learned (or even temporarily overridden) *may* have to do with the fact that all other knowledge is encoded relative to the representational medium that develops as a result of the early learning process. It does, however, almost certainly have to do with developmental declines in neural plasticity that seem to progress from the lowest to highest levels of the aforementioned hierarchy.

Assuming all of this is correct, one has to wonder whether or not the top-down effects of a career devoted to the consideration of the non-Euclidean formalisms of fundamental physics might ultimately enable, through a kind of gestalt switch, some to think the thoughts corresponding to these formalisms—that is, to really understand them. Importantly, there is nothing about either computers or neural networks per se that restricts them to the modeling the properties of three-dimensional objects. The only question, then, is whether or not the adult brain is, or can be made, plastic enough to undergo the appropriate modifications and whether or not the mere consideration of formalisms can tweak it in just the right way.

There are, as you probably know, already some who claim to have undergone such a transformation. Randy Rucker, for instance, apparently claims that with practice he has come to be able to visualize four-dimensional space for significant periods.[8] While this is small potatoes compared to what a true hyper-dimensional physicist will ultimately have to do, it is important in that (if it is not a hoax) it shows that formalisms *can* exhibit the kind of top-down effect on our way of conceiving of the world that we are looking for. (See also Schyns 1991.) Perhaps, then, we simply need to find the right protein switches and restore some level of plasticity to the brains of those who have already spent their otherwise post-plastic years steeped in the formalisms of fundamental physics. This, it seems to me, may be a quick (but also dangerous) route to the creation of actual neural systems capable of comprehending, by forming non-sentential intrinsic representations of, the world in its true hyper-dimensional glory.

These, at any rate, are some of the fun and scary implications of the model of a central facet of human cognition that I have proposed. If I am right, it is the exploration of inner space that will ultimately pave the way for exploration of outer space. If I am right, one of the great minds of physics will one day be able to confidently declare "Aha! I finally understand!"

Notes

Chapter 1

1. From the thirteenth century until (and for a while after) this development, European universities were dominated by a group of Catholic philosopher-theologians known as the scholastics. The scholastics for the most part believed that there was very little left to discover about nature, for just everything you could ever want to know could be learned by reading either recently rediscovered classic texts (e.g., those of Aristotle, Galen, and Ptolemy) or the writings of Saint Thomas Aquinas, who synthesized Aristotelian natural philosophy with the tenets of Catholicism. While there was significant disagreement about the details, the general scholastic view of nature was that all natural bodies are directed toward particular ends, or goals, which are given to them by God for the collective and ultimate purpose of man's salvation. To their credit, the post-1200 A.D. scholastics did at least have a serious interest in natural philosophy. European scholars of the preceding millennium attached little importance to natural philosophy at all.

2. The view at the time was, more specifically, that the universe consists of conglomerations of tiny bits of matter called *corpuscles*.

3. To this extent Kant is surely right, but it is doubtful that he discovered in his table of judgments the only means available to the mind for synthesizing sensations into coherent experiences. See note 11 to chapter 5.

4. That *all* mental states have this feature is debatable, but it certainly seems as though many of our mental states have it.

5. Brentano is often interpreted as arguing that this distinctive feature of mental states constitutes evidence that they are non-physical. This is a big stretch, however, given that Brentano was trying to distinguish physical *phenomena* from mental phenomena. In fact, he is far more sensibly interpreted as claiming that physical phenomena are *constitutive of* mental phenomena. Regardless, philosophers after Brentano were certainly justified in wondering whether or not the "aboutness" of mental states that is presupposed by our everyday attributions of psychological

states to one another might be cashed out in terms of physical mechanisms. This is a somewhat different concern, but a legitimate one all the same.

6. Fittingly enough, they shared the Nobel Prize for their work on neuroanatomy in 1906.

7. He has, like Wundt, been credited with setting up the first psychology lab in 1879. His, however, was geared toward demonstration rather than research.

8. A clear difference is that empiricists typically thought the associations of interest occurred between ideas rather than between stimuli and responses.

9. This is just a minor revision of Greenwood's (1999) proposal regarding the new subject matter of the psychological sciences. As Greenwood notes, many of the moderate behaviorists also posited intermediaries, but they tended to be ensnared by operationalism and thus to oversimplify.

10. Of course, with a computer, if you happen to know the program it is running, the current internal state, and the current inputs, you can predict its subsequent behavior with great accuracy. A program thus functions like a complicated law. It was for this reason that many philosophers took it that the goal of the new *cognitive* psychology should be to determine the program being run by the human brain (Putnam 1990). However, as we shall see, whatever the analogies might be between computers and humans, the project of formulating laws was never a primary goal of either cognitive psychology or any other discipline of cognitive science.

11. These can be implemented at the low level of electronic logic circuits, but it is the high-level implementation of logical operations that has, for reasons described here, been of greatest interest to cognitive scientists.

12. This description is based on use of Soar 7.0.4 and Congdon and Laird's (1997) instruction manual.

13. The modal language used here reflects the assumption that the model is trying out the various moves in its head before trying them out in the world.

14. The heuristics are very different from the probabilistic reasoning heuristics of Kahneman and Tversky (1973). Both can be viewed as fallible rules of thumb. However, the former are useful for deducing conclusions from premises, while the latter are useful for estimating either the likelihood that an event will occur or the likelihood that an individual is a member of a certain category.

15. The process just described has the same basic structure as a deductive proof. In the case of production systems, it is from a set of statements describing the current state of the world (the premises) and a set of rules for inferring how that state will change in light of various alterations (akin to the rules for natural deduction) that a statement describing the desired state (akin to the conclusion) can be derived.

There are some minor differences between the two sorts of derivation. In particular, in a natural deduction proof, the rules utilized are insensitive to the specific contents being reasoned about. Production systems, however, often encode, in the form of inference rules (i.e., operators), information that might otherwise be encoded in the form of conditional statements. This has the effect of segregating facts about the specific state of affairs being reasoned about from more general knowledge about how the world works, but the process still has the outward form of a *modus ponens* inference. There are, to complicate matters further, production system models (such as Rips' (1983) ANDS model) that utilize operators in order to represent *both* domain-specific inference rules *and* domain-general *deductive* inference rules.

16. If you have done many formal proofs, you know how useful it can be to both break a problem up into familiar chunks (i.e., sub-problems) and to reason backwards.

17. See Crevier 1993 for a very nice, and far more in-depth, history of AI.

18. See, for instance, Schank 1980; Searle 1980; Johnson-Laird 1983; Pylyshyn 1984.

19. Of course, unless the human theorist understands why the theory has the implications it does, they will be deprived of that wonderful "Aha!" moment. See chapters 7 and 9.

20. There are many gradations of this view, depending upon the level of abstraction at which one thinks the brain is a computational system. See, e.g., Clark 1990, p. 35.

21. Greenwood (1999) supplies what I consider to be the definitive analysis of the shortcomings of the intermediaries posited by many behaviorists.

22. Obviously no test is going to be truly decisive; alternative explanations for data can always be proposed. For this reason, the typical research paper in cognitive psychology describes an initial experiment and several follow-up experiments, where the goal of the latter is to show that alternative explanations for the initial set of data have implications that are not borne out. This is a bit more complicated than we need to get here, but this issue will crop up again at various points throughout the book. For another beautiful illustration of how the reaction-time method can take us deeper than introspection, see Flanagan 1991, pp. 185–188.

23. If you are not convinced, bear in mind that I will say a lot more on this topic throughout the remainder of the book (e.g., in the next chapter and in chapters 7–9).

24. This reiterates a point made by Darden and Maull (1977), with whom I agree at least this far.

25. Reichenbach (1938, 1947) and Kim (1988) make related claims.

26. The rationalists did, however, typically adopt some version of psychologism to account for this kind of knowledge (e.g., they claimed that the knowledge was innate).

27. Kitcher (1992, p. 58) likewise makes clear that anyone who takes humans to be evolved biological entities should consider the scientific study of human cognition to be relevant to the study of human knowledge.

28. Dennis Knepp, a favorite conversant of mine in the philosophy department at Washington University, was rather disgusted with the Philosophy-Neuroscience-Psychology program of which I was a part, thinking that we were all advocating that philosophers become scientists—and perhaps we were! The matter of how philosophy and *cognitive* science fit together has nagged at me ever since. This book represents my first serious attempt to resolve important facets of this issue. Thanks, Dennis! Thanks also to my colleagues at UIUC.

29. Let's face it, when it comes to arguments purporting to show how common-sense psychology has gotten things all wrong, philosophers (who are generally a bit strange to begin with) are attracted like moths to a flame. My hope is that the following chapters will redirect philosophers (viz., the up-and-coming ones who can still be reached) toward interdisciplinary tasks that are far more credible, but equally provocative.

30. An interesting tangent here is that the motivation behind the incorporation into production systems of the aforementioned strategies and heuristics was a set of introspective self-reports made by the subjects who were engaged in formal symbol-manipulation problems.

31. By 'external' I mean to draw attention to the fact that it is normal for such sentences (e.g., expressions in English or in a mathematical notation) to be found outside of the head (e.g., in spoken or written form). They are, of course, sometimes found inside of the head as well (e.g., in short-term memory).

32. Perhaps there is something akin to explanation in the realm of pure math—in fact, much of theoretical physics amounts to nearly this. I presume that there are, at the very least, important "Aha!" moments. I will leave it to those who are better acquainted with pure math to determine how similar are the causes of these "Aha!" moments to those that can occur when we seek explanations for physical events and regularities.

Chapter 2

1. While Maxi is out of the room, the candy bar is moved from its original hiding spot to a new spot (Wimmer and Perner 1983).

2. On the other hand, Stich and Ravenscroft argue, perhaps folk psychology can be construed "externally" as a body of propositions that quantify over certain theo-

retical posits and that entail platitudes that the folk find intuitive. *This* theory might turn out to be false, though at least one author has claimed that the appeal to external versions isn't the boon for eliminativists that Stich and Ravenscroft suggest it might be (Pust 1999).

3. Proponents of the LOT hypothesis typically deny that *types* of mental state are to be identified with *types* of brain states. On their view, mental states can, like computer programs, be implemented by a variety of different physical systems. Thus, while any *token* mental state is identical to some particular configuration of physical constituents or other (e.g., to a particular brain state), the *type* of which it is a token is not.

4. A notable absentee from the gauntlet is Kim's (1998) argument against mental causation. Bear in mind that if Kim is right, then cognitive science is itself illegitimate and is thus incapable of vindicating folk psychology. Here I simply assume the legitimacy of the predictive and explanatory practices of the special sciences. If I am wrong to do so, I will gladly take my lumps.

5. Fodor, of course, does not share my enthusiasm for cognitive science as a whole, preferring instead to place all of his eggs in psychology's basket. (See Fodor 1974.)

6. The basic proposal of Fodor's autonomy (a.k.a., *disunity*) thesis is that the higher-level sciences (e.g., psychology) are, in an important sense, autonomous from the lower-level sciences (e.g., neuroscience). Fodor's argument hinges on the type/token distinction described above and goes roughly as follows: There is a one-to-many mapping between the properties invoked by the higher-level sciences and those invoked by the lower-level sciences. For instance, to *be* one of the types of state that are important to psychology (e.g., a belief that there are pickles in the refrigerator) is not to have any specific material constitution—though, presumably, it is to have some constitution or other. Thus, if we understand the details of how a token mental state is realized, we still haven't learned anything about what it is to be the type of state in question; we don't know what it is, for instance, to be a belief that there are pickles in the refrigerator. Conversely, if we do know of a token mental state that it is of the type in question and why, we still may know nothing at all regarding the details of how that state is physically realized.

7. 'Intentional' in (at least roughly) Brentano's sense of the term, that is. See section 1.1.

8. Insofar as one takes productions, operators, and such to be statements of laws, traditional AI might be thought to be in the business of supplying them, but (i) the commitment to theoretical computationalism is entirely optional (see subsection 1.2.3.2), and (ii) we all know how well this project turned out (see Fodor 2000).

9. In other words, the model is thus clearly not functional in the much stronger Turing-machine sense described by Putnam (1990). 'Function', in his sense of the term, connotes mathematical functions and is simply the thesis of theoretical

computationalism. What the other sense of 'function' comes to will be discussed further in the next chapter.

10. See also Newell and Simon 1972, Fodor 1987, and Gopnik 2000. For evidence that our nearest relatives are far more prone to ineffective fumbling than we are, see Povinelli 2000.

11. See also the quotation from Chomsky 1959 in subsection 1.2.3.2.

12. Darwin himself viewed the matter in this way. Near the close of *On the Origin of Species*, he writes: "It can hardly be supposed that a false theory would explain, in so satisfactory a manner as does the theory of natural selection, the several large classes of facts above specified."

13. Even critics of the *general applicability* of natural selection accounts, including Gould and Lewontin (1979), would be unwilling to abandon the basic ontology of states and processes constituting the theory of natural selection, though they do downplay their importance.

14. We should, however, not lose sight of the fact that no new *species* has ever been created in this way.

15. There are further claims (e.g., that we are able to recognize objects, to pay attention or not, and to do things "on autopilot") endorsed by the folk that are less directly connected to our present discussion, but that are no less important to the ongoing research activities in cognitive science.

16. Horgan and Woodward (1995) claim that their theory overcomes the deficiencies of instrumentalism insofar as it invokes genuine causal explanations, but it seems that predictive power can be had merely from treating a system *as if* it were governed by certain causal interactions. For example: If the center of gravity is too far aft, this can cause a plane to stall.

17. For a more in-depth discussion of where the techniques of cognitive psychology and neuropsychology diverge, see Waskan and Bechtel 1998.

18. I wonder at Fodor's pooh-poohing of this implementation-specific research, insofar as it is the only thing that stands between him and Dennett.

19. Fodor (1987) similarly suggests that progress in psychology constitutes progress for folk psychology, though he neglects to spell out precisely how.

20. There are areas of experimental psychology (viz., mathematical psychology) where the search for other kinds of laws *is* undertaken. In later chapters I will show that mere deductions from laws never suffice to explain. For now it suffices to note that in mathematical psychology the laws in question are meant to quantify, without explaining, the interacting states of component systems specified by a given model of cognitive functioning.

21. I will argue in chapter 7 that it is seldom possible to formalize, in any fully adequate way, the reasoning that underlies particular instances of this phenomenon.

22. This is all a bit of a caricature, but it bears a close enough resemblance to Kuhn's actual thinking for present purposes. Perhaps the biggest distortion in my presentation has to do with the fact that Kuhn was, in the end, very unhappy with the strong relativistic implications of his view. He tried to counter-act them by proposing trans-paradigmatic assessment criteria, and suggested, like Popper (!) and Lakatos, that science progresses through a kind of survival of the fittest. Lakatos, however, seems to have come closest to figuring out the principles governing this competition, so I shall pay more attention to his views in what follows.

23. In fact, newcomers seem to have a remarkable track record, so if there is anything that approaches instant and objective rationality in science it is here that we are likely to find isolated instances of it which, on the aggregate, give rise to real progress. This, however, is a discussion that quickly gets very complicated, so I will set it aside for now. Still, those interested in pursuing the matter on their own might find that the model of explanation offered up in chapter 8 constitutes a very important piece of the larger puzzle.

24. The study of visual perception supplies one case-in-point. The *ur*-view, perhaps attributable to Marr (1982), seems to have been that perceptual representations are generated in a stagewise fashion with all the detail and precision that an engineer could ever desire. We now have a pretty good inkling that this is not the case, but we are all-too-often urged to throw the baby out with the bathwater—this, despite the fact that it always seems such a simple and straightforward matter to modify the *ur*-view so that it can handle the new results (e.g., see Simons 2005). Why, you might ask, should we modify the *ur*-view rather than give it up? The answer is quite simple: Giving up perceptual representations means giving up on lots of other stuff as well. For instance, if there are no perceptual representations, we will find ourselves having a dandy of a time explaining what it is that we encode, store (viz., on a short, intermediate, or long-term basis), and retrieve on so regular a basis, what the point of selective attention is, how we can think about the best way to deal with our immediate environment, and so on, and on.

25. Brooks (1991) would argue that this is like catching a glimpse of a Boeing 747 and later trying to duplicate it. It is, however, much more like being surrounded by billions of 747s and trying to engineer just one more. Of course, if the folks who are trying to do the forward engineering do not talk to those doing the reverse engineering, one should not expect much progress.

Chapter 3

1. I first encountered this wonderful term in Stich 1996.

2. Burge argued that mental contents are determined in part by facts about one's social milieu, but, in order to get to the simple point that mental contents are determined by external factors, I will focus here on non-social determinants of mental contents.

3. For an explanation of this term, see note 3 to chapter 2.

4. Egan (1999) rightly points out that we must distinguish how mental states are individuated from where they are located, but she does not tell us how to do this. She does not, in other words, tell us why the wideness of mental contents fails to imply the wideness of mental states.

5. Essentially the same point was made by Stalnaker (1989) with regard to footprints, mosquito bites, etc.

6. It may be that this problem can be rectified through only minor adjustments to the definition of 'supervenience'. Such adjustments would not, however, resuscitate the claim that mental states extend into the environment.

7. One might argue that there is at least one difference between the present case and the case of mental states—namely, that the former, but not the latter, involves derived intentionality. Below I will do my best to undermine the claim that there is a metaphysical distinction between derived and intrinsic intentionality. For present purposes, however, it suffices to note that this apparent disanalogy does not undermine the conclusion that I have here reached—namely, that supervenience does not track token identity. After all, if the *derived* dimension is stressed, we will find that there can be still other non-intrinsic differences that yield differences in representational content. Ultimately, once the derived/intrinsic dimension is softened, the same point will apply with regard to mental states.

8. I can tell you from experience that it is a lot easier to see this if one does not make the mistake rectified in the previous section. It is also easier to see this if one avoids a straightforward equating of 'content' and 'intentionality' as they are used in this context with the homonymous terminology used by Brentano (1874/1995) and Searle (1980). See note 5 to chapter 1.

9. It might be objected that attributing representational content to magnetosomes is entirely gratuitous. While I have some sympathy with this view, the consideration of how the attribution of function and content *might* work in the case of magnetosomes enables us to reach some simple conclusions about function and content, and these conclusions scale up nicely to more complex cases in which attributions of function and content are not at all gratuitous.

10. For many examples of the former, see Bechtel and Richardson 1993.

11. In cognitive science there are many cases of this sort. Cognitive scientists have been engaged in the project of trying to understand the mechanisms that underwrite the wide range of abilities discussed in subsections 2.4.3 and 2.4.4.

12. This is a mouthful of jargon, so let me elaborate a bit for those who are unfamiliar with it. To ascribe a propositional attitude to someone is just to ascribe to them one of the folk-psychological states discussed in chapter 2 (i.e., a belief that

p, a desire for *p*, a hope that *p*), etc. These states seem to comprise attitudes and what the attitude is an attitude toward, the latter of which is sometimes called a *proposition*. Philosophers have come to realize that there are generally two ways of understanding a given PA ascription. On an opaque reading, the words constituting the *proposition* ascription (usually the words coming after 'that') are taken to refer to objects and properties in the world in just the way that the ascribee takes them to. On a transparent reading, the terms refer in the way that the ascriber takes them to. An example is clearly in order. Suppose that Linda wants to yell at the man who runs a certain newspaper stand. An opaque reading of this sentence is roughly equivalent to Linda believes that there is a man who runs the newspaper stand, and Linda wants to yell at him. A transparent reading, in contrast, merely amounts to the claim that there is a man that Linda wants to yell at and who, *we* know, runs the newspaper stand (Linda may not know this; perhaps she only knows him as her handyman). True opaque PA ascriptions seem to get us closer to what we need to know in order to predict and explain behavior. For instance, if the above ascription, when read opaquely, is true, then we know something about how *Linda* sees the world, and this is what we folk need to know in order to predict and explain her behavior. Nevertheless, even opaque PA ascriptions sometimes go beyond how the ascribee thinks about the world.

13. This, I think, is implicit in Burge 1979. It is explicit in Loar 1988.

14. This, for instance, is precisely why Jackson and Pettit (1988) claim that whatever role might be played by the narrow contents posited by content internalists (see sections 2.2 and 2.5 above), it is the role of the wide contents posited by content externalists to represent the world.

15. One might try for the cheap objection that swamp humans don't really succeed, because they don't have any *real* desires, but this would just be to assume that folk semantics is the one true semantics.

16. Precedents for the claim that isomorphism is an important determinant of content can be found in McGinn 1989 and in Cummins 1996.

17. It seems to be a standard practice in the literature on externalism to speak as though some properties are causally potent while others (e.g., the relationship between sub-atomic particles and the orientation of Fodor's coin) are not. Insofar as one denies that any property is ever a cause, one may construe this practice as a kind of shorthand for some other manner of speaking. For example, as was suggested to me (in conversation) by P. Mandik, perhaps it would be more metaphysically rigorous to instead claim that it is *in virtue of* the presence of a certain property that a certain effect occurs.

18. It is for this reason, I think, that Jackson and Pettit (1988) take the solution to the problem to require an appeal to levels of explanation and multiple realizability. In particular, they propose that the property that "causally explains" is the

property that all the potential causal antecedents have in common. They call explanations that appeal to such properties "program explanations" and then make the somewhat arcane suggestion that such properties "causally program rather than produce."

19. Use of the terms 'imply' and 'inference' need not be taken to indicate a commitment to some version or other of the covering-law model of explanation. It may instead be taken in a much broader sense—in particular, one that allows for the possibility of monotonic, mechanistic, though not formal/deductive, relationships between explanantia and explananda (e.g., of the sort described in Schiffer 1991). In chapter 2, I suggested that such a construal of explanation best fits with what goes on in cognitive science. Later, I will argue that *all* explanations for physical events and regularities are like this.

20. On the importance of this qualification, see subsections 7.3.1.2 and 8.3.1.1 below.

Chapter 4

1. Povinelli (2000) also conducted an extensive series of follow-up experiments (e.g., he exaggerated the length of the prongs, varied the spatial relationships between implements and rewards, and so on), none of which reflected favorably on the chimpanzee's grasp of how implements can be used to obtain rewards.

2. This argument for productivity is a bit different from Fodor's (1987), which is based on the intuition that we seem to be capable of thinking an infinite number of thoughts.

3. I do not stick, in what follows, to letter of the usual formulations of the systematicity argument (Fodor 1987; Fodor and Pylyshyn 1988). I feel that the present formulation makes far more sense than, while remaining true to the spirit of, the original.

4. In fact, if one looks at the Chomsky-inspired tradition in linguistics, one finds a constant process, much like the addition of epicycles, of building semantic constraints into the process via the lexicon. There is, however, an upstart school of thought in linguistics, known as *cognitive grammar* (Langacker 1991; Goldberg 1995), that offers what looks to be a much more elegant account of the manner in which semantic factors influence language comprehension and language production. The key proposals advanced in this book, including my account of systematicity, all mesh quite well with this approach.

5. Also see, however, the discussions of multiple realizability in subsection 1.2.3.2.

6. The frame problem described here has, unlike Fodor's (2000), to do primarily with the human capacity to envision the consequences of alterations to our immediate environment. For Fodor, the frame problem stems from the purportedly holistic

nature of our entire belief-system. In other words, while Fodor takes the frame problem to be a worry having to do with "global properties" of our belief system, the frame problem described here has to do with properties of a comparatively local nature. For a critique of Fodor's version of the frame problem, see Waskan and Bechtel 1997.

7. PIMs need not embody the same spatial relationships as the systems they represent. For instance, by mimicking chemicals and conditions obtaining on pre-biotic Earth, Stanley Miller (1953) famously provided what may, if accurate, be viewed as a PIM of the original synthesis of organic molecules on Earth. In this case, the relevant physical isomorphisms are not spatial ones, at least not at the macro-level.

8. Craik (1952), Block (1990), and Janlert (1996) seem to have come closest to appreciating this point. Craik, however, failed to distinguish between mere isomorphism and physical isomorphism (subsection 4.6.3 above), while Block incorrectly maintains that the truth of the computational theory of mind would preclude the possibility of non-sentential cognitive models (subsection 4.6.4 above).

9. Some examples are available at www.lego.com.

10. In the latter case (and perhaps also in the former), what one builds into one's model will depend upon what kinds of properties one is interested in tracking and what the consequences are of failing to anticipate the relevance of an untracked property. For instance, if one is interested in the optimal arrangement of items in one's living room, a two-dimensional model may well suffice; and the consequences of failing to anticipate the relevance of a property (e.g., height) amounts to only a minor inconvenience. If one is interested in testing the design of a new type of spacecraft, on the other hand, it makes a good deal more sense to model the system, as is commonly done, down to the last detail, for the unforeseen importance of any given property might have dire consequences. When constructing a scale model, then, the important question is not how much should be built into a model, but rather how much one can afford to leave out.

11. See the final paragraphs of subsection 1.2.3.2.

12. To be sure, both the mental logic and scale-model metaphors imply that the systematically related representations are in some sense made of the same parts, but the parallels between the two accounts of systematicity end there.

13. Thanks to Mark Bickhard for helping me to understand the shortcomings of this way of making the distinction.

14. Dennett (1988) makes a related point.

Chapter 5

1. You will have to read the next chapter in order to *fully* understand the basis for this skepticism.

2. There are other arguments for this claim. Some of them were discussed in chapter 4; still others will be discussed in chapter 6.

3. By 'external' I mean to draw attention to the fact that it is common for sentences in such languages (viz., natural languages like English and various artificial ones) to be tokened outside the head (e.g., in spoken or written form); they are, of course, sometimes found inside the head as well (e.g., in short-term memory).

4. I have, aside from the reasons just mentioned, the following ulterior motive for entering into this discussion: Speculative though they may be, the proposals out-lined below will figure prominently in the mechanistic reformulation of the image and scale-model metaphors carried out in the next chapter. Even so, if you have little interest in the question of whether or not the scale-model metaphor can (with some outside help) be developed into a Mentalese-free account of thinking *in its entirety*, you should be able to get by with a quick skim through the remainder of section 5.2. Do have a look at the spatial proof of the Pythagorean Theorem though; it will be important later.

5. For a quick primer on the term 'propositional attitude', see note 12 to chapter 3.

6. The study of analogy is thus another case in point for the thesis that, in cognitive science, our common-sense or introspective understanding of human cognition supplies the backbone for further empirical research.

7. Another example: I may realize that stacking milk crates on their sides is a cheap way to create a set of shelves. This envisioned possibility is, however, only useful to me if I can establish correspondences between the crates in my representation of what is possible and the crates in my representation of what is actual (e.g., my representation of the contents of my storage space).

8. See Waskan 1999. Empirical studies along these lines include Smith and Ellsworth 1987, Foster and Rusbult 1999, and Nichols 2001.

9. Analogy and metaphor are closely related, though metaphorical thinking may sometimes require only one representation rather than two. In such cases, however, it is also likely to involve a more sophisticated attitude—a kind of pretense, perhaps —toward that single representation. For instance, if you were to think the thought corresponding to "Billy Graham's mind has been nailed shut," I would be surprised if you did not temporarily represent his mind as a container of some sort.

10. In the case of both electricity and light, these lacunae have more recently been filled with mathematical equations.

11. In neuroscience, the question of how we do this is one aspect of what is called the *binding problem*, and solutions to this problem have been proposed (e.g., modulation of the in-phase spiking of neurons) that are perfectly compatible with the scale-model metaphor for mental representation. (See Nieber, Koch, and Rosin 1993.) The other aspect of the binding problem has to do with the question of how

properties of an object (e.g., its shape, color, motion, distance, etc.) that are represented in several, anatomically distinct areas of the cortex might be tied to one and the same object. (See Engel and Singer 2001.) This one is more like Kant's version of the problem than the one that concerns enemies of the image metaphor. The solution may, however, be quite similar.

12. Fodor (1975) has argued that pictures can only be used to pick out particular properties of particular objects if they are accompanied by sentences that provide an "interpretation." Imagine, for instance, being asked by a detective to help identify the kind of car that was used to commit a particular crime. Upon being shown various pictures, one might say to the detective "The car was this color," or "The headlights had this shape," or "It was this make and model." Still, it seems downright obvious that the purpose of such statements would be to direct the detective's attention to particular properties at the expense of others.

13. Proponents of the former position deny this because they deny that there are (with the exception, perhaps, of words themselves) any universals to represent; proponents of the latter position deny it because they think direct contact with some transcendent realm is required.

14. This, you are probably aware, is also how the rule Universal Introduction works in predicate calculus. Thus, even if we follow proponents of the logic metaphor and take our inspiration from formal deduction systems such as predicate calculus, we may *still* be led to the conclusion that our knowledge of what holds for all members of a category at least sometimes consists in having reasoned about some arbitrarily chosen member of that category.

15. This kind of knowledge is constitutive of the semantic side of the episodic/semantic distinction (Tulving 1983, 1987; Dagenbach, Carr, and Horst 1990). Semantic memory is memory for both word meanings (e.g., the meaning of 'hammer') and facts about the world of a public, and often general, nature (e.g., the fact that John Wilkes Booth assassinated Lincoln or that water is H_2O). Episodic memory, in contrast, is memory for facts that are personal and specific (e.g., the events in the road portion of your first driving test).

16. Empirical support for this plausible claim can be found in Martin and Chao 2001.

17. To be a psychological essentialist is roughly to believe (justifiably or not) that certain superficial clusterings of properties found in nature (e.g., the properties that dogs, cats, etc. tend to have in common) have an underlying, possibly unknown cause (Gelman 2004).

18. The need for metaphors is not a clear implication of the logic metaphor. At the same time, however, social-group metaphors invoked when talking about categories will raise problems for the scale-model metaphor unless we have a scale-model-metaphor-friendly explanation for beliefs about social group membership. This

explanation will probably require further, separate explanations for beliefs about normative properties (subsection 5.2.2) and beliefs about other minds (subsection 8.3.6).

19. Johnson-Laird is a conflicted proponent of the scale-model metaphor (more on which below). He drops the ball, for instance, when it comes to negations and claims that (for lack of a better term) negative thoughts contain arbitrary symbols that mean the same thing as "it is not the case that."

20. In his discussion of the frame problem, Chater cites McCarthy and Hayes, but he also cites Fodor, and he really seems to have the latter's version of the problem in mind. (See note 6 to chapter 4.) The former version, we shall see in chapters 7 and 8, must also be solved in order for abduction to be modeled effectively.

21. In order to convince a career philosopher of science that this is true, one would need to defend a monotonic-reasoning-based model of explanation itself. I do just this in chapters 7–9. For present purposes, however, I think the following considerations will at least show the prima facie plausibility of the claim that abductive reasoning is at least oftentimes constituted by monotonic reasoning.

22. As any philosophers of science will tell you, there are numerous assumptions built into inferences of this sort. The rejection of these assumptions is what in many cases allows us to hang onto the core of a theory despite what would otherwise appear to be countervailing evidence (subsection 2.6.1). Far from undermining the present point, however, this just reinforce the point that explanatory inference is indefeasible (i.e., that if the conclusion is false, at least one of the premises must be as well). I'll have a great deal more to say on this count in chapters 7 and 8.

23. Also see the discussion of the sufficient conditions for genuine explanation described in subsection 3.9.4.

24. The claim that deduction is formal rather than contentful might raise hackles in certain corners of philosophy. Some have claimed, for instance, that the principles of deductive logic concern highly general properties of the world (Russell 1919). On this view, deductive reasoning cannot be said to involve abstracting away from content entirely. Even so, one could still say that there is a form of monotonic reasoning—which I am, in accordance with relatively common usage, calling 'deduction'—in which the derivation of conclusions from premises depends entirely on the meanings of logical operators rather than what they operate over.

25. The Latin word 'deduce' means *lead away from*, with a connotation that the leading is by force. 'Abduce' means *lead away*, with a connotation that the leading is by persuasion. 'Induce' means simply *persuade*. 'Exduce' is a term made from Latin roots that means *lead out of*.

26. The symbol ¬ means *it is not the case that*.

27. J-L&B also offer variants on the approach illustrated here in order to account for more complicated forms of deductive reasoning (e.g., quantificational).

28. To opine a bit, I do think that the vast majority of what J-L&B have to say about reasoning (and they say a lot) is worth preserving. However, in keeping with the claims made in section 5.2, I would suggest that they take more seriously the possibility that deduction does not require the explicit mental representation of negations and that metaphor and analogy may play a larger role in reasoning (e.g., in categorical reasoning) than they acknowledge.

29. See note 15 above.

30. This passage is also directly relevant to theses advanced earlier and later in this book.

31. As Detlefsen puts it in conversation, when engaging in symbol manipulation one's mind often goes "dead" to the meanings of the symbols expressed.

32. This is reminiscent of the objection to the image metaphor for thought I discussed in section 5.2. However, because it touts the advantages of *artificial* languages over the kinds of geometrical thinking to which mankind was restricted before the advent of such languages, it only *strengthens* my own contention that mental representations are unavoidably specific in the ways implied by the image and scale-model metaphors.

Chapter 6

1. Marr (1982) conveys the same idea, but his use of the terminology is slightly different (e.g., what he means by 'algorithm' is closer to what I call an effective procedure).

2. Where computational systems are concerned, there is no fixed number of distinct levels of abstraction at which their behavior can be understood. In principle, there is no upper limit on the number of levels, because one language can be, and often is, implemented by another language or by a virtual machine (e.g., a Java virtual machine), which is itself just a program (written in still another language) that simulates a type of computational architecture that is capable of implementing the higher-level program. The lower limit on the number of applicable levels is just the case where a system is "hard-wired" to implement a certain effective procedure.

3. Of course, if it is in virtue of implementing these procedures that *we* have mental states, then we will also have to attribute mental states to any computers that implement a sufficiently similar set of procedures. It is hardly surprising that such claims have generated considerable controversy.

4. Bear in mind once again that, although the claim that the brain computes in the strict sense just described *is* a foundational assumption for many philosophical

debates, it in no way constitutes a foundational assumption for cognitive science. (See chapter 2.)

5. Mere isomorphism seems to have been what Wittgenstein (1961) had in mind when he equated such seemingly diverse sorts of representation as pictures and sentences.

6. This does not mean that we have to appeal to isomorphism when fleshing out our theory of content, but, since it is there anyway, it makes sense to do so.

7. This means, roughly, that activity in adjacent areas of the retina causes activity in adjacent areas on the surface of the brain, resulting in what amounts to a map of the retina in the cortex.

8. Neural impulses generated in the retina are first propagated to a set of neurons lying deep within the brain and then on to the primary visual cortex (V1).

9. There may be a visuospatial array in some weaker, functional sense. This seems to be what Thomas (1999) has in mind when he writes "... we might have multiple arrays, one for each sort of quality, so long as the accessing routines *treat* them as a single, superposed, array...." Yet, as I will explain, this is an entirely different proposal that has its own set of objections.

10. The constituents of the hypothesized Mentalese sentences and inference rules are taken to be like the constituents of the sentences and rules characterizing production systems; they represent various objects, properties, and relationships. Put differently, they have something close to a one-to-one correspondence with the constituents of natural language sentences (Haselager 1998).

11. I can, however, imagine someone arguing that they are merely non-representational symbol strings.

12. Johnson-Laird is perhaps the only theorist to have recognized the relevance of levels of description to the discussion of CMRs. What strikes Johnson-Laird as interesting is the fact that programmers working with computational matrices devise algorithms for their manipulation without worrying about the details of machine code—that is, they think in spatial terms. Programmers can do this because array languages capture the properties of real spatial matrices. That is, the programmer operates on a high level program that functions like a real spatial array would. Says Johnson-Laird: "The moral is that although at one level a psychological process may use only strings of symbols, at a higher level it may use various sorts of representation." (1983, p. 153) Although this is major step in the right direction, part of what is required in order to support a truly robust format distinction is a conclusive demonstration that computational matrix representations are intrinsic.

13. In such cases, the representational medium is constituted by ordered memory registers *and* control processes. It is conceivable that some will take issue with this

way of viewing the matter—for instance, it runs somewhat counter to the claims made by Anderson (1978)—but it is no different from the claim that production systems represent objects and the effects of alterations thereto in terms of the sentential contents of short-term memory *and* the inference rules (i.e., operators, a.k.a. frame axioms) that operate over those contents.

14. Though it is almost not worth mentioning, this clearly need not be the case *all* of the time due to automaticity phenomena—which, mind you, obviously *presuppose* such prior short-term-memory-and-attention demanding processes as forethought. More specifically, the cerebellum and basal ganglia appear to be involved in picking up on, and taking over the execution of, frequently occurring goal/motor patterns so as to free up memory and attentional resources. (See Thach, Goodkin, and Keating 1992; Mink 1996.) This, for instance, is what allows you, *after the first several passes*, to drive home from work while thinking about everything but the drive.

15. This is the case, specifically, when objects are assigned physical properties through the command "Apply Physical Effects." It is apparently due to the use of a so-called a posteriori method of collision detection: "In the a posteriori case, we advance the physical simulation by a small time step, then check if any objects are intersecting, or are somehow so close to each other that we deem them to be intersecting. At each simulation step, a list of all intersecting bodies is created, and the positions and trajectories of these objects is somehow "fixed" to account for the collision. We say that this method is a posteriori because we typically miss the actual instant of collision, and only catch the collision after it's actually happened. . . . A posteriori algorithms cause problems in the "fixing" step, where intersections (which aren't physically correct) need to be corrected. In fact, there are some who believe that such an algorithm is inherently flawed and unstable, especially when it comes to resting contacts." (http://en.wikipedia.org/wiki/Collision_detection). The a priori method, in contrast, is computationally more expensive, but it also has a much higher fidelity. It involves precise predictions of the moments of contact so that interpenetration, which demands correction, never occurs.

16. This might seem less surprising if members of the Ray Dream programming team happen to be physics-naive. It is more likely, however, they are physics savvy and recognize a computation-sparing shortcut when they see one.

17. Although Hayes (1995) has famously suggested that AI researchers incorporate the principles of naive physics in their models of cognitive processing, the present model-based approach to representation is very much at odds with his call for an expert-systems-style axiomatization.

18. For some beautiful illustrations, visit http://www.arasvo.com/impact.htm and http://www-explorer.ornl.gov/newexplorer/main.html.

19. Because of its tremendous short-term memory capacity, even Ray Dream can be used to represent systems of far greater complexity than those that we humans can

represent in short-term memory. Our limitations in this regard apparently force us to adopt the strategy of modeling, in piecemeal fashion, the activities of individual parts of complicated mechanical systems and tracing their affects to other parts of those systems (Hegarty 1992).

20. It is the unavoidable degree of specificity exhibited by scale models and virtual-reality models that seems to give rise to each of these concerns. Interestingly enough, this kind of specificity may be necessary (though not sufficient) for avoiding the frame problem. Stenning and Oberlander (1995) make a similar claim, and even contend that this kind of specificity suffices to distinguish imagistic from sentential representations. By itself, however, a mere appeal to specificity does not provide a sufficient basis for distinguishing between sentential and imagistic representations. Stenning and Oberlander contend, for instance, that a tightly constrained notation styled after PC would be imagistic. In the absence of a distinction between levels of description, however, critics of mental imagery can simply charge that such representations are at best functionally isomorphic with images. Moreover, a tightly constrained PC-style notation need not inherit the distinguishing characteristics of images and models discussed in this section, nor does mere specificity (e.g., a reliance upon microfeatures) suffice to solve the frame problem. (See subsection 4.5.2.)

21. Representations of alterations emanate, in some sense, from outside the models, whether it be from long-term memory, language comprehension, creativity, or some other source. I do not have a full-blown account of how such alterations make their way into the models, but the fact that we can perform this feat with regard to external models shows that the basic kind of cognitive activity that is required lies well within our power.

Chapter 7

1. Scriven (1962, p. 63), based on a misreading of Hempel and Oppenheim (1948), makes a similar point. More recently, Wright and Bechtel (forthcoming) have offered a critique of Salmon's anti-psychologism that parallels my own critique in this and other respects. Also see Bechtel and Abrahamsen 2005.

2. Though it is hard to fathom how he could consistently hold that the psychological-uneasiness account is an account *of any sort*, considering that he denies the possibility of incorrect explanations.

3. This wonderful metaphor was, along with the accompanying notion of metaphilosophical intuitions, first brought to my attention by Gary Ebbs in the context of a discussion of King 2001.

4. For a list of reasons, see Fodor 1978.

5. Canfield and Lehrer (1961) clarify this point quite nicely. They, however, mistakenly take this to be an indication that the relationship between explanans and

explanandum is one of non-monotonic implication.

6. Thanks to Bob Barrett for suggesting this inane-objection-forestalling variant of the problem.

7. As I explained in section 4.3, Salmon ought to agree. As I explain in the next note, however, he would not agree.

8. In point of fact, Salmon (1988, p. 103) agrees with Scriven that this would constitute a genuine explanation—this, despite the fact that this case is a straightforward instance of the mere identification of a statistical-relevance relation. Sometimes one sees what one wants, I suppose.

9. Churchland offers a connectionist-inspired alternative to the D-N model's explanation. His general strategy is to show that his preferred model overcomes the limitations of the D-N model, but we have just seen that his critique of the D-N model misses its mark. To show that his model overcomes the limitations of the D-N model, he would thus have to show first what the actual limitations of that model are. What he offers as an alternative is also vague and ultimately unsatisfying. Churchland seems to view the recognition of patterns, the possession of concepts, and the having of theories as basically the same: They are all underwritten principally by the partitioning of neural state space. Thus, on his view there is no qualitative difference between recognizing a friend and having a theory of where the Hawaiian Islands came from.

10. The information can also be built into the consequent, since (P & Q) → R is logically equivalent to P → (Q → R).

11. An adequate model will, of course, have to explain not only how we are able to test theories, but also how we are able to hang onto them if things do not go the way we expect. This just means that an adequate model must simultaneously solve both the oversimplification problem and the problem of provisos.

12. Explanations of statistical regularities themselves could, Hempel thought, be handled with the apparatus of the original D-N model.

13. Humphreys makes a similar point (1992, p. 293).

14. Of course, I do disagree with the contention that explanations are constituted by descriptions. Admittedly, *giving* an explanation typically (though not always) involves verbiage. We have already seen, however, that explanations themselves are the sorts of things that one can *have* without ever *giving* to others, and so descriptions are in no way constitutive of them.

Chapter 8

1. Mxs means "the mass of x is s." F_{xy} means "the force of gravitation between x and y." G is the gravitational constant, and d is the distance between x and y.

2. I will be willing to replace "if and only if" with "only if" if I find compelling evidence that explanations sometimes require both ICMs and a set of mathematical formalisms. There simply cannot, however, be explanations for events and (physical) regularities without ICMs. Also, though I will not talk about metaphorical explanations here, you should be able to fill in those blanks with relative ease.

3. I do, however, have a strong suspicion that the entire explanatory process is on a par with, and even has much the same structure as, the process of planning. (See subsection 4.3.1.)

4. I say 'certain' because it could be argued that there are mereological explanations for static properties (e.g., for why a gas has the shape of its container) that appeal to underlying dynamic properties.

5. There can also be mereological explanations for dynamic properties that involve the modeling of how lower-level processes produce higher-level ones in a non-causal (synchronic) sense of the term 'produce', but in which the models of the processes occurring at each level will typically involve representations of production-relations in the causal (diachronic) sense. This is in some ways similar to explanations that appeal to causally impotent isomorphisms (subsection 3.9.4).

6. I do not re-use the example from subsection 7.3.1.1 (i.e., the putative explanation for why a certain sample of liquid floats to the top when mixed with another sample) here, for later I argued that inferences of that sort have, at best, very limited explanatory import. This matter will be discussed further in subsection 8.3.2.

7. Provided, of course, that certain provisos are satisfied (more on which in subsection 8.3.1.1).

8. See subsection 5.2.4.1 for further discussion of how non-sentential mental representations can be used in the service of formulating universal generalizations.

9. This is just the Model model's far more intuitive—especially in light of the explanatory import problem—alternative to Hempel's (1965) D-S explanations.

10. In subsection 7.3.1.1 we saw how D-N theorists were able to counter the objection that people offer explanations without citing any laws through an appeal to tacit knowledge of such laws. In *that* context, 'tacit' was meant to denote the fact that there may be representations of such laws in the heads of individuals even if they are not able to articulate them. In the present context, 'tacit' is meant to refer to the fact that the knowledge in question may never have been explicitly represented anywhere in memory, but it can easily be generated on demand. For instance, in the same way that we have tacit knowledge of the countless defeaters of a regularity, we also have tacit knowledge of the fact that a fully grown elephant cannot fit into a typical Coke bottle.

11. Cf. Wimsatt 1990; Krohn 1990.

12. I am assuming that your knowledge of this regularity is not based on a simple inductive generalization. If it is, then you lack the kind of open-ended tacit knowledge of which I speak (more on which below).

13. A simplistic (albeit, once again, tellingly hard to describe) version of such a model would be one whereby light, which passes through empty space and air but not through opaque objects such as the ground or flagpoles, emanates from an object (i.e., the sun) and illuminates those opaque objects on which it falls while leaving those on which it does not fall (e.g., those that have an object, such as a flagpole, directly between them and the light source) in relative darkness. Other processes (including refraction and reflection) must be added to the model, however, in order to account for the fact that the patch of ground that falls in the shadow of the pole is not completely dark.

14. If these are taken as specifications of actual physical principles, they are, because (inter alia) of the problem of provisos, strictly speaking false. They can, however, nevertheless be good enough for the purposes at hand — namely, for the construction of intrinsic models of the system in which we are interested that accurately represent many of its most salient properties. As we saw in subsection 6.4.4.1.2, relying upon inaccurate but useful principles is a common practice among scientists and laypeople. This will be discussed at greater length below.

15. Wilson and Keil (1998) make much of this shallow-to-deep explanatory continuum. From here on, I shall follow suit. I shall, moreover, offer an explanation for it (in subsection 8.3.4).

16. Quote from http://access.ncsa.uiuc.edu/Stories/supertwister/.

17. Ibid.

18. As was suggested in subsection 6.5.6, another likely difference is that the low-level constraints governing the medium are implemented through the kind of parallel constraint satisfaction at which neural networks excel rather than through the massive syntax-crunching process on which computers rely.

19. Not surprisingly, this parallels the concern, described in subsection 6.3.2, that if the brain is a computational system then it can only harbor sentential representations of the world.

20. Tad Zawidski has expressed this concern quite eloquently in conversation.

21. If he has this kind of knowledge, he will also have tacit knowledge of the countless exceptions to the rule; otherwise, he will lack this tacit knowledge.

22. What I am claiming here is not unlike what Glennan (1996) and Machamer, Darden, and Craver (2000) claim about mechanistic explanations. There are very important differences, however. First of all, Machamer et al. claim (see subsection 7.4.3) that explanations require descriptions of mechanisms rather than merely

requiring cognitive models of them. In addition, they try, without much success, to resist the claim that the bottom-out level is laws, presumably because they do not wish their account to turn into a variant of the D-N model. We have just seen that resistance to this claim is both futile and unnecessary. Differences between my analysis and Glennan's will be discussed below.

23. That is to say, keeping all factors constant, if the first event occurs so does the second, and if the first event does not occur neither does the second.

24. This is similar to Glennan's (1996) analysis of the metaphysics of causal relations. According to Glennan (p. 64), "two events are *causally* connected when and only when there is a mechanism connecting them" (emphasis added here), where a mechanism is constituted by (p. 52) "the interaction of a number of parts according to direct *causal* laws" (emphasis added here). The regress ends, according to Glennan, at fundamental physics, where, we have been told, laws are no longer sustained by underlying mechanisms. Ending the regress in this way will not work, however, for if these laws are not produced by underlying mechanisms, then they are not causal laws. And if there are no causal laws at the level of fundamental physics, there can be no mechanisms that produce the regularities at the next level up (e.g., chemistry), and so on up until all causality has been expunged from the world. In order to rescue Glennan's account of the metaphysics of causation, one would at least need to drop the stricture that the interactions between the parts of a mechanism need to be causal. To be fair, Glennan spent considerable energy grappling with this very issue, and, if I read him aright, he comes very close to making this very move (p. 60). Another concern about Glennan's analysis, however, is that it does not, as it is stated, account for the asymmetry of causal relations.

25. A complete analysis would require showing that the account satisfies our philosophical and metaphilosophical intuitions about causation by correctly classifying well-known cases, leaving room for the influence of individual interests, and so forth.

26. This is similar what Glennan (1996, see p. 50) claims.

27. We have a means of representing to ourselves the physical compulsion that we feel every time we pick something up, walk around, sit down, etc. Many have suspected that these very personal experiences underlie our comprehension of causal terminology (Talmy 1988; Machamer, Darden, and Craver 2000; Prinz 2002). While this account is of little use if our interest is a solution to the flagpole problem, I suspect these authors are correct if what they are claiming is that when we believe that events are causally related, there is typically a kind of transference going on whereby our representations of non-bodily goings on are somehow infused with somatosensory sensations.

28. Hume (1748/1993) did, in fact, recognize that this occurred to some extent—see, e.g., pp. 57 and 58 of that work.

29. Glennan makes a similar point (1996, p. 64).

30. Once again, however, your pragmatic purposes may be unaffected by the depth of your knowledge. For instance, maybe what you really want to know is whether or not you can place candles beside each of the objects without risk of them melting because the warm rock is going to stay warm, one of the other rocks is going to become warm and stay that way, one of the rocks will go from warm to hot, etc.

31. Indeed, quite strangely, in its original (non-psychological) formulation, knowledge that is not needed to complete the deduction apparently plays no role at all!

32. For instance, a somewhat imperfect and shallow understanding of the warmth of the glubice constructed on the basis of A2 might be articulated as follows: For some apparent reason, certain types of atomic nuclei have a tendency to fall apart. Substances made up of atoms whose nuclei have a very high tendency to fall apart are said to have a very short half-life. Maybe there's a way to explain this, rather like the way one might explain why AMCs had a high tendency to fall apart. Anyway, when nuclei do fall apart, they release either high-velocity sub-atomic particles or energy (maybe both), which tends to result in increased vibratory motion of any atoms or molecules that get in the way. So if you have a large enough, solid sample of material that is composed of a substance that has a very short half-life (e.g., glubice), you will have lots of particles or energy interacting with the other atoms that make up the sample. You will therefore have lots of highly energetic atoms. If the kinetic theory of heat is to be believed, this means that the sample will feel warm.

33. Salmon's argument here is—as are virtually all the arguments he offers in this piece—just an offshoot of Scriven's (1959; 1962) repeated claim that there are adequate explanations that elucidate necessary, but not sufficient conditions for the occurrence of an event. If these gentlemen are correct, then those of us who maintain that all explanations are based on monotonic inferences must be mistaken. Monotonic inferences necessarily specify conditions that would suffice for the truth of the conclusion. A statistical inference, in contrast, need not specify sufficient conditions (e.g., it may specify merely necessary conditions). Thus, if the conclusion of the former sort of inference is false, the grounds for the conclusion must be in some way mistaken (this is just the definition of 'monotonic'). However, if the conclusion of a statistical inference is false, the grounds given may in certain cases be maintained.

34. In fact, if explanations did not have parts, cognitive limitations would preclude us from being able to formulate adequate explanations for most events. (See Schwartz and Black 1996.)

35. See http://www.cdc.gov/ncidod/dbmd/diseaseinfo/legionellosis_g.htm and http://www.hcinfo.com/ldfaq.htm.

36. Though, we shall see in a moment, the adequacy of the overall account would not necessarily be undermined even if it did.

37. Researchers do have at their disposal theories that specify the different ways in which a mutation can occur, some of which bottom out at brute quantum events. Still, researchers were able to construct fully adequate evolutionary explanations for particular traits even before such theories existed.

38. Scriven 1959, Scriven 1962, and Salmon 1988 are full of descriptions of cases in which researchers are reputed to have hypotheses concerning the conditions that were necessary, but not sufficient for the occurrence of an event. The point of these examples is to falsify any monotonic-inference-based account of explanation, but it appears to me that all these cases can be analyzed in the manner just described. Indeed, *only* an analysis along these lines makes sense of the fact that the explanations offered are, despite their appeal to inexplicable events, nevertheless genuinely enlightening.

39. The degree of insight that computer models afford can also be quite limited—even if the model represents how certain events produce others, it still often has to be analyzed thoroughly. One advantage of computer models is that they can be analyzed with greater ease than the systems they represent (e.g., brains, tornados, or supernovae); they can be slowed down, component processes can be highlighted, etc. Still, the case of connectionist modeling seems fairly representative, and here we have seen an entire sub-industry spring up around the project of devising methods of representing, in a manner befitting our limited cognitive capacities, why particular models behave as they do.

40. If it were, then one wonders what use we would have for present-day cognitive science. We could instead spend our time trying to tease out, and render explicit, the implicit knowledge we all have of the inner workings of the human mind. This new science would thus look a good deal like linguistics (see Perner (1996) for a related claim). As near as I can tell, philosophers who are in the grips of both the ML hypothesis and the Theory theory seem to think that the goal of present-day cognitive science is just to reinvent the wheel (section 2.3)—that is, they think that mature cognitive science will end up formulating a body of laws that is a great deal like the body of laws upon which we all tacitly rely, but cognitive science will formulate those laws on independent grounds.

41. This may require imagining what it is like to *not have* certain convictions. There may be other complications as well, but the basic idea seems sufficiently clear.

42. I do not mean here to rule out the possibility that theoretical knowledge plays some role. It seems plausible, in fact, that our folk-psychological activities are informed not just by simulation, but by induced or derived principles as well (e.g., Fred does not deal with stress well; people with kids are unusually sensitive to criticism from their kids, or what-have-you).

43. It is, admittedly, a model that runs fairly deep insofar as the central monotonic inference processes are concerned but that is, at present, quite shallow when it comes to accounting for how it is that the interests of explainers determine what kind of exductive inference will suffice to explain an event or regularity in a given case (see section 8.2).

44. A full analysis would be a bit more involved than I care to undertake here. It would (inter alia) make reference to mereological explanations of processes and make note of the fact that while both the ML hypothesis and the ICM hypothesis are valued for their monotonic implications, neither runs as deep as we should like (i.e., as deep as plausible neural underpinnings).

Chapter 9

1. This appears to be what some have in mind when they say that experience is conceptualized, though they seem not, and perhaps forgivably so, to recognize that this does not require a commitment to the proposal that we think via the manipulation of representations in Mentalese.

2. This is something of a stretch, but it suffices for present purposes.

3. Here I am not expressing any commitment regarding the nature of things in themselves. I am merely trying to supply an illuminating analogy based on the relationships that appear to obtain between the objects of experience.

4. Feynmann is, of course, famous for his diagrams of subatomic goings on. What he has found, it appears, is set of diagrammatic techniques that enable the construction of representations that are sufficiently isomorphic to their represented objects to permit a wide range of truth-preserving inferences. He does not, however, take these diagrams to be literal depictions or physical isomorphs in the sense described in sections 4.4 and 6.3.

5. Quoted from http://www.pbs.org/wgbh/nova/elegant/dimensions.html.

6. I had planned to run a simple Searle-style syntax-manipulation-without-comprehension experiment with regard to the mathematically specifiable relationship between kinetic energy and inter-molecular attraction, but the reality of the situation is even more persuasive. For more arguments in favor of the dissociation of insight from law subsumption, see Cushing 1991.

7. For a very nice overview of how these work, see Miikkulainen 1993.

8. See http://www.earlham.edu/~peters/writing/synth.htm#geometry.

References

Adams, V., and A. Askenazi. 1999. *Building Better Products with Finite Element Analysis*. OnWord.

Anderson, J. R. 1978. Arguments Concerning Representations for Mental Imagery. *Psychological Review* 85: 249–277.

Anderson, J. R. 1983. *The Architecture of Cognition*. Harvard University Press.

Aristotle. Fourth century B.C. 1987. On the Soul. In *A New Aristotle Reader*, ed. J. Ackrill. Princeton University Press.

Asaro, P. 2005. On the Origins of the Synthetic Mind: Working Models, Mechanisms, and Simulations. Doctoral dissertation, University of Illinois, Urbana-Champaign.

Bach, K. 1993. Getting Down to Cases. *Behavioral and Brain Sciences* 16, no. 2: 334–336.

Baddeley, A. 1990. *Human Memory: Theory and Practice*. Allyn and Bacon.

Barsalou, L. W., and C. R. Hale, 1993. Components of Conceptual Representations: From Feature Lists to Recursive Frames. In *Categories and Concepts: Theoretical Views and Inductive Data Analysis*, ed. I. Van Mechelen, P. Theuns, and R. Michalski. Academic Press.

Barsalou, L. W., and J. Prinz. 1997. Mundane Creativity in Perceptual Symbol Systems. In *Creative Thought: An Investigation of Conceptual Structures and Processes*, ed. T. Ward, S. Smith, and J. Vaid. American Psychological Association.

Barsalou, L. W., K. O. Solomon, and L. L. Wu. 1999. Perceptual Simulation in Conceptual Tasks. In *Cultural, Typological, and Psychological Perspectives in Cognitive Linguistics*, ed. M. Hiraga, C. Sinha, and S. Wilcox. John Benjamins.

Barton, M., and S. D. Rajan. 2000. Finite Element Primer for Engineers. http://ceaspub.eas.asu.edu/structures/FiniteElementAnalysis.htm.

Bechtel, W., and A. Abrahamsen. 1991. *Connectionism and the Mind: An Introduction to Parallel Processing in Networks*. Blackwell.

Bechtel, W., and A. Abrahamsen. 2005. Explanation: A Mechanist Alternative. *Studies in the History and Philosophy of Biological and Biomedical Sciences* 36: 421–441.

Bechtel, W., A. Abrahamsen, and G. Graham. 1998. The Life of Cognitive Science. In *A Companion to Cognitive Science*, ed. W. Bechtel and G. Graham. Blackwell.

Bechtel, W., and R. C. Richardson. 1993. *Discovering Complexity: Decomposition and Localization as Strategies in Scientific Research*. Princeton University Press.

Berkeley, G. 1710/1982. *A Treatise Concerning the Principles of Human Knowledge*. Hackett.

Block, N. 1990. Mental Pictures and Cognitive Science. In *Mind and Cognition*, ed. W. Lycan. Blackwell.

Boole, G. 1854/1951. *An Investigation of the Laws of Thought*. Dover.

Brentano, F. 1874/1995. *Psychology from an Empirical Standpoint*, second edition. Routledge.

Brewer, W. Unpublished. Models in Science and Mental Models in Scientists and Non-Scientists.

Bromberger, S. 1966. Why-Questions. In *Mind and Cosmos*, ed. R. Colodny. University of Pittsburgh Press.

Brooks, L. R. 1968. Spatial and Verbal Components in the Act of Recall. *Canadian Journal of Psychology* 22: 349–368.

Brooks, R. A. 1991. Intelligence without Representation. *Artificial Intelligence* 47: 139–159.

Burge, T. 1979. Individualism and the Mental. *Midwest Studies in Philosophy* 4: 73–121.

Burge, T. 1986. Individualism and Psychology. *Philosophical Review* 95, no. 1: 3–45.

Canfield, J., and K. Lehrer. 1961. A Note on Prediction and Deduction. *Philosophy of Science* 28: 204–208.

Chater, N. 1993. Mental Models and Nonmonotonic Reasoning. *Behavioral and Brain Sciences* 16, no. 2: 340–341.

Chi, M. T. H., R. Glaser, and E. Rees. 1982. Expertise in Problem Solving. In *Advances in the Psychology of Human Intelligence*, ed. R. Sternberg. Erlbaum.

Chomsky, N. 1959. A Review of B. F. Skinner's *Verbal Behavior*. *Language* 35, no. 1: 26–58.

Chomsky, N. 1990. On the Nature, Use and Acquisition of Language. In *Mind and Cognition*, ed. W. Lycan. Blackwell.

Churchland, P. M. 1989. *A Neurocomputational Perspective: The Nature of Mind and the Structure of Science*. MIT Press.

Churchland, P. M. 1998. *On the Contrary: Critical Essays*. MIT Press.

Clark, A. 1990. *Microcognition*. MIT Press.

Clark, A. 1993. *Associative Engines*. MIT Press.

Clark, A., and D. Chalmers. 1998. The Extended Mind. *Analysis* 58, no. 1: 10–23.

Congdon, C. B., and J. E. Laird. 1997. The Soar User's Manual: Version 7. 0. 4. University of Michigan.

Copeland, B. J. 2002. The Church-Turing Thesis. In Stanford Encyclopedia of Philosophy. http://plato.stanford.edu.

Craik, K. J. W. 1952. *The Nature of Explanation*. Cambridge University Press.

Crane, T. 1998. How to Define Your (Mental) Terms. *Inquiry* 41, no. 3: 341–354.

Crevier, D. 1993. *AI: The Tumultuous History of the Search for Artificial Intelligence*. Basic Books.

Cruse, H. 2003. The Evolution of Cognition — A Hypothesis. *Cognitive Science* 27: 135–155.

Cummins, R. 1975. Functional Analysis. *Journal of Philosophy* 72, no. 20: 741–765.

Cummins, R. 1996. *Representations, Targets, and Attitudes*. MIT Press.

Cummins, R. 2000. "How Does It Work?" vs. "What Are the Laws?" Two Conceptions of Psychological Explanation. In *Explanation and Cognition*, ed. F. Keil and R. Wilson. MIT Press.

Cushing, J. T. 1991. Quantum Theory and Explanatory Discourse: Endgame for Understanding? *Philosophy of Science* 58, no. 3: 337–358.

Dagenbach, D., T. H. Carr, and S. Horst. 1990. Adding New Information to Semantic Memory: How Much Learning Is Enough to Produce Automatic Priming? *Journal of Experimental Psychology* 6, no. 4: 581–591.

Darden, L., and N. Maull. 1977. Interfield Theories. *Philosophy of Science* 44: 43–64.

Darwin, C. 1859. *On the Origin of Species*.

Davidson, D. 1970. Mental Events. In *Experience and Theory*, ed. L. Foster and J. Swanson. University of Massachusetts Press. Reprinted in D. Davison, *Essays on Actions and Events* (Oxford University Press, 1980).

Davidson, D. 2001. *Subjective, Intersubjective, Objective*. Clarendon.

Davies, M. 1991. Individualism and Perceptual Content. *Mind* 100, no. 4: 461–484.

De Kleer, J., and J. S. Brown. 1983. Assumptions and Ambiguities in Mechanistic Mental Models. In *Mental Models*, ed. D. Gentner and A. Stevens. Erlbaum.

Dennett, D. 1988. *Brainchildren*. MIT Press.

Dennett, D. 1991. Real Patterns. *Journal of Philosophy* 88, no. 1: 27–51.

De Renzi, E., M. Liotti, and P. Nichelli. 1987. Semantic Amnesia with Preservation of Autobiographical Memory. *Cortex* 23: 575–597.

Detlefsen, M. 2005. Formalism. In *The Oxford Handbook for Logic and the Philosophy of Mathematics*, ed. S. Shapiro. Oxford University Press.

Devitt, M., and K. Sterelny. 1987. *Language and Reality: An Introduction to the Philosophy of Language*. MIT Press.

DeYoe, E. A., and D. C. Van Essen. 1988. Concurrent Processing Streams in Monkey Visual Cortex. *Trends in Neurosciences* 11: 219–226.

DiSessa, A. 1983. Phenomenology and the Evolution of Intuition. In *Mental Models*, ed. D. Gentner and A. Stevens. Erlbaum.

Dretske, F. 1986. Misrepresentation. In *Belief: Form, Content and Function*, ed. R. Bogdan. Oxford University Press. Reprinted in *Mind and Cognition*, ed. W. Lycan (Blackwell, 1990).

Egan, F. 1995. Folk Psychology and Cognitive Architecture. *Philosophy of Science* 62, no. 2: 179–196.

Egan, F. 1999. In Defense of Narrow Mindedness. *Mind and Language* 14, no. 2: 177–194.

Einstein, A. 1949. Autobiographical Notes. In *Albert Einstein: Philosopher-Scientist*, ed. P. Schilpp. Library of Living Philosophers.

Ellis, A. W., and A. W. Young. 1988. *Human Cognitive Neuropsychology*. Erlbaum.

Engel, A. K., and W. Singer. 2001. Temporal Binding and the Neural Correlates of Sensory Awareness. *Trends in Cognitive Sciences* 5, no. 1: 16–25.

Falmagne, R. J. 1993. On Modes of Explanation. *Behavioral and Brain Sciences* 16, no. 2: 346–347.

Farah, M. J. 1988. Is Visual Imagery Really Visual? Overlooked Evidence from Neuropsychology. *Psychological Review* 95: 307–317.

Fauconnier, G. 1985. *Mental Spaces*. MIT Press.

Fernandez-Duque, D., and M. Johnson. 1999. Attention Metaphors: How Metaphors Guide the Cognitive Psychology of Attention. *Cognitive Science* 23: 83–116.

Flanagan, O. 1991. *The Science of the Mind*, second edition. MIT Press.

Fodor, J. A. 1974. Special Sciences (or: The Disunity of Science as a Working Hypothesis). *Synthese* 28: 97–115.

Fodor, J. A. 1975. *The Language of Thought*. Crowell.

Fodor, J. A. 1978. Propositional Attitudes. *The Monist* 61, no. 4: 501–523. Reprinted in *The Nature of Mind*, ed. D. Rosenthal (Oxford University Press, 1991).

Fodor, J. A. 1980. Methodological Solipsism Considered as a Research Strategy in Cognitive Psychology. *Behavioral and Brain Sciences* 3, no. 1: 63–72.

Fodor, J. A. 1981. Imagistic Representation. In *Imagery*, ed. N. Block. MIT Press.

Fodor, J. A. 1983. *The Modularity of Mind*. MIT Press.

Fodor, J. A. 1987. *Psychosemantics: The Problem of Meaning in the Philosophy of Mind*. MIT Press.

Fodor, J. A. 1991a. A Modal Argument for Narrow Content. *Journal of Philosophy* 88: 5–26.

Fodor, J. A. 1991b. You Can Fool Some of the People All of the Time, Everything Else Being Equal; Hedged Laws and Psychological Explanation. *Mind* 100, no. 1: 19–34.

Fodor, J. A. 1994. *The Elm and the Expert: Mentalese and Its Semantics*. MIT Press.

Fodor, J. A. 2000. *The Mind Doesn't Work That Way*. MIT Press.

Fodor, J. A., J. D. Fodor, and M. F. Garrett. 1975. The Psychological Unreality of Semantic Representations. *Linguistic Inquiry* 6: 515–531.

Fodor, J. A., and Z. W. Pylyshyn. 1988. Connectionism and Cognitive Architecture: A Critical Analysis. *Cognition* 28, no. 1–2: 3–71.

Foster, C. A., and C. E. Rusbult. 1999. Injustice and Powerseeking. *Personality and Social Psychology Bulletin* 25: 834–849.

Garnham, A. 1987. *Mental Models as Representations of Discourse and Text*. Wiley.

Gelman, S. A. 2004. Psychological Essentialism in Children. *Trends in Cognitive Sciences* 8, no. 9: 404–409.

Gentner, D., and D. R. Gentner. 1983. Flowing Waters or Teeming Crowds: Mental Models of Electricity. In *Mental Models*, ed. D. Gentner and A. Stevens. Erlbaum.

Gentner, D., and C. Toupin. 1986. Systematicity and Surface Similarity in the Development of Analogy. *Cognitive Science* 10, no. 3: 277–300.

Giere, R. 1988. Theories and Generalizations. In *The Limitations of Deductivism*, ed. A. Grunbaum and W. Salmon. University of California Press.

Glanzer, M., and A. R. Cunitz. 1966. Two Storage Mechanisms in Free Recall. *Journal of Verbal Learning and Verbal Behavior* 5: 351–360.

Glasgow, J., and D. Papadias. 1992. Computational Imagery. *Cognitive Science* 16: 355–394.

Glennan, S. 1996. Mechanisms and the Nature of Causation. *Erkenntnis* 44: 49–71.

Goldberg, A. E. 1995. *Constructions: A Construction Grammar Approach to Argument Structure*. University of Chicago Press.

Gopnik, A. 2000. Explanation as Orgasm and the Drive for Causal Knowledge: The Function, Evolution, and Phenomenology of the Theory Formation System. In *Explanation and Cognition*, ed. F. Keil and R. Wilson. MIT Press.

Gordon, R. 1996. Radical Simulationism. In *Theories of Theories of Mind*, ed. P. Carruthers and P. Smith. Cambridge University Press.

Gould, S. J., and R. C. Lewontin. 1979. The Spandrels of San Marco and the Panglossian Paradigm: A Critique of the Adaptationist Program. In *Proceedings of the Royal Society of London*, Series B, 205: 581–598.

Green, D. W. 1993. Mental Models: Rationality, Representation and Process. *Behavioral and Brain Sciences* 16, no. 2: 352–353.

Greenwood, J. D. 1991. Folk Psychology and Scientific Psychology. In *The Future of Folk Psychology*, ed. J. Greenwood. Cambridge University Press.

Greenwood, J. D. 1999. Understanding the "Cognitive Revolution" in Psychology. *Journal of the History of the Behavioral Sciences* 35, no. 1: 1–22.

Haselager, W. F. G. 1997. *Cognitive Science and Folk Psychology: The Right Frame of Mind*. Sage.

Haselager, W. F. G. 1998. Connectionism, Systematicity, and the Frame Problem. *Minds and Machines* 8: 161–179.

Haugeland, J. 1987. An Overview of the Frame Problem. In *Robot's Dilemma*, ed. Z. Pylyshyn. Ablex.

Hauser, L. 2002. Nixin' Goes to China. In *Views into the Chinese Room: New Essays on Searle and Artificial Intelligence*, ed. J. Preston and M. Bishop. Oxford University Press.

Hayes, P. J. 1995. The Second Naive Physics Manifesto. In *Computation and Intelligence*, ed. G. Luger. AAAI Press.

Hearnshaw, L. S. 1987. *The Shaping of Modern Psychology*. Routledge and Kegan Paul.

Hegarty, M. 1992. Mental Animation: Inferring Motion from Static Diagrams of Mechanical Systems. *Journal of Experimental Psychology: Learning, Memory, and Cognition* 18: 1084–1102.

Hegarty, M. 2004. Mechanical Reasoning by Mental Simulation. *Trends in Cognitive Sciences* 8, no. 6: 280–285.

Hempel, C. G. 1965. *Aspects of Scientific Explanation and Other Essays in the Philosophy of Science*. Free Press.

Hempel, C. G. 1988. Provisoes: A Problem Concerning the Inferential Function of Scientific Theories. *Erkenninis* 28: 147–164.

Hempel, C. G., and P. Oppenheim. 1948. Studies in the Logic of Explanation. *Philosophy of Science* 15, no. 2: 135–175.

Hobbes, T. 1651/1988. *Leviathan*. Prometheus Books.

Holyoak, K. J., and P. Thagard. 1995. *Mental Leaps: Analogy in Creative Thought*. MIT Press.

Horgan, T., and J, Woodward. 1985. Folk Psychology Is Here to Stay. *Philosophical Review* 94, no. 2: 197–226.

Houts, A. C., and C. K. Haddock. 1992. Answers to Philosophical and Sociological Uses of Psychologism in Science Studies. *Minnesota Studies in the Philosophy of Science* 15: 367–399.

Hull, D. L. 1987. Genealogical Actors in Ecological Roles. *Biology and Philosophy* 2: 168–184.

Hume, D. 1748/1993. *An Enquiry Concerning Human Understanding*, second edition. Hackett.

Humphreys, P. W. 1992. Scientific Explanation: The Causes, Some of the Causes, and Nothing But the Causes. *Minnesota Studies in the Philosophy of Science* 13: 283–306.

Huttenlocher, J., E. T. Higgins, and H, Clark. 1971. Adjectives, Comparatives, and Syllogisms. *Psychological Review* 78: 487–514.

Jackson, F. 1995. Essentialism, Mental Properties, and Causation. *Proceedings of the Aristotelian Society* 95: 253–268.

Jackson, F. 1996. Mental Causation. *Mind* 105, no. 419: 377–413.

Jackson, F., and Pettit, P. 1988. Functionalism and Broad Content. *Mind* 97, no. 387: 381–400.

James, W. 1890. *Principles of Psychology*. H. Holt.

Janlert, L. 1996. The Frame Problem: Freedom or Stability? With Pictures We Can Have Both. In *The Robot's Dilemma Revisited: The Frame Problem in Artificial Intelligence*, ed. K. Ford and Z. Pylyshyn. Ablex.

Johnson-Laird, P. N. 1983. *Mental Models: Towards a Cognitive Science of Language, Inference, and Consciousness*. Harvard University Press.

Johnson-Laird, P. N. 1988. How Is Meaning Mentally Represented? In *Meaning and Mental Representation*, ed. U. Eco, M. Santambrogio, and P. Violi. Indiana University Press.

Johnson-Laird, P. N., and R. M. J. Byrne. 1991. *Deduction*. Erlbaum.

Johnson-Laird, P. N., and R. M. J. Byrne. 1993. Précis of *Deduction*. *Behavioral and Brain Sciences* 16: 323–333.

Kahneman, D. 1973. *Attention and Effort*. Prentice-Hall.

Kahneman, D., and A. Tversky. 1973 On the Psychology of Prediction. *Psychological Review* 80, no. 4: 273–251.

Kant, I. 1787/1998. *Critique of Pure Reason*. Cambridge University Press.

Kant, I. 1992. *Lectures on Logic*. Cambridge University Press.

Karni, A., D. Tanne, B. S. Rubenstein, J. J. M. Askenasy, and D. Sagi. 1994. Dependence on REM Sleep of Overnight Improvement of a Perceptual Skill. *Science* 265: 679–682.

Keil, F. C., and R. A. Wilson. 1998. The Shadows and Shallows of Explanation. *Minds and Machines* 8, no. 1: 137–159.

Kim, J. 1988. What Is Naturalized Epistemology? *Philosophical Perspectives* 2: 381–406.

Kim, J. 1998. *Mind in a Physical World: An Essay on the Mind-body Problem and Mental Causation*. MIT Press.

King, J. C. 2001. *Complex Demonstratives: A Quantificational Account*. MIT Press.

Kitcher, P. 1989. Explanatory Unification and the Causal Structure of the World. *Minnesota Studies in the Philosophy of Science* 13: 410–505.

Kitcher, P. 1992. The Naturalists Return. *Philosophical Review* 101, no. 1: 53–114.

Köhler, W. 1938. *The Place of Value in a World of Fact*. Liveright.

Kosslyn, S. M. 1980. *Image and Mind*. Harvard University Press.

Kosslyn, S. M. 1994. *Image and Brain: The Resolution of the Imagery Debate*. MIT Press.

Krohn, R. 1990. Why are Graphs so Central in Science? *Biology and Philosophy* 6: 227–254.

Lakatos, I. 1970. Falsification and the Methodology Scientific Research Programmes. In *Criticism and the Growth of Knowledge*, ed. I. Lakatos and A. Musgrave. Cambridge University Press.

Lakoff, G. 1987. *Women, Fire, and Dangerous Things*. University of Chicago Press.

Lakoff, G. 1989. Some Empirical Results about the Nature of Concepts. *Mind and Language* 4: 103–129.

Lakoff, G. 1993. The Contemporary Theory of Metaphor. In *Metaphor and Thought*, second edition, ed. A. Ortony. Cambridge University Press.

Lakoff, G., and M. Johnson. 1980. *Metaphors We Live By*. University of Chicago Press.

Langacker, R. W. 1991. *Concept, Image, and Symbol: The Cognitive Basis of Grammar*. Mouton de Gruyter.

Larkin, J. H. 1983. The Role of Problem Representation in Physics. In *Mental Models*, ed. D. Gentner and A. Stevens. Erlbaum.

Leibniz, G. W. 1705/1997. *New Essays on Human Understanding*. Cambridge University Press.

Lewis, D. 1972. Psychophysical and Theoretical Identifications. *Australasian Journal of Philosophy* 50, no. 3: 249–258.

Lindsay, R. K. 1988. Images and Inference. *Cognition* 29: 229–250.

Loar, B. 1988. Social Content and Psychological Content. In *Contents of Thought*, ed. R. Grimm and D. Merrill. University of Arizona Press.

Locke, J. 1690/1964. *An Essay Concerning Human Understanding*. Clarendon.

Lycan, W. G. 1987. *Consciousness*. MIT Press.

Lycan, W. G. 1988. *Judgment and Justification*. Cambridge University Press.

MacCorquodale, K., and P. E. Meehl. 1948. On a Distinction between Hypothetical Constructs and Intervening Variables. *Psychological Review* 55: 95–107.

Machamer, P., L. Darden, and C. F. Craver. 2000. Thinking about Mechanisms. *Philosophy of Science* 67: 1–25.

Margenau, H. 1949. Einstein's Conception of Reality. In *Albert Einstein: Philosopher-Scientist*, ed. P. Schilpp. Library of Living Philosophers.

Marr, D. 1982. *Vision: A Computational Approach*. Freeman.

Marschark, M. 1985. Imagery and Organization in the Recall of Prose. *Journal of Memory and Language* 24: 554–564.

Martin, A., and L. L. Chao. 2001. Semantic Memory and the Brain: Structure and Processes. *Current Opinion in Neurobiology* 11, no. 2: 194–201.

Mayr, E. 1987. The Ontological Status of Species: Scientific Progress and Philosophical Terminology. *Biology and Philosophy* 2: 145–166.

Mazoyer, B. M., N. Tzourio, V. Frak, A. Syrota, N, Murayama, O. Levrier, G. Salamon, S. Dehaene, L. Cohen, and J. Mehler. 1993. The Cortical Representation of Speech. *Journal of Cognitive Neuroscience* 5, no. 4: 467–479.

McCarthy, J. 1986. Applications of Circumscription to Formalizing Common-Sense Knowledge. *Artificial Intelligence* 28: 86–116.

McCarthy, J., and P. J. Hayes. 1969. Some Philosophical Problems from the Standpoint of Artificial Intelligence. In *Machine Intelligence*, ed. B. Meltzer and D. Michie. Edinburgh University Press.

McGinn, C. 1989. *Mental Content*. Blackwell.

Miikkulainen, R. 1993. *Subsymbolic Natural Language Processing*. MIT Press.

Miller, A. I. 1984. *Imagery in Scientific Thought: Creating 20th-Century Physics*. Birkhäuser.

Miller, S. L. 1953. A Production of Amino Acids under Possible Primitive Earth Conditions. *Science* 117: 528–529.

Millikan, R. G. 1989. Biosemantics. *Journal of Philosophy* 86, no. 6: 281–297.

Mink, J. W. 1996. The Basal Ganglia: Focused Selection and Inhibition of Competing Motor Programs. *Progress in Neurobiology* 50: 381–425.

Mink, J. W. 2001. Basal ganglia motor function in relation to Hallervorden-Spatz syndrome. *Pediatric Neurology* 25, no. 2: 112–117.

Mishkin, M., L. G. Ungerleider, and K. A. Macko. 1983. Object Vision and Spatial Vision: Two Cortical Pathways. *Trends in Neurosciences* 6: 414–417.

Morris, D. 1967. *The Naked Ape*. Dell.

Newell, A., and H. A. Simon. 1972. *Human Problem Solving*. Prentice-Hall.

Nichols, S. 2001. Norms with Feeling: The Role of Affect in Moral Judgment. Paper delivered at 27th Annual Meeting of Society for Philosophy and Psychology, University of Cincinnati.

Nieber, E., C. Koch, and C. Rosin. 1993. An Oscillation-Based Model for the Neuronal Basis of Attention. *Vision Research* 33: 2789–2802.

Norman, D. A. 1983. Some Observations on Mental Models. In *Mental Models*, ed. D. Gentner and A. Stevens. Erlbaum.

Palmer, S. 1978. Fundamental Aspects of Cognitive Representation. In *Cognition and Categorization*, ed. E. Rosch and B. Lloyd. Erlbaum.

Perner, J. 1988. Developing Semantics for Theories of Mind: From Propositional Attitudes to Mental Representations. In *Developing Theories of Mind*, ed. J. Astington, P. Harris, and D. Olson. Cambridge University Press.

Perner, J. 1996. Simulation as Explicitation of Predication-Implicit Knowledge about the Mind: Arguments for a Simulation-Theory Mix. In *Theories of Theories of Mind*, ed. P. Carruthers and P. Smith. Cambridge University Press.

Popper, K. 1959. *The Logic of Scientific Discovery.* Hutchinson.

Postman, L., and L. W. Phillips. 1965. Short-Term Temporal Changes in Free Recall. *Quarterly Journal of Experimental Psychology* 17: 132–138.

Povinelli, D. J. 1999. Toward a New Theory of the Evolution of Human Social Intelligence: The Reinterpretation Hypothesis. Paper delivered at 25th Annual Meeting of Society for Philosophy and Psychology, Stanford University.

Povinelli, D. J. 2000. *Folk Physics for Apes: The Chimpanzee's Theory of How the World Works.* Oxford University Press.

Prinz, J. 2002. *Furnishing the Mind: Concepts and their Perceptual Basis.* MIT Press.

Pust, J. 1999. External Accounts of Folk Psychology, Eliminativism and the Simulation Theory. *Mind and Language* 14, no. 1: 113–130.

Putnam, H. 1990. The Nature of Mental States. In *Mind and Cognition*, ed. W. Lycan. Blackwell.

Pylyshyn, Z. 1981. The Imagery Debate: Analog Media versus Tacit Knowledge. In *Imagery*, ed. N. Block. MIT Press.

Pylyshyn, Z. W. 1984. *Computation and Cognition: Toward a Foundation for Cognitive Science.* MIT Press.

Pylyshyn, Z. W. 2002. Mental Imagery: In Search of a Theory. *Behavioral and Brain Sciences* 25, no. 2: 157–182.

Quillian, M. R. 1968. Semantic Memory. In *Semantic Information Processing*, ed. M. Minsky. MIT Press.

Ramsey, W., S. Stich, and J. Garon. 1991. Connectionism, Eliminativism, and the Future of Folk Psychology. In *The Future of Folk Psychology*, ed. J. Greenwood. Cambridge University Press.

Rawls, J. 1971. *A Theory of Justice.* Harvard University Press.

Reichenbach, H. 1938. *Experience and Prediction: An Analysis of the Foundations and the Structure of Knowledge.* University of Chicago Press.

Reichenbach, H. 1947. *Elements of Symbolic Logic.* Macmillan.

Rips, L. J. 1983. Cognitive Processes in Propositional Reasoning. *Psychological Review* 90, no. 1: 38–71.

Rips, L. J. 1990. Paralogical Reasoning: Evans, Johnson-Laird, and Byrne on Liar and Truth-teller Puzzles. *Cognition* 36: 291–314.

Russell, B. 1919. *Introduction to Mathematical Philosophy*. Macmillan.

Salmon, W. 1984. *Scientific Explanation and the Causal Structure of the World*. Princeton University Press.

Salmon, W. 1988. Deductivism Visited and Revisited. In *The Limitations of Deductivism*, ed. A. Grunbaum and W. Salmon. University of California Press.

Salmon, W. 1998. *Causality and Explanation*. Oxford University Press.

Savion, L. 1993. Unjustified Presuppositions of Competence. *Behavioral and Brain Sciences* 16, no. 2: 364–365.

Schank, R. 1980. How Much Intelligence Is there in Artificial Intelligence? *Intelligence* 4: 1–14.

Schiffer, S. 1991. Ceteris Paribus Laws. *Mind* 100, no. 1: 1–17.

Schwartz, D. L. 1999. Physical Imagery: Kinematic versus Dynamic Models. *Cognitive Psychology* 38: 433–464.

Schwartz, D. L., and J. B. Black. 1996. Shuttling between Depictive Models and Abstract Rules: Induction and Fall-back. *Cognitive Science* 20: 457–497.

Schyns, P. G. 1991. A Modular Neural Network Model of Concept Acquisition. *Cognitive Science* 15: 461–508.

Scriven, M. 1959. Explanation and Prediction in Evolutionary Theory. *Science* 130: 477–482.

Scriven, M. 1962. Explanations, Predictions and Laws. *Minnesota Studies in the Philosophy of Science* 3: 170–230. Reprinted in *Theories of Explanation*, ed. J. Pitt (Oxford University Press, 1988).

Searle, J. R. 1980. Minds, Brains, and Programs. *Behavioral and Brain Sciences* 3: 417–457.

Segal, S. J., and V. Fusella. 1970. Influence of Imaged Pictures and Sounds on Detection of Visual and Auditory Signals. *Journal of Experimental Psychology* 83: 458–464.

Selfridge, O. G. 1959. Pandemonium: A Paradigm for Learning. In *Symposium on the Mechanization of Thought Processes*. Her Majesty's Stationery Office.

Shepard, R. N., and S. Chipman. 1970. Second-Order Isomorphism of Internal Representations: Shapes of States. *Cognitive Psychology* 1: 1–17.

Shepard, R. N., and J., Metzler. 1971. Mental Rotation of Three-dimensional Objects. *Science* 171: 701–703.

Simons, D. J, and R. N. Rensink. 2005. Change Blindness: Past, Present, and Future. *Trends in Cognitive Sciences* 9, no. 1: 16–20.

Skinner, B. F. 1957. *Verbal Behavior*. Copley.

Skinner, B. F. 1963. Behaviorism at 50. *Science* 140: 951–958.

Smith, C. A., and P. C. Ellsworth. 1987. Patterns of Appraisal and Emotion Related to Taking an Exam. *Journal of Personality and Social Psychology* 52: 475–488.

Sosa, E. 1993. Abilities, Concepts, and Externalism. In *Mental Causation*, ed. J. Heil and A. Mele. Clarendon.

Stalnaker, R. 1989. On What's in the Head. In *Philosophical Perspectives, 3: Philosophy of Mind and Action Theory*. Reprinted in *The Nature of Mind*, ed. D. Rosenthal (Oxford University Press, 1991).

Stenning, K., and J. Oberlander. 1995. A Cognitive Theory of Graphical and Linguistic Reasoning: Logic and Implementation. *Cognitive Science* 19: 97–140.

Sterelny, K. 1990. The Imagery Debate. In *Mind and Cognition*, ed. W. Lycan. Blackwell.

Stevenson, R. J. 1993. Models, Rules, and Expertise. *Behavioral and Brain Sciences* 16, no. 2: 366.

Stich, S. 1978. Autonomous Psychology and the Belief-Desire Thesis. *The Monist* 61, no. 4: 573–591.

Stich, S. 1989. *From Folk Psychology to Cognitive Science: The Case against Belief*. MIT Press.

Stich, S. 1996. *Deconstructing the Mind*. Oxford University Press.

Stich, S., and I. Ravenscroft. 1994. What Is Folk Psychology? *Cognition* 50, no. 1–3: 447–468.

St. John, M. F., and J. L. McClelland. 1990. Learning and Applying Contextual Constraints in Sentence Processing. *Artificial Intelligence* 46: 217–257.

Talmy, L. 1988. Force Dynamics in Language and Cognition. *Cognitive Science* 12: 49–100.

Thach, W. T., H. P. Goodkin, and J. G. Keating. 1992. The Cerebellum and the Adaptive Coordination of Movement. *Annual Review of Neuroscience* 15: 403–442.

Thomas, N. J. T. 1999. Are Theories of Imagery Theories of Imagination? *Cognitive Science* 23: 207–245.

Tolman, E. C. 1922. A New Formula for Behaviorism. *Psychological Review* 29: 44–53.

Tolman, E. C. 1948. Cognitive Maps in Rats and Men. *Psychological Review* 55, no. 4: 189–208.

Tulving, E. 1983. *Elements of Episodic Memory*. St. Edmundsbury Press.

Tulving, E. 1987. Multiple Memory Systems and Consciousness. *Human Neurobiology* 6: 67–80.

Turing, A. 1950. Computing Machinery and Intelligence. *Mind* 59, no. 236: 433–460.

van Fraassen, B. C. 1980. *The Scientific Image*. Clarendon.

van Gelder, T., and R. Port. 1995. *Mind as Motion: Explorations in the Dynamics of Cognition*. MIT Press.

Waskan, J. A. 1997. Non-Propositional Representation and Mechanistic Justificatory Inference. Paper delivered at Annual Meeting of Eastern Division of American Philosophical Association, Washington.

Waskan, J. A. 1999. The Medium of Thought. Doctoral dissertation, Washington University, St. Louis.

Waskan, J. A. 2000. A Virtual Solution to the Frame Problem. In Proceedings of the First IEEE-RAS International Conference on Humanoid Robots.

Waskan, J. A. 2003a. Intrinsic Cognitive Models. *Cognitive Science* 27, no. 2: 259–283.

Waskan, J. A. 2003b. Folk Psychology and the Gauntlet of Irrealism. *Southern Journal of Philosophy* 41, no. 4: 627–655.

Waskan, J. A., and W. Bechtel. 1997. Directions in Connectionist Research: Tractable Computations without Syntactically Structured Representations. *Metaphilosophy* 28: 31–63.

Waskan, J. A., and W. Bechtel. 1998. The Scope of Cognitive Science: A Critical Notice of Paul Thagard's *Introduction to Cognitive Science*. *Canadian Journal of Philosophy* 28, no. 4: 587–608.

Watson, J. B. 1913. Psychology as the Behaviorist Views It. *Psychological Review* 20: 158–177.

Watt, A. 1993. *3D Computer Graphics, second edition*. Addison-Wesley Longman.

Wellman, H. M. 1990. *The Child's Theory of Mind*. MIT Press.

Wozniak, R. H. 1995. Mind and Body: Rene Déscartes to William James. http://serendip.brynmawr.edu/Mind/.

Wilson, M. A., and B. L. McNaughton. 1994. Reactivation of Hippocampal Ensemble Memories during Sleep. *Science* 265: 676–682.

Wimmer, H., and J. Perner. 1983. Beliefs about Beliefs: Representation and Constraining Function of Wrong Beliefs in Young Children's Understanding of Deception. *Cognition* 13, no. 1: 103–128.

Wimsatt, W. C. 1990. Taming the Dimensions-Visualizations in Science. *Philosophy of Science Association* 2: 111–138.

Wimsatt, W. C. 1994. The Ontology of Complex Systems: Levels of Organization, Perspectives, and Causal Thickets. *Canadian Journal of Philosophy*, Suppl. vol. 20: 207–274.

Wittgenstein, L. 1953. *Philosophical Investigations*. Macmillan.

Wittgenstein, L. 1961. *Tractatus Logico-Philosophicus*. Humanities Press.

Wright, C., and W. Bechtel. Forthcoming. Mechanisms and Psychological Explanation. In *Philosophy and Psychology of Cognitive Science*, ed. P. Thagard. Elsevier.

Zeki, S. M. 1976. The Functional Organization of Projections from Striate to Prestriate Visual Cortex in the Rhesus Monkey. *Cold Spring Harbor Symposia on Quantitative Biology* 40: 591–600.

Index